W9-AZR-331

Julie C. Meloni

Sams **Teach Yourself**

PHP, MySQL® and Apache

All in One

Fourth Edition

TIPPECANOE COUNTY PUBLIC LIBRARY
627 South St.
Lafayette, IN 47901

 800 East 96th Street, Indianapolis, Indiana, 46240 USA

Sams Teach Yourself PHP, MySQL and Apache All in One, Fourth Edition

Copyright © 2008 by Sams Publishing

All rights reserved. No part of this book shall be reproduced, stored in a retrieval system, or transmitted by any means, electronic, mechanical, photocopying, recording, or otherwise, without written permission from the publisher. No patent liability is assumed with respect to the use of the information contained herein. Although every precaution has been taken in the preparation of this book, the publisher and author assume no responsibility for errors or omissions. Nor is any liability assumed for damages resulting from the use of the information contained herein.

ISBN-13: 978-0-672-32976-0

ISBN-10: 0-672-32976-x

Library of Congress Cataloging-in-Publication data is on file.

Printed in the United States of America

First Printing June 2008

Trademarks

All terms mentioned in this book that are known to be trademarks or service marks have been appropriately capitalized. Sams Publishing cannot attest to the accuracy of this information. Use of a term in this book should not be regarded as affecting the validity of any trademark or service mark.

Warning and Disclaimer

Every effort has been made to make this book as complete and as accurate as possible, but no warranty or fitness is implied. The information provided is on an "as is" basis. The author and the publisher shall have neither liability nor responsibility to any person or entity with respect to any loss or damages arising from the information contained in this book or from the use of the CD or programs accompanying it.

Bulk Sales

Sams Publishing offers excellent discounts on this book when ordered in quantity for bulk purchases or special sales. For more information, please contact

U.S. Corporate and Government Sales
1-800-382-3419
corpsales@pearsontechgroup.com

For sales outside of the U.S., please contact

International Sales
international@pearsoned.com

005.75
M528S
2008

Acquisitions Editor
Mark Taber

Development Editor
Songlin Qiu

Managing Editor
Patrick Kanouse

Project Editor
Seth Kerney

Copy Editor
Mike Henry

Indexer
Ken Johnson

Proofreader
Debbie Williams

Technical Editor
Derek Mueller

Publishing Coordinator
Vanessa Evans

Book Designer
Gary Adair

Safari BOOKS ONLINE ENABLED — The Safari® Enabled icon on the cover of your favorite technology book means the book is available through Safari Bookshelf. When you buy this book, you get free access to the online edition for 45 days. Safari Bookshelf is an electronic reference library that lets you easily search thousands of technical books, find code samples, download chapters, and access technical information whenever and wherever you need it.

To gain 45-day Safari Enabled access to this book:

▶ Go to http://www.samspublishing.com/safarienabled
▶ Complete the brief registration form
▶ Enter the coupon code 68LV-Y3NM-EMY8-L7NK-AC54

If you have difficulty registering on Safari Bookshelf or accessing the online edition, please email customer-service@safaribooksonline.com.

Contents at a Glance

PART V: Basic Projects

PART VI: Administration and Fine-Tuning

Table of Contents

Teach Yourself PHP, MySQL and Apache All in One

About the Author

Julie C. Meloni is the technical director for i2i Interactive (http://www.i2ii.com), a multimedia company located in Los Altos, California. She has been developing web-based applications since the Web first saw the light of day and remembers the excitement surrounding the first GUI web browser. She has authored numerous books and articles on web-based programming languages and database topics, and you can find translations of her work in 15 different languages. She is also a fervent blogger and is the author of *Sams Teach Yourself Blogging in a Snap*. Most days, Julie can be found wandering the halls of Avery Hall on the campus of Washington State University, where she is a Ph.D. student in English who is quite interested in digital/social scholarship in the humanities.

Acknowledgments

The Apache Software Foundation, the PHP Group, and MySQL AB deserve much more recognition than they ever get for creating these super products that drive the vast majority of the Web.

Although this book is several editions removed from the original text by Daniel Lopez (author of *Sams Teach Yourself Apache 2 in 24 Hours*) and Matt Zandstra (author of *Sams Teach Yourself PHP in 24 Hours*), this book would not exist without their work oh so many years ago.

Great thanks especially to all the editors and layout folks at Sams who were involved with this book for all their hard work in seeing this through! Thanks as always to everyone at i2i Interactive for their never-ending support and encouragement.

Special thanks to Derek Mueller for taking time out of his dissertation-writing schedule to perform the duties of a technical editor, and to Rachael Shapiro for allowing me to borrow her Mac and install strange things on it in order to take some of the screenshots for this book.

We Want to Hear from You!

As the reader of this book, *you* are our most important critic and commentator. We value your opinion and want to know what we're doing right, what we could do better, what areas you'd like to see us publish in, and any other words of wisdom you're willing to pass our way.

You can email or write me directly to let me know what you did or didn't like about this book—as well as what we can do to make our books stronger.

Please note that I cannot help you with technical problems related to the topic of this book, and that due to the high volume of mail I receive, I might not be able to reply to every message.

When you write, please be sure to include this book's title and author as well as your name and phone or email address. I will carefully review your comments and share them with the author and editors who worked on the book.

Email: webdev@samspublishing.com

Mail: Mark Taber
          Associate Publisher
          Sams Publishing
          800 East 96th Street
          Indianapolis, IN 46240 USA

Reader Services

Visit our website and register this book at www.samspublishing.com/register for convenient access to any updates, downloads, or errata that might be available for this book.

Introduction

Welcome to *Sams Teach Yourself PHP, MySQL and Apache All in One, Fourth Edition*! In the previous edition, the majority of the modifications were around the ability to use both PHP 5 and MySQL 5 as core technologies. In the two years since the previous edition was released, little has changed: PHP 5 and MySQL 5 are solid, stable, and power a great number of the Web-based applications we use every day. Many hosting providers now offer PHP 5 by default, without support for PHP 4 (which has entered the "end of life" phase), thus ensuring that anyone who wants to use PHP 5 and MySQL 5 can do so without installing these applications on their own (although the first four chapters of this book explain how to do just that). All the code in this edition is based on PHP 5 and, where appropriate, the MySQL Improved Extension (mysqli) in PHP, using MySQL 5 as the back-end database.

Some of you might have heard of PHP 6 or have seen books touting PHP 6 as the core language used. As of this writing in May of 2008, PHP 6 is still in the development stages and has not even entered the release candidate stage of development. Although PHP 6 is likely to reach the release candidate stage before the end of 2008, hosting providers will be loath to provide new technologies for general use until the language and the engine driving it have been thoroughly tested and improved to the point at which the release is deemed stable and mature—perhaps sometime in 2009. Given this information, it seemed entirely premature for this edition to cover the aspects of the language based on a developmental release, especially when the goal of this book is to provide the concepts necessary to master the basics of programming in the PHP language—the version that is stable and widely distributed.

Over the course of this book, you'll learn the concepts necessary for configuring and managing the Apache web server, the basics of programming in PHP, and the methods for using and administering the MySQL relational database system. The overall goal of the book is to provide you with the foundation you need to understand how seamlessly these technologies integrate with one another and to give you practical knowledge of how to integrate them.

Who Should Read This Book?

This book is geared toward individuals who possess a general understanding of the concepts of working in a web-based development environment, be it Linux/UNIX, Windows, or even Mac OS X. Installation and configuration instructions assume that you have familiarity with your operating system and the basic methods of building (on Linux/UNIX systems) or installing (on Windows and Mac OS X systems) software.

The lessons that delve into programming with PHP assume no previous knowledge of the language. However, if you have experience with other programming languages, such as ASP (Active Server Pages), JSP (Java Server Pages), or Perl, you will find the going much easier. Similarly, if you have worked with other databases, such as Oracle or Microsoft SQL Server, you will already possess a solid foundation for working through the MySQL-related lessons.

The only real requirement is that you already understand static web content creation with HTML. If you are just starting out in the world of web development, you will still be able to use this book, but you should consider working through an HTML tutorial. If you are comfortable creating basic pages, you will be fine.

How This Book Is Organized

This book is divided into six parts, corresponding to particular topic groups. You should read the chapters within each part one right after another, with each chapter building on the information found in those before it:

- ▶ Part I, "Getting Up and Running," provides a quick start guide to installation and walks you through the installation and configuration of MySQL, Apache, and PHP in depth. You'll need to complete at least one version of these instructions—either the quick start installation or the longer instructions—before moving on unless you already have access to a working installation of these technologies through a hosting provider. Even if you don't need to install and configure MySQL, Apache, and PHP in your development environment, you should still skim these lessons so that you understand the basics of their interaction.

- ▶ Part II, "PHP Language Structure," is devoted to teaching you the basics of the PHP language, including structural elements such as arrays and objects. The examples will get you in the habit of writing code, uploading it to your server, and testing the results.

- ▶ Part III, "Getting Involved with the Code," consists of chapters that cover intermediate-level application development topics, including working with forms and files, restricting access, and completing other small projects designed to introduce a specific concept.

- ▶ Part IV, "PHP and MySQL Integration," contains chapters devoted to working with databases in general, such as database normalization, as well as using PHP to connect to and work with MySQL. Included is a basic SQL primer, which also includes MySQL-specific functions and other information.

▶ Part V, "Basic Projects," consists of chapters devoted to performing a particular task using PHP and MySQL, integrating all the knowledge gained so far. Projects include an address book, a discussion forum, and a basic online storefront, among others. These examples are built in a black-and-white environment, meaning the aesthetic display is minimal. This allows you to focus on the programming and logic involved in building the structures rather than making these items aesthetically pleasing.

▶ Part VI, "Administration and Fine-Tuning," is devoted to administering and tuning Apache and MySQL. It also includes information on virtual hosting and setting up a secure web server.

If you find that you are already familiar with a topic, you can skip ahead to the next chapter. However, in some instances, chapters refer to specific concepts learned in previous chapters, so be aware that you might have to skim a skipped chapter so that your development environment remains consistent with the book.

At the end of many chapters, a few quiz questions test how well you've learned the material. Additional activities provide another way to apply the information learned in the chapter and guide you toward using this newfound knowledge in the next chapter.

About the Book's Source Code

All of the code that appears in listings throughout the chapters is also available on the accompanying CD-ROM. You may also download the source code bundle from the author's website at http://www.thickbook.com/.

Typing the code on your own provides useful experience in making typos, causing errors, and performing the sometimes mind-numbing task of tracking down errant semicolons. However, if you want to skip that lesson and just upload the working code to your website, feel free!

Conventions Used in This Book

This book uses different typefaces to differentiate between code and plain English, and to help you identify important concepts. Throughout the chapters, code, commands, and text you type or see onscreen appear in a `computer typeface`. New terms appear in *italics* at the point in the text where they are defined. Additionally, icons accompany special blocks of information:

Sams Teach Yourself PHP, MySQL and Apache All in One

By the Way

A "By the Way" note presents an interesting piece of information related to the current topic.

Did you Know?

A "Did You Know" tip offers advice or teaches an easier method for performing a task.

Watch Out!

A "Watch Out!" warns you about potential pitfalls and explains how to avoid them.

PART I

Getting Up and Running

1

Installation QuickStart Guide

Chapters 2, 3, and 4 deal with obtaining and installing MySQL, Apache, and PHP from their respective locations on the Internet so that you can make sure that your versions are up-to-date. Additionally, these chapters contain extended explanatory information regarding each step along the way and other important information relevant to understanding how these technologies work together.

If you want to get started quickly, this short chapter will step you through installation from the supplied CD-ROM for Linux/UNIX, Mac OS X, and Windows systems.

Linux/UNIX Installation

Whenever you compile applications from a source archive, the build process depends on your system having the correct development tools and libraries in place. Although the following instructions were tested on Red Hat Linux and SuSE Linux systems, the steps are the same for a default installation of all other Linux or commercial UNIX distributions. Should you encounter unexpected error messages during compilation, contact your systems administrator or refer to the documentation for your particular operating system.

Begin as the superuser (either log in as root or su from a regular system user) and mount the CD-ROM under /mnt on your filesystem:

```
# mount /dev/cdrom /mnt -t iso9660
```

The following sections detail the installation processes for MySQL, Apache, and PHP from the CD-ROM.

Installing MySQL

Before installing MySQL, we need to create a user on the system that will run the MySQL server:

```
# groupadd mysql
# useradd -g mysql mysql
```

We will put the source distribution in the /usr/local/ directory, so let's extract the MySQL archive from the CD-ROM:

```
# cd /usr/local/
# gunzip < /mnt/MySQL/Linux/tarballs/source/mysql-5.0.51a.tar.gz ¦ tar xf -
```

This creates a directory called mysql-5.0.51a containing the binary distribution. Create a link with a shorter name:

```
# ln -s mysql-5.0.51a mysql
```

Change directories to the new directory:

```
# cd mysql
```

Issue the following series of commands to finish the installation and start your MySQL server:

```
# scripts/mysql_install_db --user=mysql
# chown -R root  .
# chown -R mysql mysql_data
# chgrp -R mysql .
# bin/mysqld_safe --user=mysql &
```

You can add the last command in the list, the MySQL startup command, to your system startup script to ensure that the MySQL server always starts following a reboot. For instance, on Red Hat Linux, add the command to /etc/rc.d/rc.local.

If you want to test whether MySQL is running, use the mysqladmin status command to get a short status message from a running server:

```
# /usr/local/mysql/bin/mysqladmin status
Uptime: 8826  Threads: 1  Questions: 10  Slow queries: 0  Opens: 8
Flush tables: 1  Open tables: 2  Queries per second avg: 0.000
```

Installing Apache

Extract the Apache source code from the CD-ROM to /usr/local/src and change to that directory:

```
# cd /usr/local/src
# gunzip < /mnt/Apache/Linux/source/httpd-2.2.8.tar.gz ¦ tar xf -
# cd httpd-2.2.8
```

We want to install Apache under /usr/local/apache2 and configure the web server to allow Dynamic Shared Objects (DSO), so that we don't need to rebuild Apache to add in PHP support. The configure command therefore looks like this:

```
# ./configure --prefix=/usr/local/apache2 --enable-so
```

We could specify other compile-time options at this time, but for the purposes of this book the example given will be sufficient.

Compile and install Apache, and then start the web server with the apachectl command:

```
# make
# make install
# /usr/local/apache2/bin/apachectl start
```

To test whether the web server is running, open a web browser and enter the name or IP address of your server as the location. If you have not specified a hostname in the Apache configuration, you can use localhost or 127.0.0.1 to access your server. The default page for a new installation (shown in Figure 1.1) tells you that everything has worked.

FIGURE 1.1
The default
Apache page.

Installing PHP

Extract the PHP source code from the CD-ROM to /usr/local/src and change to that directory:

```
# cd /usr/local/src
# gunzip < /mnt/PHP/Linux/source/php-5.2.5.tar.gz | tar xf -
# cd php-5.2.5
```

We need PHP to include MySQL support and to link into Apache using DSO using the apxs utility. We'll also use the prefix /usr/local/php for the essential PHP files:

```
# ./configure --prefix=/usr/local/php \
--with-mysqli=/usr/local/mysql/bin/mysql_config \
--with-apxs2=/usr/local/apache2/bin/apxs
```

We then use the make and make install commands to compile and install PHP:

```
# make
# make install
```

The apxs utility does most of the hard work here. After the PHP module is built, it should be copied to the correct location on the filesystem and the Apache configuration should be automatically modified to load the module at start time.

We need to make one more change to the Apache configuration file to instruct the web server to process any .php file as a PHP script. We'll also activate PHP for files ending in .html. Edit /usr/local/apache2/conf/httpd.conf and add the following line:

```
AddType application/x-httpd-php .php  .html
```

Restart Apache with the apachectl command to make sure that Apache acts on the changes to the configuration file:

```
# /usr/local/apache2/bin/apachectl restart
```

To test whether PHP is now a part of your web server, create a simple script as /usr/local/apache2/htdocs/phpinfo.php that looks like this:

```
<?php
phpinfo();
?>
```

In your web browser, visit http://localhost/phpinfo.php on your new server and you should see a page giving a lot of information on the PHP configuration.

Windows Installation

The setup files included on the CD-ROM are suitable for Windows XP, 2003, and Vista. Earlier versions of Windows are not supported.

Insert the CD-ROM into your PC; it should play automatically. If the menu screen shown in Figure 1.2 does not appear, double-click the drive icon for your CD-ROM under My Computer.

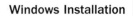

FIGURE 1.2
The Windows
CD-ROM instal-
lation menu.

Installing MySQL

Click the button in the menu to begin installing MySQL 5.0.51. At the screen shown in Figure 1.3, click the Next button to continue.

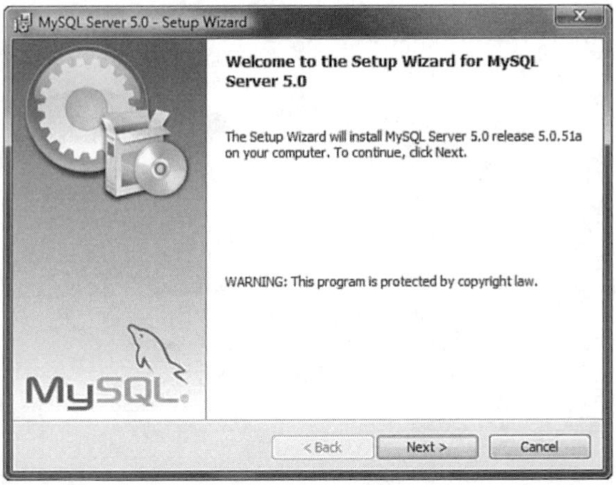

FIGURE 1.3
Beginning a
MySQL installa-
tion on
Windows.

The next few screens will contain general information regarding installation and the MySQL license. Read these screens and click the Continue button to move through them. The first important choice you will encounter is the installation type—typical, complete, or custom—as shown in Figure 1.4. A typical installation will do the job here, so leave the default item selected and click the Next button to continue installing.

FIGURE 1.4
MySQL installa-
tion type
selection.

When the installation is complete, continue to the MySQL Configuration Wizard to create a custom my.ini file tailored to your particular needs. To continue to the MySQL Configuration Wizard, check the Configure MySQL Server Now check box and click the Finish button, as shown in Figure 1.5.

FIGURE 1.5
MySQL has
been installed;
now continue to
the MySQL
Configuration
Wizard.

Select the appropriate configuration options presented on the several screens in the MySQL Configuration Wizard; consult Chapter 2, "Installing and Configuring MySQL," for detailed explanations of these options. When you have finished your configuration—which includes the addition of a password for the root user—the wizard will start the MySQL service.

Installing Apache

Click the button in the Windows CD-ROM installation menu to begin installing Apache 2.2.8. At the screen shown in Figure 1.6, click the Next button to continue.

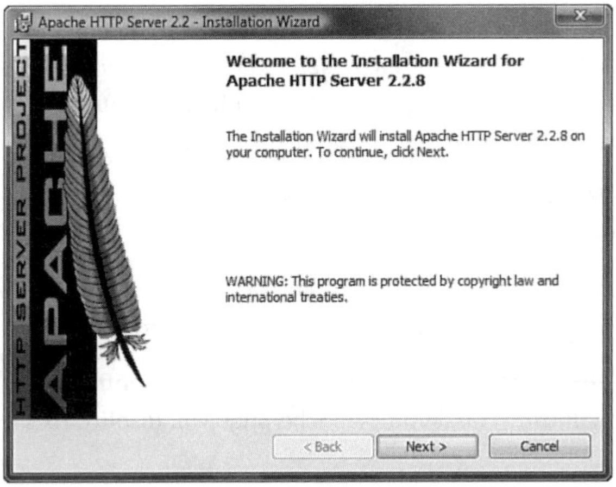

FIGURE 1.6
Beginning Apache installation on Windows.

You must accept the license terms on the next screen to continue the installation operation, after which you will see some release notes. Click the Next button after you read the notes and you will see a request for you to enter your server information, as shown in Figure 1.7.

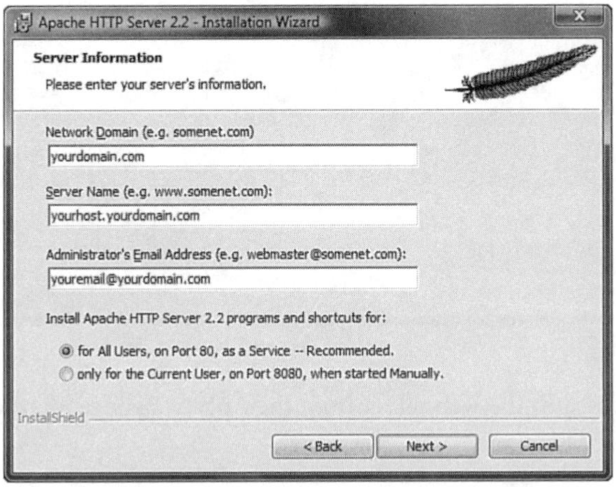

FIGURE 1.7
Entering your Apache server details.

Enter your server's domain and hostname, and your email address. If you are installing on a personal workstation, use localhost and localdomain for your server information. Leave the radio button selected on the Recommended option to install Apache on port 80.

The next screen asks you to choose a setup type, either typical or custom. The typical setup is just fine, so leave the radio button selected on that option and click Next to continue.

Then you have the opportunity to select the destination folder for the Apache files. By default this is C:\Program Files\Apache Software Foundation\Apache 2.2\—this location shouldn't cause you any problems. If you want to change it, click the Change button before you click the Next button.

Finally, Apache is ready to install. Click the Install button to start files copying to and setting up on your system.

When the installation operation is complete, the Apache server and monitor program will start and you will see a new icon in your system tray.

You can verify that Apache has started successfully by opening a web browser and visiting http://localhost/. The default Apache page will display, as shown in Figure 1.8.

FIGURE 1.8
Apache default installation page.

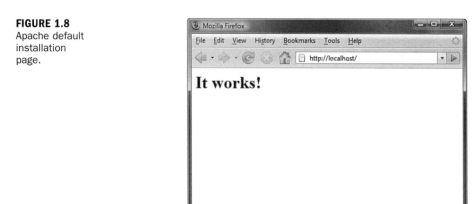

You can stop or restart the web server from the Apache Service Monitor or from the Windows Service Manager.

Installing PHP

Click the option on the Windows CD-ROM installation menu to install PHP 5.2.5; a zip archive will open, as shown in Figure 1.9.

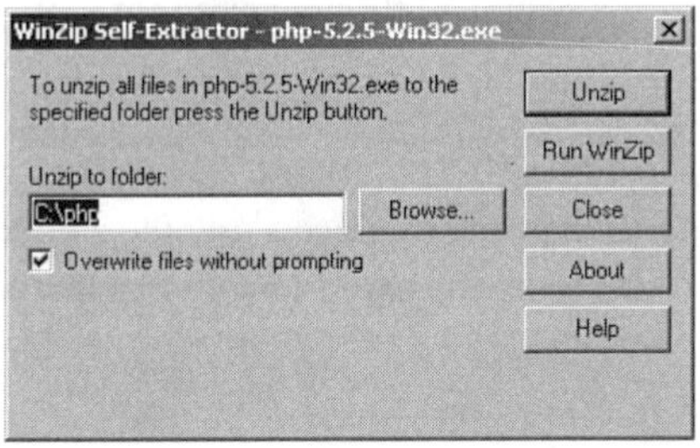

FIGURE 1.9
Beginning installation of PHP on Windows.

Extract the contents of the zip archive to C:\php. Close this window when the extraction operation has finished.

The installation process for PHP requires manual intervention to add the PHP module to Apache. Using File Explorer, open the Apache configuration directory—if you used the default location, it will be C:\Program Files\Apache Software Foundation\Apache 2.2\conf—and edit httpd.conf. Look for a section that contains a number of LoadModule directives, some prefixed with a # sign. The last few lines of this section will look like this:

```
LoadModule userdir_module modules/mod_userdir.so
#LoadModule usertrack_module modules/mod_usertrack.so
#LoadModule vhost_alias_module modules/mod_vhost_alias.so
#LoadModule ssl_module modules/mod_ssl.so
```

Add the following line to the LoadModule section to tell Apache to load the PHP module on startup:

```
LoadModule php5_module c:/php/php5apache2_2.dll
```

Additionally, add the following line to ensure that Apache knows where php.ini resides:

```
PHPIniDir "C:/php/"
```

Next, search for the AddType section with directives that look like this:

```
AddType application/x-tar .tgz
AddType image/x-icon .ico
```

Add the following line to tell Apache to process any file ending with .php or .html as a PHP script. You can add more file extensions to this line separated by spaces if you choose:

```
AddType application/x-httpd-php .php  .html
```

We also need to make a version of php.ini available. To do this, first add your PHP directory to your Windows PATH. Next, in the PHP installation directory, copy the php.ini-recommended file to php.ini. After making these changes, you must restart the Apache server—use the Apache Service Monitor or the Windows Service Manager.

If you encounter problems starting Apache, check the system events log from Control Panel and then Administrative Tools to find the error message.

Now we're ready to check whether PHP is working. In the htdocs directory in your Apache installation, create a file called phpinfo.php containing the following lines:

```
<?php
phpinfo();
?>
```

In your web browser, visit http://localhost/phpinfo.php and you should see a page giving lots of information on the PHP configuration.

Mac OS X Installation

The setup files included on the CD-ROM are suitable for Mac OS X version 10.3. Note that Apache is already installed, so no installation information is included here.

Insert the CD-ROM into your Mac; it should play automatically. If the menu screen shown in Figure 1.10 does not appear, double-click the drive icon for your CD-ROM.

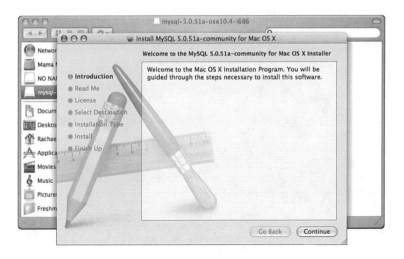

FIGURE 1.10
The Mac OS X
CD-ROM instal-
lation menu.

Installing MySQL

Click the button in the Mac OS X CD-ROM installation menu to begin installing MySQL 5.0.51. At the screen shown in Figure 1.11, click the Continue button.

FIGURE 1.11
Beginning a
MySQL installa-
tion operation
on the Mac.

Click the Continue button to move to the next step, which contains information regarding installation. Click the Continue button to move to the next step, which contains licensing information. Click the Continue button to move to the next step, which is to choose the destination. Select the appropriate drive, as shown in Figure 1.12, and then click the Continue button to move on.

FIGURE 1.12
Select the
MySQL
destination.

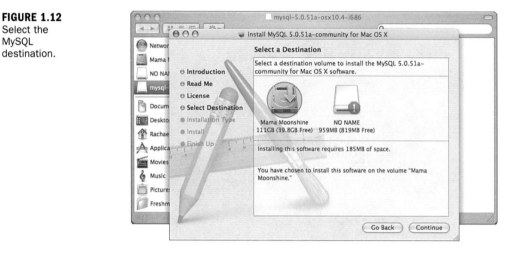

The next screen verifies your installation location and requires you to click the
Install button to continue. At this point, you receive a prompt for the administrator
username and password (unless you are installing as root) before the installation
process continues. When it continues, let the process run its course until you see the
installation is complete, as shown in Figure 1.13.

FIGURE 1.13
MySQL has
been installed.

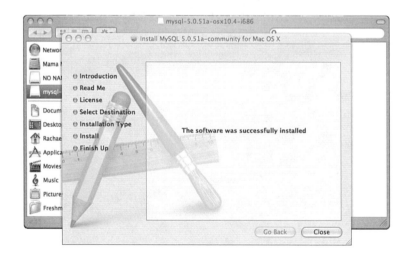

Installing PHP

Click the option on the Mac OS X CD-ROM installation menu to install PHP; an
installation package will open, as shown in Figure 1.14.

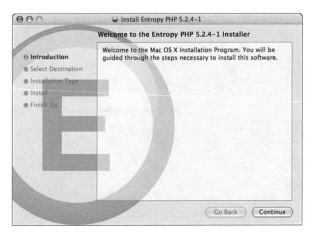

FIGURE 1.14
Beginning
installation of
PHP on
Mac OS X.

Click Continue to move to the next step, which asks you to choose the destination. Select the appropriate drive, as shown in Figure 1.15, and then click the Continue button to move on.

FIGURE 1.15
Select the PHP
destination.

The next screen verifies your installation location and requires you to click the Install button to continue. At this point, you receive a prompt for the Administrator username and password (unless you are installing as root) before the installation process continues. When it continues, let the process run its course until you see the installation is complete, as shown in Figure 1.16.

FIGURE 1.16
PHP has been
installed.

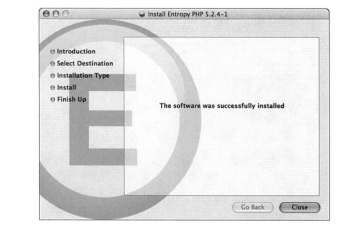

To test whether PHP is now a part of your web server, create a simple script called
phpinfo.php that looks like this:

```
<?php
phpinfo();
?>
```

Place this file in your web server document root at
/Library/WebServer/Documents. In your web browser, visit http://localhost/
phpinfo.php on your new server and you should see a page giving lots of information on the PHP configuration.

Troubleshooting

The steps in this chapter have been tested with the versions of the software supplied
on the CD-ROM that accompanies this book. If you experience installation problems, first check that you have followed the steps exactly as given in this chapter,
and then try the extended information found in Chapters 2, 3, and 4. Those chapters provide troubleshooting tips and links to additional sites that can help you work
through your installation issues.

2

Installing and Configuring MySQL

This is the first of three installation-related chapters in which you will learn how to set up your development environment. We'll tackle the MySQL installation first because building the PHP module requires bits of the MySQL installation to be complete if you're going to use MySQL with PHP.

In this chapter, you will learn

- ▶ How to install MySQL
- ▶ Basic security guidelines for running MySQL
- ▶ How to work with the MySQL user privilege system

Current and Future Versions of MySQL

The installation instructions in this chapter refer to MySQL 5.0.51, which is the current production version of the software. This version number can be read as "minor release number 51 of the major version 5.0 software." MySQL AB, now owned by Sun Microsystems, is the company responsible for creating and distributing MySQL; the company uses minor release numbers for updates containing security enhancements or bug fixes. Minor releases do not follow a set release schedule; when enhancements or fixes are added to the code and thoroughly tested, MySQL AB releases a new version with a new minor version number.

It is possible that by the time you purchase this book, the minor version number will have changed to 5.0.52 or beyond. If that is the case, you should read the list at http://dev.mysql.com/doc/refman/5.0/en/news-5-0-x.html for any changes regarding the installation or configuration process that makes up the bulk of this chapter.

Although it is unlikely that any installation instructions will change between minor version updates, you should get in the habit of always checking the changelog of software that you install and maintain. If a minor version change does occur while you are reading this book but the changelog notes no installation changes, simply make a mental note and substitute the new version number wherever it appears in the installation instructions and accompanying figures.

By the Way

> By the time this book is printed, it is likely that MySQL 5.1 will have been officially released. Although this book does not cover the enhancements to MySQL 5.1, nothing in this book is negated by the release of MySQL 5.1. In other words, if you choose to install MySQL 5.1 instead of MySQL 5.0, you will be able to perform all tasks in this book. For information on the changes between MySQL 5.0 and MySQL 5.1, please see http://dev.mysql.com/doc/refman/5.1/en/mysql-nutshell.html.

How to Get MySQL

MySQL AB, the company that develops and maintains the MySQL database server, distributes MySQL on its website: http://www.mysql.com/. Binary distributions for all platforms, installer packages for Mac OS X, and RPMs and source code files for Linux/UNIX platforms can be found at the website.

By the Way

> Linux distribution CDs usually contain some version or another of the open source MySQL software, although these are usually several minor versions behind the current release.

The installation instructions in this chapter are based on the official MySQL 5.0.x Community Server distribution from MySQL AB. All files can be downloaded from http://dev.mysql.com/downloads/mysql/5.0.html, and the current versions as of the time of writing can be found on the CD included with this book.

Installing MySQL on Linux/UNIX

The process of installing MySQL on Linux/UNIX is straightforward, whether you use RPMs or install the binaries. If you are installing from RPMs, MySQL AB provides platform-specific RPMs such as those for Red Hat, SuSE, and generic Linux running on different processor types such as x86, AMD64, and Intel IA64.

For a minimal installation from RPMs, you will need two files:

▶ `MySQL-server-type-VERSIONNUMBER.PLATFORM.rpm`—The MySQL server

▶ `MySQL-client-type-VERSIONNUMBER.PLATFORM.rpm`—The standard MySQL client libraries

To perform a minimal installation from RPMs, type the following at your prompt:

```
# rpm -i MySQL-server-VERSION.i386.rpm MySQL-client-VERSION.i386.rpm
```

By the Way

Replace *VERSIONNUMBER* in the filename with the actual version you downloaded, and *PLATFORM* with the short name of the platform you are using. For example, the current MySQL 5.0 server RPM for SuSE Linux Enterprise Server 10 is `MySQL-server-standard-5.0.51a-0.sles10.i586.rpm`, and the client libraries RPM is `MySQL-client-standard-5.0.51a-0.sles10.i586.rpm`.

Another painless (and very common) installation method is to install MySQL from a binary distribution. This method requires the `gunzip` and `tar` utilities to uncompress and unpack the distribution, and also requires the ability to create groups and users on the system. The first series of commands in the binary distribution installation process has you adding a group and a user and unpacking the distribution, as follows:

```
# groupadd mysql
# useradd -g mysql mysql
# cd /usr/local
# gunzip < /path/to/mysql-VERSION-PLATFORM.tar.gz | tar xvf -
```

By the Way

Replace *VERSION-PLATFORM* in the filename with the actual version you downloaded. For example, the current MySQL 5.0 Linux x86 binary is `mysql-standard-5.0.51a-linux-i686-glibc23.tar.gz`.

Next, the instructions tell you to create a symbolic link with a shorter name:

```
# ln -s mysql-VERSION-PLATFORM mysql
# cd mysql
```

After you unpack them, the README and INSTALL files will walk you through the remainder of the installation process for the version of MySQL you've chosen. In general, the following series of commands will be used:

```
# scripts/mysql_install_db --user=mysql
# chown -R root  .
# chown -R mysql mysql_data
# chgrp -R mysql .
# bin/mysqld_safe --user=mysql &
```

You're now ready to start the MySQL server, so skip ahead in this chapter to the section called "Basic Security Guidelines" to learn how to add passwords and users. If you had any issues with your installation, check the "Troubleshooting Your Installation" section.

Installing MySQL on Mac OS X

The MySQL installation process for Mac OS X is fairly straightforward—the developers from MySQL AB have created an installation package for Mac OS X. Go to the MySQL downloads page at http://dev.mysql.com/downloads/mysql/5.0.html and look for the section titled "Mac OS X downloads (package format)." From there, download the appropriate standard version for your system; the version you choose will depend on your Mac OS X version (10.3 or 10.4) and architecture (PowerPC, PowerPC 64-bit, or x86).

When the download is complete, unpack the installer file and double-click the *.pkg file. Follow these installation steps to complete the process:

1. The MySQL installer launches automatically, as shown in Figure 2.1. Click Continue to move to the next step.

FIGURE 2.1
The MySQL
Installer for the
Mac has
started.

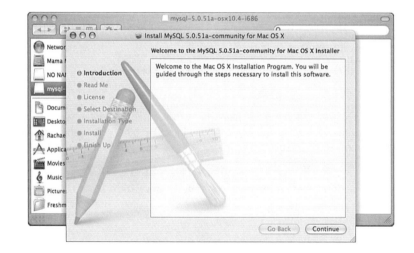

2. The next few screens contain general information regarding installation and the MySQL license. Read these screens and click Continue to move through them.

3. After stepping through the information and licensing screens, you must select an installation destination. Select the appropriate drive as shown in Figure 2.2 and then click the Continue button.

4. The next screen verifies your installation location selection and requires you to click the Install button to continue. At this point, you might be prompted to enter the administrator username and password before the installation process continues. When it continues, let the process run until you see that the installation is complete, as shown in Figure 2.3.

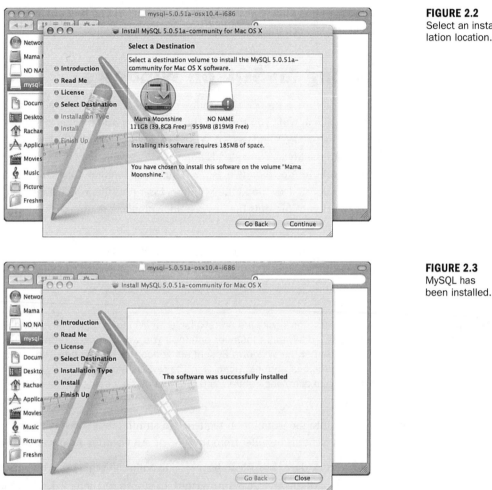

FIGURE 2.2
Select an installation location.

FIGURE 2.3
MySQL has been installed.

Also included in the installation package is the MySQL Startup Item installer. If you want MySQL to start automatically at system startup, install this additional package. Installation of the MySQL Startup Item follows the standard installation method just described—double-click the *.pkg file, select a destination disk, and allow the installation process to run to completion. After installing the MySQL Startup Item, use the following command in a terminal window to start MySQL:

```
# sudo /Library/StartupItems/MySQLCOM/MySQLCOM start
```

You might be asked to enter your account password. Press Ctrl+D to exit the shell after starting MySQL. After you have started MySQL, you can skip to the section called "Basic Security Guidelines" later in this chapter. If you had any issues with your installation, check the "Troubleshooting Your Installation" section.

Installing MySQL on Windows

The MySQL installation process on Windows uses a standard Microsoft Windows Installer (MSI) file to walk you through the installation and configuration of MySQL on your Windows 2000, Windows XP, Windows Server 2003, or Windows Vista machine. Go to the MySQL downloads page at http://dev.mysql.com/downloads/mysql/5.0.html and look for the section titled Windows Downloads. Download the Windows Essentials file, which should have an .msi file extension. When this file has been downloaded, double-click it to begin the installation process.

The following steps detail the installation of MySQL 5.0.20 on Windows using the Windows Essentials installer from MySQL AB. The installation sequence follows the same steps regardless of your Windows environment.

By the Way

Two other installation packages are available for Windows users—the Windows ZIP/Setup.EXE and Without Installer option. If you want to install either of these versions instead of the Windows Essentials version described here, be sure to read the descriptions and instructions in the MySQL Manual at http://dev.mysql.com/doc/refman/5.0/en/windows-choosing-package.html.

Jumping right into the installation sequence (assuming that you have downloaded the Windows Essentials installer from the MySQL AB website), follow these steps:

1. Double-click the *.msi file to begin the installation sequence. You will see the first screen of the MySQL Setup Wizard, as shown in Figure 2.4. Click Next to continue.

2. Select the installation method—Typical, Complete, or Custom (see Figure 2.5). The Custom option allows you to pick and choose elements of MySQL to install, whereas the Complete option installs all the components of MySQL, which range from documentation to benchmarking suites. The Typical installation method is suitable for most users because it includes the client, server, and numerous tools for general management of your MySQL installation. Select Typical as the installation method and click Next to continue.

3. Confirm your choice in the next screen and click the Install button to continue. The installation process will take over and install files in their proper locations.

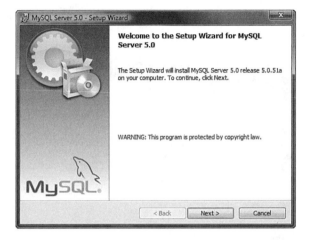

FIGURE 2.4
The first step of
the MySQL
Setup Wizard
for Windows.

FIGURE 2.5
Select an instal-
lation type.

4. When the installation is complete, you have the option of continuing to the MySQL Configuration Wizard. This wizard is highly recommended because it will create a custom my.ini file tailored to your particular needs. To continue to the MySQL Configuration Wizard, check the Configure MySQL Server Now check box and click the Finish button, as shown in Figure 2.6.

5. When you see the MySQL Configuration Wizard Welcome screen, click the Next button to go to the next step in the wizard. You will see two options for server configuration: Detailed and Standard. We will use the Detailed Configuration option so that you can see all the options available to you. If you decide to select the Standard Configuration option, you will have to manually modify the resulting my.ini file to achieve the configuration you

want. Select the Detailed Configuration radio button and then click Next to
continue.

FIGURE 2.6
MySQL has
been installed.
Now continue to
the MySQL
Configuration
Wizard.

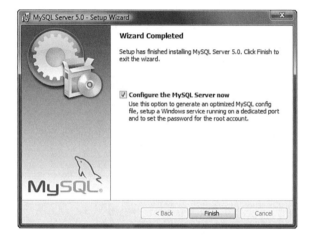

6. The next selection you must make is shown in Figure 2.7. In this step, you
   select the type of machine you are running: Developer Machine, Server
   Machine, or Dedicated MySQL Server Machine. Your selection on this screen
   determines the allotments for memory, disk, and processor usage. If you are
   using MySQL on your personal machine for testing purposes, select the
   Developer Machine option. If MySQL is running on a machine with other
   server software and can take up more system resources than if you were running it on your personal machine, select the Server Machine option. Select the
   Dedicated MySQL Server Machine option if MySQL is the primary service running on the machine and can take up the bulk of the system resources. After
   making your selection, click Next to continue.

7. The next configuration option pertains to database usage. The options are
   Multifunctional Database, for both InnoDB and MyISAM storage engines with
   resources split evenly between the two; Transactional Database, which enables
   both InnoDB and MyISAM but dedicates the most server resources to InnoDB;
   and Non-Transactional Database Only, which disables InnoDB and applies all
   resources to MyISAM. Unless you know exactly what your database will be
   used for, select the Multifunctional Database radio button and click Next to
   continue.

8. If you have selected a database usage option that includes the InnoDB storage
   engine, the next step in the configuration process enables you to configure the
   disk location and storage thresholds. The defaults are shown in Figure 2.8,

which you can simply confirm by clicking Next to continue, or you can change these settings and then click Next to continue with your custom settings in place.

FIGURE 2.7
Select your server type as part of the MySQL configuration.

FIGURE 2.8
Tune the disk usage options for the InnoDB storage engine.

9. The next configuration option determines the number of concurrent connections to your MySQL server. Your setting will depend on the amount of traffic and database usage by your website or application. The default setting is Decision Support (DSS)/OLAP, which has a maximum number of 100 concurrent connections with an average of 20 assumed. The Online Transaction Processing (OLTP) option has a maximum of 500 concurrent connections, and

the Manual setting allows you to select a number from a drop-down list or enter your own. Make your selection and click Next to continue.

10. The Networking Options screen is next in the configuration sequence. Here you will enable or disable TCP/IP networking as well as configure the port number used to connect to MySQL—the default is 3306, but you can use any unused port you choose. The other option on this screen is to enable or disable strict mode; enabling strict mode is recommended unless you know what you're changing. See http://dev.mysql.com/doc/refman/5.0/en/server-sql-mode.html for more information. Make your selections and click Next to continue.

By the Way

Remember to modify your firewall rules to allow traffic to flow on port 3306 or whichever port you decide to use for MySQL.

11. After the Networking Options screen come the character set options. The default option is Standard Character Set, which results in Latin1 being used throughout your database. You can also select the Best Support for Multilingualism option, which results in UTF8 as the character set; UTF8 allows you to store multiple languages in a single character set. If you want to use a specific character set, select the Manual Selected Default Character Set radio button and then select the appropriate character set from the drop-down list. After making your selection, click Next to continue.

12. It is recommended that MySQL be installed as a service, and the configuration screen shown in Figure 2.9 shows how this is done. Check the Install as Windows Service check box and select a name for the service. Optionally, check the Launch the MySQL Server Automatically check box. You also have the option of adding the MySQL `bin` directory to your Windows PATH for easier invocation of MySQL from the `cmd` prompt; check the box if this is appropriate for you. When you have completed your selections, click Next to continue.

13. The Security Options configuration screen is the most important screen of all. As shown in Figure 2.10, use this configuration screen to set a root password. Enter the password twice to confirm it. Do *not* check the Enable Root Access from Remote Machines check box unless you really know what you're doing; typically, root connections are allowed only from `localhost`. Additionally, you can create an anonymous account, but doing so is not recommended for security reasons. After completing the configuration options in this screen, click Next to continue.

FIGURE 2.9
Continuing the
MySQL server
instance
configuration.

FIGURE 2.10
Creating a pass-
word for root
during MySQL
configuration.

14. One step remains in the configuration sequence, and that is to click the Execute button to start the process. After the wizard has made it through the various configuration steps, you will see a confirmation screen as shown in Figure 2.11, indicating the configuration file has been created and the MySQL service has been started. Click Finish to close the wizard.

The completion of the installation and configuration wizards results in a running MySQL service and a custom my.ini file in the C:\Program Files\MySQL\MySQL Server 5.0\ directory.

FIGURE 2.11
The MySQL
Configuration
Wizard com-
pletes its tasks.

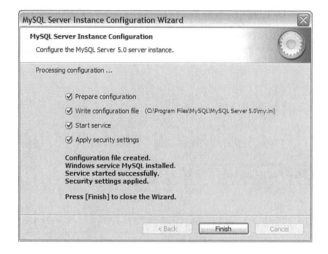

You can manually edit the `my.ini` file with any text editor. After making changes, you must restart your MySQL server.

Now that MySQL has been started, skip to the "Basic Security Guidelines" section later in this chapter. If you had any issues with your installation, check the "Troubleshooting Your Installation" section.

Troubleshooting Your Installation

If you have any problems during the installation of MySQL, the first place you should look is Appendix A, "Problems and Common Errors," in the MySQL Manual, which is located at http://dev.mysql.com/doc/refman/5.0/en/problems.html.

The following are just a few of the common installation problems:

▶ On Linux/UNIX and Mac OS X, incorrect permissions do not allow you to start the MySQL daemon. If this is the case, be sure that you have changed owners and groups to match those indicated in the installation instructions.

▶ If you see the message `Access denied` when connecting to MySQL, be sure that you are using the correct username and password.

▶ If you see the message `Can't connect to server`, make sure that the MySQL daemon is running.

If you still have trouble after reading Appendix A in the MySQL Manual, sending an email to the MySQL mailing list (see http://lists.mysql.com/ for more information) will likely produce results. You can also purchase support contracts from MySQL AB.

Basic Security Guidelines

Regardless of whether you are running MySQL on Windows, Linux/UNIX, or Mac OS X, and no matter whether you administer your own server or use a system provided to you by your Internet service provider, you must understand basic security guidelines. If you are accessing MySQL through your Internet service provider, there are several aspects of server security that you, as a non-root user, should not be able to modify or circumvent. Unfortunately, many Internet service providers pay no mind to security guidelines, leaving their clients exposed—and for the most part, unaware of the risk.

Starting MySQL

Securing MySQL begins with the server startup procedure. If you are not the administrator of the server, you won't be able to change this, but you can certainly check it out and report vulnerabilities to your Internet service provider.

If your MySQL installation is on Linux/UNIX or Mac OS X, your primary concern should be the owner of the MySQL daemon—it should not be root. Running the daemon as a non-root user such as mysql or database limits the ability of malicious individuals to gain access to the server and overwrite files.

> You can verify the owner of the process using the ps (process status) command on your Linux/UNIX or Mac OS X system.

Did you Know?

If you see that MySQL is running as root on your system, immediately contact your Internet service provider and complain. If you are the server administrator, you should start the MySQL process as a non-root user or specify the preferred username in the startup command line:

```
mysqld --user=non_root_user_name
```

For example, if you want to run MySQL as user `mysql`, use this command:

```
mysqld --user=mysql
```

However, the recommended method for starting MySQL is through the `mysqld_safe` startup script in the `bin` directory of your MySQL installation:

```
# bin/mysqld_safe --user=mysql &
```

Securing Your MySQL Connection

You can connect to the MySQL monitor or other MySQL applications in several different ways, each of which has its own security risks. If your MySQL installation is on your own workstation, you have less to worry about than users who have to use a network connection to reach their server.

If MySQL is installed on your workstation, your biggest security concern is leaving your workstation unattended with your MySQL monitor or MySQL GUI administration tool up and running. In this type of situation, anyone can walk over and delete data, insert bogus data, or shut down the server. Use a screensaver or lock screen mechanism with a password if you must leave your workstation unattended in a public area.

If MySQL is installed on a server outside your network, the security of the connection should be of some concern. As with any transmission of data over the Internet, data can be intercepted. If the transmission is unencrypted, the person who intercepted the data can piece it together and use the information. Suppose that the unencrypted transmission is your MySQL login information—a rogue individual now has access to your database, masquerading as you.

One way to prevent this from happening is to connect to MySQL through a secure connection. Instead of using Telnet to reach the remote machine, use SSH. SSH looks and acts like Telnet, but all transmissions to and from the remote machine are encrypted. Similarly, if you use a Web-based administration interface, such as the highly recommended phpMyAdmin (see http://www.phpmyadmin.net/ for more information) or another tool used by your Internet service provider, access that tool over a secure HTTP connection.

In the next section, you'll learn about the MySQL privilege system, which helps secure your database even further.

Introducing the MySQL Privilege System

The MySQL privilege system is always on. The first time you try to connect, and for each subsequent action, MySQL checks the following three things:

- Where you are accessing from (your host)

- Who you say you are (your username and password)

- What you're allowed to do (your command privileges)

All this information is stored in the database called mysql, which is automatically created when MySQL is installed. There are several privilege-related tables in the mysql database:

- **columns_priv**—Defines user privileges for specific fields within a table

- **db**—Defines the permissions for all databases on the server

- **host**—Defines the acceptable hosts that can connect to a specific database

- **procs_priv**—Defines user privileges for stored routines

- **tables_priv**—Defines user privileges for specific tables within a database

- **user**—Defines the command privileges for a specific user

These tables will become more important to you later in this chapter as you add a few sample users to MySQL. For now, just remember that these tables exist and must have relevant data in them in order for users to complete actions.

The Two-Step Authentication Process

As you've learned, MySQL checks three things during the authentication process. The actions associated with these three things are performed in two steps:

1. MySQL looks at the host you are connecting from and the username and password pair you are using. If your host is allowed to connect, your password is correct for your username, and the username matches one assigned to the host, MySQL moves to the second step.

2. For whichever SQL command you are attempting to use, MySQL verifies that you have the ability to perform that action for that database, table, and field.

If step 1 fails, you'll see an error about it and you won't be able to continue on to step 2. For example, suppose that you are connecting to MySQL with a username of joe and a password of abc123 and you want to access a database called myDB. You will receive an error message if any of those connection variables is incorrect for any of the following reasons:

▶ Your password is incorrect.

▶ Username joe doesn't exist.

▶ User joe can't connect from localhost.

▶ User joe can connect from localhost but cannot use the myDB database.

You may see an error like the following:

```
# mysql -h localhost -u joe -pabc123 test
Error 1045: Access denied for user: 'joe@localhost' (Using password: YES)
```

If user joe with a password of abc123 is allowed to connect from localhost to the myDB database, MySQL will check the actions that joe can perform in step 2 of the process. For our purposes, suppose that joe is allowed to select data but is not allowed to insert data. The sequence of events and errors would look like the following:

```
# mysql -h localhost -u joe -pabc123 test
Reading table information for completion of table and column names
You can turn off this feature to get a quicker startup with -A

Welcome to the MySQL monitor.  Commands end with ; or \g.
Your MySQL connection id is 12 to server version: 5.0.20-log
Type 'help;' or '\h' for help. Type '\c' to clear the buffer.

mysql> SELECT * FROM test_table;
+----+------------+
| id | test_field |
+----+------------+
|  1 | blah       |
|  2 | blah blah  |
+----+------------+
2 rows in set (0.0 sec)

mysql> INSERT INTO test_table VALUES ('', 'my text');
Error 1044: Access denied for user: 'joe@localhost' (Using password: YES)
```

Action-based permissions are common in applications with several levels of administration. For example, if you have created an application containing personal financial data, you might grant only SELECT privileges to entry-level staff members, but INSERT and DELETE privileges to executive-level staff with security clearances.

Working with User Privileges

In most cases when you are accessing MySQL through an Internet service provider, you will have only one user and one database available to you. By default, that user will have access to all tables in that database and will be allowed to perform all commands. In this case, the responsibility is yours as the developer to create a secure application through your programming.

However, if you are the administrator of your own server, or if your Internet service provider allows you to add as many databases and users as you want as well as to modify the access privileges of your users, these next few sections will take you through the processes of doing so.

Adding Users

Administering your server through a third-party application might afford you a simple method for adding users by using a wizard-like process or a graphical interface. However, adding users through the MySQL monitor is not difficult, especially if you understand the security checkpoints used by MySQL, which you just learned.

The simplest method for adding new users is the GRANT command. By connecting to MySQL as the root user, you can issue one command to set up a new user. The other method is to issue INSERT statements into all the relevant tables in the mysql database, which requires you to know all the fields in the tables used to store permissions. This method works just as well but is more complicated than the simple GRANT command. The simple syntax of the GRANT command is shown here:

```
GRANT privileges
ON databasename.tablename
TO username@host
IDENTIFIED BY "password";
```

Following are some of the common privileges you can grant. For a complete list, see the GRANT entry in the MySQL Manual at http://dev.mysql.com/doc/refman/5.0/en/grant.html.

- ▶ **ALL**—Gives the user all common privileges
- ▶ **ALTER**—User can alter (modify) tables, columns, and indexes
- ▶ **CREATE**—User can create databases and tables
- ▶ **DELETE**—User can delete records from tables
- ▶ **DROP**—User can drop (delete) tables and databases

▶ **FILE**—User can read and write files; this privilege is used to import or dump data

▶ **INDEX**—User can add or delete indexes

▶ **INSERT**—User can add records to tables

▶ **PROCESS**—User can view and stop system processes; only trusted users should be able to do this

▶ **RELOAD**—User can issue FLUSH statements; only trusted users should be able to do this

▶ **SELECT**—User can select records from tables

▶ **SHUTDOWN**—User can shut down the MySQL server; only trusted users should be able to do this

▶ **UPDATE**—User can update (modify) records in tables

If, for instance, you want to create a user called john with a password of 99hjc!5, with SELECT and INSERT privileges on all tables in the database called myDB, and you want this user to be able to connect from any host, use this command:

```
GRANT SELECT, INSERT
ON myDB.*
TO john@"%"
IDENTIFIED BY "99hjc!5";
```

Note the use of two wildcards: * and %. These wildcards replace values. In this example, * replaces the entire list of tables and % replaces a list of all hosts in the known world—a very long list indeed.

Here's another example of adding a user with the GRANT command, this time to add a user called jane with a password of 45sdg11, with ALL privileges on a table called employees in the database called myCompany. This new user can connect only from a specific host:

```
GRANT ALL
ON myCompany.employees
TO jane@janescomputer.company.com
IDENTIFIED BY "45sdg11";
```

If you know that janescomputer.company.com has an IP address of 63.124.45.2, you can substitute that address in the hostname portion of the command, as follows:

```
GRANT ALL
ON myCompany.employees
TO jane@'63.124.45.2'
IDENTIFIED BY "45sdg11";
```

One note about adding users: Always use a password and make sure that the password is a good one!

If you use the GRANT command to add users, the changes take immediate effect. To make absolutely sure of this, you can issue the FLUSH PRIVILEGES command in the MySQL monitor to reload the privilege tables.

Removing Privileges

Removing privileges is as simple as adding them; instead of the GRANT command, you use REVOKE. The REVOKE command syntax is as follows:

```
REVOKE privileges
ON databasename.tablename
FROM username@hostname;
```

In the same way that you can grant permissions using INSERT commands, you can also revoke permissions by issuing DELETE commands to remove records from tables in the mysql database. However, this requires that you be familiar with the fields and tables, and it's much easier and safer to use REVOKE.

To revoke the ability for user john to INSERT items in the myCompany database, you would issue this REVOKE statement:

```
REVOKE INSERT
ON myDB.*
FROM john@"%";
```

Changes made to the data in the privilege tables happen immediately, but for the server to be aware of your changes, issue the FLUSH PRIVILEGES command in the MySQL monitor.

Summary

Installing MySQL on Windows and Mac OS X is a simple process, thanks to a wizard-based installation method. Linux/UNIX users do not have a wizard-based installation process, but it's not difficult to follow a simple set of commands to unpack the MySQL client and server binaries. Linux/UNIX users can also use RPMs for installation.

Security is always a priority, and there are several steps you can take to ensure a safe and secure installation of MySQL. Even if you are not the administrator of the server, you should be able to recognize security breaches and raise a ruckus with the server administrator!

The MySQL server should never run as the root user. Additionally, named users within MySQL should always have a password, and their access privileges should be well defined.

MySQL uses the privilege tables in a two-step process for each request that is made. MySQL needs to know who you are and where you are connecting from, and each piece of this information must match an entry in its privilege tables. Also, the user whose identity you are using must have specific permission to perform the type of request you are making.

You can add user privileges using the GRANT command, which uses a simple syntax to add entries to the user table in the mysql database. The REVOKE command, which is equally simple, is used to remove those privileges.

Q&A

Q. *How do I completely remove a user? The REVOKE command just eliminates the privileges.*

A. To completely remove a user from the privilege table, you have to issue a specific DELETE query from the user table in the mysql database.

Q. *What if I tell my Internet service provider to stop running MySQL as root, and it won't?*

A. Switch providers. If your Internet service provider doesn't recognize the risks of running something as important as your database as the root user, and doesn't listen to your request, find another provider. There are providers with plans as low as $2.95/month (or even free!) that don't run important processes as the root user.

Workshop

The workshop is designed to help you anticipate possible questions, review what you've learned, and begin putting your knowledge into practice.

Quiz

1. True or False: Telnet is a perfectly acceptable method to securely connect to MySQL from a remote host.

2. Which three pieces of information does MySQL check each time a request is made?

3. What command would you use to grant SELECT, INSERT, and UPDATE privileges to a user named `bill` on `localhost` to all tables on the BillDB database? Also, what piece of information is missing from this statement that is recommended for security purposes?

Answers

1. False. The key word is *secure*, and Telnet does not encrypt data between hosts. Instead, use SSH to securely connect to your server.

2. Who you are, where you are accessing from, and what actions you're allowed to perform.

3. The command is

```
GRANT SELECT, INSERT, UPDATE
ON BillDB.*
TO bill@localhost;
```

The important missing piece is a password for the user.

Activities

1. Think of situations in which you might want to restrict command access at the table level. For example, you wouldn't want the intern-level administrator to have shutdown privileges for the corporate database.

2. If you have administrative privileges in MySQL, issue several GRANT commands to create dummy users. It doesn't matter whether the tables and databases you name are actually present.

3. Use REVOKE to remove some of the privileges of the users you created in activity 2.

3

Installing and Configuring Apache

In this second of three installation-related chapters, you will install the Apache web server and familiarize yourself with its main components, including log and configuration files.

In this chapter, you will learn

- ▶ How to install the Apache server
- ▶ How to make configuration changes to Apache
- ▶ Where Apache log and configuration files are stored

Current and Future Versions of Apache

When you visit the Apache HTTPD server website at http://httpd.apache.org, you will see announcements for releases of the Apache 1.3.x, Apache 2.0.x, and Apache 2.2.x versions. As you can imagine by the version numbers, Apache 1.3.x is the oldest of the three versions. The Apache Software Foundation maintains all three versions, but the features in Apache 2.2.x include greater support for filtering, caching, load balancing, and other system functions; it is the version used in this chapter. However, if you choose to install Apache 2.0.x or even Apache 1.3.x, all the PHP and MySQL code in this book will still work as described. In fact, you will find a considerable number of hosting providers still using the Apache 1.3.x version of the server, as well as others hosting the Apache 2.0.x version. If you have any issues with installing Apache 2.2.x as described in this chapter, try a previous version (for example, Apache 2.0.x); the installation instructions are remarkably similar. The installation instructions in this chapter refer to Apache HTTPD server version 2.2.8, which is the best available version of the software at the time of this writing.

The Apache Software Foundation uses minor release numbers for updates containing security enhancements or bug fixes. Minor releases do not follow a set release schedule. When enhancements or fixes are added to the code and thoroughly tested, the Apache Software Foundation releases a new version with a new minor version number.

It is possible that by the time you purchase this book, the minor version number will have changed to 2.2.9 or beyond. If that is the case, you should read the list of changes, which is linked from the download area at http://httpd.apache.org/download.cgi, for any changes regarding the installation or configuration process, which makes up the bulk of this chapter.

Although it is unlikely that any installation instructions will change between minor version updates, you should get in the habit of always checking the changelog of software that you install and maintain. If a minor version change does occur while you are reading this book but the changelog notes no installation changes, simply make a mental note and substitute the new version number wherever it appears in the installation instructions and accompanying figures.

Choosing the Appropriate Installation Method

You have several options when it comes to getting a basic Apache installation in place. Apache is open source, meaning that you can have access to the full source code of the software, which in turn enables you to build your own custom server. Additionally, prebuilt Apache binary distributions are available for most modern UNIX platforms. Finally, Apache comes already bundled with a variety of Linux distributions, and you can purchase commercial versions with support packages from vendors such as Covalent Technologies and IBM (among others). The examples in this chapter will teach you how to build Apache from source if you are using Linux/UNIX, and how to use the installer if you plan to run Apache on a Windows system.

Building from Source

Building from source gives you the greatest flexibility because it enables you to build a custom server, remove modules you do not need, and extend the server with third-party modules. Building Apache from source code enables you to easily upgrade to the latest versions and quickly apply security patches, whereas updated versions from vendors can take days or weeks to appear. The process of building Apache from source is not especially difficult for simple installations but can grow in complexity when third-party modules and libraries are involved.

Installing a Binary

Linux/UNIX binary installations are available from vendors or you can download them from the Apache Software Foundation website. Binary installations provide a convenient way to install Apache for users with limited system administration knowledge or with no special configuration needs. Third-party commercial vendors provide prepackaged Apache installations together with an application server, additional modules, support, and so on. The Apache Software Foundation provides an installer for Windows systems—a platform where a compiler is less commonly available than in Linux/UNIX systems.

Installing Apache on Linux/UNIX

This section explains how to install a fresh build of Apache 2.2.8 on Linux/UNIX. The general steps necessary to successfully install Apache from source are as follows:

1. Download the software

2. Run the configuration script

3. Compile the code and install it

The following sections describe these steps in detail.

Downloading the Apache Source Code

The official Apache download site is located at http://httpd.apache.org/download.cgi. You can find several versions of the Apache source code, packaged with different compression methods. The distribution files are first packed with the `tar` utility and then compressed with either the `gzip` tool or the `compress` utility. Download the `*.tar.gz` version if you have the `gunzip` utility installed on your system. This utility comes installed by default in open source operating systems such as FreeBSD and Linux. Download the `*.tar.Z` file if `gunzip` is not present in your system. (It isn't included in the default installation of many commercial UNIX operating systems.)

The file you want to download will be named something similar to `httpd-2.2.VER-SION.tar.Z` or `httpd-2.2.VERSION.tar.gz`, where `VERSION` is the most recent release of Apache. For example, Apache version 2.2.8 is distributed as a file named `httpd-2.2.8.tar.gz`. Keep the downloaded file in a directory reserved for source files, such as `/usr/src/` or `/usr/local/src/`.

Uncompressing the Source Code

If you downloaded the tarball compressed with `gzip` (it will have a `tar.gz` suffix), you can uncompress it using the `gunzip` utility (part of the `gzip` distribution).

| | Tarball is a commonly used nickname for software packed using the tar utility. |

You can uncompress and unpack the software by typing the following command:

```
# gunzip < httpd-2.2*.tar.gz ¦ tar xvf -
```

If you downloaded the tarball compressed with compress (it will have a tar.Z suffix), you can issue the following command:

```
# cat httpd-2.2*.tar.Z ¦ uncompress ¦ tar xvf -
```

Uncompressing the tarball creates a structure of directories, with the top-level directory named httpd-2.2_VERSION. Change your current directory to this top-level directory to prepare for configuring the software.

Preparing to Build Apache

You can specify which features the resulting binary will have by using the configure script in the top-level distribution directory. By default, Apache will be compiled with a set of standard modules compiled statically and will be installed in the /usr/local/apache2 directory. If you are happy with these settings, you can issue the following command to configure Apache:

```
# ./configure
```

However, in preparation for the PHP installation in Chapter 4, "Installing and Configuring PHP," you will need to make sure that mod_so is compiled into Apache. This module, named for the UNIX shared object (*.so) format, enables the use of dynamic modules such as PHP with Apache. To configure Apache to install itself in a specific location (in this case, /usr/local/apache2/) and to enable the use of mod_so, issue the following command:

```
#./configure --prefix=/usr/local/apache2 --enable-so
```

The purpose of the configure script is to figure out everything related to finding libraries, compile-time options, platform-specific differences, and so on, and to create a set of special files called *makefiles*. Makefiles contain instructions to perform different tasks, called *targets*, such as building Apache. The make utility reads these files and carries out the targets' tasks. If everything goes well, after executing configure, you will see a set of messages related to the different checks just performed and will return to the prompt:

```
...
configure ok
creating test/Makefile
```

```
config.status: creating docs/conf/httpd.conf
...
config.status: executing default commands
#
```

If the `configure` script fails, warnings will appear, alerting you to track down additional software that must be installed, such as compilers or libraries. After you install any missing software, you can try the `configure` command again, after deleting the `config.log` and `config.status` files from the top-level directory.

Building and Installing Apache

The make utility reads the information stored in the makefiles and builds the server and modules. Type **make** at the command line to build Apache. You will see several messages indicating the progress of the compilation, and you will end up back at the prompt. After compilation is finished, you can install Apache by typing **make install** at the prompt. The makefiles will install files and directories and return you to the prompt:

```
...
Installing header files
Installing build system files
Installing man pages and online manual
...
make[1]: Leaving directory '/usr/local/bin/httpd-2.2.8'
#
```

The Apache distribution files should now be in the `/usr/local/apache2` directory, as specified by the `--prefix` switch in the `configure` command. To test that the `httpd` binary built correctly, type the following at the prompt:

 # /usr/local/apache2/bin/httpd -v

You should see the following output (your version and build date will be different):

```
Server version: Apache/2.2.8
Server built:   April 12 2008 11:47:22
```

Unless you want to learn how to install Apache on Mac OS X or Windows, skip ahead to the "Apache Configuration File Structure" section to learn about the Apache configuration file.

Installing Apache on Mac OS X

Lucky you, Apache is already installed on Mac OS X! By default, the Apache server binary is located at `/usr/sbin/httpd`. Configuration files such as `httpd.conf`, the master configuration file for Apache, are in /etc/httpd. Because Apache is ready to go and fully prepared to use PHP, skip ahead to the "Apache Configuration File Structure" section to learn more about the Apache configuration file and how to use it.

Installing Apache on Windows

Apache 2.2 runs on most Windows platforms and offers increased performance and stability over the Apache 2.0 and Apache 1.3 versions for Windows. You can build Apache from source, but because not many Windows users have compilers, this section deals with the MSI installer version.

Before installing Apache, you'll probably want to make sure that you are not currently running a web server (for instance, a previous version of Apache, Microsoft Internet Information Services, or Microsoft Personal Web Server) on your machine. You might want to uninstall or otherwise disable existing servers. You can run several web servers, but they must run in different address and port combinations.

Before downloading the installer, take a moment—a very important moment—and look for a statement on the downloads page (found at http://httpd.apache.org/download.cgi) that says "If you are downloading the Win32 distribution, please read these important notes." The direct URL to these notes is http://www.apache.org/dist/httpd/binaries/win32/README.html.

The Apache Software Foundation maintains this page for the benefit of Windows users who want to run a version of the Apache server. On this page, there are notes for nearly every flavor of Windows still in use, and it is in your best interest to read the information presented. I guarantee that if you are running Apache as either a production or development server, you find relevant information on the notes page.

When you're ready to begin the installation, look for the link labeled Win32 Binary (MSI Installer). After you download the installer, double-click the file to start the installation process. You will get a welcome screen, as shown in Figure 3.1.

Click Next to continue the installation process and you will be prompted to accept the Apache license. Basically the license says that you can do whatever you want with the software—including making proprietary modifications—except claim that you wrote it, but be sure to read the license so that you fully understand the terms.

After you accept the license, the installer presents you with a brief introduction to Apache. Following that, it asks you to provide basic information about your computer, as shown in Figure 3.2. This includes the full network address for the server (for instance, mycomputer.mydomain.com) and the administrator's email address. The server name is the name your clients will use to access your server, and the administrator email address is added to error messages so that visitors know how to contact you when something goes wrong.

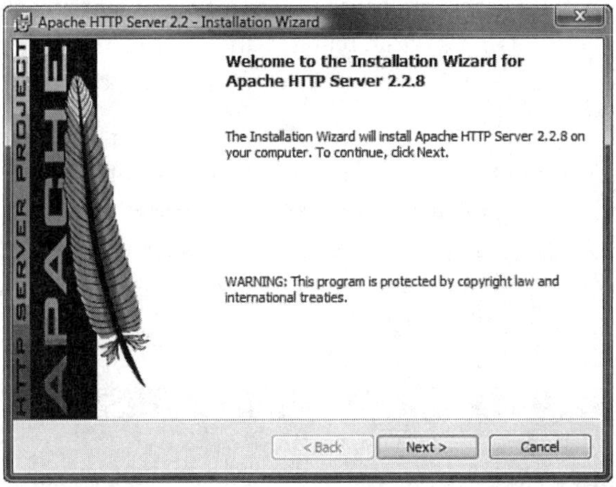

FIGURE 3.1
The Windows installer welcome screen.

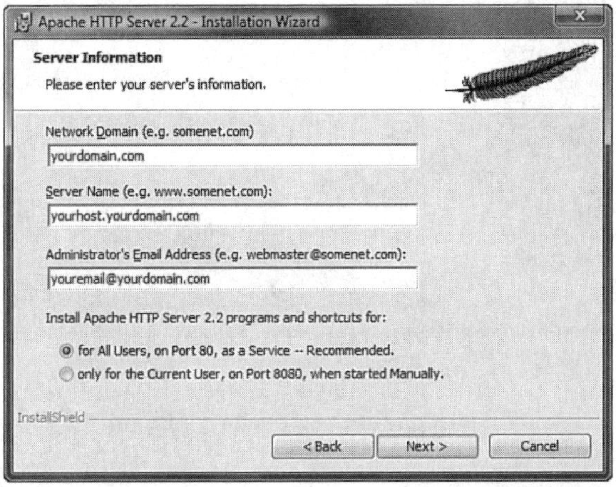

FIGURE 3.2
The basic information screen.

Also on this screen, you are prompted to select which installation shortcuts should be installed—those for starting Apache as a service or those for starting Apache manually. Installing Apache as a service causes it to run every time Windows starts, and you can control it through the standard Windows service administration tools. Installing Apache for the current user requires you to start Apache manually and set the default port on which Apache listens to requests to 8080 (instead of 80). Select the appropriate radio button and click Next to continue.

> If your machine does not have a full network address, use `localhost` or
> `127.0.0.1` as the server name.

The next screen enables you to choose the type of installation: typical or custom. A
typical installation means that Apache binaries and documentation are installed, but
headers and libraries are not. This is the best option to choose unless you plan to
compile your own modules.

A *custom installation* enables you to choose whether to install header files or documentation. After selecting the target installation directory, which defaults to
`C:\Program Files\Apache Software Foundation/Apache 2.2`, the program proceeds with the installation process. If everything goes well, it will present you with
the final screen shown in Figure 3.3.

FIGURE 3.3
The successful
installation
screen.

In the next section, you'll learn about the Apache configuration file and eventually
start up your new server.

Apache Configuration File Structure

Apache keeps all its configuration information in text files. The main file is
`httpd.conf`. This file contains directives and containers that enable you to customize your Apache installation. *Directives* configure specific settings of Apache,
such as authorization, performance, and network parameters. *Containers* specify the
context to which those settings refer. For example, authorization configuration can
refer to the server as a whole, to a directory, or to a single file.

Directives

The following rules apply for Apache directive syntax:

▶ The directive arguments follow the directive name.

▶ The directive arguments are separated by spaces.

▶ The number and type of arguments vary from directive to directive; some have no arguments.

▶ A directive occupies a single line, but you can continue it on a different line by ending the previous line with a backslash character (\).

▶ The pound sign (#) should precede the directive, and must appear on its own line.

The Apache server documentation offers a quick reference for directives at http://httpd.apache.org/docs/2.2/mod/quickreference.html. You'll soon learn about some of the basic directives, but you should supplement your knowledge using the online documentation.

The Apache documentation for directives typically follows this model:

▶ **Description**—This entry provides a brief description of the directive.

▶ **Syntax**—This entry explains the format of the directive options. Compulsory parameters appear in italics, optional parameters appear in italics and brackets.

▶ **Default**—If the directive has a default value, it will appear here.

▶ **Context**—This entry details the containers or sections in which the directive can appear. The next section explains containers. The possible values are `server config`, `virtual host`, `directory`, and `.htaccess`.

▶ **Override**—Apache directives belong to different categories. The Override field specifies which directive categories can appear in `.htaccess` per-directory configuration files.

▶ **Status**—This entry indicates whether the directive is built in Apache (`core`), belongs to one of the bundled modules (`base` or `extension`, depending on whether they are compiled by default), is part of a multi-processing module (MPM), or is bundled with Apache but not ready for use in a production server (`experimental`).

▶ **Module**—This entry indicates the module to which the directive belongs.

▶ **Compatibility**—This entry contains information about which versions of Apache support the directive.

Further explanation of the directive follows these entries in the documentation, and a reference to related directives or documentation might appear at the end.

Containers

Directive containers, also called *sections*, limit the scope for which directives apply. If directives are not inside a container, they belong to the default server scope (`server config`) and apply to the server as a whole.

These are the default Apache directive containers:

▶ **`<VirtualHost>`**—A `VirtualHost` directive specifies a virtual server. Apache enables you to host different websites with a single Apache installation. Directives inside this container apply to a particular website. This directive accepts a domain name or IP address and an optional port as arguments. You will learn more about virtual hosts in Chapter 29, "Apache Performance Tuning and Virtual Hosting."

▶ **`<Directory>`**, **`<DirectoryMatch>`**—These containers allow directives to apply to a certain directory or group of directories in the file system. `Directory` containers take a directory or directory pattern argument. Enclosed directives apply to the specified directories and their subdirectories. The `DirectoryMatch` container allows regular expression patterns to be specified as an argument. For example, the following allows a match of all second-level subdirectories of the www directory and made up of four numbers, such as a directory named after a year and month (`0906` for September 2006):

```
<DirectoryMatch "^/www/.*/[0-9]{4}">
```

▶ **`<Location>`**, **`<LocationMatch>`**—These containers allow directives to apply to certain requested URLs or URL patterns. They are similar to their `Directory` counterparts. `LocationMatch` takes a regular expression as an argument. For example, the following matches directories containing either `"/my/data"` or `"/your/data"`:

```
<LocationMatch "/(my¦your)/data">
```

▶ **`<Files>`**, **`<FilesMatch>`**—Similar to the `Directory` and `Location` containers, `Files` sections allow directives to apply to certain files or file patterns.

Containers surround directives, as shown in Listing 3.1.

LISTING 3.1   Sample Container Directives

```
 1: <Directory "/some/directory">
 2: SomeDirective1
 3: SomeDirective2
 4: </Directory>
 5: <Location "/downloads/*.html">
 6: SomeDirective3
 7: </Location>
 8: <Files "\.(gif¦jpg)">
 9: SomeDirective4
10: </Files>
```

Sample directives *SomeDirective1* and *SomeDirective2* apply to the directory
/some/directory and its subdirectories. *SomeDirective3* applies to URLs referring
to pages with the .html extension under the /downloads/ URL. *SomeDirective4*
will apply to all files with .gif or .jpg extensions.

Conditional Evaluation

Apache provides support for conditional containers. Directives enclosed in these containers will be processed only if certain conditions are met.

▶ **<IfDefine>**—Directives in this container will be processed if a specific command-line switch is passed to the Apache executable. The directive in Listing
3.2 is processed only if the -D*MyModule* switch is passed to the Apache binary
being executed. You can pass this directly or by modifying the apachectl
script, as described in the "Apache-Related Commands" section later in this
chapter.

IfDefine containers also allow you to negate the argument. That is, directives
inside a <IfDefine !*MyModule*> section—notice the exclamation point before
the *MyModule* name—are processed only if no -D*MyModule* parameter is passed
as a command-line argument.

▶ **<IfModule>**—Directives in an IfModule section will be processed only if the
module passed as an argument is present in the web server. For example,
Apache ships with a default httpd.conf configuration file that provides support for different MPMs. Only the configuration belonging to the MPM compiled into Apache will be processed, as you can see in Listing 3.3. The purpose
of the example is to illustrate that only one of the directive groups will be
evaluated.

LISTING 3.2   `IfDefine` Example

```
1: <IfDefine MyModule>
2: LoadModule my_module modules/libmymodule.so
3: </IfDefine>
```

LISTING 3.3   `IfModule` Example

```
 1: <IfModule prefork.c>
 2: StartServers          5
 3: MinSpareServers       5
 4: MaxSpareServers      10
 5: MaxClients           20
 6: MaxRequestsPerChild   0
 7: </IfModule>
 8:
 9: <IfModule worker.c>
10: StartServers          3
11: MaxClients            8
12: MinSpareThreads       5
13: MaxSpareThreads      10
14: ThreadsPerChild      25
15: MaxRequestsPerChild   0
16: </IfModule>
```

The `ServerRoot` Directive

The `ServerRoot` directive takes a single argument: a directory path pointing to the directory where the server lives. All relative path references in other directives are relative to the value of `ServerRoot`. If you compiled Apache from source on Linux/UNIX, as described earlier in this chapter, the default value of `ServerRoot` is `/usr/local/apache2`. The `ServerRoot` for Mac OS X users defaults to `/Library/WebServer`. If you used the Windows installer, the `ServerRoot` is `C:\Program Files\Apache Software Foundation\Apache 2.2\`.

Per-Directory Configuration Files

Apache uses per-directory configuration files to allow directives to exist outside the main configuration file, `httpd.conf`. These special files can be placed in the filesystem. Apache will process the content of these files if a document is requested in a directory containing one of these files or any subdirectories under it. The contents of all the applicable per-directory configuration files are merged and processed. For example, if Apache receives a request for the `/usr/local/apache2/htdocs/index.html` file, it will look for per-directory configuration files in the `/`, `/usr`, `/usr/local`, `/usr/local/apache2`, and `/usr/local/apache2/htdocs` directories, in that order.

Enabling per-directory configuration files has a performance penalty. Apache must perform expensive disk operations looking for these files in every request, even if the files do not exist.

Watch Out!

Per-directory configuration files are called `.htaccess` by default. This is for historical reasons; they originally protected access to directories containing HTML files.

The `AccessFileName` directive enables you to change the name of the per-directory configuration files from `.htaccess` to something else. It accepts a list of filenames that Apache will use when looking for per-directory configuration files.

To determine whether you can override a directive in the per-directory configuration file, check whether the `Context:` field of the directive syntax definition contains `.htaccess`. Apache directives belong to different groups, as specified in the `Override` field in the directive syntax description. Possible values for the `Override` field are as follows:

- ▶ **AuthConfig**—Directives controlling authorization
- ▶ **FileInfo**—Directives controlling document types
- ▶ **Indexes**—Directives controlling directory indexing
- ▶ **Limit**—Directives controlling host access
- ▶ **Options**—Directives controlling specific directory features

You can control which of these directive groups can appear in per-directory configuration files by using the `AllowOverride` directive. `AllowOverride` can also take an `All` or a `None` argument. `All` means that directives belonging to all groups can appear in the configuration file. `None` disables per-directory files in a directory and any of its subdirectories. Listing 3.4 shows how to disable per-directory configuration files for the server as a whole. This improves performance and is the default Apache configuration.

LISTING 3.4   Disabling Per-Directory Configuration Files

```
1: <Directory />
2: AllowOverride none
3: </Directory>
```

Apache Log Files

Apache includes two log files by default. The `access_log` file is for tracking client requests. The `error_log` file is for recording important events, such as errors or server restarts. These files don't exist until you start Apache the first time. The names of the files are `access.log` and `error.log` in Windows platforms.

The `access_log` File

When a client requests a file from the server, Apache records several parameters associated with the request, including the IP address of the client, the document requested, the HTTP status code, and the current time. Listing 3.5 shows sample log file entries. Chapter 26, "Logging and Monitoring Server Activity," shows you how to modify which parameters are logged.

LISTING 3.5   Sample `access_log` Entries

```
1: 127.0.0.1 - - [13/Apr/2008:08:33:25 -0700] "GET / HTTP/1.1" 200 44
2: 127.0.0.1 - - [13/Apr/2008:08:33:25 -0700] "GET /fav.ico HTTP/1.1" 404 209
```

The `error_log` File

The `error_log` file includes error messages, startup messages, and any other significant events in the life cycle of the server. This is the first place to look when you have a problem with Apache. Listing 3.6 shows sample `error_log` entries.

LISTING 3.6   Sample `error_log` Entries

```
1: Starting the Apache2.2 service [The Apache2.2 service is running.]
2: Apache/2.2.8 (Win32) configured -- resuming normal operations
3: [Sun Apr 13 08:29:34 2008] [notice] Server built: Jan 18 2008 00:37:19
4: [Sun Apr 13 08:29:34 2008] [notice] Parent: Created child process 3504
5: [Sun Apr 13 08:29:35 2008] [notice] Child 3504: Child process is running
6: [Sun Apr 13 08:29:35 2008] [notice] Child 3504: Acquired the start mutex.
```

Additional Files

The `httpd.pid` file contains the process ID of the running Apache server. You can use this number to send signals to Apache manually, as described in the next section. The `scoreboard` file, the present configuration file on Linux/UNIX Apache, is used by the process-based MPMs to communicate with their children. In general, you do not need to worry about these files.

Apache-Related Commands

The Apache distribution includes several executables. This section covers only the server binary and related scripts. Chapter 25, "Restricting Access to Your Applications," and Chapter 29 cover additional utilities included with the Apache distribution.

Apache Server Binary

The name of the Apache executable is `httpd` in Linux/UNIX and Mac OS X, and `apache.exe` in Windows. It accepts several command-line options, some of which are described in Table 3.1. You can get a complete listing of options by typing `/usr/local/apache2/bin/httpd -h` on Linux/UNIX, by typing `/usr/sbin/httpd -h` on Mac OS X, or by typing **apache.exe -h** from a command prompt on Windows.

TABLE 3.1 Some `httpd` Options

Option	Meaning
-D	Allows you to pass a parameter that can be used for <IfDefine> section processing
-l	Lists compiled-in modules
-v	Shows version number and server compilation time
-f	Allows you to pass the location of httpd.conf if it is different from the compile-time default

After Apache is running, you can use the `kill` command on Linux/UNIX and Mac OS X to send signals to the parent Apache process. Signals provide a mechanism to send commands to a process. To send a signal, execute the following command:

`# kill -SIGNAL pid`

In this syntax, *pid* is the process ID and *SIGNAL* is one of the following:

- ▶ **HUP**—Stop the server
- ▶ **USR1** or **WINCH**—Graceful restart; which signal to use depends on the underlying operating system
- ▶ **SIGHUP**—Restart

If you make some changes to the configuration files and you want them to take effect, you must signal Apache that the configuration has changed. You can do this by stopping and starting the server or by sending a restart signal. This tells Apache to reread its configuration.

A normal restart can result in a momentary pause in service. A graceful restart takes a different approach: Each thread or process serving a client continues processing the current request, but when it finishes, it is killed and replaced by a new thread or process with the new configuration. This allows seamless operation of the web server with no downtime.

On Windows, you can signal Apache using the apache.exe executable. Some commands are listed here:

- **apache.exe -k restart**—Tells Apache to restart
- **apache.exe -k graceful**—Tells Apache to do a graceful restart
- **apache.exe -k stop**—Tells Apache to stop

You can access shortcuts to these commands in the Start menu entries that the Apache installer created. If you installed Apache as a service, you can start or stop Apache by using the Windows service interface: In Control Panel, select Administrative Tasks and then click the Services icon.

Apache Control Script

Although it is possible to control Apache on Linux/UNIX using the httpd binary, it is recommended that you use the apachectl tool. The apachectl support program wraps common functionality in an easy-to-use script. To use apachectl, type the following:

```
# /usr/local/apache2/bin/apachectl command
```

In this syntax, command can be stop, start, restart, or graceful. You can also edit the contents of the apachectl script to add extra command-line options. Some OS distributions provide you with additional scripts to control Apache; please check the documentation included with your distribution.

Starting Apache for the First Time

Before you start Apache, you should verify that the minimal set of information is present in the Apache configuration file, httpd.conf. The following sections describe the basic information needed to configure Apache and to start the server.

Check Your Configuration File

You can edit the Apache `httpd.conf` file with your favorite text editor. In Linux/UNIX and Mac OS X, this probably means `vi` or `emacs`. In Windows, you can use Notepad or WordPad. You must remember to save the configuration file in plain text, which is the only format Apache will understand.

There are only two parameters that you might need to change to enable you to start Apache for the first time: the name of the server and the address and port to which it is listening. The name of the server is the one Apache will use when it needs to refer to itself (for example, when redirecting requests).

Apache can usually figure out its server name from the IP address of the machine, but this is not always the case. If the server does not have a valid DNS (domain name service) entry, you might need to specify one of the IP addresses of the machine. If the server is not connected to a network (you might want to test Apache on a standalone machine), you can use the value 127.0.0.1, which is the loopback address. The default port value is 80. You might need to change this value if a server is already running in the machine at port 80 or if you do not have administrator permissions—on Linux/UNIX and Mac OS X systems, only the `root` user can bind to privileged ports (those with port numbers lower than 1024).

You can change both the listening address and the port values with the `Listen` directive. The `Listen` directive takes either a port number or an IP address and a port, separated by a colon. If you specify only the port, Apache will listen on that port at all available IP addresses in the machine. If you provide an additional IP address, Apache will listen at only that address and port combination. For example, `Listen 80` tells Apache to listen for requests at all IP addresses on port 80. `Listen 10.0.0.1:443` tells Apache to listen at only 10.0.0.1 on port 443.

The `ServerName` directive enables you to define the name the server will report in any self-referencing URLs. The directive accepts a DNS name and an optional port, separated by a colon. Make sure that `ServerName` has a valid value. Otherwise, the server will not function properly; for example, it will issue incorrect redirects.

On Linux/UNIX and Mac OS X platforms, you can use the `User` and `Group` directives to specify which user and group IDs the server will run as. The `nobody` user is a good choice for most platforms. However, there are problems in the HP-UX platform with this user ID, so you must create and use a different user ID, such as www.

Starting Apache

To start Apache on Linux/UNIX, change to the directory containing the `apachectl` script and execute the following command:

```
# /usr/local/apache2/bin/apachectl start
```

Mac OS X users can type the following at the prompt:

```
# /usr/sbin/httpd
```

To manually start Apache on Windows, click the Start Apache in Console link in the Control Apache Server section, within the Apache HTTP Server 2.2 program group in the Start menu. If you installed Apache as a service, you must start the Apache service instead.

If everything goes well, you can access Apache using a browser. A default installation page displays, such as the one shown in Figure 3.4. If you cannot start the web server or an error page appears instead, please consult the "Troubleshooting" section that follows. Make sure that you are accessing Apache in one of the ports specified in the `Listen` directive—usually port 80 or 8080.

FIGURE 3.4
Apache default installation page.

Troubleshooting

The following subsections describe several common problems that you might encounter the first time you start Apache.

Already an Existing Web Server

If a server is already running on the machine and is listening to the same IP address and port combination, Apache will not be able to start successfully. You will get an entry in the error log file indicating that Apache cannot bind to the port:

```
[crit] (48)Address already in use: make_sock: could not bind...[alert] no
listening sockets available, shutting down
```

To solve this problem, you need to stop the running server or change the Apache configuration to listen on a different port.

No Permission to Bind to Port

You will get an error if you do not have administrator permissions and you try to bind to a privileged port (between 0 and 1024):

```
[crit] (13)Permission denied: make_sock: could not bind to address 10.0.0.2:80
[alert] no listening sockets available, shutting down
```

To solve this problem, you must either log on as the administrator before starting Apache or change the port number (8080 is a commonly used nonprivileged port).

Access Denied

You might not be able to start Apache if you do not have permission to read the configuration files or to write to the log files. You will get an error similar to the following:

```
(13)Permission denied: httpd: could not open error log file
```

This problem can arise if the user who built and installed Apache is different from the user trying to run it.

Wrong Group Settings

You can configure Apache to run under a certain username and group. Apache has default values for the running server username and group. Sometimes the default value is not valid and you will get an error containing `setgid: unable to set group id`.

To solve this problem on Linux/UNIX and Mac OS X, you must change the value of the `Group` directive in the configuration file to a valid value. Check the `/etc/groups` file for existing groups.

Summary

This chapter explained different ways of getting an Apache 2.2 server installed and running on your Linux/UNIX, Mac OS X, or Windows machine. It covered both binary and source installation and explained the basic build-time options. Additionally, you learned the location of the server configuration files and the syntax of the commands used to modify your Apache configuration. You learned about the two main log files: access_log and error_log. Finally, you saw how to start and stop the server using the Apache control scripts or the Apache server binary on Linux/UNIX, Mac OS X, and Windows platforms.

Q&A

Q. *How can I start a clean build?*

A. If you need to build a new Apache from source and do not want the result of earlier builds to affect the new one, it is always a good idea to run the make clean command. Doing so will take care of cleaning up any existing binaries, intermediate object files, and so on.

Q. *Why are per-directory configuration files useful?*

A. Although per-directory configuration files have an effect on server performance, they can be useful for delegated administration. Because per-directory configuration files are read every time a request is made, there is no need to restart the server when a change is made to the configuration.

You can allow users of your website to make configuration changes on their own without granting them administrator privileges. In this way, they can password-protect sections of their home pages, for example.

Q. *What do you mean by a valid* ServerName *directive?*

A. The DNS system associates IP addresses with domain names. The value of ServerName is returned when the server generates a URL. If you are using a certain domain name, you must make sure that it is included in your DNS system and will be available to clients visiting your site.

Workshop

The workshop is designed to help you anticipate possible questions, review what you've learned, and begin putting your knowledge into practice.

Quiz

1. How can you specify the location where you want to install Apache?

2. What is the main difference between the <Location> and <Directory> sections?

3. What is the difference between a restart and a graceful restart?

Answers

1. Linux/UNIX users can use the --prefix option of the configure script. If an existing installation is present at that location, the configuration files will be preserved but the binaries will be replaced. On Windows, this location is set in the Installation Wizard.

2. Directory sections refer to file system objects; Location sections refer to elements in the address bar of the web page.

3. During a normal restart, the server is stopped and then started, causing some requests to be lost. A graceful restart allows Apache children to continue to serve their current requests until they can be replaced with children running the new configuration.

Activities

1. Practice the various types of server shutdown and restart procedures.

2. Make some configuration changes, such as different port assignments and ServerName changes.

4

Installing and Configuring PHP

In this last of the three installation-related chapters, you will acquire, install, and configure PHP and make some basic changes to your Apache installation. In this chapter, you will learn

▶ How to install PHP

▶ How to test your PHP installation

▶ How to find help when things go wrong

▶ The basics of the PHP language

Current and Future Versions of PHP

The installation instructions in this chapter refer to PHP version 5.2.5, which is the current version of the software.

> **By the Way**
>
> If you are already using PHP 4.x.x in a production environment, or you want to stay with the 4.x.x development tree, please visit the Installation and Configuration section of the PHP Manual at http://www.php.net/install.
>
> Because PHP 5 has been in use for more than three years and PHP 6 will likely become production-ready in 2009, the status of PHP 4 is officially "end of life"—this means the PHP Group has not made any updates to PHP 4 since December 31, 2007. For more information, visit: http://www.php.net/archive/2007.php#2007-07-13-1.
>
> The code in this book assumes the use of PHP 5 and not PHP 4; in some instances, the code is no different between the versions, but you should familiarize yourself with the difference between the two versions so that you can make the appropriate adjustments.

The PHP Group uses minor release numbers for updates containing security enhancements or bug fixes. Minor releases do not follow a set release schedule; when enhancements or fixes are added to the code and are thoroughly tested, the PHP Group releases a new version with a new minor version number.

It is possible that by the time you purchase this book, the minor version number will have changed, to 5.2.6 or beyond. If that is the case, you should read the list of changes at http://www.php.net/ChangeLog-5.php for any changes regarding the installation or configuration process that makes up the bulk of this chapter.

Although it is unlikely that any installation instructions will change between minor version updates, you should get in the habit of always checking the changelog of software that you install and maintain. If a minor version change does occur while you are reading this book but the changelog notes no installation changes, simply make a mental note and substitute the new version number wherever it appears in the installation instructions and accompanying figures.

Building PHP on Linux/UNIX with Apache

In this section, we will look at one way of installing PHP with Apache on Linux/UNIX. The process is more or less the same for any UNIX-like operating system. Although you might be able to find prebuilt versions of PHP for your system, compiling PHP from source gives you greater control over the features built into your binary.

To download the PHP distribution files, go to the home of PHP, http://www.php.net/, and follow the link to the Downloads section. Grab the latest version of the source code—for this example, we are using 5.2.5. Your distribution will be named something similar to php-*VERSION*.tar.gz, where *VERSION* is the most recent release number. This archive will be a compressed tar file, so you will need to unpack it:

```
# gunzip < php-VERSION.tar.gz ¦ tar xvf -
```

Keep the downloaded file in a directory reserved for source files, such as /usr/src/ or /usr/local/src/. After your distribution is unpacked, you should move to the PHP distribution directory:

```
# cd php-VERSION
```

In your distribution directory, you will find a script called configure. This script accepts additional information that is provided when the configure script is run from the command line. These command-line arguments control the features that

PHP supports. In this example, we will include the basic options you need to install PHP with Apache and MySQL support. We will discuss some of the available configure options later in the chapter and throughout the book as they become relevant.

```
# ./configure  --prefix=/usr/local/php \
--with-mysqli=/usr/local/mysql/bin/mysql_config \
--with-apxs2=/usr/local/apache2/bin/apxs
```

After the configure script has run, you will be returned to the prompt, such as

```
...
Generating files
updating cache ./config.cache
creating ./config.status
creating php5.spec
creating main/build-defs.h
creating scripts/phpize
creating scripts/man1/phpize.1
creating scripts/php-config
creating scripts/man1/php-config.1
creating sapi/cli/php.1
creating main/php_config.h
creating main/internal_functions.c
creating main/internal_functions_cli.c
+---------------------------------------------------------------------+
¦ License:                                                            ¦
¦ This software is subject to the PHP License, available in this      ¦
¦ distribution in the file LICENSE.  By continuing this installation  ¦
¦ process, you are bound by the terms of this license agreement.      ¦
¦ If you do not agree with the terms of this license, you must abort  ¦
¦ the installation process at this point.                            ¦
+---------------------------------------------------------------------+

Thank you for using PHP.

#
```

From the prompt, issue the make command, followed by the make install command. These commands should end the process of PHP compilation and installation and return you to your prompt:

```
...
chmod 755 /usr/local/apache2/modules/libphp5.so
[activating module 'php5' in /usr/local/apache2/conf/httpd.conf]
Installing PHP CLI binary:        /usr/local/bin/
Installing PHP CLI man page:      /usr/local/man/man1/
Installing build environment:     /usr/local/lib/php/build/
Installing header files:          /usr/local/include/php/
Installing helper programs:       /usr/local/bin/
  program: phpize
  program: php-config
Installing man pages:             /usr/local/man/man1/
  page: phpize.1
  page: php-config.1
#
```

You will need to ensure that two very important files are copied to their correct locations. First, issue the following command to copy the recommended version of php.ini to its default location. You will learn more about php.ini later in this chapter.

```
# cp php.ini-recommended /usr/local/lib/php.ini
```

Next, copy the PHP shared object file to its proper place in the Apache installation directory, if it has not already been placed there by the installation process (it usually will be, as you can see in the make install output, just shown):

```
# cp libs/libphp5.so /usr/local/apache2/modules/
```

You should now be able to configure and run Apache, but let's cover some additional configuration options before heading on to the "Integrating PHP with Apache on Linux/UNIX" section.

Additional Linux/UNIX Configuration Options

In the previous section, when we ran the PHP configure script, we included some command-line arguments that determined some features that the PHP engine will include. The configure script itself gives you a list of available options, including the ones we used. From the PHP distribution directory, type the following:

```
# ./configure --help
```

This command produces a long list, so you might want to add it to a file and read it at your leisure:

```
# ./configure --help > configoptions.txt
```

If you discover additional functionality you want to add to PHP after you install it, simply run the configuration and build process again. Doing so creates a new version of libphp5.so and places it in the Apache directory structure. All you have to do is restart Apache to load the new file.

Integrating PHP with Apache on Linux/UNIX

To ensure that PHP and Apache get along with one another, you need to check for—and potentially add—a few items to the httpd.conf configuration file. First, look for a line like the following:

```
LoadModule php5_module        modules/libphp5.so
```

If this line is not present or only appears with a pound sign (#) at the beginning of the line, you must add the line or remove the #. This line tells Apache to use the PHP shared object file created by the PHP build process (libphp5.so).

Next, look for this section:

```
#
# AddType allows you to add to or override the MIME configuration
# file mime.types for specific file types.
#
```

Add the following line to that section:

```
AddType application/x-httpd-php .php   .html
```

This statement ensures that the PHP engine will parse files that end with the .php and .html extensions. Your selection of filenames might differ.

Save this file and then restart Apache. When you look in your error_log, you should see something like the following line:

```
[Sun Apr 13 10:42:47 2008] [notice] Apache/2.2.8 (Unix) PHP/5.2.5 configured
```

PHP is now part of the Apache web server. If you want to learn how to install PHP on a Mac OS X platform, keep reading. Otherwise, you can skip ahead to the "Testing Your Installation" section.

Installing PHP on Mac OS X

There are a few different options for installing PHP with Apache on Mac OS X, including building from source as described in the previous section. However, the simplest method is to install PHP from a precompiled binary package, such as those found here (per the PHP Manual):

▶ **Entropy**—http://www.entropy.ch/software/macosx/php/

▶ **Fink**—http://www.finkproject.org/

▶ **MacPorts**—http://www.macports.org/

By the Way

If you would like to build PHP from the source and are comfortable with the Mac OS X operating system and using the terminal, feel free to follow the instructions in the PHP Manual, at http://www.php.net/manual/en/install.macosx.php.

Previous editions of this book have pointed to the packages from Entropy and developer Marc Liyanage, and there is no reason to change that practice. The packages are complete, well-maintained, and well-documented.

To obtain the PHP installation package, go to http://www.entropy.ch/software/macosx/php/ and look for the section titled "Installation Instructions." Once there, follow the link to download PHP 5 for your version of Mac OS X. It is possible that this version of PHP will be a few versions behind the current Linux/UNIX build files or Windows installer.

When the download is complete, mount the disc image and double-click the *.pkg file. Perform the following installation steps to complete the process:

1. The PHP installer launches automatically, as shown in Figure 4.1. Click Continue to move to the next step.

FIGURE 4.1
The Mac PHP Installer has started.

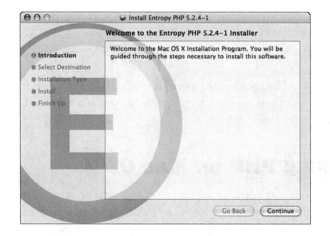

2. The next screen asks you to select the destination. Select the drive, as shown in Figure 4.2, and then click Continue.

3. You are prompted for the administration username and password, unless you are installing as root. If so, enter those values and click the Continue button.

4. The installation process continues, installing PHP and optimizing the system. When the process is complete, the installation program will say so, as shown in Figure 4.3.

The PHP installation program has made all the necessary changes to your Apache configuration, so there's nothing left for you to do except skip ahead to the "Testing Your Installation" section.

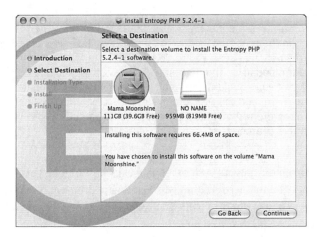

FIGURE 4.2
Select the installation location.

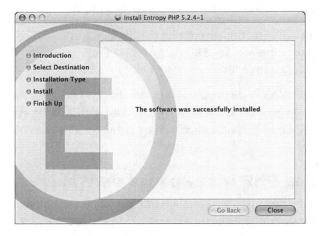

FIGURE 4.3
PHP installation is complete!

Installing PHP on Windows

Installing PHP on Windows requires nothing more than downloading the distribution file. To download the PHP distribution files, go to the home of PHP, http://www.php.net/, and follow the link to the Downloads section. Grab the latest version of the zip package (*not* the installer) from the Windows Binaries section—for this example, we are using 5.2.5. Your distribution will be named something similar to php-*VERSION*.zip, where *VERSION* is the most recent release number.

> You might ask, "Why not the installer?" The answer is simple: There are quite a few restrictions in the automatic setup of the various files, extensions, and configurations. The restrictions cause you to do more work to "fix" the installation than if you installed it manually in the first place. This situation, combined with this author's belief that you should understand how technologies are put together if you plan to use them, and the PHP Group's own recommendation that "use of the installer isn't the preferred method for installing PHP," results in the instructions you will find in this chapter.

After the file downloads to your system, double-click it to launch your unzipping software. The distribution is packed up with relative pathnames already in place, so extract the files to a new directory called C:\php\, where it will place all the files and subdirectories under that new directory.

From this point, only two basic steps need to be performed:

1. Add your PHP directory to your Windows PATH. If you do not know how to do this, see the corresponding FAQ in the PHP Manual at http://www.php.net/manual/en/faq.installation.php#faq.installation.addtopath.

2. In the PHP installation directory, copy the php.ini-recommended file to php.ini. To get a basic version of PHP working with Apache, you'll need to make a few minor modifications to the Apache configuration file.

Integrating PHP with Apache on Windows

To ensure that PHP and Apache get along with one another, you need to add a few items to the httpd.conf configuration file. First, find a section that looks like this:

```
# Example:
# LoadModule foo_module modules/mod_foo.so
#
LoadModule access_module modules/mod_access.so
...
#LoadModule ssl_module modules/mod_ssl.so
```

At the end of this section, add the following:

```
LoadModule php5_module C:/php/php5apache2_2.dll
```

Additionally, add the following to ensure Apache knows where php.ini resides:

```
PHPIniDir "C:/php/"
```

Next, look for this section:

```
#
# AddType allows you to add to or override the MIME configuration
# file mime.types for specific file types.
#
```

Add the following line:

```
AddType application/x-httpd-php .php  .html
```

This statement ensures that the PHP engine will parse files that end with the `.php` and `.html` extensions. Your selection of filenames might differ.

Save the `httpd.conf` file and then restart Apache. The server should start without warning; PHP is now part of the Apache web server.

If you have trouble getting Apache to read the correct `php.ini` file, look at the "Runtime Configuration" entry in the PHP Manual, which provides the list of locations searched for `php.ini`, at http://www.php.net/manual/en/configuration.php.

By the Way

---

php.ini **Basics**

After you have compiled or installed PHP, you can still change its behavior with the `php.ini` file. On Linux/UNIX systems, the default location for this file is `/usr/local/php/lib` or the `lib` subdirectory of the PHP installation location you used at configuration time. On a Windows system, this file should be in the PHP directory or another directory as specified by the value of `PHPIniDir` in the Apache `httpd.conf` file.

Directives in the `php.ini` file come in two forms: values and flags. Value directives take the form of a directive name and a value separated by an equal sign. Possible values vary from directive to directive. Flag directives take the form of a directive name and a positive or negative term separated by an equal sign. Positive terms include 1, On, Yes, and True. Negative terms include 0, Off, No, and False. Whitespace is ignored.

You can change your `php.ini` settings at any time, but after you do, you'll need to restart the server for the changes to take effect. At some point, take time to read through the `php.ini` file on your own to see the types of things that you can configure.

Testing Your Installation

The simplest way to test your PHP installation is to create a small test script that uses the phpinfo() function. This function will produce a long list of configuration information. Open a text editor and type the following line:

```
<?php phpinfo(); ?>
```

Save this file as phpinfo.php and place it in the document root of your web server—the htdocs subdirectory of your Apache installation or the /Library/WebServer/Documents directory on Mac OS X. Access this file using your web browser, and you should see something like what is shown in Figure 4.4.

FIGURE 4.4
The results of phpinfo().

The exact output of phpinfo() depends on your operating system, PHP version, and configuration options.

Getting Installation Help

Help is always at hand on the Internet, particularly for problems concerning open source software. Wait a moment before you click the send button, however. No matter how intractable your installation, configuration, or programming problem might seem, chances are you are not alone. Someone has probably already answered your question.

When you hit a brick wall, your first recourse should be to the official PHP site at http://www.php.net/ (particularly the annotated manual at http://www.php.net/manual/). If you still can't find your answer, don't forget that the PHP site is searchable. The advice you are seeking may be lurking in a press release or a Frequently Asked Questions file. You can also search the mailing list archives at http://www.php.net/search.php. These archives represent a huge information resource with contributions from many of the great minds in the PHP community. Spend some time trying out a few keyword combinations.

If you are still convinced that your problem has not been addressed, you might well be doing the PHP community a service by exposing it. You can join the PHP mailing lists at http://www.php.net/mailing-lists.php. Although these lists often have high volume, you can learn a lot from them. If you are serious about PHP scripting, you should certainly subscribe to at least a digest list. After you've subscribed to the list that matches your concerns, consider posting your problem.

When you post a question, it is a good idea to include as much information as possible (without writing a novel). The following items are often pertinent:

- Your operating system

- The version of PHP you are running or installing

- The configuration options you chose

- Any output from the `configure` or `make` commands that preceded an installation failure

- A reasonably complete example of the code that is causing problems

Why all these cautions about posting a question to a mailing list? First, developing research skills will stand you in good stead. A good researcher can generally solve a problem quickly and efficiently. Posting a naive question to a technical list often results in a wait rewarded only by a message or two referring you to the archives where you should have begun your search for answers in the first place.

Second, remember that a mailing list is not analogous to a technical support call center. No one is paid to answer your questions. Despite this, you have access to an impressive pool of talent and knowledge, including that of some of the creators of PHP itself. A good question and its answer will be archived to help other coders. Asking a question that has already been answered several times just adds more noise.

Having said this, don't be afraid to post a problem to the list. PHP developers are a civilized and helpful breed, and by bringing a problem to the attention of the community, you might be helping others to solve the same problem.

The Basics of PHP Scripts

Let's jump straight in with a PHP script. To begin, open your favorite text editor. Like HTML documents, PHP files are made up of plain text. You can create them with any text editor, and most popular HTML editors provide at least some support for PHP.

Did you Know? | A good website for finding PHP-friendly editors is at http://www.php-editors.com.

Type in the example in Listing 4.1 and save the file, using a name something like `first.php`.

LISTING 4.1   A Simple PHP Script

```
1: <?php
2:     echo "<h1>Hello Web!</h1>";
3: ?>
```

If you are not working directly on the machine that will be serving your PHP script, you will need to use an FTP or SCP client to upload your saved document to the server. When the document is in place on the server, you should be able to access it using your browser. If all has gone well, you should see the script's output. Figure 4.5 shows the output from the `first.php` script.

FIGURE 4.5
Success: the output from `first.php`.

Beginning and Ending a Block of PHP Statements

When writing PHP, you need to inform the PHP engine that you want it to execute your commands. If you don't do this, the code you write will be mistaken for HTML and will be output to the browser. You can designate your code as PHP with special tags that mark the beginning and end of PHP code blocks. Table 4.1 shows four such PHP delimiter tags.

TABLE 4.1   PHP Start and End Tags

Tag Style	Start Tag	End Tag
Standard tags	`<?php`	`?>`
Short tags	`<?`	`?>`
ASP tags	`<%`	`%>`
Script tags	`<script language="php">`	`</script>`

Of the tags in Table 4.1, only the standard and script tags are guaranteed to work on any configuration. You must explicitly enable the short and ASP-style tags in your `php.ini` file.

To activate recognition for short tags, you must make sure that the `short_open_tag` switch is set to `On` in `php.ini`:

```
Short_open_tag = On;
```

To activate recognition for the ASP-style tags, you must enable the `asp_tags` setting in `php.ini`:

```
asp_tags = On;
```

> To ensure portable, reusable code, it's best to use the standard tags instead of short tags or ASP-style tags for the simple reason that server configurations are unique—use the standard style because you know you can count on it as part of any configuration.

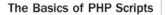
By the Way

After you have edited `php.ini` and restarted Apache, you should be able to use any of the four styles in your scripts. This is largely a matter of preference, although if you intend to include XML in your script, you should disable the short tags (`<? ?>`) and work with the standard tags (`<?php ?>`).

> The character sequence <? tells an XML parser to expect a processing instruction
> and is therefore frequently included in XML documents. If you include XML in your
> script and have short tags enabled, the PHP engine is likely to confuse XML pro-
> cessing instructions and PHP start tags. Disable short tags if you intend to incor-
> porate XML in your document.

Let's run through some of the ways in which you can legally write the code in
Listing 4.1. Given the configuration changes shown earlier, you can use any of the
four PHP start and end tags that you have seen:

```
<?
Echo "Hello Web!";
?>
```

```
<?php
echo "Hello Web!";
?>
```

```
<%
echo "Hello Web!";
%>
```

```
<script language="php">
echo "Hello Web!";
</script>
```

You can also put single lines of code in PHP on the same line as the PHP start and
end tags:

```
<? echo "Hello Web!"; ?>
```

Now that you know how to define a block of PHP code, let's take a closer look at the
code in Listing 4.1 itself.

The echo **Statement and** print() **Function**

Simply put, you use the echo statement to output data. In most cases, anything output by echo ends up viewable in the browser. Alternatively, you could have used the
print() function in place of the echo statement. Using echo or print() is a matter
of taste; when you look at other people's scripts, you might see either used.

Whereas echo is a statement, print() is a function. A *function* is a command that
performs an action, usually modified in some way by data provided for it. Data sent
to a function is almost always placed in parentheses after the function name. In this
case, you could have sent the print() function a collection of characters, or a

string. Strings must always be enclosed in quotation marks, either single or double, as in this example:

```
<?
print("Hello Web!");
?>
```

The only line of code in Listing 4.1 ended with a semicolon. The semicolon informs the PHP engine that you have completed a statement.

A *statement* represents an instruction to the PHP engine. Broadly, it is to PHP what a sentence is to written or spoken English. A sentence should usually end with a period; a statement should usually end with a semicolon. Exceptions to this rule include statements that enclose other statements and statements that end a block of code. In most cases, however, failure to end a statement with a semicolon will confuse the PHP engine and result in an error.

Combining HTML and PHP

The script in Listing 4.1 is pure PHP. You can incorporate this into an HTML document by simply adding HTML outside the PHP start and end tags, as shown in Listing 4.2.

LISTING 4.2   A PHP Script Incorporated into HTML

```
1: <html>
2: <head>
3: <title>A PHP script including HTML</title>
4: </head>
5: <body>
6: <h1><?php echo "hello world"; ?></h1>
7: </body>
8: </html>
```

As you can see, incorporating PHP code into a predominantly HTML document is simply a matter of typing in the code. The PHP engine ignores everything outside the PHP open and close tags. If you were to save the contents of Listing 4.2 as helloworld.php, place it in your document root, and then view it with a browser, as shown in Figure 4.6, you would see the string hello world in a bold heading. If you were to view the document source, as shown in Figure 4.7, the listing would look exactly like a normal HTML document.

You can include as many blocks of PHP code as you need in a single document, interspersing them with HTML as required. Although you can have multiple blocks of code in a single document, they combine to form a single script. Any variables defined in the first block will usually be available to subsequent blocks.

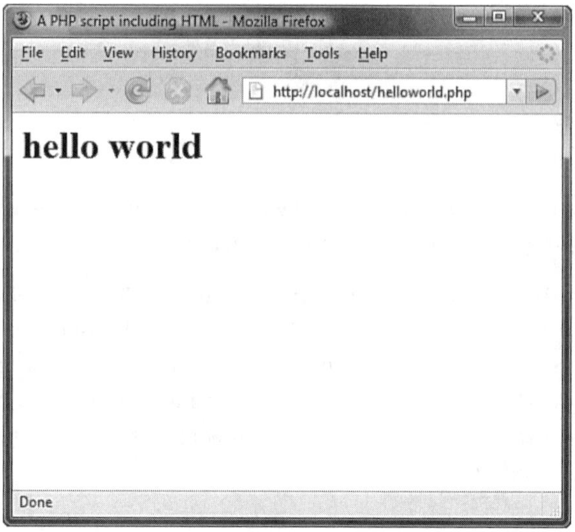

FIGURE 4.6
The output of
helloworld.php
as viewed in a
browser.

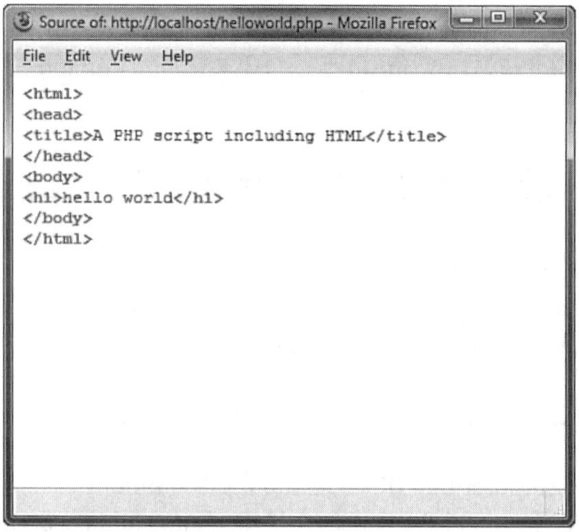

FIGURE 4.7
The output of
helloworld.php
as HTML source
code.

Adding Comments to PHP Code

Code that seems clear at the time you write it can seem like a hopeless tangle when you try to amend it six months later. Adding comments to your code as you write can save you time later on and make it easier for other programmers to work with your code.

A *comment* is text in a script that is ignored by the PHP engine. Comments can make code more readable or annotate a script.

Single-line comments begin with two forward slashes (//)—the preferred style—or a single hash or pound sign (#). The PHP engine ignores all text between these marks and either the end of the line or the PHP close tag:

```
// this is a comment
#  this is another comment
```

Multiline comments begin with a forward slash followed by an asterisk (/*) and end with an asterisk followed by a forward slash (*/):

```
/*
this is a comment
none of this will
be parsed by the
PHP engine
*/
```

Summary

In this chapter, you learned how to install and configure PHP 5.2.5 for use with Apache on Linux/UNIX, Mac OS X, or Windows. You learned that various config-ure options in the Linux/UNIX build script can change the features that are supported. You learned about php.ini and how to change the values of its directives.

Using the phpinfo() function, you tested your installation and produced a list of its configuration values. You created a simple PHP script using a text editor. You examined four sets of tags that you can use to begin and end blocks of PHP code.

Finally, you learned how to use the echo statement or print() function to send data to the browser, and you brought HTML and PHP together into the same script. In the next chapter, you will use these skills to test some of the fundamental building blocks of the PHP language, including variables, data types, and operators.

Q&A

Q. *You have covered an installation for Linux/UNIX, Mac OS X, or Windows, and the Apache web server. Does this mean that the material presented in this book will not apply to my server and operating system?*

A. No. One of PHP's great strengths is that it runs on multiple platforms. You can find installation instructions for different web servers and configuration directives for database support in the PHP Manual. Although the examples throughout this book are specifically geared toward the combination of PHP, MySQL, and Apache, only slight modifications would be needed to work with the examples using different web servers or databases.

Q. *Which are the best start and end tags to use?*

A. It is largely a matter of preference. For the sake of portability, the standard tags (<?php ?>) are preferred.

Q. *What editors should I avoid when creating PHP code?*

A. Do not use word processors that format text for printing (such as Microsoft Word, for example). Even if you save files created using this type of editor in plain text format, hidden characters are likely to creep into your code.

Q. *When should I comment my code?*

A. Again, this is a matter of preference. Some short scripts will be self-explanatory even after a long interval. For scripts of any length or complexity, you should comment your code. Comments in your code often save you time and frustration in the long run.

Workshop

The workshop is designed to help you anticipate possible questions, review what you've learned, and begin putting your knowledge into practice.

Quiz

1. From a Linux/UNIX operating system, how would you get help on configuration options (the options that you pass to the `configure` script in your PHP distribution)?

2. What line should you add to the Apache configuration file to ensure that the `.php` extension is recognized?

3. What is PHP's configuration file called?

4. Can a person browsing your website read the source code of PHP script you have successfully installed?

Answers

1. You can get help on configuration options by calling the `configure` script in the PHP distribution folder and passing it the `--help` argument:

```
./configure --help
```

2. This line ensures that Apache will treat files ending with the `.php` extension as PHP scripts:

```
AddType application/x-httpd-php .php
```

3. PHP's configuration file is called `php.ini`.

4. No, the user will see only the output of your script.

Activities

1. Install PHP on your system. If it is already in place, review your `php.ini` file and check your configuration.

2. Familiarize yourself with the process of creating, uploading, and running PHP scripts. In particular, create your own "hello world" script. Add HTML code to it, and add additional blocks of PHP. Experiment with the different PHP delimiter tags. Which ones are enabled in your configuration? Take a look at your `php.ini` file to confirm your findings. Don't forget to add some comments to your code.

PART II

PHP Language Structure

5

The Building Blocks of PHP

In this chapter, you will get your hands dirty with some of the nuts and bolts of the PHP scripting language. Those of you new to programming might feel overwhelmed at times, but don't worry—you can always refer to this chapter later on. Concentrate on understanding the concepts, rather than memorizing the features covered, because these elements will be repeated throughout the scripts in this book. Eventually you'll get it, if not the first time!

If you're already an experienced programmer, you should at least skim this chapter because it covers a few PHP-specific features with regards to global variables, data types, and changing types.

In this chapter, you will learn

▶ About variables—what they are, why you need to use them, and how to use them

▶ How to define and access variables

▶ About data types

▶ About some of the more commonly used operators

▶ How to use operators to create expressions

▶ How to define and use constants

Variables

A *variable* is a special container that you can define, which will then "hold" a value, such as a number, string, object, array, or a Boolean. Variables are fundamental to programming. Without variables, you would be forced to hard-code each specific value used in your scripts. The following hard-coded statement adds two numbers together and prints the result, which solves a simple mathematics problem:

```
echo (2 + 4);
```

However, this snippet of code is useful only for people who specifically want to know the sum of 2 and 4. To get past this limitation, you could write a script for finding the sum of another set of numbers, say 3 and 5. However, this approach to programming is clearly absurd, and this is where variables come into play.

Variables allow you to create templates for operations, such as adding two numbers, without worrying about the specific values the variables represent. Values will be given to the variables when the script is run, possibly through user input, through a database query, or from the result of another action earlier in the script. In other words, variables should be used whenever the data in your script is liable to change—either during the lifetime of the script, or when it is passed to another script for later use.

A variable consists of a name of your choosing, preceded by a dollar sign ($). Variable names can include letters, numbers, and the underscore character (_), but they cannot include spaces. Names must begin with a letter or an underscore. The following list shows some legal variables:

```
$a;
```

```
$a_longish_variable_name;
```

```
$2453;
```

```
$sleepyZZZZ;
```

By the Way

> Your variable names should be meaningful as well as consistent in style. For example, if your script deals with name and password values, don't create a variable called $n for the name and $p for the password—those are not meaningful names for anyone other than you, at that particular moment. If you pick up that script weeks later, you might think that $n is the variable for "number" rather than "name" and that $p stands for "page" rather than "password." And what if a coworker has to modify your script? How will that person know what $n and $p stood for? You can use whatever naming convention you want for variables in your scripts, as long as the names are descriptive and follow some sort of pattern that others can understand.

A semicolon (;)—also known as the *instruction terminator*—is used to end a PHP statement. The semicolons in the previous fragment of code are not part of the variable names, but are used to end the statement that declares the variable as "alive and kicking," if you will. To declare a variable, you need only include it in your script. When you declare a variable, you usually assign a value to it in the same statement, as shown here:

```
$num1 = 8;

$num2 = 23;
```

The preceding lines declare two variables and use the assignment operator (=) to assign values to them. You will learn about assignment in more detail in the "Operators and Expressions" section later in this chapter. After you assign values to your variables, you can treat them exactly as if they were the values themselves. In other words

```
echo $num1;
```

is equivalent to

```
echo 8;
```

as long as $num1 is assigned a value of 8.

Globals and Superglobals

In addition to the rules for naming variables, there are rules regarding the availability of variables. In general, the assigned value of a variable is present only within the function or script where it resides. For example, if you have scriptA.php that holds a variable called $name with a value of joe, and you want to create scriptB.php that also uses a $name variable, you can assign to that second $name variable a value of jane without affecting the variable in scriptA.php. The value of the $name variable is local to each script, and the assigned values are independent of each other.

However, you can also define the $name variable as global within a script or function. If the $name variable is defined as a global variable in both scriptA.php and scriptB.php, and these scripts are connected to each other (that is, one script calls the other or includes the other), there will only be one value for the now-shared $name variable. Examples of global variable scope will be explained in more detail in Chapter 7, "Working with Functions."

In addition to global variables of your own creation, PHP has several predefined variables called superglobals. These variables are always present, and their values are available to all your scripts. Each of the following superglobals is actually an array of other variables:

▶ $_GET contains any variables provided to a script through the GET method.

▶ $_POST contains any variables provided to a script through the POST method.

- ▶ $_COOKIE contains any variables provided to a script through a cookie.

- ▶ $_FILES contains any variables provided to a script through file uploads.

- ▶ $_SERVER contains information such as headers, file paths, and script locations.

- ▶ $_ENV contains any variables provided to a script as part of the server environment.

- ▶ $_REQUEST contains any variables provided to a script via GET, POST, or COOKIE input mechanisms.

- ▶ $_SESSION contains any variables that are currently registered in a session.

The examples in this book will use superglobals wherever possible. Using superglobals within your scripts is important in creating secure applications because superglobals reduce the likelihood of user-injected input to your scripts. By coding your scripts to accept only what you want, in the manner defined by you (from a form using the POST method, or from a session, for example), you can eliminate some of the problems created by loosely written scripts.

Data Types

Different types of data take up different amounts of memory and may be treated differently when they are manipulated in a script. Some programming languages therefore demand that the programmer declare in advance which type of data a variable will contain. By contrast, PHP is *loosely typed*, meaning that it will determine the data type at the time data is assigned to each variable.

This automatic typing is a mixed blessing. On the one hand, it means that variables can be used flexibly—in one instance, a variable can hold a string and then later in the script it can hold an integer or some other data type. On the other hand, this flexibility can lead to problems in larger scripts if you are specifically expecting a variable to hold one data type when in fact it holds something completely different. For example, suppose that you have created code to manipulate an array variable. If the variable in question instead contains a number value and no array structure is in place, errors will occur when the code attempts to perform array-specific operations on the variable.

Table 5.1 shows the eight standard data types available in PHP.

TABLE 5.1 Standard Data Types

Type	Example	Description
Boolean	`true`	One of the special values `true` or `false`
Integer	5	A whole number
Float or double	`3.234`	A floating-point number
String	`"hello"`	A collection of characters
Object		An instance of a class
Array		An ordered set of keys and values
Resource		Reference to a third-party resource (a database, for example)
NULL		An uninitialized variable

Resource types are often returned by functions that deal with external applications or files. For example, you will see references to "the MySQL resource ID" in Chapter 18, "Interacting with MySQL Using PHP." The NULL type is reserved for variables that have been declared, but no value has been assigned to them.

PHP has several functions available to test the validity of a particular type of variable—one for each type, in fact. The is_* family of functions, such as is_bool(), tests whether a given value is a Boolean. Listing 5.1 assigns different data types to a single variable and then tests the variable with the appropriate is_* function. The comments in the code show you where the script is in the process.

> You can read more about calling functions in Chapter 7.

By the Way

LISTING 5.1 Testing the Type of a Variable

```
1:  <?php
2:  $testing; // declare without assigning
3:  echo "is null? ".is_null($testing); // checks if null
4:  echo "<br/>";
5:  $testing = 5;
6:  echo "is an integer? ".is_int($testing); // checks if integer
7:  echo "<br/>";
8:  $testing = "five";
9:  echo "is a string? ".is_string($testing); // checks if string
10: echo "<br/>";
11: $testing = 5.024;
12: echo "is a double? ".is_double($testing); // checks if double
13: echo "<br/>";
14: $testing = true;
15: echo "is boolean? ".is_bool($testing); // checks if boolean
16: echo "<br/>";
17: $testing = array('apple', 'orange', 'pear');
```

LISTING 5.1 Continued

```
18: echo "is an array? ".is_array($testing); // checks if array
19: echo "<br/>";
20: echo "is numeric? ".is_numeric($testing); // checks if is numeric
21: echo "<br/>";
22: echo "is a resource? ".is_resource($testing); // checks if is a resource
23: echo "<br/>";
24: echo "is an array? ".is_array($testing); // checks if is an array
25: echo "<br/>";
26: ?>
```

Put these lines into a text file called `testtype.php`, and place this file in your web server document root. When you access this script through your web browser, it produces the following output:

```
is null? 1
is an integer? 1
is a string? 1
is a double? 1
is boolean? 1
is an array? 1
is numeric?
is a resource?
is an array? 1
```

When the `$testing` variable is declared in line 2, no value is assigned to it, so when the variable is tested in line 3 to see whether it is null (using `is_null()`), the result is 1 (true). After this, values are assigned to `$testing` by using the = sign before testing it with the appropriate `is_*` function. An integer, assigned to the `$testing` variable in line 5, is a whole or real number. In simple terms, you can think of a whole number as a number without a decimal point. A string, assigned to the `$testing` variable in line 8, is a collection of characters. When you work with strings in your scripts, they should always be surrounded by double or single quotation marks (`"` or `'`). A double, assigned to the `$testing` variable in line 11, is a floating-point number (that is, a number that includes a decimal point). A Boolean, assigned to the `$testing` variable in line 14, can have one of two special values: `true` or `false`. In line 17, an array is created using the `array()` function, which you'll learn more about in Chapter 8, "Working with Arrays." This particular array contains three items, and the script dutifully reports `$testing` to have a type of "array."

From line 20 through the end of the script, no value is reassigned to `$testing`—only the type is tested. Lines 20 and 22 test whether `$testing` is a numeric or resource type, respectively, and because it is not, no value is displayed to the user. In line 24, the script tests again to see whether `$testing` is an array, and because it is, the value of 1 is displayed.

Changing Type with settype()

PHP also provides the function settype(), which is used to change the type of a variable. To use settype(), you place the variable to change and the type to change it to between the parentheses and separate the elements with a comma, like this:

```
settype($variabletochange, 'new type');
```

Listing 5.2 converts the value 3.14 (a float) to each of the four standard types examined in this chapter.

LISTING 5.2   Changing the Type of a Variable with settype()

```
1:  <?php
2:  $undecided = 3.14;
3:  echo "is ".$undecided." a double? ".is_double($undecided)."<br/>"; // double
4:  settype($undecided, 'string');
5:  echo "is ".$undecided." a string? ".is_string($undecided)."<br/>"; // string
6:  settype($undecided, 'integer');
7:  echo "is ".$undecided." an integer? ".is_integer($undecided)."<br/>"; //
➥int
8:  settype($undecided, 'double');
9:  echo "is ".$undecided." a double? ".is_double($undecided)."<br/>"; // double
10: settype($undecided, 'bool');
11: echo "is ".$undecided." a boolean? ".is_bool($undecided)."<br/>"; // boolean
12: ?>
```

> Per the PHP Manual, "double" is returned in case of a float, and not simply "float". Your eyes are not deceiving you.

By the Way

In each case, we use the appropriate is_* function to confirm the new data type and to print the value of the variable $undecided to the browser using echo. When we convert the string "3.14" to an integer in line 6, any information beyond the decimal point is lost forever. That's why $undecided contains 3 after we change it back to a double in line 8. Finally, in line 10, we convert $undecided to a Boolean. Any number other than 0 becomes true when converted to a Boolean. When printing a Boolean in PHP, true is represented as 1 and false is represented as an empty string, so in line 11, $undecided is printed as 1.

Put these lines into a text file called settype.php and place this file in your web server document root. When you access this script through your web browser, it produces the following output:

```
is 3.14 a double? 1
is 3.14 a string? 1
is 3 an integer? 1
is 3 a double? 1
is 1 a boolean? 1
```

Changing Type by Casting

The principal difference between using settype() to change the type of an existing variable and changing type by *casting* is the fact that casting produces a copy, leaving the original variable untouched. To change type through casting, you indicate the name of a data type, in parentheses, in front of the variable you are copying. For example, the following line creates a copy of the $originalvar variable, with a specific type (integer) and a new name $newvar. The $originalvar variable will still be available, and will be its original type; $newvar is a completely new variable.

```
$newvar = (integer) $originalvar
```

Listing 5.3 illustrates changing data types through casting.

LISTING 5.3   Casting a Variable

```
1:  <?php
2:  $undecided = 3.14;
3:  $holder = (double) $undecided;
4:  echo "is ".$holder." a double? ".is_double($holder)."<br/>"; // double
5:  $holder = (string) $undecided;
6:  echo "is ".$holder." a string? ".is_string($holder)."<br/>"; // string
7:  $holder = (integer) $undecided;
8:  echo "is ".$holder." an integer? ".is_integer($holder)."<br/>"; // integer
9:  $holder = (double) $undecided;
10: echo "is ".$holder." a double? ".is_double($holder)."<br/>"; // double
11: $holder = (boolean) $undecided;
12: echo "is ".$holder." a boolean? ".is_bool($holder)."<br/>"; // boolean
13: echo "<hr/>";
14: echo "original variable type of $undecided: ";
15: echo gettype($undecided); // double
16: ?>
```

Listing 5.3 never actually changes the type of the $undecided variable, which remains a double throughout this script, as illustrated on line 15, where the gettype() function is used to determine the type of $undecided.

By the Way

> Despite its usage here, don't use gettype() to test for a certain type because it can be slow and is likely to be deprecated in future versions. Use the is_* family of functions to test type in production. This usage is simply for illustrative purposes.

In fact, casting $undecided creates a copy that is then converted to the type specified at the time of the cast, and stored in the variable $holder. This casting occurs first in line 3, and again in lines 5, 7, 9, and 11. Because the code is working with only a copy of $undecided and not the original variable, it never lost its original value, as the $undecided variable did in line 6 of Listing 5.2 when its type changed from a string to an integer.

Put the contents of Listing 5.3 into a text file called `casttype.php` and place this file in your web server document root. When you access this script through your web browser, it produces the following output:

```
is 3.14 a double? 1
is 3.14 a string? 1
is 3 an integer? 1
is 3.14 a double? 1
is 1 a boolean? 1
original variable type of 3.14: double
```

Now that you've seen how to change the contents of a variable from one type to another either by using `settype()` or by casting, consider why this might be useful. It is not a procedure that you will have to use often because PHP automatically casts your variables for you when the context of the script requires a change. However, such an automatic cast is temporary, and you might want to make a variable persistently hold a particular data type—thus, the ability to specifically change types.

For example, the numbers that a user types into an HTML form will be made available to your script as the string type. If you try to add two strings together because they contain numbers, PHP will helpfully convert these strings into numbers while the addition is taking place. So

```
"30cm" + "40cm"
```

results in an answer of 70.

> The generic term *number* is used here to mean integers and floats. If the user input is in float form, and the strings added together were "3.14cm" and "4.12cm", the answer provided would be 7.26.

During the casting of a string into an integer or float, PHP will ignore any non-numeric characters. The string will be truncated, and any characters from the location of the first non-numeric character onward are ignored. So, whereas "30cm" is transformed into "30", the string "6ft2in" becomes just 6 because the rest of the string evaluates to zero.

You might want to clean up the user input yourself and use it in a particular way in your script. Imagine that the user has been asked to submit a number. We can simulate this by declaring a variable and assigning the user's input to it:

```
$test = "30cm";
```

As you can see, the user has added units to his number—instead of entering "30", the user has entered "30cm". You can make sure that the user input is clean by casting it as an integer:

```
$newtest = (integer) $test;
echo "Your imaginary box has a width of $newtest centimeters.";
```

The resulting output would be

```
Your imaginary box has a width of 30 centimeters.
```

Had the the user input not been cast, and the value of the original variable, $test, been used in place of $newtest when printing the statement regarding the width of a box, the result would have been

```
Your imaginary box has a width of 30cm centimeters.
```

This output looks strange; in fact, it looks like parroted user input that hadn't been cleaned up (which is exactly what it is).

Why Test Type?

Why might it be useful to know the type of a variable? There are often circumstances in programming in which data is passed to you from another source. In Chapter 7, you will learn how to create functions in your scripts, and data is often passed between one or more functions because they can accept information from calling code in the form of arguments. For the function to work with the data it is given, it is a good idea to first verify that the function has been given values of the correct data type. For example, a function expecting data that has a type of "resource" will not work well when passed a string.

Operators and Expressions

With what you have learned so far, you can assign data to variables, and you can even investigate and change the data type of a variable. A programming language isn't very useful, though, unless you can manipulate the data you have stored. Operators are symbols used to manipulate data stored in variables, to make it possible to use one or more values to produce a new value, or to check the validity of data to determine the next step in a condition, and so forth. A value operated on by an operator is referred to as an operand.

> An *operator* is a symbol or series of symbols that, when used in conjunction with values, performs an action and usually produces a new value.
>
> An *operand* is a value used in conjunction with an operator. There are usually two or more operands to one operator.

By the Way

In this simple example, two operands are combined with an operator to produce a new value:

```
(4 + 5)
```

The integers 4 and 5 are operands. The addition operator (+) operates on these operands to produce the integer 9. Operators almost always sit between two operands, although you will see a few exceptions later in this chapter.

The combination of operands with an operator to produce a result is called an *expression*. Although operators and their operands form the basis of expressions, an expression need not contain an operator. In fact, an expression in PHP is defined as anything that can be used as a value. This includes integer constants such as 654, variables such as $user, and function calls such as gettype(). The expression (4 + 5), for example, consists of two expressions (4 and 5) and an operator (+). When an expression produces a value, it is often said to *resolve to* that value. That is, when all subexpressions are taken into account, the expression can be treated as if it were a code for the value itself. In this case, the expression (4 + 5) resolves to 9.

> An *expression* is any combination of functions, values, and operators that resolves to a value. As a rule of thumb, if you can use it as if it were a value, it is an expression.

By the Way

Now that you have the principles out of the way, it's time to take a tour of the operators commonly used in PHP programming.

The Assignment Operator

You have seen the assignment operator in use each time a variable was declared in an example; the assignment operator consists of the single character: =. The assignment operator takes the value of the right-side operand and assigns it to the left-side operand:

```
$name = "jimbo";
```

The variable $name now contains the string "jimbo". This construct is also an expression. Although it might seem at first glance that the assignment operator simply changes the variable $name without producing a value, in fact, a statement that uses the assignment operator always resolves to a copy of the value of the right operand. Thus

```
echo $name = "jimbo";
```

prints the string "jimbo" to the browser while it also assigns the value "jimbo" to the $name variable.

Arithmetic Operators

The arithmetic operators do exactly what you would expect—they perform arithmetic operations. Table 5.2 lists these operators along with examples of their usage and results.

TABLE 5.2 Arithmetic Operators

Operator	Name	Example	Sample Result
+	Addition	10+3	13
-	Subtraction	10-3	7
/	Division	10/3	3.3333333333333
*	Multiplication	10*3	30
%	Modulus	10%3	1

The addition operator adds the right-side operand to the left-side operand. The subtraction operator subtracts the right-side operand from the left-side operand. The division operator divides the left-side operand by the right-side operand. The multiplication operator multiplies the left-side operand by the right-side operand. The modulus operator returns the remainder of the left-side operand divided by the right-side operand.

The Concatenation Operator

The concatenation operator is represented by a single period (.). Treating both operands as strings, this operator appends the right-side operand to the left-side operand. So

```
"hello"." world"
```

returns

```
"hello world"
```

Note that the resulting space between the words occurs because there is a leading space in the second operand (`" world"` instead of `"world"`). The concatenation operator literally smashes together two strings without adding any padding. So, if you tried to concatenate two strings without leading or trailing spaces, such as

`"hello"."world"`

you would get this as your result:

`"helloworld"`

Regardless of the data types of the operands used with the concatenation operator, they are treated as strings, and the result will always be of the string type. You will encounter concatenation frequently throughout this book when the results of an expression of some kind must be combined with a string, as in

```
$cm = 212;
echo "the width is ".($cm/100)." meters";
```

Combined Assignment Operators

Although there is only one true assignment operator, PHP provides a number of combination operators that transform the left-side operand and return a result, while also modifying the original value of the variable. As a rule, operators use operands but do not change their original values, but combined assignment operators break this rule. A combined assignment operator consists of a standard operator symbol followed by an equal sign. Combination assignment operators save you the trouble of using two operators in two different steps within your script. For example, if you have a variable with a value of 4, and you want to increase this value to 4 more, you might see:

```
$x = 4;
$x = $x + 4; // $x now equals 8
```

However, you can also use a combination assignment operator (+=) to add and return the new value, as shown here:

```
$x = 4;
$x += 4; // $x now equals 8
```

Each arithmetic operator, as well as the concatenation operator, also has a corresponding combination assignment operator. Table 5.3 lists these new operators and shows an example of their usage.

TABLE 5.3   Some Combined Assignment Operators

Operator	Example	Equivalent To
+=	$x += 5	$x = $x + 5
-=	$x -= 5	$x = $x - 5
/=	$x /= 5	$x = $x / 5
*=	$x *= 5	$x = $x * 5
%=	$x %= 5	$x = $x % 5
.=	$x .= " test"	$x = $x." test"

Each of the examples in Table 5.3 transforms the value of $x using the value of the right-side operand. Subsequent uses of $x will refer to the new value. For example

```
$x = 4;
$x += 4; // $x now equals 8
$x += 4; // $x now equals 12
$x -= 3; // $x now equals 9
```

These operators will be used throughout the scripts in the book. You will frequently see the combined concatenation assignment operator when you begin to create dynamic text; looping through a script and adding content to a string, such as dynamically building the HTML code to represent a table, is a prime example of the use of a combined assignment operator.

Automatically Incrementing and Decrementing an Integer Variable

When coding in PHP, you will often find it necessary to increment or decrement a variable that is an integer type. You will usually need to do this when you are counting the iterations of a loop. You have already learned two ways of doing this—either by incrementing the value of $x using the addition operator

```
$x = $x + 1; // $x is incremented by 1
```

or by using a combined assignment operator

```
$x += 1; // $x is incremented by 1
```

In both cases, the new value is assigned to $x. Because expressions of this kind are common, PHP provides some special operators that allow you to add or subtract the integer constant 1 from an integer variable, assigning the result to the variable itself. These are known as the *post-increment* and *post-decrement* operators. The post-increment operator consists of two plus symbols appended to a variable name:

```
$x++; // $x is incremented by 1
```

This expression increments the value represented by the variable $x by one. Using two minus symbols in the same way will decrement the variable:

```
$x--; // $x is decremented by 1
```

If you use the post-increment or post-decrement operators in conjunction with a conditional operator, the operand will be modified only after the first operation has finished:

```
$x = 3;
$y = $x++ + 3;
```

In this instance, $y first becomes 6 (the result of 3 + 3) and then $x is incremented.

In some circumstances, you might want to increment or decrement a variable in a test expression before the test is carried out. PHP provides the pre-increment and pre-decrement operators for this purpose. These operators behave in the same way as the post-increment and post-decrement operators, but they are written with the plus or minus symbols preceding the variable:

```
++$x; // $x is incremented by 1
--$x; // $x is decremented by 1
```

If these operators are used as part of a test expression, incrementing occurs before the test is carried out. For example, in the next fragment, $x is incremented before it is tested against 4.

```
$x = 3;
++$x < 4; // false
```

The test expression returns false because 4 is not smaller than 4.

Comparison Operators

Comparison operators perform comparative tests using their operands and return the Boolean value true if the test is successful or false if the test fails. This type of expression is useful when using control structures in your scripts, such as if and while statements. This book covers if and while statements in Chapter 6, "Flow Control Functions in PHP."

For example, to test whether the value contained in $x is smaller than 5, you can use the less-than operator as part of your expression:

```
$x < 5
```

If $x contains the value 3, this expression will have the value true. If $x contains 7, the expression resolves to false.

Table 5.4 lists the comparison operators.

TABLE 5.4   Comparison Operators

Operator	Name	Returns True If...	Example ($x **Is** 4)	Result
==	Equivalence	Left is equivalent to right	$x == 5	false
!=	Non-equivalence	Left is not equivalent to right	$x != 5	true
===	Identical	Left is equivalent to right and they are the same type	$x === 4	true
	Non-equivalence	Left is equivalent to right but they are not the same type	$x === "4"	false
>	Greater than	Left is greater than right	$x > 4	false
>=	Greater than or equal to	Left is greater than or equal to right	$x >= 4	true
<	Less than	Left is less than right	$x < 4	false
<=	Less than or equal to	Left is less than or equal to right	$x <= 4	true

These operators are most commonly used with integers or doubles, although the equivalence operator is also used to compare strings. Be very sure to understand the difference between the == and = operators. The == operator tests equivalence, whereas the = operator assigns value. Also, remember that === tests equivalence with regards to both value and type.

Creating Complex Test Expressions with the Logical Operators

Logical operators test combinations of Boolean values. For example, the or operator, which is indicated by two pipe characters (¦¦) or simply the word or, returns the Boolean value true if either the left or the right operand is true:

```
true ¦¦ false
```

This expression returns true.

The and operator, which is indicated by two ampersand characters (&&) or simply the word and, returns the Boolean value true only if both the left and right operands are true:

```
true && false
```

This expression returns the Boolean value false. It's unlikely that you will use a logical operator to test Boolean constants because it makes more sense to test two or more expressions that resolve to a Boolean. For example

```
($x > 2) && ($x < 15)
```

returns the Boolean value true if $x contains a value that is greater than 2 and smaller than 15. Parentheses are used when comparing expressions to make the code easier to read and to indicate the precedence of expression evaluation. Table 5.5 lists the logical operators.

TABLE 5.5 Logical Operators

Operator	Name	Returns True If...	Example	Result
||	Or	Left or right is true	true || false	true
or	Or	Left or right is true	true or false	true
xor	Xor	Left or right is true but not both	true xor true	false
&&	And	Left and right are true	true && false	false
and	And	Left and right are true	true and false	false
!	Not	The single operand is not true	! true	false

You might wonder why are there two versions of both the or and the and operators, and that's a good question. The answer lies in operator precedence, which you will examine next.

Operator Precedence

When you use an operator within an expression, the PHP engine usually reads your expression from left to right. For complex expressions that use more than one operator, though, the PHP engine could be led astray without some guidance. First, consider a simple case:

```
4 + 5
```

There's no room for confusion here—PHP simply adds 4 to 5. But what about the following fragment, with two operators:

```
4 + 5 * 2
```

This presents a problem. Should PHP find the sum of 4 and 5, and then multiply it by 2, providing the result 18? Or does it mean 4 plus the result of 5 multiplied by 2, resolving to 14? If you were simply to read from left to right, the former would be true. However, PHP attaches different precedence to different operators, and because the multiplication operator has higher precedence than the addition operator, the second solution to the problem is the correct one: 4 plus the result of 5 multiplied by 2.

However, you can override operator precedence by putting parentheses around your expressions. In the following fragment, the addition expression will be evaluated before the multiplication expression:

```
(4 + 5) * 2
```

Whatever the precedence of the operators in a complex expression, it is a good idea to use parentheses to make your code clearer and to save you from bugs such as applying sales tax to the wrong subtotal in a shopping cart situation. The following is a list of the operators covered in this chapter in precedence order (those with highest precedence are listed first):

```
++, --, (cast)
/, *, %
+, -
<, <=, =>, >
==, ===, !=
&&
||
=, +=, -=, /=, *=, %=, .=
and
xor
or
```

As you can see, or has a lower precedence than ||, and and has a lower precedence than &&, so you can use the lower-precedence logical operators to change the way a complex test expression is read. In the following fragment, the two expressions are equivalent, but the second is much easier to read:

```
$x and $y || $z
```

```
$x && ($y || $z)
```

Taking it one step further, the following fragment is easier still:

```
$x and ($y or $z)
```

However, all three examples are equivalent.

The order of precedence is the only reason that both && and and are available in PHP. The same is true of || and or. In most circumstances, the use of parentheses makes for clearer code and fewer bugs than code that takes advantage of the difference in precedence of these operators. This book will tend to use the more common || and && operators, and rely on parenthetical statements to set specific operator precedence.

Constants

Variables offer a flexible way of storing data because you can change their values and the type of data they store at any time during the execution of your scripts. However, if you want to work with a value that must remain unchanged throughout your script's execution, you can define and use a *constant*. You must use PHP's built-in define() function to create a constant, which subsequently cannot be changed unless you specifically define() it again. To use the define() function, place the name of the constant and the value you want to give it, within parentheses and separated by a comma:

```
define("YOUR_CONSTANT_NAME", 42);
```

The value you want to set can be a number, a string, or a Boolean. By convention, the name of the constant should be in capital letters. Constants are accessed with the constant name only; no dollar symbol is required. Listing 5.4 shows you how to define and access a constant.

LISTING 5.4 Defining and Accessing a Constant

```
1: <?php
2: define("THE_YEAR", "2008");
3: echo "It is the year ".THE_YEAR;
4: ?>
```

Did you
Know?

> Constants can be used anywhere in your scripts, including in functions stored in
> external files.

Notice that in line 3 the concatenation operator is used to append the value held by
the constant to the string "It is the year " because PHP does not distinguish
between a constant and a string within quotation marks.

Put these few lines into a text file called constant.php and place this file in your
web server document root. When you access this script through your web browser, it
produces the following output:

```
It is the year 2008
```

The define() function can also accept a third Boolean argument that determines
whether the constant name should be case sensitive. By default, constant names are
case sensitive. However, by passing true to the define() function, you can change
this behavior, so if you were to set up our THE_YEAR constant as

```
define("THE_YEAR", "2008", true);
```

you could access its value without worrying about case:

```
echo the_year;
echo ThE_YeAr;
echo THE_YEAR;
```

The preceding three expressions are equivalent, and all would result in an output of
2008. This feature can make scripts a little friendlier for other programmers who
work with our code because they will not need to consider case when accessing a
constant we have already defined. On the other hand, given the fact that other constants *are* case sensitive, this might make for more, rather than less, confusion as
programmers forget which constants to treat in which way. Unless you have a com-
pelling reason to do otherwise, the safest course is to keep your constants case sensitive and define them using uppercase characters, which is an easy-to-remember (not
to mention standard) convention.

Predefined Constants

PHP automatically provides some built-in constants for you. For example, the constant __FILE__ returns the name of the file that the PHP engine is currently reading.
The constant __LINE__ returns the current line number of the file. These constants
are useful for generating error messages. You can also find out which version of PHP
is interpreting the script with the PHP_VERSION constant. This constant can be useful

if you need version information included in script output when sending a bug report.

Summary

This chapter covered some of the basic features of the PHP language. You learned about variables and how to assign values to them using the assignment operator, as well as received an introduction to the scope of variables and built-in superglobals. You got an introduction to operators and learned how to combine some of the most common of these into expressions. Finally, you learned how to define and access constants.

Now that you have mastered some of the fundamentals of PHP, the next chapter will really put you in the driver's seat. You will learn how to make scripts that can make decisions and repeat tasks, with help from variables, expressions, and operators.

Q&A

Q. *Why is it useful to know the type of data that a variable holds?*

A. Often the data type of a variable constrains what you can do with it. For example, you can't perform array-related functions on simple strings. Similarly, you might want to make sure that a variable contains an integer or a float before using it in a mathematical calculation, even though PHP will often help you by changing data types for you in this situation.

Q. *Should I obey any conventions when naming variables?*

A. Your goal should always be to make your code easy to read and understand. A variable such as $ab123245 tells you nothing about its role in your script and invites typos. Keep your variable names short and descriptive.

A variable named $f is unlikely to mean much to you when you return to your code after a month or so. A variable named $filename, on the other hand, should make more sense.

Q. *Should I learn the operator precedence table?*

A. There is no reason you shouldn't, but I would save the effort for more useful tasks. By using parentheses in your expressions, you can make your code easy to read while defining your own order of precedence.

Workshop

The workshop is designed to help you anticipate possible questions, review what you've learned, and begin putting your knowledge into practice.

Quiz

1. Which of the following variable names are not valid?

```
$a_value_submitted_by_a_user
$666666xyz
$xyz666666
$_____counter_____
$the first
$file-name
```

2. What will the following code fragment output?

```
$num = 33;
(boolean) $num;
echo $num;
```

3. What will the following statement output?

```
echo gettype("4");
```

4. What will be the output from the following code fragment?

```
$test_val = 5.5466;
settype($test_val, "integer");
echo $test_val;
```

5. Which of the following statements does not contain an expression?

```
4;
gettype(44);
5/12;
```

6. Which of the statements in question 5 contains an operator?

7. What value will the following expression return?

```
5 < 2
```

What data type will the returned value be?

Answers

1. The variable name $666666xyz is not valid because it does not begin with a letter or an underscore character. The variable name $the first is not valid because it contains a space. $file-name is also invalid because it contains a nonalphanumeric character (-).

2. The fragment will print the integer 33. The cast to Boolean produces a converted copy of the value stored in $num. It does not alter the value actually stored there.

3. The statement will output the string "string".

4. The code will output the value 5. When a float is converted to an integer, any information beyond the decimal point is lost.

5. They are all expressions because they all resolve to values.

6. The statement 5/12; contains a division operator.

7. The expression will resolve to false, which is a Boolean value.

Activities

1. Create a script that contains at least five different variables. Populate them with values of different data types and use the gettype() function to print each type to the browser.

2. Assign values to two variables. Use comparison operators to test whether the first value is

   ▶ The same as the second

   ▶ Less than the second

   ▶ Greater than the second

   ▶ Less than or equal to the second

   Print the result of each test to the browser.

   Change the values assigned to your test variables and run the script again.

6

Flow Control Functions in PHP

The scripts created in the previous chapter flow only in a single direction—forward. That is, the same statements execute in the same order every time a script is run. This does not allow for much flexibility because any sort of dynamic programming will at the very least need to have a loop or two, not to mention the ability to check for the validity of certain conditions before proceeding onward.

You will now learn about the programming structures that enable your scripts to adapt to circumstances. In this chapter, you will learn

- ▶ How to use the `if` statement to execute code if a test expression evaluates to `true`
- ▶ How to execute alternative blocks of code when the test expression of an `if` statement evaluates to `false`
- ▶ How to use the `switch` statement to execute code based on the value returned by a test expression
- ▶ How to repeat execution of code using a `while` statement
- ▶ How to use `for` statements to make neater loops
- ▶ How to break out of loops
- ▶ How to nest one loop within another
- ▶ How to use PHP start and end tags within control structures

Switching Flow

It is common for scripts to evaluate conditions and change their behavior accordingly. These decisions are what make your PHP pages dynamic—that is, able to change output according to circumstances. Like most programming languages, PHP allows you to do this with an `if` statement.

The `if` **Statement**

The `if` statement is a way of controlling the execution of a statement that follows it (that is, a single statement or a block of code inside braces). The `if` statement evaluates an expression found between parentheses—if this expression results in a `true` value, the statement is executed. Otherwise, the statement is skipped entirely. This functionality enables scripts to make decisions based on any number of factors:

```
if (expression) {
    // code to execute if the expression evaluates to true
}
```

Listing 6.1 executes a block of code only if a variable contains the string `"happy"`.

LISTING 6.1   An `if` Statement

```
1: <?php
2: $mood = "happy";
3: if ($mood == "happy") {
4:      echo "Hooray, I'm in a good mood!";
5: }
6: ?>
```

In line 2, the value `"happy"` is assigned to the variable $mood. In line 3, the comparison operator == compares the value of the variable $mood with the string `"happy"`. If they match, the expression evaluates to `true`, and the subsequent code is executed until the closing bracket is found (in this case, in line 5).

Put these lines into a text file called `testif.php` and place this file in your web server document root. When you access this script through your web browser, it produces the following output:

```
Hooray, I'm in a good mood!
```

If you change the assigned value of $mood to `"sad"` or any other string besides `"happy"`, and then run the script again, the expression in the `if` statement will evaluate to `false` and the code block will be skipped. The script remains silent, which leads to the `else` clause.

Using the `else` **Clause with the** `if` **Statement**

When working with an `if` statement, you might want to define an alternative block of code that should be executed if the expression you are testing evaluates to `false`. You can do this by adding `else` to the `if` statement followed by a further block of code:

```
if (expression) {
   // code to execute if the expression evaluates to true
} else {
   // code to execute in all other cases
}
```

Listing 6.2 amends the example in Listing 6.1 so that a default block of code is executed if the value of $mood is not equivalent to "happy".

LISTING 6.2   An if Statement That Uses else

```
1: <?php
2: $mood = "sad";
3: if ($mood == "happy") {
4:     echo "Hooray, I'm in a good mood!";
5: } else {
6:     echo "I'm in a $mood mood.";
7: }
8: ?>
```

Put these lines into a text file called testifelse.php and place this file in your web server document root. When you access this script through your web browser, it produces the following output:

```
I'm in a sad mood.
```

Notice in line 2 that the value of $mood is the string "sad", which obviously is not equal to "happy", so the expression in the if statement in line 3 evaluates to false. This results in the first block of code (line 4) being skipped. However, the block of code after else *is* executed, and the alternate message is printed: I'm in a sad mood. The string "sad" is the value assigned to the variable $mood.

Using an else clause in conjunction with an if statement allows scripts to make decisions regarding code execution. However, your options are limited to an either-or branch: either the code block following the if statement or the code block following the else statement. You'll now learn about additional options for the evaluation of multiple expressions, one after another.

Using the elseif Clause with the if Statement

You can use an if...elseif...else clause to test multiple expressions (the if...else portion) before offering a default block of code (the elseif portion):

```
if (expression) {
   // code to execute if the expression evaluates to true
} elseif (another expression) {
   // code to execute if the previous expression failed
   // and this one evaluates to true
```

```
} else {
    // code to execute in all other cases
}
```

If the initial if expression does not evaluate to true, the first block of code will be ignored. The elseif clause presents another expression for evaluation; if it evaluates to true, its corresponding block of code is executed. Otherwise, the block of code associated with the else clause is executed. You can include as many elseif clauses as you want, and if you don't need a default action, you can omit the else clause.

By the Way

> The elseif clause can also be written as two words (else if). The syntax you employ is a matter of taste, but coding standards employed by PEAR (the PHP extension and application repository) and PECL (the PHP extension community library) use elseif.

Listing 6.3 adds an elseif clause to the previous example.

LISTING 6.3   An if Statement That Uses else and elseif

```
 1:  <?php
 2:  $mood = "sad";
 3:  if ($mood == "happy") {
 4:      echo "Hooray, I'm in a good mood!";
 5:  } elseif ($mood == "sad") {
 6:      echo "Awww. Don't be down!";
 7:  } else {
 8:      echo "Neither happy nor sad but $mood.";
 9:  }
10:  ?>
```

Once again, the $mood variable has a value of "sad", as shown in line 2. This value is not equal to "happy", so the code in line 4 is ignored. The elseif clause in line 5 tests for equivalence between the value of $mood and the value "sad", which in this case evaluates to true. The code in line 6 is therefore executed. In lines 7 through 9, a default behavior is provided, which would be invoked if the previous test conditions were all false. In that case, we would simply print a message including the actual value of the $mood variable.

Put these lines into a text file called testifelseif.php and place this file in your web server document root. When you access this script through your web browser, it produces the following output:

```
Awww. Don't be down!
```

Change the value of $mood to `"iffy"` and run the script, and it will produce the following output:

```
Neither happy nor sad but iffy.
```

The switch **Statement**

The switch statement is an alternative way of changing flow, based on the evaluation of an expression. Using the if statement in conjunction with elseif, you can evaluate multiple expressions, as you've just seen. However, a switch statement evaluates only one expression in a list of expressions, selecting the correct one based on a specific bit of matching code. Whereas the result of an expression evaluated as part of an if statement is interpreted as either true or false, the expression portion of a switch statement is subsequently tested against any number of values, in hopes of finding a match:

```
switch (expression) {
      case result1:
            // execute this if expression results in result1
            break;
      case result2:
            // execute this if expression results in result2
            break;
      default:
            // execute this if no break statement
            // has been encountered hitherto
            break;
}
```

The expression used in a switch statement is often just a variable, such as $mood. Within the switch statement, you find a number of case statements. Each of these cases tests a value against the value of the switch expression. If the case value is equivalent to the expression value, the code within the case statement is executed. The break statement ends the execution of the switch statement altogether.

If the break statement is omitted, the next case statement is executed, regardless of whether a previous match has been found. If the optional default statement is reached without a previous matching value having been found, its code is executed.

It is important to include a break statement at the end of any code that will be executed as part of a case statement. Without a break statement, the program flow will continue to the next case statement and ultimately to the default statement. In most cases, this will result in unexpected behavior, likely incorrect!

Watch Out!

Listing 6.4 re-creates the functionality of the if statement example using the switch statement.

LISTING 6.4   A switch Statement

```
1: <?php
2: $mood = "sad";
3: switch ($mood) {
4:     case "happy":
5:         echo "Hooray, I'm in a good mood!";
6:         break;
7:     case "sad":
8:         echo "Awww. Don't be down!";
9:         break;
10:    default:
11:        echo "Neither happy nor sad but $mood.";
12:        break;
13: }
14: ?>
```

Once again, in line 2 the $mood variable is initialized with a value of "sad". The switch statement in line 3 uses this variable as its expression. The first case state-ment in line 4 tests for equivalence between "happy" and the value of $mood. There is no match in this case, so script execution moves on to the second case statement in line 7. The string "sad" is equivalent to the value of $mood, so this block of code is executed. The break statement in line 9 ends the process. Lines 10 through 12 provide the default action, should neither of the previous cases evaluate as true.

Put these lines into a text file called testswitch.php and place this file in your web server document root. When you access this script through your web browser, it pro-duces the following output:

```
Awww. Don't be down!
```

Change the value of $mood to "happy" and run the script, and it will produce the following output:

```
Hooray, I'm in a good mood!
```

To emphasize the caution regarding the importance of the break statement, try run-ning this script without the second break statement. Be sure to change the value of $mood back to "sad" and then run the script. Your output will be as follows:

```
Awww. Don't be down!Neither happy nor sad but sad.
```

This is definitely not the desired output, so be sure to include break statements where appropriate!

Using the ? Operator

The ? or *ternary* operator is similar to the if statement, except that it returns a value derived from one of two expressions separated by a colon. This construct will provide you with three parts of the whole, hence the name *ternary*. The expression used to generate the returned value depends on the result of a test expression:

```
(expression) ? returned_if_expression_is_true : returned_if_expression_is_false;
```

If the test expression evaluates to `true`, the result of the second expression is returned; otherwise, the value of the third expression is returned. Listing 6.5 uses the ternary operator to set the value of a variable according to the value of $mood.

LISTING 6.5   Using the ? Operator

```
1: <?php
2: $mood = "sad";
3: $text = ($mood == "happy") ? "I'm in a good mood!" : "I am in a $mood mood.";
4: echo "$text";
5: ?>
```

In line 2, $mood is set to `"sad"`. In line 3, $mood is tested for equivalence to the string `"happy"`. Because this test returns `false`, the result of the third of the three expressions is returned.

Put these lines into a text file called `testtern.php` and place this file in your web server document root. When you access this script through your web browser, it produces the following output:

```
I am in a sad mood.
```

The ternary operator can be difficult to read, but is useful if you are dealing with only two alternatives and want to write compact code.

Loops

So far you've looked at decisions that a script can make about what code to execute. Scripts can also decide how many times to execute a block of code. Loop statements are specifically designed to enable you to perform repetitive tasks because they continue to operate until a specified condition is achieved or until you explicitly choose to exit the loop.

The while Statement

The while statement looks similar in structure to a basic if statement, but has the ability to loop:

```
while (expression) {
    // do something
}
```

Unlike an if statement, a while statement will execute for as long as the expression evaluates to true, over and over again if need be. Each execution of a code block within a loop is called an *iteration*. Within the block, you usually change something that affects the while statement's expression; otherwise, your loop continues indefinitely. For example, you might use a variable to count the number of iterations and act accordingly. Listing 6.6 creates a while loop that calculates and prints multiples of 2 up to 24.

LISTING 6.6   A while **Statement**

```
1: <?php
2: $counter = 1;
3: while ($counter <= 12) {
4:     echo $counter." times 2 is ".($counter * 2)."<br />";
5:     $counter++;
6: }
7: ?>
```

This example initializes the variable $counter in line 2 with a value of 1. The while statement in line 3 tests the $counter variable so that as long as the value of $counter is less than or equal to 12, the loop will continue to run. Within the while statement's code block, the value of $counter is multiplied by 2 and the result is printed to the browser. In line 5, the value of $counter is incremented by 1. This step is extremely important because if you did not increment the value of the $counter variable, the while expression would never resolve to false and the loop would never end.

Put these lines into a text file called testwhile.php and place this file in your web server document root. When you access this script through your web browser, it produces the following output:

```
1 times 2 is 2
2 times 2 is 4
3 times 2 is 6
4 times 2 is 8
5 times 2 is 10
6 times 2 is 12
7 times 2 is 14
8 times 2 is 16
9 times 2 is 18
10 times 2 is 20
11 times 2 is 22
12 times 2 is 24
```

The do...while **Statement**

A do...while statement looks a little like a while statement turned on its head. The essential difference between the two is that the code block is executed *before* the truth test and not after it:

```
do {
    // code to be executed
} while (expression);
```

> The test expression of a do...while statement should always end with a semi-colon.

Watch Out!

This type of statement is useful when you want the code block to be executed at least once, even if the while expression evaluates to false. Listing 6.7 creates a do...while statement. The code block is executed a minimum of one time.

LISTING 6.7 The do...while **Statement**

```
1: <?php
2: $num = 1;
3: do {
4:     echo "The number is: ".$num."<br />";
5:     $num++;
6: } while (($num > 200) && ($num < 400));
7: ?>
```

The do...while statement tests whether the variable $num contains a value that is greater than 200 and less than 400. Line 2 initializes $num to 1, so this expression returns false. Nonetheless, the code block is executed at least one time before the expression is evaluated, so the statement will print a single line to the browser.

Put these lines into a text file called testdowhile.php and place this file in your web server document root. When you access this script through your web browser, it produces the following output:

```
The number is: 1
```

If you change the value of $num in line 2 to 300 and then run the script, the loop will display

```
The number is: 300
```

and will continue to print similar lines, with increasing numbers, through

```
The number is: 399
```

The for **Statement**

Anything you want to do with a for statement can also be done with a while statement, but a for statement is often a more efficient method of achieving the same effect. In Listing 6.6, you saw how a variable was initialized outside the while statement, and then tested within its expression, and incremented within the code block. The for statement allows you to achieve this same series of events, but in a single line of code. This allows for more compact code and makes it less likely that you will forget to increment a counter variable, thereby creating an infinite loop:

```
for (initialization expression; test expression; modification expression) {
    // code to be executed
}
```

By the Way

> *Infinite loops* are, as the name suggests, loops that run without bounds. If your loop is running infinitely, your script is running for an infinite amount of time. This behavior is very stressful on your web server and renders the web page unusable.

The expressions within the parentheses of the for statement are separated by semi-colons. Usually, the first expression initializes a counter variable, the second expression is the test condition for the loop, and the third expression increments the counter. Listing 6.8 shows a for statement that re-creates the example in Listing 6.6, which multiplies 12 numbers by 2.

LISTING 6.8   Using the for **Statement**

```
1: <?php
2: for ($counter=1; $counter<=12; $counter++) {
3:     echo $counter." times 2 is ".($counter * 2)."<br />";
4: }
5: ?>
```

Put these lines into a text file called testfor.php and place this file in your web server document root. When you access this script through your web browser, it produces the following output:

```
1 times 2 is 2
2 times 2 is 4
3 times 2 is 6
4 times 2 is 8
5 times 2 is 10
6 times 2 is 12
7 times 2 is 14
8 times 2 is 16
9 times 2 is 18
10 times 2 is 20
11 times 2 is 22
12 times 2 is 24
```

The results of Listings 6.6 and 6.8 are the same, but the for statement makes the code in Listing 6.8 more compact. Because the $counter variable is initialized and incremented at the beginning of the statement, the logic of the loop is clear at a glance. That is, as shown in line 2, the first expression initializes the $counter variable and assigns a value of 1, the test expression verifies that $counter contains a value that is less than or equal to 12, and the final expression increments the $counter variable. Each of these items is found in the single line of code.

When the sequence of script execution reaches the for loop, the $counter variable is initialized and the test expression is evaluated. If the expression evaluates to true, the code block is executed. The $counter variable is then incremented and the test expression is evaluated again. This process continues until the test expression evaluates to false.

Breaking Out of Loops with the break Statement

Both while and for statements incorporate a built-in test expression with which you can end a loop. However, the break statement enables you to break out of a loop based on the results of additional tests. This can provide a safeguard against error. Listing 6.9 creates a simple for statement that divides a large number by a variable that is incremented, printing the result to the screen.

LISTING 6.9 A for Loop That Divides 4000 by 10 Incremental Numbers

```
1: <?php
2: for ($counter=1; $counter <= 10; $counter++) {
3:     $temp = 4000/$counter;
4:     echo "4000 divided by ".$counter." is...".$temp."<br />";
5: }
6: ?>
```

In line 2, this example initializes the variable $counter and assigns a value of 1. The test expression in the for statement verifies that the value of $counter is less than or equal to 10. Within the code block, 4000 is divided by $counter, printing the result to the browser.

Put these lines into a text file called testfor2.php and place this file in your web server document root. When you access this script through your web browser, it produces the following output:

```
4000 divided by 1 is... 4000
4000 divided by 2 is... 2000
4000 divided by 3 is... 1333.33333333
4000 divided by 4 is... 1000
4000 divided by 5 is... 800
4000 divided by 6 is... 666.666666667
```

```
4000 divided by 7 is... 571.428571429
4000 divided by 8 is... 500
4000 divided by 9 is... 444.444444444
4000 divided by 10 is... 400
```

This seems straightforward enough. But what if the value you place in $counter comes from user input? The value could be a negative number or even a string. Let's take the first instance, where the user input value is a negative number. Changing the initial value of $counter from 1 to -4 causes **4000** to be divided by 0 when the code block is executed for the fifth time. It is generally not a good idea for your code to divide by zero because such an operation results in an answer of "undefined." Listing 6.10 guards against this occurrence by breaking out of the loop if the value of the $counter variable equals zero.

LISTING 6.10   Using the break **Statement**

```
1: <?php
2: $counter = -4;
3: for (; $counter <= 10; $counter++) {
4:     if ($counter == 0) {
5:         break;
6:     } else {
7:         $temp = 4000/$counter;
8:         echo  "4000 divided by ".$counter." is...".$temp."<br />";
9:     }
10: }
11 ?>:
```

<table>
<tr><td>**By the**
Way</td><td>Dividing a number by zero does not cause a fatal error in PHP. Instead, PHP generates a warning and execution continues.</td></tr>
</table>

Listing 6.10 uses an if statement, shown in line 4, to test the value of $counter before attempting mathematical operations using this value. If the value of $counter is equal to zero, the break statement immediately halts execution of the code block, and program flow continues after the for statement (line 11).

Put these lines into a text file called testfor3.php and place this file in your web server document root. When you access this script through your web browser, it produces the following output:

```
4000 divided by -4 is... -1000
4000 divided by -3 is... -1333.33333333
4000 divided by -2 is... -2000
4000 divided by -1 is... -4000
```

Notice that the $counter variable was initialized in line 2, outside the for statement's parentheses. This method was used to simulate a situation in which the value of $counter is set from outside the script.

You can omit any of the expressions from a for statement, but you must remember to retain the separation semicolons.

Did you Know?

Skipping an Iteration with the continue Statement

The continue statement ends execution of the current iteration but doesn't cause the loop as a whole to end. Instead, the next iteration begins immediately. Using the break statement as in Listing 6.10 is a little drastic; with the continue statement in Listing 6.11, you can avoid a divide-by-zero error without ending the loop completely.

LISTING 6.11   Using the continue Statement

```
1:  <?php
2:  $counter = -4;
3:  for (; $counter <= 10; $counter++) {
4:      if ($counter == 0) {
5:          continue;
6:      }
7:      $temp = 4000/$counter;
8:      echo "4000 divided by ".$counter." is...".$temp."<br />";
9:  }
10: ?>
```

Line 5 swaps the break statement for a continue statement. If the value of the $counter variable is equivalent to zero, the iteration is skipped and the next one starts immediately.

Put these lines into a text file called testcontinue.php and place this file in your web server document root. When you access this script through your web browser, it produces the following output:

```
4000 divided by -4 is... -1000
4000 divided by -3 is... -1333.33333333
4000 divided by -2 is... -2000
4000 divided by -1 is... -4000
4000 divided by 1 is... 4000
4000 divided by 2 is... 2000
4000 divided by 3 is... 1333.33333333
4000 divided by 4 is... 1000
4000 divided by 5 is... 800
4000 divided by 6 is... 666.666666667
4000 divided by 7 is... 571.428571429
4000 divided by 8 is... 500
```

Watch
Out!

Using the break and continue statements can make code more difficult to read because they often add layers of complexity to the logic of the loop statements that contain them. Use these statements with care, or comment your code to show other programmers (or yourself) just what you're trying to achieve with these statements.

Nesting Loops

Loops can contain other loop statements, as long as the logic is valid and the loops are tidy. The combination of such statements is particularly useful when working with dynamically created HTML tables. Listing 6.12 uses two for statements to print a multiplication table to the browser.

LISTING 6.12   Nesting Two for Loops

```
1:  <?php
2:  echo "<table style=\"border: 1px solid black;\"> \n";
3:  for ($y=1; $y<=12; $y++) {
4:      echo "<tr> \n";
5:      for ($x=1; $x<=12; $x++) {
6:          echo "<td style=\"border: 1px solid #000; width: 25px; padding: 4px;
7:                  text-align:center;\">";
8:          echo ($x * $y);
9:          echo "</td> \n";
10:     }
11:     echo "</tr> \n";
12: }
13: echo "</table>";
14: ?>
```

Before you examine the for loops, take a closer look at line 2 in Listing 6.12:

```
echo "<table style=\"border: 1px solid black;\"> \n";
```

Notice that Listing 6.12 uses the backslash character (\) before each of the quotation marks within the string containing the style information for the table. These backslashes also appear in lines 6 and 7, in the style information for the table data cell. This is necessary because it tells the PHP engine that we want to use the quotation mark character, rather than have PHP interpret it as the beginning or end of a string. If you did not "escape" the quotation marks with the backslash character, the statement would not make sense to the engine (it would read it as a string followed by a number followed by another string). Such a construct would generate an error. This line also uses \n to represent a newline character, which will make the source easier to read when it is rendered by the browser.

The outer for statement (line 3) initializes a variable called $y, assigning to it a starting value of 1. This for statement defines an expression that intends to verify that the value of $y is less than or equal to 12, and then defines the increment that will be used. In each iteration, the code block prints a tr (table row) HTML element (line 4) and begins another for statement (line 5). This inner loop initializes a variable called $x and defines expressions along the same lines as for the outer loop. For each iteration, the inner loop prints a td (table cell) element to the browser (lines 6 and 7), as well as the result of $x multiplied by $y (line 8). Line 9 closes the table cell. After the inner loop has finished, execution falls back through to the outer loop, where the table row closes on line 11, ready for the process to begin again. When the outer loop has finished, the result is a neatly formatted multiplication table. Listing 6.12 wraps things up by closing the table on line 13.

Put these lines into a text file called testnestfor.php and place this file in your web server document root. When you access this script through your web browser, it should look like Figure 6.1.

FIGURE 6.1
Output of testnestfor. php.

Code Blocks and Browser Output

In Chapter 4, "Installing and Configuring PHP," you learned that you can slip in and out of HTML mode at will using the PHP start and end tags. In this chapter, you have discovered that you can present distinct output to the user according to a decision-making process you can control with if and switch statements. This section will combine these two techniques.

Imagine a script that outputs a table of values only when a variable is set to the Boolean value true. Listing 6.13 shows a simplified HTML table constructed with the code block of an if statement.

LISTING 6.13   A Code Block Containing Multiple echo Statements

```
1: <?php
2: $display_prices = true;
3: if ($display_prices) {
4:     echo "<table style=\"border: 1px solid black;\">\n";
5:     echo "<tr><td colspan=\"3\">";
6:     echo "today's prices in dollars";
7:     echo "</td></tr>";
8:     echo "<tr><td>\$14.00</td><td>\$32.00</td><td>\$71.00</td></tr>\n";
9:     echo "</table>";
10: }
11: ?>
```

Watch Out!

> In line 8 you will note the dollar sign, when meant literally and not as part of a variable declaration, must be escaped with a backslash for it to be interpreted as the dollar sign character.

If the value of $display_prices is set to true in line 2, the table is printed. For the sake of readability, we split the output into multiple echo() statements, and once again use the backslash to escape any quotation marks used in the HTML output.

Put these lines into a text file called testmultiecho.php and place this file in your web server document root. When you access this script through your web browser, it should look like Figure 6.2.

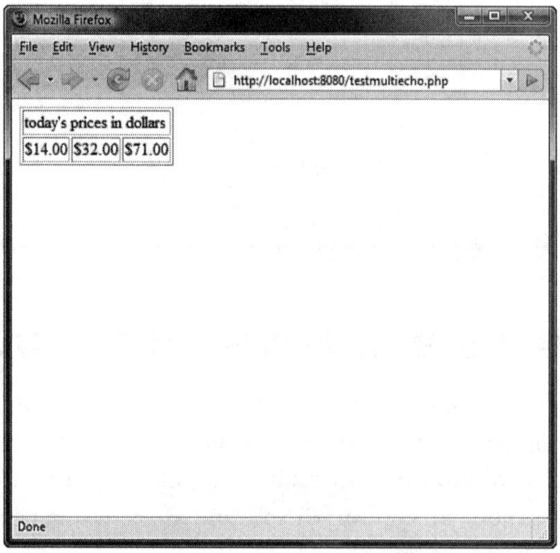

FIGURE 6.2
Output of test-multiecho.php.

There's nothing wrong with the way this is coded, but you can save yourself some typing by simply slipping back into HTML mode within the code block. Listing 6.14 does just that.

LISTING 6.14   **Returning to HTML Mode Within a Code Block**

```
1: <?php
2: $display_prices = true;
3: if ($display_prices) {
4: ?>
5: <table style="border: 1px solid black;">
6: <tr><td colspan="3">today's prices in dollars</td></tr>
7: <tr><td>$14.00</td><td>$32.00</td><td>$71.00</td></tr>
8: </table>
9: <?php
10: }
11: ?>
```

The important thing to note here is that the shift to HTML mode on line 4 occurs only if the condition of the `if` statement is fulfilled. This can save you the bother of escaping quotation marks and wrapping your output in `echo()` statements. This approach might, however, affect the readability of the code in the long run, especially if the script grows larger.

Summary

In this chapter, you learned about control structures and the ways in which they can help to make your scripts flexible and dynamic. Most of these structures will reappear regularly throughout the rest of the book.

You learned how to define an `if` statement and how to provide for alternative actions with the `elseif` and `else` clauses. You learned how to use the `switch` statement to change flow according to multiple equivalence tests on the result of an expression. You learned about loops—in particular, the `while` and `for` statements—and you learned how to use `break` and `continue` to prematurely end the execution of a loop or to skip an iteration. You learned how to nest one loop within another and saw a typical use for this structure. Finally, you looked at a technique for using PHP start and end tags in conjunction with conditional code blocks, to alleviate having to escape (use the backslash in front of) special characters such as the quotation mark and dollar sign.

You should now know enough of the basics to write scripts of your own that make decisions and perform repetitive tasks. In the next chapter, you will look at a way of adding even more power to your applications. You will learn how functions enable you to organize your code, preventing duplication and improving reusability.

Q&A

Q. *Must a control structure's test expression result in a Boolean value?*

A. Ultimately, yes, but in the context of a test expression, zero, an undefined variable, or an empty string will be converted to `false`. All other values will evaluate to `true`.

Q. *Must I always surround a code block in a control statement with brackets?*

A. If the code you want executed as part of a control structure consists of only a single line, you can omit the brackets. However, the habit of always using opening and closing brackets, regardless of structure length, is a good one.

Workshop

The workshop is designed to help you anticipate possible questions, review what you've learned, and begin putting your knowledge into practice.

Quiz

1. How would you use an `if` statement to print the string `"Youth message"` to the browser if an integer variable, $age, is between 18 and 35? If $age contains any other value, the string `"Generic message"` should be printed to the browser.

2. How would you extend your code in question 1 to print the string `"Child message"` if the $age variable is between 1 and 17?

3. How would you create a `while` statement that increments through and prints every odd number between 1 and 49?

4. How would you convert the `while` statement you created in question 3 into a `for` statement?

Answers

1.
```
$age = 22;

if (($age >= 18) && ($age <= 35)) {
    echo "Youth message";
} else {
    echo "Generic message";
}
```

2.

```php
$age = 12;

if (($age >= 18) && ($age <= 35)) {
    echo "Youth message";
} elseif (($age >= 1) && ($age <= 17)) {
    echo "Child message";
} else {
    echo "Generic message";
}
```

3.

```php
$num = 1;

while ($num <= 49) {
    echo $num."<br />";
    $num += 2;
}
```

4.

```php
for ($num = 1; $num <= 49; $num += 2) {
    echo $num."<br />";
}
```

Activity

Review the syntax for control structures. Think about how the techniques you've learned will help you in your scripting. Perhaps some of the script ideas you develop will be able to behave in different ways according to user input or will loop to display an HTML table. Start to build the control structures you will be using. Use temporary variables to mimic user input or database queries for the time being.

7

Working with Functions

Functions are at the heart of a well-organized script and will make your code easy to read and reuse. No large project would be manageable without them because the problem of repetitive code would bog down the development process. Throughout this chapter, you will investigate functions and demonstrate some of the ways functions can save you from repetitive work. In this chapter, you will learn

- ▶ How to define and call functions from within your scripts
- ▶ How to pass values to functions and receive values in return
- ▶ How to call a function dynamically using a string stored in a variable
- ▶ How to access global variables from within a function
- ▶ How to give a function a "memory"
- ▶ How to pass data to functions by reference
- ▶ How to create anonymous functions
- ▶ How to verify that a function exists before calling it

What Is a Function?

You can think of a function as an input/output machine. This machine takes the raw materials you feed it (input) and works with them to produce a product (output). A function accepts values, processes them, and then performs an action (printing to the browser, for example), returns a new value, or both.

If you needed to bake a single cake, you would probably do it yourself, in your own kitchen with your standard oven. But if you needed to bake thousands of cakes, you would probably build or acquire a special cake-baking machine, built for baking cakes in massive quantities. Similarly, when deciding whether to create a function for reuse, the most important factor to consider is the extent to which it can save you from writing repetitive code.

A *function* is a self-contained block of code that can be called by your scripts. When called, the function's code is executed and performs a particular task. You can pass values to a function, which then uses the values appropriately—storing them, transforming them, displaying them, whatever the function is told to do. When finished, a function can also pass a value back to the original code that called it into action.

Calling Functions

Functions come in two flavors—those built in to the language and those you define yourself. PHP has hundreds of built-in functions. Look at the following snippet for an example of a function in use:

```
strtoupper("Hello Web!");
```

This example calls the `strtoupper()` function, passing it the string `"Hello Web!"`. The function then goes about its business of changing the contents of the string to uppercase letters. A function call consists of the function name (`strtoupper` in this case) followed by parentheses. If you want to pass information to the function, you place it between these parentheses. A piece of information passed to a function in this way is called an *argument*. Some functions require that more than one argument be passed to them, separated by commas:

```
some_function($an_argument, $another_argument);
```

`strtoupper()` is typical for a function in that it returns a value. Most functions return some information back after they've completed their task—they usually at least tell whether their mission was successful. `strtoupper()` returns a string value, so its usage requires the presence of a variable to accept the new string, such as

```
$new_string = strtoupper("Hello Web!");
```

You may now use $new_string in your code, such as to print it to the screen:

```
echo $new_string;
```

This code will result in the following text on the screen:

```
HELLO WEB!
```

By the Way

> The `print()` and `echo()` functions are not actually functions, they're language constructs designed to output strings to the browser. However, you will find them in the PHP function list, at http://www.php.net/print and http://www.php.net/echo, respectively. These constructs are similar in functionality and can be used interchangably. Whichever one you use is a matter of taste.

The abs() function, for example, requires a signed numeric value and returns the absolute value of that number. Let's try it out in Listing 7.1.

LISTING 7.1 Calling the Built-in abs() Function

```
1: <?php
2: $num = -321;
3: $newnum = abs($num);
4: echo $newnum;
5: //prints "321"
6: ?>
```

This example assigns the value -321 to a variable $num. It then passes that variable to the abs() function, which makes the necessary calculation and returns a new value. The code assigns this to the variable $newnum and displays the result.

Put these lines into a text file called abs.php and place this file in your web server document root. When you access this script through your web browser, it produces the following:

```
321
```

In fact, Listing 7.1 could have dispensed with temporary variables altogether, passing the number straight to the abs() function and directly printing the result:

```
echo abs(-321);
```

This example uses the temporary variables $num and $newnum, though, to make each step of the process as clear as possible. Sometimes you can make your code more readable by breaking it up into a greater number of simple expressions.

You can call user-defined functions in exactly the same way that we have been calling built-in functions.

Defining a Function

You can define your own functions using the function statement:

```
function some_function($argument1, $argument2) {
    //function code here
}
```

The name of the function follows the function statement and precedes a set of parentheses. If your function requires arguments, you must place comma-separated variable names within the parentheses. These variables will be filled by the values passed to your function. Even if your function doesn't require arguments, you must nevertheless supply the parentheses.

> The naming rules for functions are similar to the naming rules for variables, which you learned in Chapter 5, "The Building Blocks of PHP." Names cannot include spaces, and they must begin with a letter or an underscore. As with variables, your function names should be meaningful as well as consistent in style. The capitalization of function names is one such stylistic touch you can add to your code; using mixed case in names, such as `myFunction()` or `handleSomeDifficultTask()`, makes your code much easier to read.

Listing 7.2 declares and calls a function.

LISTING 7.2   Declaring and Calling a Function

```
1: <?php
2: function bighello() {
3:     echo "<h1>HELLO!</h1>";
4: }
5: bighello();
6: ?>
```

The script in Listing 7.2 simply outputs the string `"HELLO!"` wrapped in an HTML h1 element.

Put these lines into a text file called `bighello.php` and place this file in your web server document root. When you access this script through your web browser, it should look like Figure 7.1.

FIGURE 7.1
Output of
`bighello.php`.

Listing 7.2 declares a function, `bighello()`, that requires no arguments. Because of this, the parentheses are left empty. Although `bighello()` is a working function, it is not terribly useful. Listing 7.3 creates a function that requires an argument and actually does something with it.

LISTING 7.3   Declaring a Function That Requires an Argument

```
1: <?php
2: function printBR($txt) {
3:      echo $txt."<br/>";
4: }
5: printBR("This is a line.");
6: printBR("This is a new line.");
7: printBR("This is yet another line.");
8: ?>
```

> Unlike variable names, function names are not case sensitive. In Listing 7.3, the `printBR()` function could have been called as `printbr()`, `PRINTBR()`, or any combination thereof, with success.

Put these lines into a text file called `printbr.php` and place this file in your web server document root. When you access this script through your web browser, it should look like Figure 7.2.

FIGURE 7.2
A function that prints a string with an appended `<br/>` tag.

In line 2, the `printBR()` function expects a string, so the variable name `$txt` is placed between the parentheses when the function is declared. Whatever is passed to `printBR()` will be stored in this `$txt` variable. Within the body of the function, line 3 prints the `$txt` variable, appending a `<br/>` element to it.

When you want to print a line to the browser, such as in line 5, 6, or 7, you can call `printBR()` instead of the built-in `print()`, saving you the bother of typing the `<br/>` element.

Returning Values from User-Defined Functions

The previous example output an amended string to the browser within the printBR() function. Sometimes, however, you will want a function to provide a value that you can work with yourself. If your function has transformed a string that you have provided, you might want to get the amended string back so that you can pass it to other functions. A function can return a value using the return state-ment in conjunction with a value. The return statement stops the execution of the function and sends the value back to the calling code.

Listing 7.4 creates a function that returns the sum of two numbers.

LISTING 7.4   A Function That Returns a Value

```
1: <?php
2: function addNums($firstnum, $secondnum) {
3:      $result = $firstnum + $secondnum;
4:      return $result;
5: }
6: echo addNums(3,5);
7: //will print "8"
8: ?>
```

Put these lines into a text file called addnums.php and place this file in your web server document root. When you access this script through your web browser, it pro-duces the following:

8

Notice in line 2 that addNums() should be called with two numeric arguments (line 6 shows those to be 3 and 5 in this case). These values are stored in the variables $firstnum and $secondnum. Predictably, addNums() adds the numbers contained in these variables and stores the result in a variable called $result.

The return statement can return a value or nothing at all. How you arrive at a value passed by return can vary. The value can be hard-coded:

```
return 4;
```

It can be the result of an expression:

```
return $a/$b;
```

It can be the value returned by yet another function call:

```
return another_function($an_argument);
```

Variable Scope

A variable declared within a function remains local to that function. In other words, it will not be available outside the function or within other functions. In larger projects, this can save you from accidentally overwriting the contents of a variable when you declare two variables with the same name in separate functions.

Listing 7.5 creates a variable within a function and then attempts to print it outside the function.

LISTING 7.5   Variable Scope: A Variable Declared Within a Function Is Unavailable Outside the Function

```
1: <?php
2: function test() {
3:     $testvariable = "this is a test variable";
4: }
5: echo "test variable: ".$testvariable."<br/>";
6: ?>
```

Put these lines into a text file called scopetest.php and place this file in your web server document root. When you access this script through your web browser, it should look like Figure 7.3.

FIGURE 7.3
Output of
scopetest.php.

The exact output you see depends on your PHP error settings. That is, it might or might not produce a "notice" as shown in Figure 7.3, but it will show the lack of an additional string after "test variable".

The value of the variable $testvariable is not printed because no such variable exists outside the test() function. Remember that the attempt in line 5 to access a nonexistent variable produces a notice such as the one displayed only if your PHP settings are set to display all errors, notices, and warnings; if your error settings are not strictly set, only the string "test variable:" will be shown.

Similarly, a variable declared outside a function will not automatically be available within it.

Accessing Variables with the global Statement

From within one function, you cannot (by default) access a variable defined in another function or elsewhere in the script. Within a function, if you attempt to use a variable with the same name, you will only set or access a local variable. Let's put this to the test in Listing 7.6.

LISTING 7.6　　Variables Defined Outside Functions Are Inaccessible from Within a Function by Default

```
1: <?php
2: $life = 42;
3: function meaningOfLife() {
4:     echo "The meaning of life is ".$life";
5: }
6: meaningOfLife();
7: ?>
```

Put these lines into a text file called scopetest2.php and place this file in your web server document root. When you access this script through your web browser, it should look like Figure 7.4.

FIGURE 7.4
Attempting to reference a variable from outside the scope of a function.

As you might expect, the meaningOfLife() function does not have access to the $life variable in line 2; $life is empty when the function attempts to print it. On the whole, this is a good thing because it saves you from potential clashes between identically named variables, and a function can always demand an argument if it needs information about the outside world. Occasionally, you might want to access an important variable from within a function without passing it in as an argument. This is where the global statement comes into play. Listing 7.7 uses global to restore order to the universe.

LISTING 7.7   Accessing Global Variables with the global Statement

```
1: <?php
2: $life=42;
3: function meaningOfLife() {
4:     global $life;
5:     echo "The meaning of life is ".$life";
6: }
7: meaningOfLife();
8: ?>
```

Put these lines into a text file called scopetest3.php and place this file in your web server document root. When you access this script through your web browser, it should look like Figure 7.5.

FIGURE 7.5
Successfully accessing a global variable from within a function using the global statement.

By placing the global statement in front of the $life variable when it is declared in the meaningOfLife() function (line 4), it now refers to the $life variable declared outside the function (line 2).

You will need to use the global statement within every function that needs to access a particular named global variable. Be careful, though: If you manipulate the contents of the variable within the function, the value of the variable will be changed for the script as a whole.

You can declare more than one variable at a time with the global statement by simply separating each of the variables you want to access with commas:

```
global $var1, $var2, $var3;
```

Usually, an argument is a copy of whatever value is passed by the calling code; changing it in a function has no effect beyond the function block. Changing a global variable within a function, on the other hand, changes the original and not a copy. Use the global statement carefully.

Saving State Between Function Calls with the static Statement

Local variables within functions have a short but happy life—they come into being when the function is called and die when execution is finished, as they should. Occasionally, however, you might want to give a function a rudimentary memory.

Assume that you want a function to keep track of the number of times it has been called so that numbered headings can be created by a script. You could, of course, use the global statement to do this, as shown in Listing 7.8.

LISTING 7.8   Using the global Statement to Remember the Value of a Variable Between Function Calls

```
1:   <?php
2:   $num_of_calls = 0;
3:   function numberedHeading($txt) {
4:       global $num_of_calls;
5:       $num_of_calls++;
6:       echo "<h1>".$num_of_calls." ".$txt."</h1>";
7:   }
8:   numberedHeading("Widgets");
9:   echo "<p>We build a fine range of widgets.</p>";
10:  numberedHeading("Doodads");
11:  echo "<p>Finest in the world.</p>";
12:  ?>
```

Put these lines into a text file called numberedheading.php and place this file in your web server document root. When you access this script through your web browser, it should look like Figure 7.6.

FIGURE 7.6
Using the glob-
al statement to
keep track of
the number of
times a function
has been
called.

This does the job. Listing 7.8 declares a variable, $num_of_calls, in line 2, outside the function numberedHeading(). Line 4 makes this variable available to the function by using the global statement.

Every time numberedHeading() is called, the value of $num_of_calls is incremented (line 5). You can then print out the heading complete with the properly incremented heading number.

This is not the most elegant solution, however. Functions that use the global statement cannot be read as standalone blocks of code. In reading or reusing them, we need to look out for the global variables that they manipulate.

This is where the static statement can be useful. If you declare a variable within a function in conjunction with the static statement, the variable remains local to the function, and the function "remembers" the value of the variable from execution to execution. Listing 7.9 adapts the code from Listing 7.8 to use the static statement.

LISTING 7.9   Using the static Statement to Remember the Value of a Variable Between Function Calls

```
1: <?php
2: function numberedHeading($txt) {
3:     static $num_of_calls = 0;
4:     $num_of_calls++;
5:     echo "<h1>".$num_of_calls." ". $txt."</h1>";
6: }
7: numberedHeading("Widgets");
8: echo "<p>We build a fine range of widgets.</p>";
9: numberedHeading("Doodads");
10: echo "<p>Finest in the world.</p>";
11: ?>
```

The `numberedHeading()` function has become entirely self-contained. When the `$num_of_calls` variable is declared on line 3, an initial value is assigned to it. This assignment is made when the function is first called on line 7. This initial assignment is ignored when the function is called a second time on line 9. Instead, the code remembers the previous value of `$num_of_calls`. You can now paste the `numberedHeading()` function into other scripts without worrying about global variables. Although the output of Listing 7.9 is the same as that of Listing 7.8, the code is a bit more elegant.

More About Arguments

You've already seen how to pass arguments to functions, but there's plenty more to cover. In this section, you'll look at a technique for giving your arguments default values and explore a method of passing variables by reference rather than by value. This means that the function is given an alias of the original value rather than a copy of it.

Setting Default Values for Arguments

PHP provides a nifty feature to help build flexible functions. Until now, you've heard that some functions require one or more arguments. By making some arguments optional, you can render your functions a little less autocratic.

Listing 7.10 creates a useful little function that wraps a string in an HTML span element. To give the user of the function the chance to change the `font-size` style, you can demand a `$fontsize` argument in addition to the string (line 2).

LISTING 7.10   A Function Requiring Two Arguments

```
1: <?php
2: function fontWrap($txt, $fontsize) {
3:      echo "<span style=\"font-size:$fontsize\">".$txt."</span>";
4: }
5: fontWrap("A Heading<br/>","24pt");
6: fontWrap("some body text<br/>","16pt");
7: fontWrap("smaller body text<br/>","12pt");
8: fontWrap("even smaller body text<br/>","10pt");
9: ?>
```

Put these lines into a text file called `fontwrap.php` and place this file in your web server document root. When you access this script through your web browser, it should look like Figure 7.7.

FIGURE 7.7
A function that
formats and
outputs strings.

By assigning a value to an argument variable within the function definition's parentheses, you can make the $fontsize argument optional. If the function call doesn't define an argument for this argument, the value you have assigned to the argument is used instead. Listing 7.11 uses this technique to make the $fontsize argument optional.

LISTING 7.11 A Function with an Optional Argument

```php
1: <?php
2: function fontWrap($txt, $fontsize = "12pt") {
3:     echo "<span style=\"font-size:$fontsize\">".$txt."</span>";
4: }
5: fontWrap("A Heading<br/>","24pt");
6: fontWrap("some body text<br/>");
7: fontWrap("smaller body text<br/>");
8: fontWrap("even smaller body text<br/>");
9: ?>
```

When the fontWrap() function is called with a second argument, as in line 5, this value is used to set the font-size attribute of the span element. When this argument is omitted, as in lines 6, 7, and 8, the default value of "12pt" is used instead. You can create as many optional arguments as you want, but when you've given an argument a default value, all subsequent arguments should also be given defaults.

Passing Variable References to Functions

When you pass arguments to functions, they are stored as copies in parameter variables. Any changes made to these variables in the body of the function are local to that function and are not reflected beyond it. This is illustrated in Listing 7.12.

LISTING 7.12   Passing an Argument to a Function by Value

```
1: <?php
2: function addFive($num) {
3:       $num += 5;
4: }
5: $orignum = 10;
6: addFive($orignum);
7: echo $orignum;
8: ?>
```

Put these lines into a text file called addfive.php and place this file in your web server document root. When you access this script through your web browser, it produces the following:

10

The addFive() function accepts a single numeric value and adds 5 to it, but it returns nothing. A value is assigned to a variable $orignum in line 5 and then this variable is passed to addFive() in line 6. A copy of the contents of $orignum is stored in the variable $num. Although $num is incremented by 5, this has no effect on the value of $orignum. When $orignum is printed, you find that its value is still 10. By default, variables passed to functions are passed by value. In other words, local copies of the values of the variables are made.

You can change this behavior by creating a reference to your original variable. You can think of a reference as a signpost that points to a variable. In working with the reference, you are manipulating the value to which it points.

Listing 7.13 shows this technique in action. When you pass an argument to a function by reference, as in line 6, the contents of the variable you pass ($orignum) are accessed by the argument variable and manipulated within the function, rather than just a copy of the variable's value (10). Any changes made to an argument in these cases will change the value of the original variable. You can pass an argument by reference by adding an ampersand to the argument name in the function definition, as shown in line 2.

LISTING 7.13   Using a Function Definition to Pass an Argument to a Function by Reference

```
1: <?php
2: function addFive(&$num) {
3:       $num += 5;
4: }
5: $orignum = 10;
6: addFive($orignum);
7: echo $orignum;
8: ?>
```

Put these lines into a text file called addfive2.php and place this file in your web server document root. When you access this script through your web browser, it produces the following:

15

Testing for the Existence of a Function

You do not always know that a function exists before you try to invoke it. Different builds of the PHP engine might include different functionality, and if you are writing a script that may be run on multiple servers, you might want to verify that key features are available. For instance, you might want to write code that will use MySQL if MySQL-related functions are available but simply log data to a text file otherwise.

You can use function_exists() to check for the availability of a function. function_exists() requires a string representing a function name. It returns true if the function can be located and false otherwise.

Listing 7.14 shows function_exists() in action and illustrates some of the other topics we have covered in this chapter.

LISTING 7.14   Testing for a Function's Existence

```
1:  <?php
2:  function tagWrap($tag, $txt, $func = "") {
3:      if ((!empty($txt)) && (function_exists($func))) {
4:          $txt = $func($txt);
5:          return "<".$tag.">".$txt."</".$tag."><br/>";
6:      } else {
7:          return "<b>".$txt."</b><br/>";
8:      }
9:  }
10:
11: function underline($txt) {
12: return "<span style=\"text-decoration:underline;\">".$txt."</span>";
13: }
14: echo tagWrap('b', 'make me bold');
15: echo tagWrap('i', 'underline me too', "underline");
16: echo tagWrap('i', 'make me italic and quote me',
17: create_function('$txt', 'return "&quot;$txt&quot;";'));
18: ?>
```

Listing 7.14 defines two functions, tagWrap() (line 2) and underline() (line 11). The tagWrap() function accepts three strings: a tag, the text to format, and an optional function name. It returns a formatted string. The underline() function requires a single argument—the text to be formatted—and returns the text wrapped in <span> tags with appropriate style attributes.

When you first call `tagWrap()` on line 14, you pass it the character b and the string `"make me bold"`. Because you haven't passed a value for the function argument, the default value (an empty string) is used. Line 3 checks whether the `$func` variable contains characters, and, if it is not empty, `function_exists()` is called to check for a function by that name. Of course, in this case, the `$func` variable is empty, so the `$txt` variable is wrapped in `<b>` tags in the `else` clause on lines 6–7 and the result is returned.

The code calls `tagWrap()` on line 15 with the string `'i'`, some text, and a third argument: `"underline"`. `function_exists()` finds a function called `underline()` (line 11), so it calls this function and passes the `$txt` argument variable to it before any further formatting is done. The result is an italicized, underlined string.

Finally, on line 16, the code calls `tagWrap()`, which wraps text in quotation entities. It would be quicker to simply add the entities to the text to be transformed ourselves, but this example serves to illustrate the point that `function_exists()` works as well on anonymous functions as it does on strings representing function names.

Put these lines into a text file called `exists.php` and place this file in your web server document root. When you access this script through your web browser, it should look like Figure 7.8.

FIGURE 7.8
Output of
`exists.php`.

Summary

This chapter taught you about functions and how to deploy them. You learned how to define and pass arguments to a function, how to use the `global` and `static` statements, how to pass references to functions, and how to create default values for function arguments. Finally, you learned to test for the existence of functions.

Q&A

Q. Can I include a function call within a double- or single-quoted string, as I can with a variable?

A. No. You must call functions outside quotation marks. However, you can break the string apart and place the function call between the parts of the string, using the concatenation operator to tie them together. For example

```
$newstring = "I purchased".numPurchase($somenum)." items.";
```

Q. What will happen if I call a function that does not exist, or if I declare a function with a name already in use?

A. Calling a function that does not exist or declaring a function with the same name as another existing function will cause the script to stop execution. Whether or not an error message is displayed in the browser will depend on the error settings in your php.ini file.

Workshop

The workshop is designed to help you anticipate possible questions, review what you've learned, and begin putting your knowledge into practice.

Quiz

1. True or false: If a function doesn't require an argument, you can omit the parentheses in the function call.

2. How do you return a value from a function?

3. What would the following code fragment print to the browser?

```
$number = 50;

function tenTimes() {
    $number = $number * 10;
}

tenTimes();
echo $number;
```

4. What would the following code fragment print to the browser?

```
$number = 50;

function tenTimes() {
    global $number;
    $number = $number * 10;
}

tenTimes();
echo $number;
```

5. What would the following code fragment print to the browser?

```
$number = 50;

function tenTimes( &$n ) {
    $n = $n * 10;
}

tenTimes( $number );
echo $number;
```

Answers

1. The statement is false. You must always include the parentheses in your function calls, whether or not you are passing arguments to the function.

2. You must use the `return` keyword.

3. It would print 50. The `tenTimes()` function has no access to the global `$number` variable. When it is called, it will manipulate its own local `$number` variable.

4. It would print 500. This example uses the `global` statement, which gives the `tenTimes()` function access to the `$number` variable.

5. It would print 500. By adding the ampersand to the parameter variable `$n`, you ensure that this argument is passed by reference. `$n` and `$number` point to the same value, so any changes to `$n` will be reflected when you access `$number`.

Activity

Create a function that accepts four string variables and returns a string that contains an HTML table element, enclosing each of the variables in its own cell.

8

Working with Arrays

Arrays are used to store and organize data. PHP includes many functions that enable you to create, modify, and manipulate arrays, which you will use frequently throughout the procedural programming method described in this book.

In this chapter, you learn the basics of working with arrays, including

▶ How to create associative and multidimensional arrays

▶ How to use the myriad array-related functions built into PHP

What Are Arrays?

You've already learned about and used scalar variables in the earlier chapters in this book, and thus you know that these variables are used to store values. But scalar variables can store only one value at a time—the $color variable can hold only a value of red or blue, and so forth, but it cannot be used to hold a list of colors in the rainbow. But arrays are special types of variables that enable you to store as many values as you want, including all seven of those rainbow colors.

Arrays are indexed, which means that each entry is made up of a *key* and a *value*. The key is the index position, beginning with 0 and increasing incrementally by 1 with each new element in the array. The value is whatever value you associate with that position—a string, an integer, or whatever you want. Think of an array as a filing cabinet and each key/value pair as a file folder. The key is the label written on the top of the folder, and the value is what is inside. You'll see this type of structure in action as you create arrays in the next section.

Watch
Out!

Although you can store as many values as you want in an array, some array func-tions have an upper limit of 100,000 values. If you are storing large amounts of data in your arrays, be sure to read the PHP Manual entry for array functions you want to use and find out whether the function has an upper limit for working with data.

Creating Arrays

You can create an array using either the array() function or the array operator []. The array() function is usually used when you want to create a new array and populate it with more than one element, all in one fell swoop. The array operator is often used when you want to create a new array with just one element at the outset, or when you want to add to an existing array element.

The following code snippet shows how to create an array called $rainbow using the array() function, containing all its various colors:

```
$rainbow = array("red", "orange", "yellow", "green", "blue", "indigo",
"violet");
```

The following snippet shows the same array being created incrementally using the array operator:

```
$rainbow[] = "red";
$rainbow[] = "orange";
$rainbow[] = "yellow";
$rainbow[] = "green";
$rainbow[] = "blue";
$rainbow[] = "indigo";
$rainbow[] = "violet";
```

Both snippets create a seven-element array called $rainbow, with values starting at index position 0 and ending at index position 6. If you wanted to be literal about it, you could have specified the index positions, such as in this code:

```
$rainbow[0] = "red";
$rainbow[1] = "orange";
$rainbow[2] = "yellow";
$rainbow[3] = "green";
$rainbow[4] = "blue";
$rainbow[5] = "indigo";
$rainbow[6] = "violet";
```

However, PHP does this for you when positions are not specified, and that eliminates the possibility that you will misnumber your elements, as in this example:

```
$rainbow[0] = "red";
$rainbow[1] = "orange";
$rainbow[2] = "yellow";
$rainbow[5] = "green";
$rainbow[6] = "blue";
$rainbow[7] = "indigo";
$rainbow[8] = "violet";
```

Regardless of whether you initially create your array using the array() function or the array operator, you can still add to it using the array operator. In the first line of the following snippet, six elements are added to the array, and one more element is added to the end of the array in the second line:

```
$rainbow = array("red", "orange", "yellow", "green", "blue", "indigo");
$rainbow[] = "violet";
```

The examples used in this section are of numerically indexed arrays, arguably the most common type you'll see. In the next two sections, you learn about two other types of arrays: associative and multidimensional.

Creating Associative Arrays

Whereas numerically indexed arrays use an index position as the key—0, 1, 2, and so forth—associative arrays utilize actual named keys. The following example demonstrates this by creating an array called $character with four elements:

```
$character = array(
            "name" => "Bob",
            "occupation" => "superhero",
            "age" => 30,
            "special power" => "x-ray vision"
            );
```

The four keys in the $character array are name, occupation, age, and special power. The associated values are Bob, superhero, 30, and x-ray vision, respectively. You can reference specific elements of an associative array using the specific key, such as in this example:

```
echo $character['occupation'];
```

The output of this snippet would be

```
superhero
```

As with numerically indexed arrays, you can use the array operator to add to an associative array:

```
$character['supername'] = "Mega X-Ray Guy";
```

This example adds a key called `supername` with a value of `Mega X-Ray Guy`.

The only difference between an associative array and a numerically indexed array is the key name; in a numerically indexed array, the key name is a number; in an associative array, the key name is a meaningful word.

Creating Multidimensional Arrays

The first two types of arrays hold strings and integers, whereas this third type holds other arrays. If each set of key/value pairs constitutes a dimension, a multidimensional array holds more than one series of these key/value pairs. For example, Listing 8.1 defines a multidimensional array called `$characters`, each element of which contains an associative array. This might sound confusing, but it's really only an array that contains another array.

LISTING 8.1   Defining a Multidimensional Array

```
1:  <?php
2:  $characters = array(
3:              array(
4:                "name" => "Bob",
5:                "occupation" => "superhero",
6:                "age" => 30,
7:                "special power" => "x-ray vision"
8:                ),
9:              array(
10:                "name" => "Sally",
11:                "occupation" => "superhero",
12:                "age" => 24,
13:                "special power" => "superhuman strength"
14:                ),
15:              array(
16:                "name" => "Jane",
17:                "occupation" => "arch villain",
18:                "age" => 45,
19:                "special power" => "nanotechnology"
20:                )
21:              );
22: ?>
```

In line 2, the $characters array is initialized using the array() function. Lines 3–8 represent the first element, lines 9–14 represent the second element, and lines 15–20 represent the third element. These elements can be referenced as $characters[0], $characters[1], and $characters[2].

Each element consists of an associative array, itself containing four elements: name, occupation, age, and special_power.

However, if you attempt to print the master elements like so

```
echo $characters[1];
```

the output will be

```
Array
```

because the master element indeed holds an array as its content. To really get to the content you want, that is, the specific information found within the inner array element, you need to access the master element index position plus the associative name of the value you want to view.

Take a look at this example:

```
echo $characters[1]['occupation'];
```

It will print this:

```
superhero
```

If you add the following lines to the end of the code in Listing 8.1, it prints the information stored in each element:

```
foreach ($characters as $c) {
        while (list($k, $v) = each ($c)) {
                echo "$k ... $v <br/>";
        }
}
```

The foreach loop is concerned with the master array element, $characters. It loops through this array and assigns the temporary name $c to the element contained within each position. Next, the code begins a while loop. This loop uses two functions to extract the contents of the inner array. First, the list() function names placeholder variables, $k and $v, which will be populated with the keys and values gathered from the each() function. The each() function looks at each element of the $c array and extracts the information accordingly.

The echo statement simply prints each key and value ($k and $v) extracted from the $c array using the each() function and adds a line break for display purposes. Figure 8.1 shows the result of this file, called mdarray.php.

FIGURE 8.1
Looping through
a multidimen-
sional array.

Some Array-Related Functions

More than 70 array-related functions are built into PHP, which you can read about in detail at http://www.php.net/array. Some of the more common (and useful) functions are explained in this section.

▶ **count()** and **sizeof()**—Each of these functions counts the number of elements in an array. Given the following array

```
$colors = array("blue", "black", "red", "green");
```

both count($colors); and sizeof($colors); return a value of 4.

▶ **each()** and **list()**—These functions usually appear together, in the context of stepping through an array and returning its keys and values. You saw an example of this previously, where we stepped through the $c array and printed its contents.

▶ **foreach()**—This function is also used to step through an array, assigning the value of an element to a given variable, as you saw in the previous section.

▶ **reset()**—This function rewinds the pointer to the beginning of an array, as in this example:

```
reset($character);
```

This function is useful when you are performing multiple manipulations on an array, such as sorting, extracting values, and so forth.

▶ **array_push()**—This function adds one or more elements to the end of an existing array, as in this example:

```
array_push($existingArray, "element 1", "element 2", "element 3");
```

▶ **array_pop()**—This function removes (and returns) the last element of an existing array, as in this example:

```
$last_element = array_pop($existingArray);
```

▶ **array_unshift()**—This function adds one or more elements to the beginning of an existing array, as in this example:

```
array_unshift($existingArray, "element 1", "element 2", "element 3");
```

▶ **array_shift()**—This function removes (and returns) the first element of an existing array, as in this example, where the value of the element in the first position of $existingArray is assigned to the variable $first_element:

```
$first_element = array_shift($existingArray);
```

▶ **array_merge()**—This function combines two or more existing arrays, as in this example:

```
$newArray = array_merge($array1, $array2);
```

▶ **array_keys()**—This function returns an array containing all the key names within a given array, as in this example:

```
$keysArray = array_keys($existingArray);
```

▶ **array_values()**—This function returns an array containing all the values within a given array, as in this example:

```
$valuesArray = array_values($existingArray);
```

▶ **shuffle()**—This function randomizes the elements of a given array. The syntax of this function is simply as follows:

```
shuffle($existingArray);
```

This brief rundown of array-related functions only scratches the surface of using arrays. However, arrays and array-related functions are used in the code examples throughout this book, so you will get your fill soon enough. If you don't, there's always the array section of the PHP Manual at http://www.php.net/array, which discusses all array-related functions in great detail, including more than 10 different methods for sorting your arrays.

Summary

This chapter introduced you to the concepts of arrays, including how they are created and referenced. The three array types are the numerically indexed array, associative array, and multidimensional array. Additionally, you saw examples of some of the numerous array-related functions already built into PHP. These functions can be used to manipulate and modify existing arrays, sometimes even creating entirely new ones.

Q&A

Q. *How many dimensions can multidimensional arrays have?*

A. You can create as many dimensions in your multidimensional array as you can manage, but remember the more dimensions you have, the more you'll have to manage. If you have data with more than a few dimensions, it might be wise to ask yourself whether that data should be stored differently, such as in a database and accessed that way.

Workshop

The workshop is designed to help you anticipate possible questions, review what you've learned, and begin putting your knowledge into practice.

Quiz

1. What construct can you use to define an array?

2. What function would you use to join two arrays?

Answers

1. `array()`

2. `array_merge()`

Activity

Create a multidimensional array of movies organized by genre. This should take the form of an associative array with genres as keys, such as `Science Fiction`, `Action`, `Adventure`, and so forth. Each of the array's elements should be an array containing movie names, such as *Alien*, *Terminator 3*, *Star Wars*, and so on. When your arrays are created, loop through them, printing the name of each genre and its associated movie(s).

9

Working with Objects

Programmers use objects to store and organize data. Object-oriented programming structures found in many programming languages are also evident in PHP. However, in PHP, it is not required that you write your scripts in an object-oriented manner. Many PHP scripts, in fact most of the ones you will find in this book, are procedural rather than object-oriented. If you are coming to PHP with a background in object-oriented programming, this chapter will help you to understand the object model in PHP. If you are altogether new to programming, it's important to understand the basics of object-oriented programming, but you might want to gain experience in procedural programming and the fundamentals of the PHP language before you tackle a topic that has entire books written about it.

In this chapter, you learn the basics of working with objects, including

▶ Understanding the basic structure of an object

▶ How to create and manipulate objects and the data they contain

Creating an Object

Explaining the concept of an object is a little difficult: It's a sort of theoretical box of things—variables, functions, and so forth—that exists in a templated structure called a class. Although it's easy to visualize a scalar variable, such as $color, with a value of red, or an array called $character with three or four different elements inside it, some people have a difficult time visualizing objects.

For now, try to think of an object as a little box with inputs and outputs on either side of it. The input mechanisms are *methods*, and methods have properties. Throughout this section, we will look at how classes, methods, and properties work together to produce various outputs.

By the Way

> If the concept of classes is completely foreign to you, you can supplement your knowledge by reading the chapter called "Classes and Objects" of the PHP manual. You can find it at http://www.php.net/manual/en/language.oop5.php.

The section opened with saying that an object exists in a structure called a class. In each class, you define a set of characteristics. For example, say that you have created an automobile class. In the automobile class, you might have color, make, and model characteristics. Each automobile object uses all the characteristics, but each object initializes the characteristics to different values, such as silver, Mazda, and Protege5, or red, Porsche, and Boxter.

The whole purpose of using objects is to create reusable code. Because classes are so tightly structured but self-contained and independent of one another, you can reuse them from one application to another. For example, suppose that you write a text-formatting class for one project and decide you can use that class in another project. Because a class is just a set of characteristics, you can pick up the code and use it in the second project, reaching into it with methods specific to the second application but using the inner workings of the existing code to achieve new results.

Creating an object is simple; you simply declare it to be in existence:

```
class myClass {
    //code will go here
}
```

Now that you have a class, you can create a new instance of an object:

```
$object1 = new myClass();
```

In Listing 9.1, you have proof that your object exists, even though there's nothing in it—it's just been named.

LISTING 9.1   Proof That Your Object Exists

```
1:  <?php
2:  class myClass {
3:      //code will go here
4:  }
5:  $object1 = new myClass();
6:  echo "\$object1 is an ".gettype($object1).".<br/>";
7:
8:  if (is_object($object1)) {
9:      echo "Really! I swear \$object1 is an object!";
10: }
11: ?>
```

If you save this code as `proofofclass.php`, place it in your document root, and access it with your web browser, you will see the following on your screen:

```
$object1 is an object.
Really! I swear $object1 is an object!
```

This is not a particularly useful class because it does absolutely nothing, but it is valid and shows you how the class template works in lines 2 through 5. Lines 8 through 10 use the `is_object()` function to test whether something is an object; in this case the *something* is `$object1`. Because the test of `is_object()` evaluates to true, the string within the `if` statement is printed to the screen.

Next, you'll learn about using object properties and methods within the class template.

Properties of Objects

The variables declared inside an object are called *properties*. It is standard practice to declare your variables at the top of the class. These properties can be values, arrays, or even other objects. The following snippet uses simple scalar variables inside the class, prefaced with the `var` keyword:

```
class myCar {
     var $color = "silver";
     var $make = "Mazda";
     var $model = "Protege5";
}
```

Now when you create a `myCar` object, it will always have those three properties. Listing 9.2 shows you how to access properties after they have been declared and values have been assigned to them.

LISTING 9.2   Showing Object Properties

```
1:  <?php
2:  class myCar {
3:      var $color = "silver";
4:      var $make = "Mazda";
5:      var $model = "Protege5";
6:  }
7:  $car = new myCar();
8:  echo "I drive a: ".$car -> color." ".$car -> make." ".$car -> model;
9:  ?>
```

If you save this code as `objproperties.php`, place it in your document root, and access it with your web browser, you will see the following on your screen:

```
I drive a: silver Mazda Protege5
```

Because the odds are low that you also drive a silver Mazda Protege5, you'll want to change the properties of the myCar object. Listing 9.3 shows you how to do just that.

LISTING 9.3   Changing Object Properties

```
1:  <?php
2:  class myCar {
3:      var $color = "silver";
4:      var $make = "Mazda";
5:      var $model = "Protege5";
6:  }
7:  $car = new myCar();
8:  $car -> color = "red";
9:  $car -> make = "Porsche";
10: $car -> model = "Boxter";
11: echo "I drive a: ".$car -> color." ".$car -> make." ".$car -> model;
12: ?>
```

If you save this code as objproperties2.php, place it in your document root, and access it with your web browser, you will see the following on your screen:

```
I drive a: red Porsche Boxter
```

By the Way

In this instance, even if the $color, $make, and $model properties had no initial values when declared, lines 8 through 10 would assign a value to them. As long as the properties are declared, you can use them later—initial values or not.

The purpose of Listing 9.3 is to show that as long as you have a well-defined class with properties, you can easily change the values of the properties to fit your needs.

Object Methods

Methods add functionality to your objects. No longer will your objects just sit there, holding on to their properties for dear life—they'll actually do something! Listing 9.4 shows just that.

LISTING 9.4   A Class with a Method

```
1: <?php
2: class myClass {
3:     function sayHello() {
4:             echo "HELLO!";
5:     }
6: }
7: $object1 = new myClass();
8: $object1 -> sayHello();
9: ?>
```

Although it's not the most thrilling example of action, if you save this code as helloclass.php, place it in your document root, and access it with your web browser, you will see the following on your screen:

HELLO!

A method looks and acts like a normal function but is defined within the framework of a class. The -> operator is used to call the object method in the context of your script. Had there been any variables stored in the object, the method would have been capable of accessing them for its own purposes. This is illustrated in Listing 9.5.

LISTING 9.5   Accessing Class Properties Within a Method

```
1:  <?php
2:  class myClass {
3:      var $name = "Jimbo";
4:      function sayHello() {
5:            echo "HELLO! My name is ".$this->name;
6:      }
7:  }
8:  $object1 = new myClass();
9:  $object1 -> sayHello();
10: ?>
```

If you save this code as helloclass2.php, place it in your document root, and access it with your web browser, you will see the following on your screen:

HELLO! My name is Jimbo

The special variable $this is used to refer to the currently instantiated object as you see on line 5. Anytime an object refers to itself, you must use the $this variable. Using the $this variable in conjunction with the -> operator enables you to access any property or method in a class, within the class itself.

One final tidbit regarding the basics of working with an object's properties is how to change a property from within a method. Previously, a property's value changed outside the method in which it was contained. Listing 9.6 shows how to make the change from inside a method.

LISTING 9.6   Changing the Value of a Property from Within a Method

```
1: <?php
2: class myClass {
3:     var $name = "Jimbo";
4:     function setName($n) {
5:           $this->name = $n;
6:     }
7:     function sayHello() {
8:           echo "HELLO! My name is ".$this->name;
9:     }
```

LISTING 9.6   Continued

```
10: }
11: $object1 = new myClass();
12: $object1 -> setName("Julie");
13: $object1 -> sayHello();
14: ?>
```

If you save this code as `helloclass3.php`, place it in your document root, and access it with your web browser, you will see the following on your screen:

```
HELLO! My name is Julie
```

Why? Because in lines 4–6, a new function called `setName()` was created. When it is called in line 12, it changes the value of $name to `Julie`. Thus, when the `sayHello()` function is called in line 13 and it looks for `$this->name`, it uses `Julie`, which is the new value that was just set by the `setName()` function. In other words, an object is capable of modifying its own property—in this case, the $name variable.

Constructors

A *constructor* is a function that lives within a class and, given the same name as the class, is automatically called when a new instance of the class is created using `new classname`. Using constructors enables you to provide arguments to your class, which will then be processed immediately when the class is called. You see constructors in action in the next section on object inheritance.

Object Inheritance

Having learned the absolute basics of objects, properties, and methods, you can start to look at object inheritance. Inheritance with regard to classes is just what it sounds like: One class inherits functionality from its parent class. Listing 9.7 shows an example.

LISTING 9.7   A Class Inheriting from Its Parent

```
1:  <?php
2:  class myClass {
3:      var $name = "Matt";
4:      function myClass($n) {
5:          $this->name = $n;
6:      }
7:      function sayHello() {
8:          echo "HELLO! My name is ".$this->name;
9:      }
10: }
11: class childClass extends myClass {
```

LISTING 9.7 Continued

```
12: //code goes here
13: }
14: $object1 = new childClass("Baby Matt");
15: $object1 -> sayHello();
16: ?>
```

If you save this code as inheritance.php, place it in your document root, and access it with your web browser, you will see the following on your screen:

```
HELLO! My name is Baby Matt
```

Lines 4–6 make up a constructor. Notice that the name of this function is the same as the class in which it is contained: myClass. Lines 11–13 define a second class, childClass, that contains no code. That's fine because, in this example, the class exists only to demonstrate inheritance from the parent class. The inheritance occurs through the extends clause shown in line 11. The second class inherits the elements of the first class because this clause is used.

Listing 9.8 shows you one last example of how a child class can override the methods of the parent class.

LISTING 9.8 The Method of a Child Class Overriding That of Its Parent

```
1:  <?php
2:  class myClass {
3:      var $name = "Matt";
4:      function myClass($n) {
5:          $this->name = $n;
6:      }
7:      function sayHello() {
8:          echo "HELLO! My name is ".$this->name;
9:      }
10: }
11: class childClass extends myClass {
12:     function sayHello() {
13:         echo "I will not tell you my name.";
14:     }
15: }
16: $object1 = new childClass("Baby Matt");
17: $object1 -> sayHello();
18: ?>
```

The only changes in this code from Listing 9.7 are the new lines 12–14. In these lines, a function is created called sayHello() that, instead of printing HELLO! My name is..., prints the message I will not tell you my name. Because the sayHello() function now exists in childClass, and childClass is the class called in line 16, its version of sayHello() is the one used.

If you save this code as `inheritance2.php`, place it in your document root, and access it with your web browser, you will see the following on your screen:

```
I will not tell you my name
```

Like most elements of object-oriented programming, inheritance is useful when attempting to make your code flexible. Suppose that you created a text-formatting class that organized and stored data, formatted it in HTML, and output the result to a browser—your own personal masterpiece. Now suppose that you had a client who wanted to use that concept, but instead of formatting the content into HTML and sending it to a browser, he wanted to format it for plain text and save it to a text file. No problem—you just add a few methods and properties, and away you go. Finally, the client comes back and says that he really wants the data to be formatted and sent as an email—and then, what the heck, why not create XML-formatted files as well?

Although you might want to pull your hair out in frustration, you're really not in a bad situation. If you separate the compilation and storage classes from the formatting classes—one for each of the various delivery methods (HTML, text, email, XML)—you essentially have a parent-child relationship. Consider the parent class the one that holds the compilation and storage methods. The formatting classes are the children: They inherit the information from the parent and output the result based on their own functionality. Everybody wins.

Summary

This chapter provided a foundation for working with object-oriented code. In no way does this content cover all the aspects of object-oriented programming—universities teach entire series of classes (no pun intended) devoted to this topic, so you can imagine that these pages are a little light. However, you did learn to create classes and instantiate objects from them. You learned how to create and access the properties and methods of a class, how to build new classes, and how to inherit features from parent classes. That's not too shabby!

Q&A

Q. *Do I have to understand object-oriented programming to become a good PHP programmer or even to finish this book?*

A. Not at all. In fact, the projects in this book are procedural and do *not* contain object-oriented programming! Object-oriented programming is an organizational approach intended to improve the reusability and extensibility of the code that makes up a given application. You might not know enough about your project in the beginning stages of development to fully plan for an object-oriented design. When it is complete—or, at least, approaching a solid state—you might start to see areas in which an object-oriented approach can be taken, and you might start to combine your code into classes, properties, and methods. But for the most part, you won't write simple scripts performing particular duties in object-oriented fashion unless it is your background and comes naturally to you. For a great deal more information on the object model in PHP 5, see the appropriate section of the PHP Manual, at http://www.php.net/manual/en/language.oop5.php.

Workshop

The workshop is designed to help you anticipate possible questions, review what you've learned, and begin putting your knowledge into practice.

Quiz

1. How would you declare a class called `emptyClass` that has no methods or properties?

2. How would you choose a name for a constructor method?

Answers

1. Use the `class` keyword:

```
class emptyClass {
}
```

2. You don't—a constructor is named for the class in which it resides.

Activity

Create a class called `baseCalc()` that stores two numbers as properties. Next, create a `calculate()` method that prints the numbers to the browser. Finally, create classes called `addCalc()`, `subCalc()`, `mulCalc()`, and `divCalc()` that inherit functionality from `baseCalc()` but override the `calculate()` method and print appropriate totals to the browser.

PART III

Getting Involved with the Code

10

Working with Strings, Dates, and Time

No matter how rich web content becomes, HTML lies behind it all, pushing string-based content out to web browsers. It is no accident, then, that PHP provides many functions with which you can format and manipulate strings. Similarly, dates and times are so much a part of everyday life that it becomes easy to use them without thinking. However, because the quirks of the Gregorian calendar can be difficult to work with, PHP provides powerful tools that make date manipulation an easy task.

Numerous PHP functions are available to you, and this chapter does not begin to cover all of them. However, this chapter does provide a foundation for using some of the basic string, date, and time functions, and an idea of how to begin thinking about using these types of functions in your code. The rule of thumb is this: If you want to transform, manipulate, or display a string, date, or time, don't build your own custom solution without first visiting the PHP Manual because chances are good that a function already exists for your desired task.

In this chapter, you will learn

- ▶ How to format strings

- ▶ How to determine the length of a string

- ▶ How to find a substring within a string

- ▶ How to break a string down into component parts

- ▶ How to remove whitespace from the beginning or end of a string

- ▶ How to replace substrings

- ▶ How to change the case of a string

- ▶ How to acquire the current date and time

- ▶ How to get information about a date and time

- ▶ How to format date and time information

- ▶ How to test dates for validity

- ▶ How to set dates and times

Formatting Strings with PHP

Until now, you have simply printed any strings you want to display directly to the browser in their original state. PHP provides two functions that allow you first to apply formatting, whether to round doubles to a given number of decimal places, define alignment within a field, or display data according to different number systems. In this section, you will look at a few of the formatting options provided by printf() and sprintf().

Working with printf()

If you have any experience with a C-like programming language, you will be familiar with the concept of the printf() function. The printf() function requires a string argument, known as a *format control string*. It also accepts additional arguments of different types, which you'll learn about in a moment. The format control string contains instructions regarding the display of these additional arguments. The following fragment, for example, uses printf() to output an integer as an octal (or base-8) number:

```php
<?php
printf("This is my number: %o", 55);
// prints "This is my number: 67"
?>
```

Included within the format control string (the first argument) is a special code, known as a *conversion specification*. A conversion specification begins with a percent (%) symbol and defines how to treat the corresponding argument to printf(). You can include as many conversion specifications as you want within the format control string, as long as you send an equivalent number of arguments to printf().

The following fragment outputs two floating-point numbers using printf():

```php
<?php
printf("First number: %f<br/>Second number: %f<br/>", 55, 66);
// Prints:
// First number: 55.000000
// Second number: 66.000000
?>
```

The first conversion specification corresponds to the first of the additional arguments to printf(), or 55. The second conversion specification corresponds to 66. The f following the percent symbol requires that the data be treated as a floating-point number. This part of the conversion specification is the *type specifier*.

`printf()` **and Type Specifiers**

You have already come across two type specifiers, o, which displays integers as octals, and f, which displays integers as floating-point numbers. Table 10.1 lists the other type specifiers available.

TABLE 10.1   Type Specifiers

Specifier	Description
d	Display argument as a decimal number
b	Display an integer as a binary number
c	Display an integer as ASCII equivalent
f	Display an integer as a floating-point number (double)
o	Display an integer as an octal number (base 8)
s	Display argument as a string
x	Display an integer as a lowercase hexadecimal number (base 16)
X	Display an integer as an uppercase hexadecimal number (base 16)

Listing 10.1 uses `printf()` to display a single number according to some of the type specifiers listed in Table 10.1. Notice that the listing does not only add conversion specifications to the format control string. Any additional text included is also printed.

LISTING 10.1   Demonstrating Some Type Specifiers

```
1: <?php
2: $number = 543;
3: printf("Decimal: %d<br/>", $number);
4: printf("Binary: %b<br/>", $number);
5: printf("Double: %f<br/>", $number);
6: printf("Octal: %o<br/>", $number);
7: printf("String: %s<br/>", $number);
8: printf("Hex (lower): %x<br/>", $number);
9: printf("Hex (upper): %X<br/>", $number);
10: ?>
```

Put these lines into a text file called `printftest.php` and place this file in your web server document root. When you access this script through your web browser, it should look something like Figure 10.1. As you can see, `printf()` is a quick way of converting data from one number system to another and outputting the result.

FIGURE 10.1
Demonstrating
conversion
specifiers.

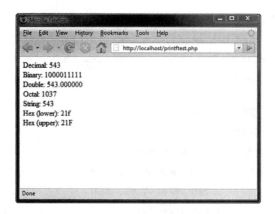

FIGURE 10.1
Demonstrating
conversion
specifiers.

When specifying a color in HTML, you combine three hexadecimal numbers
between 00 and FF, representing the values for red, green, and blue. You can use
printf() to convert three decimal numbers between 0 and 255 to their hexadecimal equivalents:

```php
<?php
$red = 204;
$green = 204;
$blue = 204;
printf("#%X%X%X", $red, $green, $blue);
// prints "#CCCCCC"
?>
```

Although you can use the type specifier to convert from decimal to hexadecimal
numbers, you can't use it to determine how many characters the output for each
argument should occupy. Within an HTML color code, each hexadecimal number
should be padded to two characters, which would become a problem if you changed
the $red, $green, and $blue variables in the previous fragment to contain 1, for
example. You would end up with the output #111. You can force the output of leading zeroes by using a *padding specifier*.

Padding Output with a Padding Specifier

You can require that output be padded by leading characters. The padding specifier
should directly follow the percent sign that begins a conversion specification. To pad
output with leading zeroes, the padding specifier should consist of a zero followed by
the number of characters you want the output to take up. If the output occupies
fewer characters than this total, zeroes will fill the difference:

```php
<?php
printf("%04d", 36);
// prints "0036"
?>
```

To pad output with leading spaces, the padding specifier should consist of a space character followed by the number of characters that the output should occupy:

```
<?php
printf("% 4d", 36)
// prints "  36"
?>
```

A browser will not display multiple spaces in an HTML document. You can force the display of spaces and newlines by placing <pre> tags around your output:

```
<pre>
<?php
echo "The        spaces        will be visible";
?>
</pre>
```

If you want to format an entire document as text, you can use the header() function to change the Content-Type header:

```
header("Content-Type: text/plain");
```

Remember that your script must not have sent any output to the browser for the header() function to work as desired.

Did you Know?

You can specify any character other than a space or a zero in your padding specifier with a single quotation mark followed by the character you want to use:

```
<?php
printf ("%'x4d", 36);
// prints "xx36"
?>
```

You now have the tools you need to complete your HTML code example. Until now, you could convert three numbers to hexadecimal, but could not pad the hexadecimal values with leading zeroes:

```
<?php
$red = 1;
$green = 1;
$blue = 1;
printf("#%02X%02X%02X", $red, $green, $blue);
// prints "#010101"
?>
```

Each variable is output as a hexadecimal number. If the output occupies fewer than two spaces, leading zeroes will be added.

Specifying a Field Width

You can specify the number of spaces within which your output should sit. A *field width specifier* is an integer that should be placed after the percent sign that begins a conversion specification (assuming that no padding specifier is defined). The following fragment outputs a list of four items, all of which sit within a field of 20 spaces. To make the spaces visible on the browser, place all the output within a pre element:

```php
<?php
echo "<pre>";
printf("%20s\n", "Books");
printf("%20s\n", "CDs");
printf("%20s\n", "DVDs");
printf("%20s\n", "Games");
printf("%20s\n", "Magazines");
echo "</pre>";
?>
```

Figure 10.2 shows the output of this fragment.

FIGURE 10.2
Aligning with
field width
specifiers.

By default, output is right-aligned within the field you specify. You can make it left-aligned by prepending a minus (–) symbol to the field width specifier:

```php
printf("%-20s\n", "Left aligned");
```

Note that alignment applies to the decimal portion of any number that you output. In other words, only the portion before the decimal point of a double will sit flush to the end of the field width when right-aligned.

Specifying Precision

If you want to output data in floating-point format, you can specify the precision to which you want to round your data. This is particularly useful when dealing with currency. The precision identifier should be placed directly before the type specifier.

It consists of a dot followed by the number of decimal places to which you want to round. This specifier only has an effect on data that is output with the f type specifier:

```php
<?php
printf("%.2f", 5.333333);
// prints "5.33"
?>
```

By the Way

> In the C language, it is possible to use a precision specifier with printf() to specify padding for decimal output. The precision specifier will have no effect on decimal output in PHP. Use the padding specifier to add leading zeroes to integers.

Conversion Specifications: A Recap

Table 10.2 lists the specifiers that can make up a conversion specification in the order that they would be included. Note that it is difficult to use both a padding specifier and a field width specifier. You should choose to use one or the other, but not both.

TABLE 10.2   Components of Conversion Specification

Name	Description	Example
Padding specifier	Determines the number of characters that output should occupy, and the characters to add otherwise	' 4'
Field width specifier	Determines the space within which output should be formatted	'20'
Precision specifier	Determines the number of decimal places to which a double should be rounded	'.4'
Type specifier	Determines the data type that should be output	'd'

Listing 10.2 uses printf() to output a list of products

LISTING 10.2   Using printf() to Format a List of Product Prices

```php
1:  <?php
2:  $products = array("Green armchair" => "222.4",
3:  "Candlestick"=> "4",
4:  "Coffee table"=> "80.6");
5:  echo "<pre>";
6:  printf("%-20s%20s\n", "Name", "Price");
7:  printf("%'-40s\n", "");
8:  foreach ($products as $key=>$val) {
9:      printf( "%-20s%20.2f\n", $key, $val );
```

LISTING 10.2   Continued

```
10: }
11: echo "</pre>";
12: ?>
```

The listing first defines an associative array containing product names and prices in lines 2 through 4. It prints the opening tag of the pre element, in line 5, so that the browser will recognize the spaces and newlines. The first printf() call on line 6 uses the following format control string:

```
"%-20s%20s\n"
```

The first conversion specification in the format control string ("%-20s") defines a width specifier of 20 characters, with the output to be left-justified. The string type specifier is also used. The second conversion specification ("%20s") sets up a right-aligned field width. This printf() call will output our field headers.

The second printf() function call on line 7 draws a line containing – characters, 40 characters wide. You achieve this with a padding specifier, which adds padding to an empty string.

The final printf() call on line 9 is part of a foreach statement that loops through the product array. The code uses two conversion specifications here—the first ("%-20s") prints the product name as a string left-justified within a 20-character field, and the second ("%20.2f") uses a field width specifier to ensure that output will be right-aligned within a 20-character field. It also uses a precision specifier to ensure that the output is rounded to two decimal places.

Put these lines into a text file called printftest2.php and place this file in your web server document root. When you access this script through your web browser, it should look like Figure 10.3.

FIGURE 10.3
Products and prices formatted with printf().

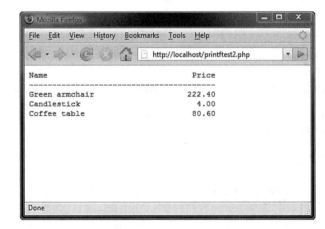

Argument Swapping

Imagine that you are printing dates to the browser. As shown in the snippet below, assume the dates are in a multidimensional array and you are using `printf()` to format the output.

```php
<?php
$dates = array(
        array('mon'=> 12, 'mday'=>25, 'year'=>2007),
        array('mon'=>  1, 'mday'=>23, 'year'=>2008),
        array('mon'=> 10, 'mday'=>29, 'year'=>2007)
        );
$format = include("local_format.php");
foreach($dates as $date) {
    printf("$format", $date['mon'], $date['mday'], $date['year']);
}
?>
```

In the preceding snippet, the format control string comes from an include file called `local_format.php`. Assuming that this file contains only

```php
<?php
return "%02d/%02d/%d<br/>";
?>
```

the output will be in the format `mm/dd/yyyy`:

```
12/25/2007
01/23/2008
10/29/2007
```

Imagine now that you are installing your script for a European site, where dates are commonly presented with days before months (dd/mm/yyyy). Assume that the core code is written in stone and cannot be changed. What should you do? Luckily you can now alter the order in which the arguments are presented from within the format control code by changing the `return` statement to

```php
return "%2\$02d/%1\$02d/%3\$d<br/>";
```

You can insert the argument number you are interested in after the initial percentage character that marks each conversion specification, followed by an escaped dollar ($) character. So, in the fragment, you are demanding that the second argument be presented:

```
%2\$02d
```

followed by the first argument:

```
%1\$02d
```

and concluded with the third argument:

```
%3\$d
```

The result of the new code is a list of dates in British format:

```
25/12/2007
23/01/2008
29/10/2007
```

Storing a Formatted String

The printf() function outputs data to the browser, which means that the results are not available to your scripts. You can, however, use the function sprintf(), which is used just like printf() except that it returns a string that can be stored in a variable for later use. The following fragment uses sprintf() to round a double to two decimal places, storing the result in $cash:

```php
<?php
$cash = sprintf("%.2f", 21.334454);
echo "You have \$$cash to spend.";
// Prints "You have $21.33 to spend."
?>
```

One particular use of sprintf() is to write formatted data to a file—you can call sprintf() and assign its return value to a variable that can then be printed to a file with fputs().

Investigating Strings in PHP

You do not always know everything about the data you are working with. Strings can arrive from many sources, including user input, databases, files, and web pages. Before you begin to work with data from an external source, you often will need to find out more about the data. PHP provides many functions that enable you to acquire information about strings.

A Note About Indexing Strings

This book frequently uses the word *index* in relation to strings. You will have come across this word in the context of arrays, such as in Chapter 8, "Working with Arrays." In fact, strings and arrays are not as different as you might imagine. You can think of a string as an array of characters, thus you can access the individual characters of a string as if they were elements of an array:

```php
<?php
$test = "phpcoder";
echo $test[0]; // prints "p"
echo $test[4]; // prints "o"
?>
```

It is important to remember that when this book discusses the position or index of a character within a string, the characters, just like array elements, have a starting index value of 0, not 1.

Finding the Length of a String with `strlen()`

You can use the built-in `strlen()` function to determine the length of a string. This function requires a string as its argument and returns an integer representing the number of characters in the string you passed to it. `strlen()` might be used to check the length of user input, as in the following fragment, which tests a membership code to ensure that it is exactly four characters long:

```php
<?php
if (strlen($membership) == 4) {
    echo "<p>Thank you!</p>";
} else {
    echo "<p>Your membership number must be four characters long.</p>";
}
?>
```

The user is thanked for his input only if the $membership variable holds a string that is exactly four characters long. Otherwise, an error message is presented.

Finding a Substring Within a String with `strstr()`

You can use the `strstr()` function to test whether a string exists within another string. This function requires two arguments: the source string and the substring you want to find within it. The function returns `false` if it cannot find the substring; otherwise, it returns the portion of the source string, beginning with the substring. For the following example, imagine that you want to treat membership codes that contain the string AB differently from those that do not:

```php
<?php
$membership = "pAB7";
if (strstr($membership, "AB")) {
    echo "<p>Your membership expires soon!</p>";
} else {
    echo "<p>Thank you!</p>";
}
?>
```

Because the value of the $membership variable contains the substring AB, the `strstr()` function returns the string AB7. The function resolves to `true` when tested, so the code prints the appropriate message, "Your membership expires soon!". But what happens if you search for "pab7"? Because `strstr()` is case sensitive, AB will not be found. The `if` statement's original test will fail, and the default message ("Thank you!") will be printed to the browser. If you want to search for either AB or ab within the string, you must use `strstr()` in place of `substr()`; the function is used in exactly the same way, but its search is not case sensitive.

Finding the Position of a Substring with `strpos()`

The `strpos()` function tells you whether a string exists within a larger string as well as where it is found. The `strpos()` function requires two arguments: the source string and the substring you are seeking. The function also accepts an optional third argument, an integer representing the index from which you want to start searching. If the substring does not exist, `strpos()` returns `false`; otherwise, it returns the index at which the substring begins. The following fragment uses `strpos()` to ensure that a string begins with the string `mz`:

```php
<?php
$membership = "mz00xyz";
if (strpos($membership, "mz") === 0) {
    echo "Hello mz!";
}
?>
```

Notice the trick that had to be played to get the expected results. Although the `strpos()` function finds `mz` in the string, it finds it at the first element—the 0 position. Returning zero will resolve to `false` in the `if` condition test. To work around this, the code uses the equivalence operator `===`, which returns `true` if the left and right operands are equivalent and of the same type, as they are in this case.

This is just one of several variations on string-related functions meant to find needles in haystacks. Visiting the PHP Manual page for this function provides links to many other related functions.

Extracting Part of a String with `substr()`

The `substr()` function returns a string based on the start index and length of the characters you are looking for. This function requires two arguments: a source string and the starting index. Using these arguments, the function returns all the characters from the starting index to the end of the string you are searching. You can also (optionally) provide a third argument—an integer representing the length of the string you want returned. If this third argument is present, `substr()` returns only that number of characters, from the start index onward.

```php
<?php
$test = "phpcoder";
echo substr($test,3)."<br/>";  // prints "coder"
echo substr($test,3,2)."<br/>"; // prints "co"
?>
```

If you pass substr() a negative number as its second (starting index) argument, it will count from the end rather than the beginning of the string. The following fragment writes a specific message to people who have submitted an email address ending in .fr:

```php
<?php
$test = "pierre@wanadoo.fr";
if ($test = substr($test, -3) == ".fr") {
    echo "<p>Bonjour! Nous avons des prix spéciaux de vous.</p>";
} else {
    echo "<p>Welcome to our store.</p>";
}
?>
```

Tokenizing a String with strtok()

You can parse a string word by word using the strtok() function. This function requires two arguments: the string to tokenize and the delimiters by which to split the string. The delimiter string can include as many characters as you want, and the function will return the first token found. After strtok() has been called for the first time, the source string will be cached—for subsequent calls, you should pass only the delimiter string to the strtok() function. The function will return the next found token every time it is called, returning false when the end of the string is reached. The strtok() function will usually be called repeatedly, within a loop. Listing 10.3 uses strtok() to tokenize a URL, splitting the host and path from the query string, and further dividing the name/value pairs of the query string.

LISTING 10.3   Dividing a String into Tokens with strtok()

```php
1: <?php
2: $test  = "http://www.google.com/search?";
3: $test .= "hl=en&ie=UTF-8&q=php+development+books&btnG=Google+Search";
4: $delims = "?&";
5: $word = strtok($test, $delims);
6: while (is_string($word)) {
7:    if ($word) {
8:        echo $word."<br/>";
9:    }
10:    $word = strtok($delims);
11: }
12: ?>
```

Put these lines into a text file called teststrtotok.php and place this file in your web server document root. When you access this script through your web browser, it should look like Figure 10.4.

FIGURE 10.4
Output of test-strtotok.php, a tokenized string.

The strtok() function is something of a blunt instrument, and a few tricks are required to work with it. The code first stores the delimiters to work with in a variable, $delims, on line 4. It calls strtok() on line 5, passing it the URL to tokenize and the $delims string, and stores the first result in $word. Within the conditional expression of the while loop on line 6, the code tests that $word is a string. If it isn't, the end of the string has been reached and no further action is required.

Listing 10.3 tests the return type because a string containing two delimiters in a row would cause strtok() to return an empty string when it reaches the first of these delimiters. So, a more conventional test such as

```
while ($word) {
    $word = strtok($delims);
}
```

would fail if $word is an empty string, even if the end of the source string has not yet been reached.

Having established that $word contains a string, the code can go on to work with it. If $word does not contain an empty string, print it to the browser on line 8. The code must then call strtok() again on line 10 to repopulate the $word variable for the next test. Notice that the source string to strtok() is not passed a second time—if you did this, the first word of the source string would be returned once again, and you would find yourself in an infinite loop.

Manipulating Strings with PHP

PHP provides many functions that will transform a string argument, subtly or radically, as you'll soon see.

Cleaning Up a String with `trim()`, `ltrim()`, and `strip_tags()`

When you acquire text from user input or an external file, you can't always be sure that you haven't also picked up whitespace at the beginning and end of your data. The `trim()` function shaves any whitespace characters, including newlines, tabs, and spaces, from both the start and end of a string. It accepts the string to modify, returning the cleaned-up version. For example:

```
<?php
$text = "\t\tlots of room to breathe        ";
echo "<pre>$text</pre>";
// prints "        lots of room to breathe        ";
$text = trim($text);
echo "<pre>$text</pre>";
// prints "lots of room to breathe";
?>
```

Of course this might be more work than you require. You might want to keep whitespace at the beginning of a string but remove it from the end. You can use PHP's `rtrim()` function exactly as you would use `trim()`. However, `rtrim()` removes whitespace at only the end of the string argument:

```
<?php
$text = "\t\tlots of room to breathe        ";
echo "<pre>$text</pre>";
// prints "        lots of room to breathe        ";
$text = rtrim($text);
echo "<pre>$text</pre>";
// prints "        lots of room to breathe";
?>
```

PHP provides the `ltrim()` function to strip whitespace from only the beginning of a string. Once again, you call this function with the string you want to transform and it returns a new string, shorn of tabs, newlines, and spaces:

```
<?php
$text = "\t\tlots of room to breathe        ";
echo "<pre>$text</pre>";
// prints "        lots of room to breathe        ";
$text = ltrim($text);
echo "<pre>$text</pre>";
// prints "lots of room to breathe        ";
?>
```

It is not unusual to have to remove tags from a block of text to display it without any HTML formatting. PHP provides the `strip_tags()` function for this purpose. The `strip_tags()` function accepts two arguments: the text to transform and an optional set of HTML tags that `strip_tags()` can leave in place. The tags in this list should not be separated by any characters.

```php
<?php
$string = "<p>\"I <i>simply</i> will not have it,\" <br/>said Mr Dean.</p>
<p><b>The end.</b></p>";
echo strip_tags($string, "<br/><p>");
?>
```

The previous code fragment creates an HTML-formatted string. When you call `strip_tags()`, you pass it the $string variable and a list of exceptions. The result is that the <br/> and <p> tags are left in place and all other tags are stripped out. In addition, the matching tag for <p>—</p>—is removed as well.

The output of this snippet is

```
"I simply will not have it,"
said Mr Dean.

The end.
```

Note that the italics and bold formatting are gone, but the paragraphs and line breaks remain.

Replacing a Portion of a String Using `substr_replace()`

The `substr_replace()` function works similarly to the `substr()` function, except it allows you to replace the portion of the string that you extract. The function requires three arguments: the string to transform, the text to add to it, and the starting index; it also accepts an optional length argument. The `substr_replace()` function finds the portion of a string specified by the starting index and length arguments, replaces this portion with the string provided, and returns the entire transformed string.

The following code fragment for renewing a user's membership number changes its second two characters:

```php
<?php
$membership = "mz07xyz";
$membership = substr_replace($membership, "08", 2, 2);
echo "New membership number: $membership";
// prints "New membership number: mz06xyz"
?>
```

The result of this code is that the old membership number, "mz07xyz", is transformed into the new membership number, "mz08xyz".

Replacing Substrings Using `str_replace`

The `str_replace()` function is used to replace all instances of a given string within another string. It requires three arguments: the search string, the replacement string, and the master string. The function returns the transformed string.

The following example uses `str_replace()` to change all references to 2005 to 2008 within a master string:

```php
<?php
$string = "<h1>The 2005 Guide to All Things Good in the World</h1>";
$string .= "<p>Site contents copyright 2005.</p>";
echo str_replace("2005","2008",$string);
?>
```

The `str_replace()` function accepts arrays as well as strings for all its arguments. This allows you to perform multiple search and replace operations on a subject string, and even on more than one subject string. Take the following snippet, for instance:

```php
<?php
$source = array(
    "The package which is at version 4.2 was released in 2005.",
    "The year 2005 was an excellent time for PointyThing 4.2!");
$search  = array("4.2", "2005");
$replace = array("6.3", "2008");
$source = str_replace($search, $replace, $source);
foreach($source as $str) {
    echo "$str<br>";
}
?>
```

The output is of this snippet is

```
The package which is at version 6.3 was released in 2008.
The year 2008 was an excellent time for PointyThing 6.3!
```

When an array of strings is passed to `str_replace()` for its first and second arguments, it attempts to switch each search string with its corresponding replace string in the text to be transformed. When the third argument is an array, the `str_replace()` function returns an array of strings. The search and replace operation will have been executed on each string in the array.

Converting Case

PHP provides several functions that allow you to convert the case of a string. Changing case is often useful for string comparisons. To get an uppercase version of a string, use the `strtoupper()` function. This function requires only the string that you want to convert and returns the converted string:

```php
<?php
$membership = "mz08xyz";
$membership = strtoupper($membership);
echo "$membership"; // prints "MZ08XYZ"
?>
```

To convert a string to lowercase characters, use the `strtolower()` function. Once again, this function requires the string you want to convert and returns the converted version:

```php
<?php
$membership = "MZ08XYZ";
$membership = strtolower($membership);
echo "$membership"; // prints "mz08xyz"
?>
```

PHP also provides a case function that has a useful cosmetic purpose. The `ucwords()` function makes the first letter of every word in a string uppercase. The following fragment makes the first letter of every word in a user-submitted string uppercase:

```php
<?php
$full_name = "violet elizabeth bott";
$full_name = ucwords($full_name);
echo $full_name; // prints "Violet Elizabeth Bott"
?>
```

Although this function makes the first letter of each word uppercase, it does not touch any other letters. So, if the user had had problems with her Shift key in the previous example and submitted VIolEt eLIZaBeTH bOTt, the preceding approach would not have done much to fix the string. The output would have been VIolEt ELIZaBeTH BOTt, which isn't much of an improvement. You can deal with this by making the submitted string lowercase with the `strtolower()` function before invoking `ucwords()`:

```php
<?php
$full_name = "VIolEt eLIZaBeTH bOTt";
$full_name = ucwords(strtolower($full_name));
echo $full_name; // prints "Violet Elizabeth Bott"
?>
```

Finally, the `ucfirst()` function capitalizes only the first letter in a string. The following fragment capitalizes the first letter in a user-submitted string:

```php
<?php
$myString = "this is my string.";
$myString = ucfirst($myString);
echo $myString; // prints "This is my string."
?>
```

Working with case-related string functions can prove useful when attempting to authenticate passwords that are not case sensitive, for example. If the user inputs "MyPass" and the stored password is "mypass" but you do not want the match to be case sensitive, you can attempt to match a lowercase (or uppercase) version of the user input with the lowercase (or uppercase) version of the stored password. If they match in their similarly cased format, the user can be authenticated even if he typed something different from what was actually stored.

Wrapping Text with `wordwrap()` and `nl2br()`

When you present plain text within a web page, you are often faced with a problem in which new lines are not displayed and your text runs together into one big mess. The `nl2br()` function conveniently converts every new line into an HTML break. So

```php
<?php
$string  = "one line\n";
$string .= "another line\n";
$string .= "a third for luck\n";
echo nl2br($string);
?>
```

outputs

```
one line<br />
another line<br />
a third for luck<br />
```

> The <br> tags are output in XHTML-compliant format (<br />).

By the Way

The `nl2br()` function is great for maintaining newlines that are already in the text you are converting. Occasionally, you might want to add arbitrary line breaks to format a column of text. The `wordwrap()` function is perfect for this. `wordwrap()` requires one argument: the string to transform. By default, `wordwrap()` wraps lines every 75 characters and uses \n as its line break character. So, the code fragment

```php
<?php
$string  = "Given a long line, wordwrap() is useful as a means of ";
$string .= "breaking it into a column and thereby making it easier to read";
echo wordwrap($string);
?>
```

would output

```
Given a long line, wordwrap() is useful as a means of breaking it into a
column and thereby making it easier to read
```

Because the lines are broken with the character \n, the formatting does not show up in HTML code, of course. The wordwrap() function has two more optional arguments: a number representing the maximum number of characters per line and a string representing the end of line string you want to use. So, applying the function call

```
echo wordwrap($string, 24, "<br/>\n");
```

to the $string variable used earlier, the output would be

```
Given a long line,<br/>
wordwrap() is useful as<br/>
a means of breaking it<br/>
into a column and<br/>
thereby making it easier<br/>
to read
```

The wordwrap() function won't automatically break at your line limit if a word has more characters than the limit. You can, however, use an optional fourth argument to enforce this. The argument should be a positive integer. So, using wordwrap() in conjunction with the fourth argument, you can wrap a string even when it contains words that extend beyond the limit you are setting. This fragment

```
<?php
$string  = "As usual you will find me at http://www.witteringonaboutit.com/";
$string .= "chat/eating_green_cheese/forum.php. Hope to see you there!";
echo wordwrap($string, 24, "<br/>\n", 1);
?>
```

outputs

```
As usual you will find<br/>
me at<br/>
http://www.witteringonab<br/>
outit.com/chat/eating_gr<br/>
een_cheese/forum.php.<br/>
Hope to see you there!
```

instead of

```
As usual you will find<br/>
me at<br/>
http://www.witteringonaboutit.com/chat/eating_green_cheese/forum.php. <br/>
Hope to see you there!
```

Breaking Strings into Arrays with explode()

The delightfully named explode() function is similar in some ways to strtok(). But explode() breaks up a string into an array, which you can then store, sort, or examine as you want. The explode() function requires two arguments: the delimiter string that you want to use to break up the source string and the source string itself. The function optionally accepts a third argument that determines the maximum number of pieces the string can be broken into. The delimiter string can include more than one character, all of which form a single delimiter (unlike multiple delimiter characters passed to strtok(), each of which will be a delimiter in its own right). The following fragment breaks up a date and stores the result in an array:

```php
<?php
$start_date = "2008-02-19";
$date_array = explode("-", $start_date);
// $date_array[0] == "2008"
// $date_array[1] == "02"
// $date_array[2] == "19"
echo $date_array[0]."-".$date_array[1]."-".$date_array[2];
//prints 2008-02-19
?>
```

Now that your head is full with some common PHP string functions, let's move on to date and time functions.

Using Date and Time Functions in PHP

The following sections introduce you to the date- and time-related functions specifically in PHP. Try out each listing for yourself to see how simple and powerful these functions can be.

Getting the Date with time()

PHP's time() function gives you all the information you need about the current date and time. It requires no arguments and returns an integer. For us humans, the returned number is a little hard on the eyes, but it's extremely useful nonetheless.

```php
echo time();
// sample output: 1202082227
// this represents February 3, 2008 at 03:44PM
```

The integer returned by time() represents the number of seconds elapsed since midnight GMT on January 1, 1970. This moment is known as the *UNIX epoch*, and the number of seconds that have elapsed since then is referred to as a *time stamp*. PHP offers excellent tools to convert a time stamp into a form that humans are comfortable with. Even so, you might think, "Isn't a time stamp a needlessly convoluted way of storing a date?" In fact, the opposite is true. From just one number, you can extract enormous amounts of information. Even better, a time stamp can make date arithmetic much easier than you might imagine.

Think of a homegrown date system in which you record days of the month as well as months and years. Now imagine a script that must add one day to a given date. If this date happened to be 31 December 1999, rather than adding 1 to the date, you'd have to write code to set the day of the month to 1, the month to January, and the year to 2000. Using a time stamp, you need add only a day's worth of seconds (60 * 60 * 24, or 86400) to your current figure and you're done. You can convert this new figure into something friendlier, at your leisure.

Converting a Time Stamp with getdate()

Now that you have a time stamp to work with, you must convert it before you present it to the user. getdate() optionally accepts a time stamp and returns an associative array containing information about the date. If you omit the time stamp, getdate() works with the current time stamp as returned by time(). Table 10.3 lists the elements contained in the array returned by getdate().

TABLE 10.3   The Associative Array Returned by getdate()

Key	Description	Example
seconds	Seconds past the minute (0–59)	53
minutes	Minutes past the hour (0–59)	44
hours	Hours of the day (0–23)	17
mday	Day of the month (1–31)	3
wday	Day of the week (0–6)	0
mon	Month of the year (1–12)	2
year	Year (4 digits)	2008
yday	Day of year (0–365)	33
weekday	Day of the week (name)	Sunday
month	Month of the year (name)	February
0	Time stamp	1202082293

Listing 10.4 uses getdate() in line 2 to extract information from a time stamp, employing a foreach statement to print each element (line 3). You can see typical output of this script, called getdate.php, in Figure 10.5.

LISTING 10.4   Acquiring Date Information with getdate()

```
1: <?php
2: $date_array = getdate(); // no argument passed so today's date will be used
3: foreach ($date_array as $key => $val) {
4:     echo "$key = $val<br>";
5: }
```

LISTING 10.4   Continued

```
6:  ?>
7:  <hr/>
8:  <?php
9:  echo "<p>Today's date: ".$date_array['mon']."/".$date_array['mday']."/".
10:     $date_array['year']."</p>";
11: ?>
```

FIGURE 10.5
Using
getdate().

```
seconds = 53
minutes = 44
hours = 17
mday = 3
wday = 0
mon = 2
year = 2008
yday = 33
weekday = Sunday
month = February
0 = 1202082293
```

Today's date: 2/3/2008

Converting a Time Stamp with date()

You can use getdate() when you want to work with the elements that it outputs. Sometimes, though, you want to display the date as a string. The date() function returns a formatted string that represents a date. You can exercise an enormous amount of control over the format that date() returns with a string argument that you must pass to it. In addition to the format string, date() optionally accepts a time stamp. Table 10.4 lists some of the codes that a format string can contain. You can find the complete list at http://www.php.net/date. Any other data you include in the format string passed to date() is included in the return value.

TABLE 10.4   Some Format Codes for Use with date()

Format	Description	Example
a	am or pm (lowercase)	am
A	AM or PM (uppercase)	AM
d	Day of month (number with leading zeroes)	28
D	Day of week (three letters)	Tue

TABLE 10.4   Continued

Format	Description	Example
e	Timezone identifier	America/ Los_Angeles
F	Month name	February
h	Hour (12-hour format—leading zeroes)	06
H	Hour (24-hour format—leading zeroes)	06
g	Hour (12-hour format—no leading zeroes)	6
G	Hour (24-hour format—no leading zeroes)	6
i	Minutes	45
j	Day of the month (no leading zeroes)	28
l	Day of the week (name)	Tuesday
L	Leap year (1 for yes, 0 for no)	0
m	Month of year (number—leading zeroes)	02
M	Month of year (three letters)	Feb
n	Month of year (number—no leading zeroes)	2
s	Seconds of hour	26
S	Ordinal suffix for the day of the month	th
r	Full date standardized to RFC 822 (http://www.faqs.org/rfcs/rfc822.html)	Tue, 28 Feb 2006 06:45:26 -0800
U	Time stamp	1141137926
y	Year (two digits)	06
Y	Year (four digits)	2006
z	Day of year (0–365)	28
Z	Offset in seconds from GMT	-28800

Listing 10.5 puts a few of these formats to the test.

LISTING 10.5   Formatting a Date with `date()`

```
1: <?php
2: $time = time(); //stores the exact timestamp to use in this script
3: echo date("m/d/y G:i:s e", $time);
4: echo "<br/>";
5: echo "Today is ";
6: echo date("jS \o\f F Y, \a\\t g:ia \i\\n e", $time);
7: ?>
```

Listing 10.5 calls date() twice: the first time on line 3 to output an abbreviated date format, and the second time on line 6 for a longer format. Save the text of this listing in a file called datetest.php and open it in your web browser. Your date will differ from the following, obviously, but here's some sample output:

```
02/03/08 15:50:26 America/Los_Angeles
Today is 3rd of February 2008, at 3:50pm in America/Los_Angeles
```

Although the format string looks arcane, it's easy to build. If you want to add a string that contains letters that are also format codes to the format, you can escape them by placing a backslash (\) in front of them. For characters that become control characters when escaped, you must escape the backslash that precedes them. For example, \t is a format code for a tab, so to ensure that the tab prints, use \\t as in the example in Listing 10.5.

Another example is in the context of a word you are adding to a string; for example, *the*. The word *the* is made up of three format codes, so all must be escaped:

```php
<?php
echo date("l \\t\h\e jS");
//prints Tuesday the 3rd
?>
```

Also note that the date() function returns information according to your local time zone. If you want to format a date in GMT, you use the gmdate() function, which works in exactly the same way.

Creating Time Stamps with mktime()

You can already get information about the current time, but you cannot yet work with arbitrary dates. mktime() returns a time stamp that you can then use with date() or getdate(). mktime() accepts up to six integer arguments in the following order:

Hour

Minute

Second

Month

Day of month

Year

Listing 10.6 uses mktime() to get a time stamp it then uses with the date() function.

LISTING 10.6   Creating a Time Stamp with `mktime()`

```
1: <?php
2: // make a timestamp for Feb 3 2008 at 2:13 pm
3: $ts = mktime(2, 13, 0, 2, 3, 2008);
4: echo date("m/d/y G:i:s e", $ts);
5: echo "<br/>";
6: echo "The date is ";
7: echo date("jS \o\f F Y, \a\\t g:ia \i\\n e", $ts );
8: ?>
```

This code calls `mktime()` on line 3 and assigns the returned time stamp to the `$ts` variable. It then uses the `date()` function on lines 4 and 7 to output formatted versions of the date using `$ts`. You can choose to omit some of or all the arguments to `mktime()`, and the value appropriate to the current time is used instead. `mktime()` also adjusts for values that go beyond the relevant range, so an hour argument of 25 translates to 1:00 a.m. on the day after that specified in the month, day, and year arguments.

Save the text of this listing in a file called `mktimetest.php` and open it in your web browser. You should see

```
02/03/08 2:13:00 America/Chicago
The date is 3rd of February 2008, at 2:13am in America/Chicago
```

Testing a Date with `checkdate()`

You might need to accept date information from user input. Before you work with a user-entered date or store it in a database, make sure that the date is valid. `checkdate()` accepts three integers: month, day, and year. `checkdate()` returns `true` if the month is between 1 and 12, the day is acceptable for the given month and year (accounting for leap years), and the year is between 0 and 32767. Be careful, though: A date might be valid but not acceptable to other date functions. For example, the following line returns `true`:

```
checkdate(4, 4, 1066)
```

If you were to attempt to build a date with `mktime()` using these values, you'd end up with a time stamp of `-1`. As a rule of thumb, don't use `mktime()` with years before 1902, and be cautious of using date functions with any date before 1970 because negative numbers are not valid dates. Because the UNIX epoch began January 1, 1970, anything before that is an invalid (negative) time stamp.

Other String, Date, and Time Functions

PHP does not lack for functions, especially for common items such as strings and dates. It is worth your while to bookmark the following chapters in the PHP Manual:

▶ "Strings" at http://www.php.net/manual/en/ref.strings.php

▶ "Date/Time" at http://www.php.net/manual/en/ref.datetime.php

In addition to keeping up with functions as they are added to PHP, the user-contributed notes for each function often offer solutions to various programming tasks that you might find useful as you build your own applications.

Summary

In this chapter, you learned about some of the functions that enable you to take control of the strings in your PHP scripts. You learned how to format strings with `printf()` and `sprint()`. You should be able to use these functions to create strings that both transform and format data. You learned about functions that investigate strings. You should be able to discover the length of a string with `strlen()`, determine the presence of a substring with `strpos()`, and extract a substring with `substr()`. You should be able to tokenize a string with `strtok()`.

You also learned about functions that transform strings. You can now remove whitespace from the beginning or end of a string with `trim()`, `ltrim()`, or `rtrim()`. You can change the case of characters in a string with `strtoupper()`, `strtolower()`, or `ucwords()`. You can replace all instances of a string with `str_replace()`.

You also learned how to use various PHP functions to perform date- and time-related actions. The `time()` function gets a date stamp for the current date and time, and you can use `getdate()` to extract date information from a time stamp and `date()` to convert a time stamp into a formatted string. You learned how to create a time stamp using `mktime()`, and how to test a date for validity with `checkdate()`. You will learn many more powerful date-related functions in Chapter 16, "Learning Basic SQL Commands," so much so that you might find yourself using MySQL and not PHP for many of your date-related needs.

Workshop

The workshop is designed to help you anticipate possible questions, review what you've learned, and begin putting your knowledge into practice.

Q&A

Q. *Can I combine multiple string functions?*

A. Yes. You can nest any function, not just string functions. Just remember to count your opening and closing parentheses to ensure that you've nested your functions appropriately.

Quiz

1. What conversion specifier would you use with `printf()` to format an integer as a double? Indicate the full syntax required to convert the integer 33.

2. How would you pad the conversion you effected in question 1 with zeroes so that the part before the decimal point is four characters long?

3. How would you specify a precision of two decimal places for the floating-point number you have been formatting in the previous questions?

4. What function would you use to extract a substring from a string?

5. How might you remove whitespace from the beginning of a string?

6. How would you break up a delimited string into an array of substrings?

7. Using PHP, how do you acquire a UNIX time stamp that represents the current date and time?

8. Which PHP function accepts a time stamp and returns an associative array that represents the given date?

9. Which PHP function do you use to format date information?

10. Which PHP function could you use to check the validity of a date?

Answers

1. The conversion specifier `f` is used to format an integer as a double:

```
printf("%f", 33);
```

2. You can pad the output from `printf()` with the padding specifier—that is, a space or a zero followed by a number representing the number of characters you want to pad by:

```
printf("%04f", 33);
```

3. The precision specifier consists of a dot (.) followed by a number representing the precision you want to apply. You should place the precision specifier before the conversion specifier:

```
printf("%04.2f", 33);
```

4. The `substr()` function extracts and returns a substring.

5. The `ltrim()` function removes whitespace from the start of a string.

6. The `explode()` function splits up a string into an array.

7. Use `time()`.

8. The `getdate()` function returns an associative array whose elements contain aspects of the given date.

9. Use `date()`.

10. You can check a date with the `checkdate()` function.

Activities

1. Create a feedback form that accepts a user's full name and an email address. Use case conversion functions to capitalize the first letter of each name the user submits and print the result back to the browser. Check that the user's email address contains the @ symbol and print a warning otherwise.

2. Create an array of doubles and integers. Loop through the array, converting each element to a floating-point number with a precision of 2. Right-align the output within a field of 20 characters.

3. Create a birthday countdown script. Given form input of month, day, and year, output a message that tells the user how many days, hours, minutes, and seconds until the big day.

11

Working with Forms

Until now, the PHP examples in this book have been missing a crucial dimension. Sure, you know the basics, can set variables and arrays, create and call functions, and work with strings. But that's all meaningless if users can't interact in a meaningful way with your website. HTML forms are the principal means by which substantial amounts of information pass from the user to the server, so this chapter moves into this dimension and looks at strategies for acquiring and working with user input.

In this chapter, you will learn

▶ How to access information from form fields

▶ How to work with form elements that allow multiple selections

▶ How to create a single document that contains both an HTML form and the PHP code that handles its submission

▶ How to save state with hidden fields

▶ How to redirect the user to a new page

▶ How to build HTML forms and PHP code that send mail

▶ How to build HTML forms that upload files and write the PHP code to handle the uploads

Creating a Simple Input Form

For now, let's keep the HTML separate from the PHP code. Listing 11.1 builds a simple HTML form.

LISTING 11.1   A Simple HTML Form

```
 1: <html>
 2: <head>
 3: <title>A simple HTML form</title>
 4: </head>
 5: <body>
 6: <form action="send_simpleform.php" method="POST">
 7: <p><strong>Name:</strong><br/>
 8. <input type="text" name="user"/></p>
 9: <p><strong>Message:</strong><br/>
10: <textarea name="message" rows="5" cols="40"></textarea></p>
11: <p><input type="submit" value="send"/></p>
12: </form>
13: </body>
14: </html>
```

Put these lines into a text file called `simpleform.html` and place that file in your web server document root. This listing defines a form that contains a text field with the name `"user"` on line 8, a text area with the name `"message"` on line 10, and a submit button on line 11. The FORM element's ACTION argument points to a file called `send_simpleform.php`, which processes the form information. The method of this form is POST, so the variables are stored in the $_POST superglobal.

Listing 11.2 creates the code that receives our users' input.

LISTING 11.2   Reading Input from a Form

```
1: <?php
2: echo "<p>Welcome <b>".$_POST["user"]."</b>!</p>";
3: echo "<p>Your message is:<br/><b>".$_POST["message"]."</b></p>";
4:?>
```

Put these lines into a text file called `send_simpleform.php` and place that file in your web server document root. Now access the form itself (`simpleform.html`) with your web browser, and you should see something like Figure 11.1.

The script in Listing 11.2 is called when the user submits the form created in Listing 11.1. The code in Listing 11.2 accesses two variables: $_POST["user"] and $_POST["message"]. These are references to the variables in the $_POST superglobal, which contain the values that the user entered in the user text field and the message text area. Forms in PHP really *are* as simple as that.

Enter some information in the form fields and click the send button. You should see your input echoed to the screen.

FIGURE 11.1
The form creat-
ed by simple-
form.html.

You could also use the GET method in this form (and others). POST can handle
more data than GET and does not pass the data in the query string. If you use the
GET method, be sure to change your superglobal to $_GET and not $_POST.

By the
Way

Accessing Form Input with User-Defined Arrays

The previous example showed how to gather information from HTML elements that
submit a single value per element name, such as text fields, text areas, and radio
buttons. This leaves you with a problem when working with elements such as
SELECT because it is possible for the user to choose one or more items from a multiple SELECT list. If you name the SELECT element with a plain name, like so

```
<select name="products" multiple>
```

the script that receives this data has access to only a single value corresponding to
this name ($_POST["products"]). You can change this behavior by renaming an
element of this kind so that its name ends with an empty set of square brackets.
Listing 11.3 does this.

LISTING 11.3   An HTML Form Including a SELECT Element

```
1: <html>
2: <head>
3: <title>An HTML form including a SELECT element</title>
4: </head>
5: <body>
```

LISTING 11.3   Continued

```
 6: <form action="send_formwithselect.php" method="POST">
 7: <p><strong>Name:</strong><br/>
 8: <input type="text" name="user"/>
 9: <p><strong>Select Some Products:</strong><br/>
10: <select name="products[]" multiple="multiple">
11: <option value="Sonic Screwdriver">Sonic Screwdriver</option>
12: <option value="Tricoder">Tricorder</option>
13: <option value="ORAC AI">ORAC AI</option>
14: <option value="HAL 2000">HAL 2000</option>
15: </select>
16: <p><input type="submit" value="send"/></p>
17: </form>
18: </body>
19: </html>
```

Put these lines into a text file called formwithselect.html and place that file in
your web server document root. Next, in the script that processes the form input,
you find that input from the "products[]" form element created on line 10 is
available in an array called $_POST["products"]. Because products[] is a SELECT
element, offer the user multiple choices using the option elements on lines 11
through 14. That the user's choices are made available is demonstrated in an array
in Listing 11.4.

LISTING 11.4   Reading Input from the Form in Listing 11.3

```
 1: <?php
 2: echo "<p>Welcome <b>".$_POST["user"]."</b>!</p>";
 3: echo "<p>Your product choices are:<br/>";
 4: if (!empty($_POST["products"])) {
 5:     echo "<ul>";
 6:     foreach ($_POST["products"] as $value) {
 7:         echo "<li>$value</li>";
 8:     }
 9:     echo "</ul>";
10: }
11: ?>
```

Put these lines into a text file called send_formwithselect.php and place that file
in your web server document root. Now access the form with your web browser and
fill out the fields. Figure 11.2 shows an example.

Line 2 of the script in Listing 11.4 accesses the $_POST["user"] variable, which is
derived from the user form element. On line 4, the code tests for the $_POST["prod-
ucts"] variable. If $_POST["products"] is present, execution loops through it on
line 6, and outputs each choice to the browser on line 7. The text within the value
attribute of the selected OPTION element becomes one of the stored values in the array.

Submit the form, and you might see something like that shown in Figure 11.3.

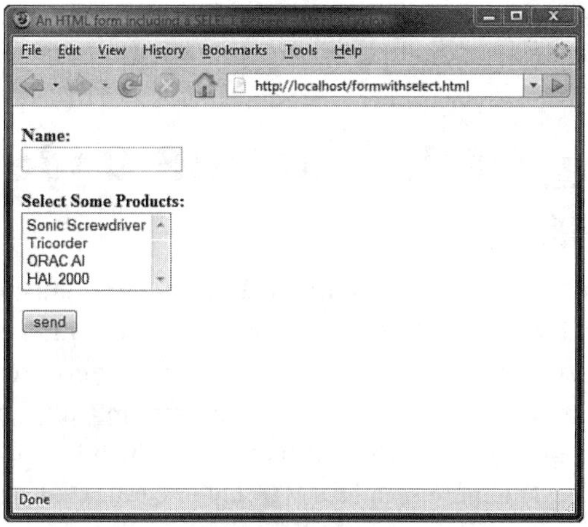

FIGURE 11.2
The form created in Listing 11.3.

FIGURE 11.3
Sample output of send_formwith select.php.

Although the looping technique is particularly useful with the SELECT element, it can work with other types of form elements as well. For example, by giving a number of check boxes the same name, you can enable a user to choose many values within a single field name.

As long as the name you choose ends with empty square brackets, PHP compiles the user input for this field into an array. We can replace the SELECT elements from lines 11–14 in Listing 11.3 with a series of check boxes to achieve the same effect:

```
<input type="checkbox" name="products[]"
       value="Sonic Screwdriver"/>Sonic Screwdriver<br/>
<input type="checkbox" name="products[]" value="Tricorder"/>Tricorder<br/>
<input type="checkbox" name="products[]" value="ORAC AI"/>ORAC AI<br/>
<input type="checkbox" name="products[]" value="HAL 2000"/>HAL 2000<br/>
```

The selected values will still be accessible using the $_POST["products"] variable, just as if they came from the multiple SELECT list in Listing 11.4.

Combining HTML and PHP Code on a Single Page

In some circumstances, you might want to include the form-parsing PHP code on the same page as a hard-coded HTML form. Such a combination can be useful if you need to present the same form to the user more than once. You would have more flexibility if you were to write the entire page dynamically, of course, but you would miss out on one of the great strengths of PHP, which is that it mingles well with standard HTML. The more standard HTML you can include in your pages, the easier they are for designers and page builders to amend without asking you, the programmer, for help. For the following examples, imagine that you're creating a site that teaches basic math to preschool children and have been asked to create a script that takes a number from form input and tells the user whether it's larger or smaller than a predefined integer.

Listing 11.5 creates the HTML. For this example, you need only a single text field, but even so, the code listing includes a little PHP.

LISTING 11.5   An HTML Form That Calls Itself

```
 1: <html>
 2: <head>
 3: <title>An HTML form that calls itself</title>
 4: </head>
 5: <body>
 6: <form action="<?php echo $_SERVER["PHP_SELF"]; ?>" method="POST">
 7: <p><strong>Type your guess here:</strong>
 8: <input type="text" name="guess"/></p>
 9: <p><input type="submit" value="submit your guess"/></p>
10: </form>
11: </body>
12: </html>
```

The action of this script is $_SERVER["PHP_SELF"], as shown in line 6. This global variable represents the name of the current script. In other words, the action tells the script to reload itself. The script in Listing 11.5 doesn't produce any output, but if you upload the script to your web server, access the page, and view the source of the page, you will notice that the form action now contains the name of the script itself.

In Listing 11.6, you begin to build up the PHP element of the page.

LISTING 11.6 A PHP Number-Guessing Script

```
 1: <?php
 2: $num_to_guess = 42;
 3: if (!isset($_POST["guess"])) {
 4:     $message = "Welcome to the guessing machine!";
 5: } else if ($_POST["guess"] > $num_to_guess) {
 6:     $message = $_POST["guess"]." is too big! Try a smaller number.";
 7: } else if ($_POST["guess"] < $num_to_guess) {
 8:     $message = $_POST["guess"]." is too small! Try a larger number.";
 9: } else { // must be equivalent
10:     $message = "Well done!";
11: }
12: ?>
```

First, you must define the number that the user guesses, and this is done in line 2 when 42 is assigned to the $num_to_guess variable. Next, you must determine whether the form has been submitted; you can test for submission by looking for the existence of the variable $_POST["guess"], which will be available only if your script has been submitted with a value in the guess field. If a value for $_POST["guess"] isn't present, you can safely assume that the user arrived at the page without submitting a form. If the value *is* present, you can test the value it contains. The test for the presence of the $_POST["guess"] variable takes place on line 3.

Lines 3 through 11 represent an if...else if...else control structure. Only one of these conditions will be true at any given time, depending on what (if anything) was submitted from the form. Depending on the condition, a different value will be assigned to the $message variable. That variable is then printed to the screen in line 18, which is part of the HTML portion of the script.

LISTING 11.6 A PHP Number-Guessing Script (continued)

```
13: <html>
14: <head>
15: <title>A PHP number guessing script</title>
16: </head>
17: <body>
18: <h1><?php echo $message; ?></h1>
19: <form action="<?php echo $_SERVER["PHP_SELF"]; ?>" method="POST">
20: <p><strong>Type your guess here:</strong>
21: <input type="text" name="guess" /></p>
22: <p><input type="submit" value="submit your guess" /></p>
23: </form>
24: </body>
25: </html>
```

Place the PHP and HTML code (all the lines in Listing 11.6, above) into a text file called numguess.php and put this file in your web server document root. Now access the script with your web browser, and you should see something like Figure 11.4.

FIGURE 11.4
The form
created in
Listing 11.6.

There are still a few more additions you could make, but you can probably see how simple it would be to hand the code to a designer for aesthetic treatment. The designer can do her part without having to disturb the programming in any way—the PHP code is at the top, and the rest is 99% HTML.

Using Hidden Fields to Save State

The script in Listing 11.6 has no way of knowing how many guesses a user has made, but you can use a hidden field to keep track of this value. A hidden field behaves the same as a text field, except that the user cannot see it unless he views the HTML source of the document that contains it.

Take the original numguess.php script and save a copy as numguess2.php. In the new version, add a line after the initial assignment of the $num_to_guess variable:

```
$num_tries = (isset($_POST["num_tries"])) ? $num_tries + 1 : 1;
```

This line initializes a variable called $num_tries and assigns a value to it. If the form has not yet been submitted (if $_POST["num_tries"] is empty), the value of the $num_tries variable is 1 because you are on your first attempt at guessing the number. If the form has already been sent, the new value is the value of $_POST["num_tries"] plus 1.

The next change comes after the HTML level H1 heading:

```
<p><strong>Guess number:</strong> <?php echo $num_tries; ?></p>
```

This new line simply prints the current value of $num_tries to the screen.

Finally, before the HTML code for the form submission button, add the hidden field. This field saves the incremented value of $num_tries:

```
<input type="hidden" name="num_tries" value="<?php echo $num_tries; ?>"/>
```

Listing 11.7 shows the new script in its entirety.

LISTING 11.7   Saving State with a Hidden Field

```
 1: <?php
 2: $num_to_guess = 42;
 3: $num_tries = (isset($_POST["num_tries"])) ? $_POST["num_tries"]  + 1 : 1;
 4: if (!isset($_POST["guess"])) {
 5:     $message = "Welcome to the guessing machine!";
 6: } else if ($_POST["guess"] > $num_to_guess) {
 7:     $message = $_POST["guess"]." is too big! Try a smaller number.";
 8: } else if ($_POST["guess"] < $num_to_guess) {
 9:     $message = $_POST["guess"]." is too small! Try a larger number.";
10: } else { // must be equivalent
11:     $message = "Well done!";
12: }
13: $guess = $_POST["guess"];
14: ?>
15: <html>
16: <head>
17: <title>Saving state with a hidden field</title>
18: </head>
19: <body>
20: <h1><?php echo $message; ?></h1>
21: <p><strong>Guess number:</strong> <?php echo $num_tries; ?></p>
22: <form action="<?php echo $_SERVER["PHP_SELF"]; ?>" method="POST">
23: <p><strong>Type your guess here:</strong></p>
24: <input type="text" name="guess" value="<?php echo $guess; ?>" />
25: <input type="hidden" name="num_tries" value="<?php echo $num_tries; ?>" />
26: <p><input type="submit" value="submit your guess" /></p>
27: </form>
28: </body>
29: </html>
```

Save the numguess2.php file and place it in your web server document root. Access the form a few times with your web browser and try to guess the number (pretend you don't already know it). The counter should increment by 1 each time you access the form.

Redirecting the User

Our simple script still has one major drawback—the form is reloaded whether or not the user guesses correctly. The fact that the HTML is hard-coded makes it difficult to avoid writing the entire page. You can, however, redirect the user to a congratulations page, thereby sidestepping the issue altogether.

When a server script communicates with a client, it must first send some headers that provide information about the document to follow. PHP usually handles this for you automatically, but you can choose to send your own header lines with PHP's header() function.

To call the header() function, you must be absolutely sure that no output has been sent to the browser. The first time content is sent to the browser, PHP sends out headers of its own, and it's too late for you to send any more. Any output from your document, even a line break or a space outside your script tags, causes headers to be sent. If you intend to use the header() function in a script, you must make certain that nothing precedes the PHP code that contains the function call. You should also check any libraries that you might be using.

Listing 11.8 shows typical headers sent to the browser by PHP, beginning with line 3, in response to the request in line 1.

LISTING 11.8   Typical Server Headers Sent from a PHP Script

```
1: HTTP/1.1 200 OK
2: Date: Sun,  03 Feb 2008 15:50:28 PST
3: Server: Apache/2.2.8 (Win32) PHP/5.2.5
4: X-Powered-By: PHP/5.2.5
5: Connection: close
6: Content-Type: text/html
```

By sending a Location header instead of PHP's default header, you can cause the browser to be redirected to a new page, such as

```
header("Location: http://www.samspublishing.com");
```

Assuming that you've created a suitably upbeat page called congrats.html, we can amend the number-guessing script to redirect the user if she guesses correctly, as shown in Listing 11.9. The only change between this and Listing 11.7 comes after the else clause on line 10.

LISTING 11.9   Using header() to Redirect User

```
1: <?php
2: $num_to_guess = 42;
3: $num_tries = (isset($_POST["num_tries"])) ? $_POST["num_tries"] + 1 : 1;
4: if (!isset($_POST["guess"])) {
5:     $message = "Welcome to the guessing machine!";
6: } elseif ($_POST["guess"] > $num_to_guess) {
7:     $message = $_POST["guess"]." is too big! Try a smaller number";
8: } elseif ($_POST["guess"] < $num_to_guess) {
9:     $message = $_POST["guess"]." is too small! Try a larger number";
10: } else { // must be equivalent
11:     header("Location: congrats.html");
```

LISTING 11.9 Continued

```
12:    exit;
13: }
14: $guess = $_POST["guess"];
15: ?>
16: <html>
17: <head>
18: <title>Using header() to Redirect User</title>
19: </head>
20: <body>
21: <h1><?php echo $message; ?></h1>
22: <p><strong>Guess number:</strong> <?php echo $num_tries; ?></p>
23: <form action="<?php echo $_SERVER["PHP_SELF"]; ?>" method="POST">
24: <p><strong>Type your guess here:</strong>
25: <input type="text" name="guess" value="<?php echo $guess; ?>" />
26: <input type="hidden" name="num_tries" value="<?php echo $num_tries; ?>" />
27: <p><input type="submit" value="submit your guess" /></p>
28: </form>
29: </body>
30: </html>
```

The else clause of the if statement on line 10 now causes the browser to send the user away to a page called congrats.html. The exit statement on line 12 immediately ends execution and output of this script, which ensures that all output from the current page is aborted.

Sending Mail on Form Submission

You've already seen how to take form responses and print the results to the screen, so you're only one step away from sending those responses in an email message. Before learning about sending mail, however, read through the next section to make sure that your system is properly configured.

System Configuration for the mail() Function

Before you can use the mail() function to send mail, a few directives must be set up in the php.ini file so that the function works properly. Open php.ini with a text editor and look for these lines:

```
[mail function]
; For Win32 only.
SMTP = localhost

; For Win32 only.
sendmail_from = me@localhost.com

; For Unix only.  You may supply arguments as well (default: "sendmail -t -i").
;sendmail_path =
```

If you're using Windows as your web server platform, the first two directives apply to you. For the mail() function to send mail, it must be able to access a valid outgoing mail server. If you plan to use the outgoing mail server of your ISP (the following example uses EarthLink), the entry in php.ini should look like this:

```
SMTP = mail.earthlink.net
```

The second configuration directive is sendmail_from, which is the email address used in the From header of the outgoing email. It can be overwritten in the mail script itself but normally operates as the default value, as in this example:

```
sendmail_from = youraddress@yourdomain.com
```

A good rule of thumb for Windows users is that whatever outgoing mail server you've set up in your email client on that machine, you should also use as the value of SMTP in php.ini.

If your web server is running on a Linux/UNIX platform, you use the sendmail functionality of that particular machine. In this case, only the last directive applies to you: sendmail_path. The default is sendmail -t -i, but if sendmail is in an odd place or if you need to specify different arguments, feel free to do so, as in the following example, which does not use real values:

```
sendmail_path = /opt/sendmail -odd -arguments
```

After making any changes to php.ini on any platform, you must restart the web server process for the changes to take effect.

Creating the Form

In Listing 11.10, you see the basic HTML for creating a simple feedback form named feedback.html. This form has an action of sendmail.php, which you will create in the next section. The fields in feedback.html are simple: Line 7 contains a name field, line 8 contains the return email address field, and line 10 contains the text area for the user's message.

LISTING 11.10   Creating a Simple Feedback Form

```
1:  <html>
2:  <head>
3:  <title>E-Mail Form</title>
4:  </head>
5:  <body>
6:  <form action="sendmail.php" method="POST">
7:  <p><strong>Name:</strong><br/>
8:  <input type="text" size="25" name="name" /></p>
9:  <p><strong>E-Mail Address:</strong><br />
```

LISTING 11.10   Continued

```
10: <input type="text" size="25" name="email" /></p>
11: <p><strong>Message:</strong><br />
12: <textarea name="message" cols="30" rows="5"></textarea></p>
13: <p><input type="submit" value="send" /></p>
14: </form>
15: </body>
16: </html>
```

Put all the lines shown in Listing 11.10 into a text file called feedback.html and place this file in your web server document root. Now access the script with your web browser, and you should see something like Figure 11.5.

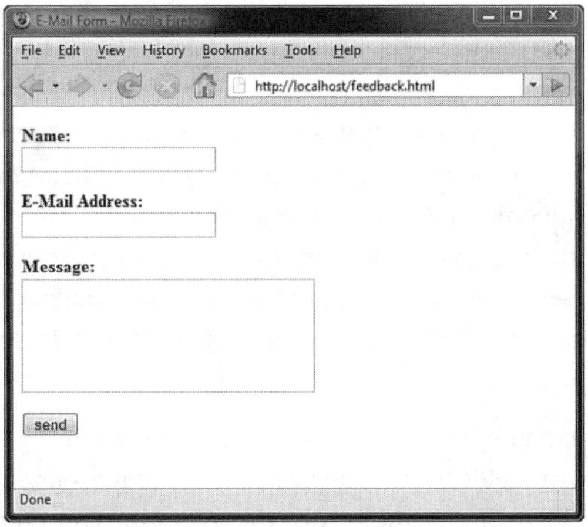

FIGURE 11.5
The form created in Listing 11.10.

In the next section, you create the script that sends this form to a recipient.

Creating the Script to Send the Mail

This script is only slightly different in concept from the script in Listing 11.4, which simply printed form responses to the screen. In the script shown in Listing 11.11, in addition to printing the responses to the screen, you send them to an email address.

LISTING 11.11   Sending the Simple Feedback Form

```
1: <html>
2: <head>
3: <title>Sending mail from the form in Listing 11.10</title>
4: </head>
5: <body>
6: <?php
7: echo "<p>Thank you, <b>".$_POST["name"]."</b>, for your message!</p>";
```

LISTING 11.11   Continued

```
 8: echo "<p>Your e-mail address is: <b>".$_POST["email"]."</b>.</p>";
 9: echo "<p>Your message was:<br />";
10: echo $_POST["message"]."</p>";
11: //start building the mail string
12: $msg = "Name:     ".$_POST["name"]."\n";
13: $msg .= "E-Mail:   ".$_POST["email"]."\n";
14: $msg .= "Message: ".$_POST["message"]."\n";
15: //set up the mail
16: $recipient = "you@yourdomain.com";
17: $subject = "Form Submission Results";
18: $mailheaders = "From: My Web Site <defaultaddress@yourdomain.com> \n";
19: $mailheaders .= "Reply-To: ".$_POST["email"];
20: //send the mail
21: mail($recipient, $subject, $msg, $mailheaders);
22: ?>
23: </body>
24: </html>
```

The variables used in lines 7–9 are $_POST["name"], $_POST["email"], and $_POST["message"]—the names of the fields in the form, their values saved as part of the $_POST superglobal. That's all well and good for printing the information to the screen, but in this script, you also want to create a string that's sent in email. For this task, you essentially build the email by concatenating strings to form one long message string, using the newline (\n) character to add line breaks where appropriate.

Lines 12 through 14 create the $msg variable, a string containing the values typed by the user in the form fields (and some introductory text for good measure). This string will form the body of the email. Note the use of the concatenation operator (.=) when adding to the $msg variable in lines 13 and 14.

Lines 16 and 17 are hard-coded variables for the email recipient and the subject of the email message. Replace you@yourdomain.com with your own email address, obviously. If you want to change the subject, feel free to do that, too!

Lines 18 and 19 set up some mail headers, namely the From: and Reply-to: headers. You could put any value in the From: header; this is the information that displays in the From or Sender column of your email application when you receive this mail.

By the Way

If your outbound mail server is a Windows machine, the \n newline character should be replaced with \r\n.

The mail() function requires four parameters: the recipient, the subject, the message, and any additional mail headers. The order of these parameters is shown in line 21, and your script is complete after you close up your PHP block and your HTML elements in lines 22–24.

Put these lines into a text file called sendmail.php and place that file in your web server document root. Use your web browser and go back to the form, enter some information, and click the submission button. You should see something like Figure 11.6 in your browser.

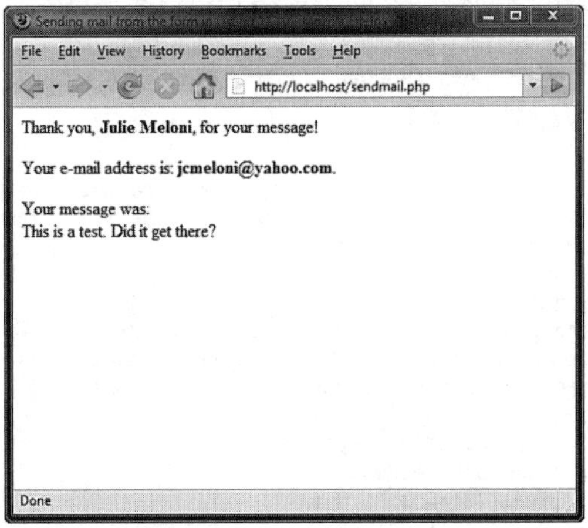

FIGURE 11.6
Sample results from sendmail.php.

If you then check your email, you should have a message waiting for you. It might look something like Figure 11.7.

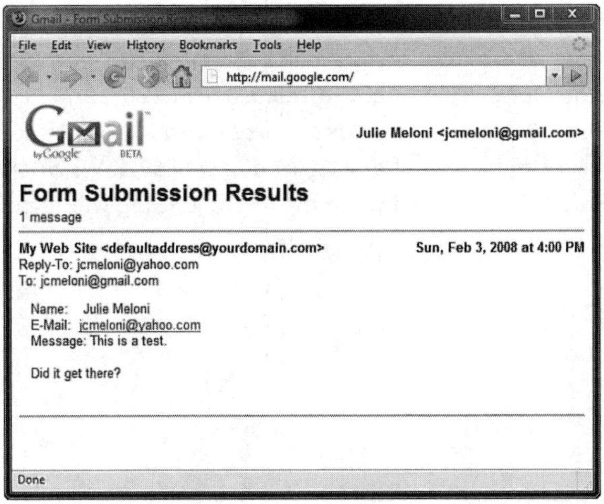

FIGURE 11.7
Email sent from sendmail.php.

Formatting Your Mail with HTML

The "trick" to sending HTML-formatted email is not a trick at all. In fact, it only involves writing the actual HTML and modifying the headers sent by the mail() function. In Listing 11.12, a variation of Listing 11.11, changes were made in lines 12–14 and lines 18–19.

LISTING 11.12   Sending the Simple Feedback Form—HTML Version

```
 1:  <html>
 2:  <head>
 3:  <title>Sending the Simple Feedback Form - HTML Version</title>
 4:  </head>
 5:  <body>
 6:  <?php
 7:  echo "<p>Thank you, <b>".$_POST["name"]."</b>, for your message!</p>";
 8:  echo "<p>Your e-mail address is: <b>".$_POST["email"]."</b>.</p>";
 9:  echo "<p>Your message was:<br />";
10:  echo $_POST["message"]."</p>";
11:  //start building the mail string
12:  $msg = "<p><strong>Name:</strong>    ".$_POST["name"]."</p>";
13:  $msg .= "<p><strong>E-Mail:</strong>   ".$_POST["email"]."</p>";
14:  $msg .= "<p><strong>Message:</strong> ".$_POST["message"]."</p>";
15:  //set up the mail
16:  $recipient = "you@yourdomain.com";
17:  $subject = "Form Submission Results";
18:  $mailheaders = "MIME-Version: 1.0\r\n";
19:  $mailheaders .= "Content-type: text/html; charset=ISO-8859-1\r\n";
20:  $mailheaders .= "From: My Web Site <defaultaddress@yourdomain.com> \n";
21:  $mailheaders .= "Reply-To: ".$_POST["email"];
22:  //send the mail
23:  mail($recipient, $subject, $msg, $mailheaders);
24:  ?>
25:  </body>
26:  </html>
```

In lines 12–14, the message string now contains HTML code. Additional headers are created in lines 18–19, which set the Mime Version header to 1.0 and the Content-type header to text/html with a character set of ISO-8859-1. When opened in an HTML-enabled mail client, the HTML in the message string will appear as intended, as shown in Figure 11.8.

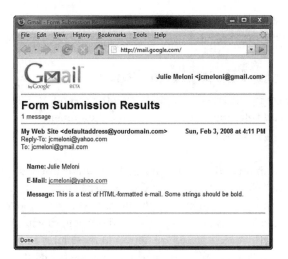

FIGURE 11.8
Email sent from
Listing 11.12.

Working with File Uploads

So far, you've looked at simple form input. However, web browsers support file uploads, and so, of course, does PHP. In this section, you examine the features that PHP makes available to deal with this kind of input.

Information about the uploaded file becomes available to you in the $_FILES super-global, which is indexed by the name of the upload field (or fields) in the form. The corresponding value for each of these keys is an associative array. These fields are described in Table 11.1, using fileupload as the name of the form field used for the upload.

TABLE 11.1 File Upload Global Variables

Element	Contains	Example
$_FILES["fileupload"]["name"]	Original name of uploaded file	test.gif
$_FILES["fileupload"]["tmp_name"]	Path to temporary file	/tmp/phprDfZvN
$_FILES["fileupload"]["size"]	Size (in bytes) of uploaded file	6835
$_FILES["fileupload"]["type"]	MIME type of uploaded file (where given by client)	image/gif

Keep these elements in the back of your mind for a moment, while you create the upload form in the next section.

Creating the File Upload Form

First, you must create the HTML form to handle the upload. HTML forms that include file upload fields must include an ENCTYPE argument:

```
ENCTYPE="multipart/form-data"
```

PHP also works with an optional hidden field that can be inserted before the file upload field. This field must be called MAX_FILE_SIZE and should have a value representing the maximum size in bytes of the file that you're willing to accept. The MAX_FILE_SIZE field is obeyed at the browser's discretion, so you should rely on the php.ini setting, upload_max_filesize, to cap unreasonably large uploads. After the MAX_FILE_SIZE field has been entered, you're ready to add the upload field itself. This is simply an INPUT element with a TYPE argument of "file". You can give it any name you want. Listing 11.13 brings all this together into an HTML upload form.

LISTING 11.13   A Simple File Upload Form

```
 1: <html>
 2: <head>
 3: <title>A simple file upload form</title>
 4: </head>
 5: <body>
 6: <form action="do_upload.php" enctype="multipart/form-data" method="POST">
 7: <input type="hidden" name="MAX_FILE_SIZE" value="51200" />
 8: <p><strong>File to Upload:</strong>
 9: <input type="file" name="fileupload" /></p>
10: <p><input type="submit" value="upload!" /></p>
11: </form>
12: </body>
13: </html>
```

As you can see, file uploads are limited to 50KB on line 7, and the name of the file upload field is fileupload, as shown on line 8. Save this listing in a text file called fileupload.html and place that file in your web server document root. Use your web browser to access this form and you should see something like Figure 11.9.

This form calls the do_upload.php script, which you will create next.

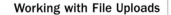

FIGURE 11.9
The form created by Listing 11.13.

Creating the File Upload Script

If you remember the information regarding the $_FILES superglobal, you have all the information you need to write a simple file upload script. This script is the backend for the form created in Listing 11.14.

LISTING 11.14   A File Upload Script

```
1: <?php
2: $file_dir = "/path/to/upload/directory";
3: foreach($_FILES as $file_name => $file_array) {
4:      echo "path: ".$file_array['"tmp_'name"]."<br />\n";
5:      echo "name: ".$file_array['''"name"]."<br />\n";
6:      echo "type: ".$file_array['"type'"]."<br />\n";
7:      echo "size: ".$file_array['''"size"]."<br />\n";
8:
9:      if (is_uploaded_file($file_array['"tmp_'name"])) {
10:         move_uploaded_file($file_array['"tmp_'name"],
11:            "$file_dir/".$file_array["name"]) or die ("Couldn't copy");
12:         echo "file was moved!<br />";
13:      }
14: }
15: ?>
```

In Listing 11.14, you first create the $file_dir variable on line 2 to store path information. This path should be one that exists on your system, and the web server user (for example, httpd, www, nobody) must have write permissions for it.

> The path used in line 2 is a Linux/UNIX path. Windows users would use escaped backslashes, such as
>
> $file_dir = "C:\\Documents and Settings\\Owner\\Desktop\\";

By the Way

Line 3 begins a `foreach` statement that loops through every element in the `$_FILES` array. A loop is used rather than an `if` statement to make the script capable of scaling to deal with multiple uploads on the same page. The `foreach` loop on line 3 stores the upload file's name in the `$file_name` variable and the file information in the `$file_array` variable. You can then output the information you have about the upload.

Before moving the uploaded file from its temporary position to the location specified in line 2, first check that it exists. The code does so on line 9, using the `is_uploaded_file()` function. This function accepts a path to an uploaded file and returns `true` only if the file in question is a valid upload file. This function therefore enhances the security of your scripts.

Assuming that all is well, the file is copied from its temporary home to a new directory on lines 10 and 11. Another function, `move_uploaded_file()`, is used for this purpose. This function copies a file from one place to another, first performing the same security checks as those performed by `is_uploaded_file()`. The `move_uploaded_file()` function requires a path to the source file and a path to the destination. It returns `true` if the move is successful and `false` if the file isn't a valid upload file or if the file couldn't be found.

Watch Out!

> Beware of the names of uploaded files. Operating systems such as Mac OS and Windows are pretty relaxed when it comes to file naming, so expect uploaded files to come complete with spaces, quotation marks, and all manner of other unexpected characters. Therefore, it's a good idea to filter filenames.

Put all the code in Listing 11.14 into a text file called do_upload.php and place that file in your web server document root. Use your web browser to go back to the form and then try to upload a file. If successful, you should see something like Figure 11.10 in your browser.

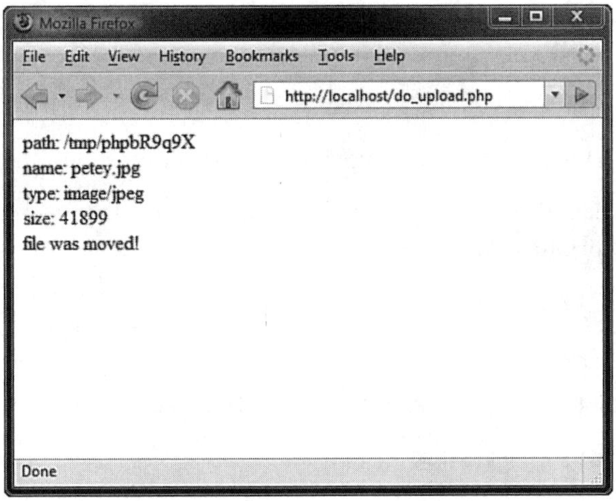

FIGURE 11.10
Sample results
from Listing
11.14.

Summary

Things are really getting exciting now! A few items are still missing, of course, but there's plenty of book left. Now that you can get information from the user, it would be nice to be able to do something with it—write it to a file, perhaps? That's the subject of an upcoming chapter.

In this chapter, you learned how to work with various superglobals and form input. You also learned how to send raw headers to the client to redirect a browser. You learned how to acquire list information from form submissions and how to pass information from script call to script call using hidden fields. Finally, you learned how to send your form results in email, and how to upload files through your web browser using a PHP script.

Workshop

The workshop is designed to help you anticipate possible questions, review what you've learned, and begin putting your knowledge into practice.

Quiz

1. Which predefined variable do you use to find the name of the script?

2. Which built-in associative array contains all values submitted as part of a POST request?

3. Which built-in associative array contains all values submitted as part of a file upload?

4. What function do you use to redirect the browser to a new page?

5. What are the four arguments used by the `mail()` function?

6. On the client side, how do you limit the size of a file that a user can submit via a particular upload form?

Answers

1. The variable `$_SERVER["PHP_SELF"]` holds the name of the script.

2. The `$_POST` superglobal.

3. The `$_FILES` superglobal.

4. The `header()` function, along with a location.

5. The recipient, the subject, the message string, and additional headers.

6. Use a hidden field called `MAX_FILE_SIZE` in your form.

Activities

1. Create a calculator script that enables the user to submit two numbers and choose an operation (addition, multiplication, division, or subtraction) to perform on them.

2. Use hidden fields with the script you created in activity 1 to store and display the number of requests that the user submitted.

12

Working with Cookies and User Sessions

PHP contains numerous functions for managing and keeping track of user information, including both simple cookies and all-encompassing user sessions. Sessions use techniques built into the PHP language, making the act of saving state as easy as referencing a super-global variable.

In this chapter, you will learn

- ▶ How to store and retrieve cookie information
- ▶ What session variables are and how they work
- ▶ How to start or resume a session
- ▶ How to store variables in a session
- ▶ How to destroy a session
- ▶ How to unset session variables

Introducing Cookies

You can use cookies within your PHP scripts to store small bits of information about a user. A *cookie* is a small amount of data stored by the user's browser in compliance with a request from a server or script. A single host can request that up to 20 cookies be stored by a user's browser. Each cookie consists of a name, value, and expiration date, as well as host and path information. The size of an individual cookie is limited to 4KB.

After a cookie is set, only the originating host can read the data, ensuring that the user's privacy is respected. Furthermore, the user can configure her browser to notify her upon receipt of all cookies, or even to refuse all cookie requests. For this reason, cookies should be used in moderation and should not be relied on as an essential element of an environment design without first warning the user.

The Anatomy of a Cookie

A PHP script that sets a cookie might send headers that look something like this:

```
HTTP/1.1 200 OK
Date: Sun, 03 Feb 2008 13:39:58 GMT
Server: Apache/2.2.8 (Unix) PHP/5.2.5
X-Powered-By: PHP/5.2.5
Set-Cookie: vegetable=artichoke; path=/; domain=yourdomain.com
Connection: close
Content-Type: text/html
```

As you can see, this Set-Cookie header contains a name/value pair, a path, and a domain. If set, the expiration field provides the date at which the browser should "forget" the value of the cookie. If no expiration date is set, the cookie expires when the user's session expires—that is, when he closes his browser.

The path and domain fields work together: The path is a directory found on the domain, below which the cookie should be sent back to the server. If the path is "/", which is common, that means the cookie can be read by any files below the document root. If the path is "/products/", the cookie can be read only by files within the /products directory of the website.

The domain field represents the Internet domain from which cookie-based communication is allowed. For example, if your domain is www.yourdomain.com and you use www.yourdomain.com as the domain value for the cookie, the cookie will be valid only when browsing the www.domain.com website. This could pose a problem if you send the user to some domain like www2.domain.com or billing.domain.com within the course of his browsing experience because the original cookie will no longer work. Thus, it is common simply to begin the value of the domain slot in cookie definitions with a dot, leaving off the host; for example, .domain.com. In this manner, the cookie will be valid for all hosts on the domain. The domain cannot be different from the domain from which the cookie was sent; otherwise, the cookie will not function properly, if at all, or the web browser will refuse the cookie in its entirety.

Accessing Cookies

If your web browser is configured to store cookies, it keeps the cookie-based information until the expiration date. If the user points the browser at any page that matches the path and domain of the cookie, it will resend the cookie to the server. The browser's headers might look something like this:

```
GET / HTTP/1.0
Connection: Keep-Alive
User-Agent: Mozilla/5.0 (Windows; U; Windows NT 6.0; en-US; rv:1.8.1.11)
        Gecko/20071127 Firefox/2.0.0.11
```

```
Host: www.yourdomain.com
Accept: image/gif, image/x-xbitmap, image/jpeg, image/pjpeg, image/png, */*
Accept-Encoding: gzip
Accept-Language: en,pdf
Accept-Charset: iso-8859-1,*,utf-8
Cookie: vegetable=artichoke
```

A PHP script will then have access to the cookie in the environment variable HTTP_COOKIE or as part of the $_COOKIE superglobal variable, which you may access three different ways:

```
echo $_SERVER["HTTP_COOKIE"];   // will print "vegetable=artichoke"

echo getenv("HTTP_COOKIE");  // will print "vegetable=artichoke"

echo $_COOKIE["vegetable"];  // will print "artichoke"
```

Setting a Cookie with PHP

You can set a cookie in a PHP script in two ways. First, you could use the header() function to set the Set-Cookie header. The header() function requires a string that will then be included in the header section of the server response. Because headers are sent automatically for you, header() must be called before any output at all is sent to the browser:

```
header ("Set-Cookie: vegetable=artichoke; expires=Mon, 04-Feb-08 14:39:58 GMT;
path=/; domain=yourdomain.com");
```

Although not difficult, this method of setting a cookie would require you to build a function to construct the header string. Although formatting the date as in this example and URL-encoding the name/value pair would not be a particularly arduous task, it would be a repetitive one because PHP provides a function that does just that—setcookie().

The setcookie() function does what its name suggests—it outputs a Set-Cookie header. For this reason, it should be called before any other content is sent to the browser. The function accepts the cookie name, cookie value, expiration date in UNIX epoch format, path, domain, and integer that should be set to 1 if the cookie is only to be sent over a secure connection. All arguments to this function are optional apart from the first (cookie name) parameter.

Listing 12.1 uses setcookie() to set a cookie.

LISTING 12.1   Setting and Printing a Cookie Value

```
1: <?php
2: setcookie("vegetable", "artichoke", time()+3600, "/", ".yourdomain.com", 0);
3:
4: if (isset($_COOKIE["vegetable"])) {
5:     echo "<p>Hello again, you have chosen:  ".$_COOKIE["vegetable"].".</p>";
6: } else {
7:   echo "<p>Hello you. This may be your first visit.</p>";
8: }
9: ?>
```

Even though the listing sets the cookie (line 2) when the script is run for the first time, the $_COOKIE["vegetable"] variable will not be created at this point. Because a cookie is read only when the browser sends it to the server, you won't be able to read it until the user revisits a page within this domain.

The cookie name is set to "vegetable" on line 2 and the cookie value to "artichoke". The time() function gets the current time stamp and adds 3600 to it (there are 3,600 seconds in an hour). This total represents the expiration date. The code defines a path of "/", which means that a cookie should be sent for any page within this server environment. The domain argument is set to ".yourdomain.com" (you should make the change relevant to your own domain or use localhost), which means that a cookie will be sent to any server in that group. Finally, the code passes 0 to setcookie(), signaling that cookies can be sent in an insecure environment.

Passing setcookie() an empty string ("") for string arguments or 0 for integer fields causes these arguments to be skipped.

By the Way

With using a dynamically created expiration time in a cookie, as in Listing 12.1, note the expiration time is created by adding a certain number of seconds to the current system time of the machine running Apache and PHP. If this system clock is not accurate, the machine may send the cookie at an expiration time that has already passed.

You can view your cookies in most modern web browsers. Figure 12.1 shows the cookie information stored for Listing 12.1. The cookie name, content, and expiration date appear as expected; the domain name will differ when you run this script on your own domain.

For more information on using cookies, and the setcookie() function in particular, see the PHP Manual entry at http://www.php.net/setcookie.

FIGURE 12.1
Viewing a
stored cookie in
a web browser.

Deleting a Cookie with PHP

Officially, to delete a cookie, you call `setcookie()` with the name argument only:

```
setcookie("vegetable");
```

This approach does not always work well, however, and you should not rely on it. Instead, to delete a cookie, it is safest to set the cookie with a date that you are sure has already expired:

```
setcookie("vegetable", "", time()-60, "/", "yourdomain.com", 0);
```

Also make sure that you pass `setcookie()` the same path, domain, and secure parameters as you did when originally setting the cookie.

Session Function Overview

Session functions provide a unique identifier to a user, which can then be used to store and acquire information linked to that ID. When a visitor accesses a session-enabled page, either a new identifier is allocated or the user is reassociated with one that was already established in a previous visit. Any variables that have been associated with the session become available to your code through the `$_SESSION` super-global.

Session state is usually stored in a temporary file, although you can implement database storage using a function called `session_set_save_handler()`. The use of `session_set_save_handler()` and a discussion about other advanced session functionality are beyond the scope of this book, but you can find more information in the PHP Manual section for sessions for all items not discussed here.

Starting a Session

To work with a session, you need to explicitly start or resume that session *unless* you have changed your `php.ini` configuration file. By default, sessions do not start automatically. If you want to start a session this way, you will have to find the following line in your `php.ini` file and change the value from 0 to 1 (and restart the web server):

```
session.auto_start = 0
```

By changing the value of `session.auto_start` to 1, you ensure that a session initiates for every PHP document. If you don't change this setting, you need to call the `session_start()` function in each script.

After a session is started, you instantly have access to the user's session ID via the `session_id()` function. The `session_id()` function allows you to either set or retrieve a session ID. Listing 12.2 starts a session and prints the session ID to the browser.

LISTING 12.2   Starting or Resuming a Session

```
1: <?php
2: session_start();
3: echo "<p>Your session ID is ".session_id().".</p>";
4: ?>
```

When this script is run for the first time from a browser, a session ID is generated by the `session_start()` function call on line 2. If the script is later reloaded or revisited, the same session ID is allocated to the user. This action assumes that the user has cookies enabled. For example, when I run this script the first time, the output is

```
Your session ID is fa963e3e49186764b0218e82d050de7b
```

When I reload the page, the output is still

```
Your session ID is fa963e3e49186764b0218e82d050de7b
```

because I have cookies enabled and the session ID still exists.

Because start_session() attempts to set a cookie when initiating a session for the first time, it is imperative that you call this function before you output anything else at all to the browser. If you do not follow this rule, your session will not be set, and you will likely see warnings on your page.

Sessions remain current as long as the web browser is active. When the user restarts the browser, the cookie is no longer stored. You can change this behavior by altering the session.cookie_lifetime setting in your php.ini file. The default value is 0, but you can set an expiry period in seconds.

Working with Session Variables

Accessing a unique session identifier in each of your PHP documents is only the start of session functionality. When a session is started, you can store any number of variables in the $_SESSION superglobal and then access them on any session-enabled page.

Listing 12.3 adds two variables into the $_SESSION superglobal: product1 and product2 (lines 3 and 4).

LISTING 12.3 Storing Variables in a Session

```
1: <?php
2: session_start();
3: $_SESSION["product1"] = "Sonic Screwdriver";
4: $_SESSION["product2"] = "HAL 2000";
5: echo "The products have been registered.";
6: ?>
```

The magic in Listing 12.3 will not become apparent until the user moves to a new page. Listing 12.4 creates a separate PHP script that accesses the variables stored in the $_SESSION superglobal.

LISTING 12.4 Accessing Stored Session Variables

```
1: <?php
2: session_start();
3: echo "Your chosen products are:";
4: echo "<ul>";
5: echo "<li>".$_SESSION["product1"]."</li>";
6: echo "<li>".$_SESSION["product2"]."</li>";
7: echo "</ul>";
8: ?>
```

Figure 12.2 shows the output from Listing 12.4. As you can see, you have access to the $_SESSION["product1"] and $_SESSION["product2"] variables in an entirely new page.

FIGURE 12.2
Accessing
stored session
variables.

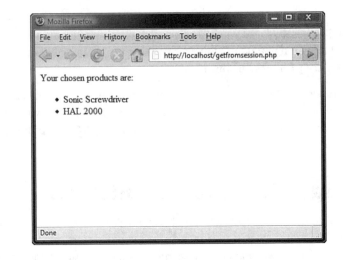

Although not a terribly interesting or useful example, the script does show how to access stored session variables. Behind the scenes, PHP writes information to a temporary file. You can find out where this file is being written on your system by using the session_save_path() function. This function optionally accepts a path to a directory and then writes all session files to it. If you pass it no arguments, it returns a string representing the current directory to which it saves session files. On my system,

```
echo session_save_path();
```

prints /tmp. A glance at my /tmp directory reveals a number of files with names like the following:

```
sess_fa963e3e49186764b0218e82d050de7b
sess_76cae8ac1231b11afa2c69935c11dd95
sess_bb50771a769c605ab77424d59c784ea0
```

Opening the file that matches the session ID I was allocated when I first ran Listing 12.2, I can see how the registered variables have been stored:

```
product1|s:17:"Sonic Screwdriver";product2|s:8:"HAL 2000";
```

When a value is placed in the $_SESSION superglobal, PHP writes the variable name and value to a file. This information can be read and the variables resurrected later—as you have already seen. After you add a variable to the $_SESSION superglobal, you can still change its value at any time during the execution of your script, but the altered value won't be reflected in the global setting until you reassign the variable to the $_SESSION superglobal.

The example in Listing 12.3 demonstrates the process of adding variables to the $_SESSION superglobal. This example is not very flexible, however. Ideally, you should be able to register a varying number of values. You might want to let users pick products from a list, for example. In this case, you can use the serialize() function to store an array in your session.

Listing 12.5 creates a form that allows a user to choose multiple products. You will use the session variables to create a rudimentary shopping cart.

LISTING 12.5 Adding an Array Variable to a Session Variable

```
1: <?php
2: session_start();
3: ?>
4: <html>
5: <head>
6: <title>Storing an array with a session</title>
7: </head>
8: <body>
9: <h1>Product Choice Page</h1>
10: <?php
11: if (isset($_POST["form_products"])) {
12:     if (!empty($_SESSION["products"])) {
13:         $products = array_unique(
14:         array_merge(unserialize($_SESSION["products"]),
15:         $_POST["form_products"]));
16:         $_SESSION["products"] = serialize($products);
17:     } else {
18:         $_SESSION["products"] = serialize($_POST["form_products"]);
19:     }
20:     echo "<p>Your products have been registered!</p>";
21: }
22: ?>
23: <form method="POST" action="<?php echo $_SERVER["PHP_SELF"]; ?>">
24: <P><strong>Select some products:</strong><br>
25: <select name="form_products[]" multiple="multiple" size="3">
26: <option value="Sonic Screwdriver">Sonic Screwdriver</option>
27: <option value="Hal 2000">Hal 2000</option>
28: <option value="Tardis">Tardis</option>
29: <option value="ORAC">ORAC</option>
30: <option value="Transporter bracelet">Transporter bracelet</option>
31: </select>
32: <P><input type="submit" value="choose" /></p>
33: </form>
34: <p><a href="session1.php">go to content page</a></p>
35: </body>
36: </html>
```

The listing starts or resumes a session by calling session_start() on line 2. This call gives access to any previously set session variables. An HTML form begins on line 23 and, on line 25, creates a SELECT element named form_products[], which contains OPTION elements for a number of products.

> Remember that HTML form elements that allow multiple selections should have square brackets appended to the value of their NAME arguments. This makes the user's choices available in an array.

The block of PHP code beginning on line 10 tests for the presence of the $_POST["form_products"] array (line 11). If the variable is present, you can assume that the form has been submitted and information has already been stored in the $_SESSION superglobal.

Line 12 tests for an array called $_SESSION["products"]. If the array exists, it was populated on a previous visit to this script, so the code merges it with the $_POST["form_products"] array, extracts the unique elements, and assigns the result back to the $products array (lines 13–15). Then the $products array is added to the $_SESSION superglobal on line 16.

Line 34 contains a link to another script, which will demonstrate access to the products the user has chosen. This new script is created in Listing 12.6, but in the meantime you can save the code in Listing 12.5 as arraysession.php.

Moving on to Listing 12.6, you see how to access the items stored in the session created in arraysession.php.

LISTING 12.6   Accessing Session Variables

```
 1: <?php
 2: session_start();
 3: ?>
 4: <html>
 5: <head>
 6: <title>Accessing session variables</title>
 7: </head>
 8: <body>
 9: <h1>Content Page</h1>
10: <?php
11: if (isset($_SESSION["products"])) {
12:     echo "<strong>Your cart:</strong><ol>";
13:     foreach (unserialize($_SESSION["products"]) as $p) {
14:         echo "<li>".$p."</li>";
15:     }
16:     echo "</ol>";
17: }
18: ?>
19: <p><a href="arraysession.php">return to product choice page</a></p>
20: </body>
21: </html>
```

Once again, session_start() resumes the session on line 2. Line 11 tests for the presence of the $_SESSION["products"] variable. If it exists, it is unserialized and looped through on lines 13–15, printing each of the user's chosen items to the browser. Figure 12.3 shows an example.

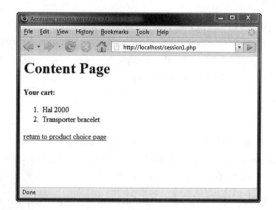

FIGURE 12.3
Accessing an array of session variables.

For a real shopping cart program, of course, you would keep product details in a database and test user input, rather than blindly store and present it, but Listings 12.5 and 12.6 demonstrate the ease with which you can use session functions to access array variables set in other pages.

Passing Session IDs in the Query String

So far you have relied on a cookie to save the session ID between script requests. On its own, this method is not the most reliable way of saving state because you cannot be sure that the browser will accept cookies. You can build in a failsafe, however, by passing the session ID from script to script embedded in a query string. PHP makes a name/value pair available in a constant named SID if a cookie value for a session ID cannot be found. You can add this string to any HTML links in session-enabled pages:

```
<a href="page2.html?<?php echo SID; ?>">Another page</a>
```

It will reach the browser as

```
<a href="page2.html?PHPSESSID=08ecedf79fe34561fa82591401a01da1">Another page</a>
```

A session ID passed in this way will automatically be recognized in the target page when session_start() is called, and you will have access to session variables in the usual way.

Destroying Sessions and Unsetting Variables

You can use session_destroy() to end a session, erasing all session variables. The session_destroy() function requires no arguments. You should have an established session for this function to work as expected. The following code fragment resumes a session and abruptly destroys it:

```
session_start();
session_destroy();
```

When you move on to other pages that work with a session, the session you have destroyed will not be available to them, forcing them to initiate new sessions of their own. Any registered variables will be lost.

The session_destroy() function does not instantly destroy registered variables, however. They remain accessible to the script in which session_destroy() is called (until it is reloaded). The following code fragment resumes or initiates a session and registers a variable called test, set to 5. Destroying the session does not destroy the registered variable.

```
session_start();
$_SESSION["test"] = 5;
session_destroy();
echo $_SESSION["test"]; // prints 5
```

To remove all registered variables from a session, you simply unset the variable:

```
session_start();
$_SESSION["test"] = 5;
session_destroy();
unset($_SESSION["test"]);
echo $_SESSION["test"]; // prints nothing.
```

Using Sessions in an Environment with Registered Users

The examples you've seen so far have gotten your feet wet with sessions, but perhaps additional explanation is warranted for using sessions "in the wild," so to speak. The following two sections outline some examples of common session usage. In later chapters of this book, sessions will be used in the sample applications you will build.

Working with Registered Users

Suppose that you've created an online community, or a portal, or some other type of application that users can "join." The process usually involves a registration form, where the user creates a username and password and completes an identification profile. From that point forward, each time a registered user logs in to the system, you can grab the user's identification information and store it in the user's session.

The items you decide to store in the user's session should be those items you can imagine using quite a bit—and that would be inefficient to continually extract from the database. For example, suppose that you have created a portal in which users are assigned a certain level, such as administrator, registered user, anonymous guest, and so forth. Within your display modules, you would always want to check to verify that the user accessing the module has the proper permissions to do so. Thus, "user level" would be an example of a value stored in the user's session, so that the authentication script used in the display of the requested module only has to check a session variable—there would be no need to connect to, select, and query the database.

Working with User Preferences

If you were feeling adventurous in the design phase of a user-based application, you might build a system in which registered users could set specific preferences that would affect the way they viewed your site. For example, you may allow your users to select from a predetermined color scheme, font type and size, and so forth. Or, you may allow users to turn "off" (or "on") the visibility of certain content groupings.

Each of those functional elements could be stored in a session. When the user logs in, the application would load all relevant values into the user's session and would react accordingly for each subsequently requested page. Should the user decide to change her preferences, she could do so while logged in—you could even prepopulate a "preferences" form based on the items stored in the session rather than going back to the database to retrieve them. If the user changes any preferences while she is logged in, simply replace the value stored in the $_SESSION superglobal with the new selection—no need to force the user to log out and then log back in again.

Summary

In this chapter, you looked at different ways of saving state in a stateless protocol, including setting a cookie and starting a session. All methods of saving state use some manner of cookies or query strings, sometimes combined with the use of files or databases. These approaches all have their benefits and problems.

You learned that a cookie alone is not intrinsically reliable and cannot store much information. On the other hand, it can persist over a long period. Approaches that write information to a file or database involve some cost to speed and might become a problem on a popular site. Nonetheless, a simple ID can unlock large amounts of data stored on disk. To ensure that as many users as possible get the benefit of your session-enabled environment, you can use the SID constant to pass a session ID to the server as part of a query string.

In regard to sessions themselves, you learned how to initiate or resume a session with session_start(). When in a session, you learned how to add variables to the $_SESSION superglobal, check that they exist, unset them if you want, and destroy the entire session.

Q&A

Q. *What will happen to my application if users disable cookies?*

A. Simply put, if your application relies heavily on cookies and users have cookies disabled, your application won't work. However, you can do your part to warn users that cookies are coming by announcing your intention to use cookies, and also by checking that cookies are enabled before doing anything "important" with your application. The idea being, of course, that even if users ignore your note that cookies must be turned on in order to use your application, specifically disallowing users to perform an action if your cookie test fails will get their attention!

Q. *Should I be aware of any pitfalls with session functions?*

A. The session functions are generally reliable. However, remember that cookies cannot be read across multiple domains, so if your project uses more than one domain name on the same server (perhaps as part of an e-commerce environment), you might need to consider disabling cookies for sessions by setting the

```
session.use_cookies
```

directive to 0 in the php.ini file.

Workshop

The workshop is designed to help you anticipate possible questions, review what you've learned, and begin putting your knowledge into practice.

Quiz

1. Which function would you use to start or resume a session within a PHP script?

2. Which function can return the current session's ID?

3. How would you end a session and erase all traces of it for future visits?

4. What does the SID constant return?

Answers

1. You can start a session by using the `session_start()` function within your script.

2. You can access the session's ID by using the `session_id()` function.

3. The `session_destroy()` function removes all traces of a session for future requests.

4. If cookies are not available, the SID constant contains a name/value pair that can be incorporated in a query string. It will pass the session ID from script request to script request.

Activity

Create a script that uses session functions to remember which pages in your environment the user has visited. Provide the user with a list of links on each page to make it easy for her to retrace her steps.

13

Working with Files and Directories

Testing for the existence of files, plus reading from them and writing to them, are important features of any rich programming language. PHP is no exception in that it provides functions that make these processes straightforward. Additionally, because PHP, Apache, and MySQL are not the only applications on your machine, there might come a time when you need to access those other applications from within your PHP code; elements in this chapter show you how to access other applications from within your PHP code. In this chapter, you will learn

- ▶ How to include other files in your documents
- ▶ How to test for the existence of files and directories
- ▶ How to open a file before working with it
- ▶ How to read data from files
- ▶ How to write or append to a file
- ▶ How to lock a file
- ▶ How to work with directories
- ▶ How to pipe data to and from external applications
- ▶ How to send shell commands and display results in the browser

Including Files with `include()`

The `include()` statement enables you to incorporate other files (usually other PHP scripts) into your PHP documents. PHP code in these included files will then be executed as if it were part of the main document. This is useful for including code libraries within multiple pages.

Say you create a really useful function. Without the include() function, your only option until now would have been to paste it into every document that needs to use it. Of course, if you discover a bug or want to add a feature, you would have to find every page you pasted the function into and make the change—over and over again. The include() statement saves you from such a chore. You can add your newly created function to a single document, such as myinclude.php and, at run-time, read it into any page that needs it.

The include() statement requires a single argument: a relative path to the file to include. Listing 13.1 creates a simple PHP script that uses include() to incorporate and output the contents of a file.

LISTING 13.1   Using include()

```
1: <?php
2: include("myinclude.php");
3: ?>
```

The include() statement in Listing 13.1 incorporates the document myinclude.php, the contents of which you can see in Listing 13.2.

LISTING 13.2   The File Included in Listing 13.1

```
1: I have been included!!
```

Put the contents of Listing 13.1 in a file named test_include.php, and the contents of Listing 13.2 in a file named myinclude.php. Place both files in your web server document root. When you access test_include.php through your web browser, the output on the screen is

```
I have been included!!
```

This might seem strange to you, given that you're including plain text within a block of PHP code. In fact, the contents of an included file display as text by default. *If* you want to execute PHP code in an included file, you must enclose it in PHP start and end tags. Listing 13.3 amends the contents of myinclude.php so that code is executed in the included file.

LISTING 13.3   An Include File Containing PHP Code

```
1: <?php
2: echo "I have been included!!<br/>";
3: echo "But now I can add up...   4 + 4 = ".(4 + 4);
4: ?>
```

Put the contents of Listing 13.3 in a file called `myinclude2.php` and change the value of the included file in `test_include.php` to point to this new file. Place both these files in your web server document root. Now, when you access `test_include.php` through your web browser, the output on the screen is

```
I have been included!!
But now I can add up... 4 + 4 = 8
```

The only way you would see the number 8 is if the code for adding 4 and 4 were executed as PHP, and it was.

Returning a Value from an Included Document

Included files in PHP can return a value in the same way that functions do. As in a function, using the `return` statement ends the execution of code within the included file. Additionally, no further HTML is included. Listings 13.4 and 13.5 include a file and assign its return value to a variable.

LISTING 13.4   Using `include()` to Execute PHP and Assign the Return Value

```
1: <?php
2: $addResult = include("returnvalue.php");
3: echo "The include file returned ".$addResult;
4: ?>
```

LISTING 13.5   An Include File That Returns a Value

```
1: <?php
2: $retval = ( 4 + 4 );
3: return $retval;
4: ?>
5: This HTML will never be displayed because it comes after a return statement!
```

Put the contents of Listing 13.4 in a file named `test_returnvalue.php`; put the contents of Listing 13.5 in a file named `returnvalue.php`. Place both of these files in your web server document root. When you access `test_returnvalue.php` through your web browser, the output is

```
The include file returned 8.
```

Just as the string suggests on line 5 of Listing 13.5, anything outside the PHP block will not be displayed, if there *is* a PHP block present in the included file.

Using `include()` **Within Control Structures**

If you want to use an `include()` statement within a conditional statement, it will be treated like any other code—the file will be included only if the condition is met. For example, the `include()` statement in the following fragment will never be called:

```
$test = "1";
if ($test == "2") {
    include("file.txt"); // won't be included
}
```

If you use an `include()` statement within a loop, the file will literally be included each time the loop iterates. Listing 13.6 illustrates this concept by using an `include()` statement in a `for` loop. The `include()` statement references a different file for each iteration.

LISTING 13.6   Using `include()` **Within a Loop**

```
1: <?php
2: for ($x = 1; $x<=3; $x++) {
3:     $incfile = "incfile".$x.".txt";
4:     echo "Attempting to include ".$incfile."<br/>";
5:     include("$incfile");
6:     echo "<br/>";
7: }
8: ?>
```

Save the contents of Listing 13.6 in a file called `loopy_include.php` and place it in the document root of the web server, along with three different files: `incfile1.txt`, `incfile2.txt`, and `incfile3.txt`. Assuming that each of these files simply contains a confirmation of its own name, the output should look like Figure 13.1.

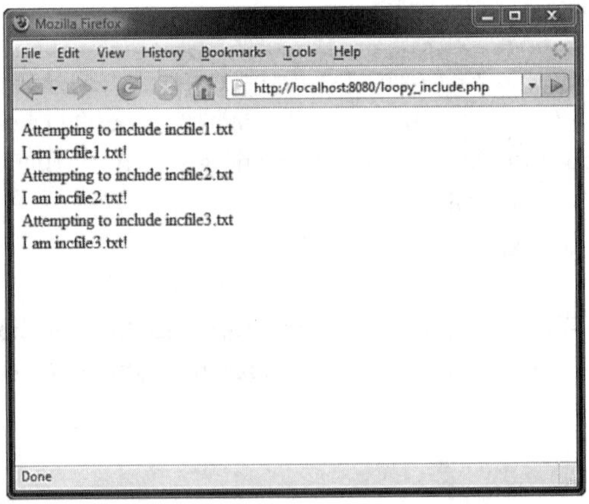

FIGURE 13.1
Output of
`loopy_include`
`.php`.

Although this code worked fine, there are some instances in which using the `include()` function in this manner would not be such a great idea, as you'll see in the next section.

Using `include_once()`

One problem caused by using several different libraries of code within your code is the danger of calling `include()` twice on the same file. This sometimes happens in larger projects when different library files call `include()` on a common file. Including the same file twice often results in repeated declarations of functions and classes, thereby causing the PHP engine great unhappiness.

This situation is remedied by using the `include_once()` function in place of the `include()` function. The `include_once()` function requires the path to an include file and otherwise behaves the same way as the `include()` function the first time it's called. However, if `include_once()` is called again for the same file during script execution, the file will *not* be included again. This makes `include_once()` an excellent tool for the creation of reusable code libraries!

The `include_path` **Directive**

Using `include()` and `include_once()` to access your code libraries can increase the flexibility and reusability of your projects. However, there are still headaches to overcome. Portability, in particular, can suffer if you hard-code the paths to included files. Imagine that you create a `lib` directory and reference it throughout your project:

```
include_once("/home/user/bob/htdocs/project4/lib/mylib.inc.php");
```

When you move your project to a new server, you might find that you have to change a hundred or more `include` paths, if this is hard-coded in a hundred or more files. You can escape this fate by setting the `include_path` directive in your `php.ini` file:

```
include_path  .:/home/user/bob/htdocs/project4/lib/
```

The `include_path` value can include as many directories as you want, separated by colons (semicolons in Windows). The order of the items in the `include_path` directive determines the order in which the directories are searched for the named file. The first dot (.) before the first colon indicates "current directory," and should be present. Now any path used in `include()` or `include_once()` can be relative to the value of `include_path`:

```
include_once("mylib.inc.php");
```

When you move your project, you need to change only the `include_path` directive.

By the Way

PHP also has a `require()` statement, which performs a similar function to `include()`, and a `require_once()` statement.

Anything pulled into your code by `require()` is executed regardless of a script's flow, and therefore shouldn't be used as part of conditional or loop structures.

Also, be aware that a file included as the result of a `require()` statement cannot return a value.

Validating Files

Before you work with a file or directory within your code, it's often a good idea to learn more about it, and whether it actually exists is a pretty good start! PHP provides many functions to help you to discover information about files on your system. This section briefly covers some of the most useful functions.

Checking for Existence with `file_exists()`

You can test for the existence of a file with the `file_exists()` function. This function requires a string representation of an absolute or relative path to a file, which might or might not be present. If the file is found, the `file_exists()` function returns `true`; otherwise, it returns `false`.

```
if (file_exists("test.txt")) {
        echo "The file exists!";
}
```

This is all well and good, but what if you're unsure whether something is a file or a directory, and you really need to know? Read on!

A File or a Directory?

You can confirm that the entity you're testing is a file, as opposed to a directory, using the `is_file()` function. The `is_file()` function requires the file path and returns a Boolean value.

```
if (is_file("test.txt")) {
        echo "test.txt is a file!";
}
```

Conversely, you might want to check that the entity you're testing is a directory. You can do this with the `is_dir()` function. `is_dir()` requires the path to the directory and returns a Boolean value.

```
if (is_dir("/tmp")) {
        echo "/tmp is a directory";
}
```

After you know a file or directory exists, you might need to test its permissions. You'll learn about this in the next section.

Checking the Status of a File

When you know that a particular entity exists, and it's what you expect it to be (either a directory or a file), you'll need to know what you can do with it. Typically, you might want to read, write to, or execute a file. PHP can help you determine whether you can perform these operations.

The is_readable() function tells you whether you can read a file. On UNIX systems, you might be able to see a file but still be barred from reading its contents because of its user permissions. The is_readable() function accepts the file path as a string and returns a Boolean value.

```
if (is_readable("test.txt")) {
        echo "test.txt is readable";
}
```

The is_writable() function tells you whether you have the proper permission to write to a file. As with is_readable(), the is_writable() function requires the file path and returns a Boolean value.

```
if (is_writable("test.txt")) {
        echo "test.txt is writable";
}
```

The is_executable() function tells you whether you can execute the given file, relying on either the file's permissions or its extension, depending on your platform. The function accepts the file path and returns a Boolean value.

```
if (is_executable("test.txt")) {
        echo "test.txt is executable";
}
```

Permission-related information isn't all you might need to know about a file. The next section shows how to determine the file size.

Determining File Size with filesize()

Given the path to a file, the filesize() function attempts to determine and return its size in bytes. It returns false if it encounters problems.

```
echo "The size of test.txt is ".filesize("test.txt");
```

Finding the specific file size is important in situations where you want to attach a file to an email or stream a file to the user—you'll need to know the size so as to properly create the headers (in the case of the email) or know when to stop sending bytes to the user (in the case of the stream). For more general purposes, you might want to get the file size so that you can display it to the user before she attempts to download some monstrous application or high-resolution photograph from your site.

Getting Date Information About a File

Sometimes you need to know when a file was last written to or accessed. PHP provides several functions that can provide this information.

You can find out the last-accessed time of a file using the `fileatime()` function. This function requires the file path and returns the date that the file was last accessed. To *access* a file means either to read or write to it. Dates are returned from all the date information functions in time stamp—that is, the number of seconds since January 1, 1970. The examples in this book use the `date()` function to translate this value into human-readable form.

```
$atime = fileatime("test.txt");
echo "test.txt was last accessed on ".date("D d M Y g:i A", $atime);
// Sample output: test.txt was last accessed on Sun 13 Jan 2008 5:33 AM
```

You can discover the modification date of a file with the function `filemtime()`, which requires the file path and returns the date in UNIX epoch format. To *modify* a file means to change its contents in some way.

```
$mtime = filemtime("test.txt");
echo "test.txt was last modified on ".date("D d M Y g:i A", $mtime);
// Sample output: test.txt was last modified on Sun 13 Jan 2008 5:47 AM
```

PHP also enables you to test the change time of a document with the `filectime()` function. On UNIX systems, the change time is set when a file's contents are modified or when changes are made to its permissions or ownership. On other platforms, the `filectime()` returns the creation date.

```
$ctime = filectime("test.txt");
echo "test.txt was last changed on ".date("D d M Y g:i A", $ctime);
// Sample output: test.txt was last changed on Sun 13 Jan 2008 5:47
```

Creating a Function That Performs Multiple File Tests

Listing 13.7 creates a function that brings together the file-related functions just discussed into one script.

LISTING 13.7   A Function to Output the Results of Multiple File Tests

```
1:  <?php
2:  function outputFileTestInfo($f) {
3:      if (!file_exists($f)) {
4:          echo "<p>$f does not exist</p>";
5:          return;
6:      }
7:      echo "<p>$f is ".(is_file($f) ? "" : "not ")."a file</p>";
8:      echo "<p>$f is ".(is_dir($f) ? "" : "not ")."a directory</p>";
9:      echo "<p>$f is ".(is_readable($f) ? "": "not ")."readable</p>";
10:     echo "<p>$f is ".(is_writable($f) ? "": "not ")."writable</p>";
11:     echo "<p>$f is ".(is_executable($f) ? "": "not ")."executable</p>";
12:     echo "<p>$f is ".(filesize($f))." bytes</p>";
13:     echo "<p>$f was accessed on
14:         ".date( "D d M Y g:i A",fileatime($f))."</p>";
15:     echo "<p>$f was modified on
16:         ".date( "D d M Y g:i A",filemtime($f))."</p>";
17:     echo "<p>$f was changed on
18:         ".date( "D d M Y g:i A",filectime($f) )."</p>";
19: }
20: $file = "test.txt";
21: outputFileTestInfo($file);
22: ?>
```

If this code were saved to the document root of your web server as `filetests.php` and run through your web browser, the output would look something like Figure 13.2 (provided you had a file called `test.txt` also in the document root).

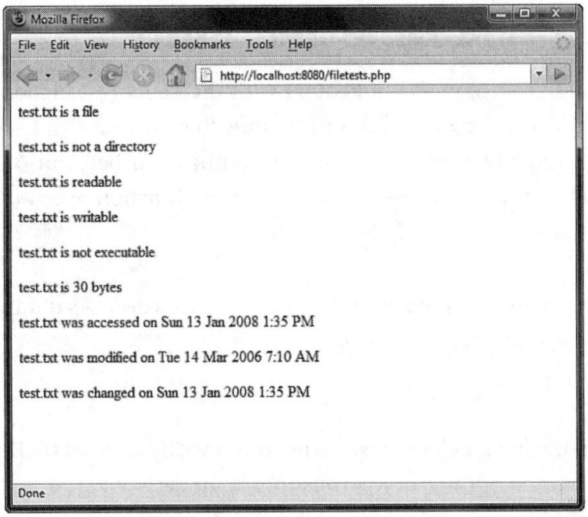

FIGURE 13.2
Output of
`filetests.php`.

Notice that the ternary operator is used as a compact way of working with some of these tests. Let's look at one such test, found in line 7, in more detail:

```
echo "<p>$f is ".(is_file($f) ? "" : "not ")."a file</p>";
```

The is_file() function is used as the left-side expression of the ternary operator. If it returns true, an empty string is returned. Otherwise, the string "not " is returned. The return value of the ternary expression is added to the string to be printed with concatenation operators. This statement could be made clearer, but less compact, as follows:

```
$is_it = is_file($f) ? "" : "not ";
echo "<p>".$f." is ".$is_it." a file</p>";
```

You could, of course, be even clearer with an if statement, but imagine how large the function would become if you used the following:

```
if (is_file($f)) {
        echo "<p>$f is a file</p>";
} else {
        echo "<p>$f is not a file</p>";
}
```

Because the result of these three approaches is the same, the approach you take becomes a matter of preference.

Creating and Deleting Files

If a file does not yet exist, you can create it with the touch() function. Given a string representing a file path, touch() attempts to create an empty file of that name. If the file already exists, its contents won't be disturbed, but the modification date will be updated to reflect the time at which the function executed.

```
touch("myfile.txt");
```

You can remove an existing file with the unlink() function. As did the touch() function, unlink() accepts a file path:

```
unlink("myfile.txt");
```

All functions that create, delete, read, write, and modify files on UNIX systems require the correct file or directory permissions to be set.

Opening a File for Writing, Reading, or Appending

Before you can work with a file, you must first open it for reading or writing, or for performing both tasks. PHP provides the `fopen()` function for doing so, and this function requires a string that contains the file path, followed by a string that contains the mode in which the file is to be opened. The most common modes are read (r), write (w), and append (a).

The `fopen()` function returns a file resource you'll use later to work with the open file. To open a file for reading, you use the following:

```
$fp = fopen("test.txt", "r");
```

You use the following to open a file for writing:

```
$fp = fopen("test.txt", "w");
```

To open a file for *appending* (that is, to add data to the end of a file), you use this:

```
$fp = fopen("test.txt", "a");
```

The `fopen()` function returns `false` if the file cannot be opened for any reason. Therefore, it's a good idea to test the function's return value before proceeding to work with it. You can do so with an `if` statement:

```
if ($fp = fopen("test.txt", "w")) {
    // do something with the $fp resource
}
```

Or, you can use a logical operator to end execution if an essential file can't be opened:

```
($fp = fopen("test.txt", "w")) or die("Couldn't open file, sorry");
```

If the `fopen()` function returns `true`, the rest of the expression won't be parsed, and the `die()` function (which writes a message to the browser and ends the script) is never reached. Otherwise, the right side of the `or` operator is parsed and the `die()` function is called.

Assuming that all is well and you go on to work with your open file, you should remember to close it when you finish. You can do so by calling `fclose()`, which requires the file resource returned from a successful `fopen()` call as its argument:

```
fclose($fp);
```

The resource that became available ($fp) is now unavailable to you.

Reading from Files

PHP provides a number of functions for reading data from files. These functions enable you to read by the byte, by the whole line, and even by the single character.

Reading Lines from a File with `fgets()` and `feof()`

When you open a file for reading, you might want to access it line by line. To read a line from an open file, you can use the `fgets()` function, which requires the file resource returned from `fopen()` as its argument. You must also pass `fgets()` an integer as a second argument, which specifies the number of bytes that the function should read if it doesn't first encounter a line end or the end of the file. The `fgets()` function reads the file until it reaches a newline character (`"\n"`), the number of bytes specified in the length argument, or the end of the file—whichever comes first.

```
$line = fgets($fp, 1024); // where $fp is the file resource returned by fopen()
```

Although you can read lines with `fgets()`, you need some way to tell when you reach the end of the file. The `feof()` function does this by returning `true` when the end of the file has been reached and `false` otherwise. The `feof()` function requires a file resource as its argument:

```
feof($fp); // where $fp is the file resource returned by fopen()
```

You now have enough information to read a file line by line, as shown in Listing 13.8.

LISTING 13.8   Opening and Reading a File Line by Line

```
1: <?php
2: $filename = "test.txt";
3: $fp = fopen($filename, "r") or die("Couldn't open $filename");
4: while (!feof($fp)) {
5:     $line = fgets($fp, 1024);
6:     echo $line."<br/>";
7: }
8: ?>
```

If this code were saved to the document root of your web server as `readlines.php` and run through your web browser, the output would look something like Figure 13.3 (the contents of your sample text file might be different).

The code calls `fopen()` on line 3, using the name of the file that you want to read as its argument. The `or die()` construct is used to ensure that script execution ends if the file cannot be read. This usually occurs if the file does not exist or if the file's permissions don't allow read access to the file.

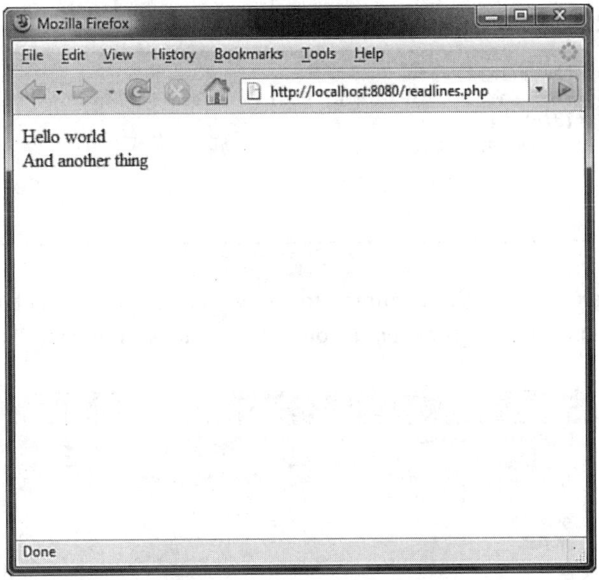

FIGURE 13.3
Output of read-
lines.php.

The actual reading of the file contents takes place in the while statement on line 4. The while statement's test expression calls feof() for each iteration, ending the loop when it returns true. In other words, the loop continues until it reaches the end of the file. Within the code block, fgets() on line 5 extracts a line (or 1024 bytes, whichever comes first) from the file. The result is assigned to $line and printed to the browser on line 6, appending a <br/> tag for the sake of readability.

Reading Arbitrary Amounts of Data from a File with fread()

Rather than reading text by the line, you can choose to read a file in arbitrarily defined chunks. The fread() function accepts a file resource as an argument, as well as the number of bytes you want to read. The fread() function returns the amount of data you requested, unless the end of the file is reached first.

```
$chunk = fread($fp, 16);
```

Listing 13.9 amends the previous example so that it reads data in chunks of eight bytes rather than by the line.

LISTING 13.9   Reading a File with `fread()`

```
1: <?php
2: $filename = "test.txt";
3: $fp = fopen($filename, "r") or die("Couldn't open $filename");
4: while (!feof($fp)) {
5:     $chunk = fread($fp, 8);
6:     echo $chunk."<br/>";
7: }
8: ?>
```

If this code were saved to the document root of your web server as `readlines2.php` and run through your web browser, the output could look something like Figure 13.4.

FIGURE 13.4
Output of `read-lines2.php`.

Although the `fread()` function enables you to define the amount of data acquired from a file, it doesn't let you decide the position from which the acquisition begins. You can set this manually with the `fseek()` function.

The `fseek()` function enables you to change your current position within a file. It requires a file resource and an integer that represents the offset from the start of the file (in bytes) to which you want to jump:

```
fseek($fp, 64);
```

Listing 13.10 uses `fseek()` and `fread()` to output the second half of a file to the browser.

LISTING 13.10   Moving Around a File with `fseek()`

```
 1: <?php
 2: $filename = "test.txt";
 3: $fp = fopen($filename, "r") or die("Couldn't open $filename");
 4: $fsize = filesize($filename);
 5: $halfway = (int)($fsize / 2);
 6: echo "Halfway point: ".$halfway." <br/>\n";
 7: fseek($fp, $halfway);
 8: $chunk = fread($fp, ($fsize - $halfway));
 9: echo $chunk;
10: ?>
```

If this code were saved to the document root of your web server as `readseek.php` and run through your web browser, the output could look something like Figure 13.5.

FIGURE 13.5
Output of read-seek.php.

The code calculates the halfway point of our file on line 5, by dividing the return value of `filesize()` by 2. It uses this as the second argument to `fseek()` on line 7, jumping to the halfway point of the text file. Finally, on line 8, `fread()` is called to extract the second half of the file and then the result is printed to the browser.

Reading Characters from a File with `fgetc()`

The `fgetc()` function is similar to `fgets()` except that it returns only a single character from a file every time it is called. Because a character is always one byte in size, `fgetc()` doesn't require a length argument. You must simply pass it a file resource:

```
$char = fgetc($fp);
```

Listing 13.11 creates a loop that reads the file `test.txt` one character at a time, outputting each character to the browser on its own line.

LISTING 13.11   Moving Around a File with `fgetc()`

```
1: <?php
2: $filename = "test.txt";
3: $fp = fopen($filename, "r") or die("Couldn't open $filename");
4: while (!feof($fp)) {
5:     $char = fgetc($fp);
6:     echo $char."<br/>";
7: }
8: ?>
```

If this code were saved to the document root of your web server as `readchars.php` and run through your web browser, the output could look something like Figure 13.6.

FIGURE 13.6
Output of read-chars.php.

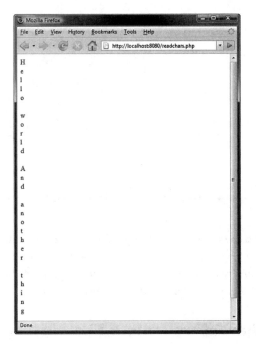

Writing or Appending to a File

The processes for writing to and appending to a file are the same—the difference lies in the mode with which you call the `fopen()` function. When you write to a file, you use the mode argument `"w"` when you call `fopen()`:

```
$fp = fopen("test.txt", "w");
```

All subsequent writing occurs from the start of the file. If the file doesn't already exist, it is created. If the file already exists, any prior content is destroyed and replaced by the data you write.

When you append to a file, you use the mode argument `"a"` in your `fopen()` call:

```
$fp = fopen("test.txt", "a");
```

Any subsequent writes to your file are added to the end of your existing content, but if you attempt to append content to a nonexistent file, the file is created first.

Writing to a File with `fwrite()` or `fputs()`

The `fwrite()` function accepts a file resource and a string, and then writes the string to the file. The `fputs()` function works in exactly the same way:

```
fwrite($fp, "hello world");
fputs($fp, "hello world");
```

Writing to files is as straightforward as that. Listing 13.12 uses `fwrite()` to print to a file. It then appends an additional string to the same file using `fputs()`.

LISTING 13.12   Writing and Appending to a File

```
 1: <?php
 2: $filename = "test.txt";
 3: echo "<p>Writing to ".$filename." ... </p>";
 4: $fp = fopen($filename, "w") or die("Couldn't open $filename");
 5: fwrite($fp, "Hello world\n");
 6: fclose($fp);
 7: echo "<p>Appending to ".$filename." ...</p>";
 8: $fp = fopen($filename, "a") or die("Couldn't open $filename");
 9: fputs($fp, "And another thing\n");
10: fclose($fp);
11: ?>
```

The screen output of this script, when run from your web browser, is

```
Writing to test.txt ...
Appending to test.txt ...
```

If you open the `test.txt` file or use `readlines.php` to read its contents, you'll find the file now contains:

```
Hello world
And another thing
```

Locking Files with `flock()`

The techniques you just learned for reading and amending files work fine if only a single user is accessing your script. In the real world, however, you would expect many users to access your website, and the scripts within it, at more or less the same time. Imagine what would happen if two users were to execute a script that writes to one file at the same moment—the file would quickly become corrupt.

PHP provides the `flock()` function to forestall this eventuality. The `flock()` function locks a file to warn other processes against writing to or reading from that file while the current process is working with it. The `flock()` function requires a valid file resource from an open file and an integer representing the kind of lock you want to set. PHP provides predefined constants for each of the integers you're likely to need. Table 13.1 lists three kinds of locks you can apply to a file.

TABLE 13.1   Integer Arguments to the `flock()` Function

Constant	Integer	Lock Type	Description
LOCK_SH	1	Shared	Allows other processes to read the file but prevents writing (used when reading a file)
LOCK_EX	2	Exclusive	Prevents other processes from either reading from or writing to a file (used when writing to a file)
LOCK_UN	3	Release	Releases a shared or exclusive lock

You should call `flock()` directly after calling `fopen()` and then call it again to release the lock before closing the file. If the lock is not released, you will not be able to read from or write to the file. Here is an example of this sequence of events:

```
$fp = fopen("test.txt", "a") or die("Couldn't open file.");
flock($fp, LOCK_EX); // create exclusive lock
// write to the file
flock($fp, LOCK_UN); // release the lock
fclose($fp);
```

Did you Know?

For more information on file locking, see the PHP Manual entry for the `flock()` function at http://www.php.net/flock.

Working with Directories

Now that you can test, read, and write to files, let's turn our attention to directories. PHP provides many functions for working with directories. Let's look at how to create, remove, and read from them.

Creating Directories with `mkdir()`

The `mkdir()` function enables you to create a directory. The `mkdir()` function requires a string that represents the path to the directory you want to create and an octal number integer that represents the mode you want to set for the directory. Remember, you specify an octal (base 8) number using a leading 0; for example, 0777 or 0400.

The mode argument has an effect only on UNIX systems. The mode should consist of three numbers between 0 and 7, representing permissions for the directory owner, group, and everyone, respectively. The `mkdir()` function returns `true` if it successfully creates a directory or `false` if it doesn't. If `mkdir()` fails, it's usually because the containing directory has permissions that preclude processes with the script's user ID from writing.

If you're not comfortable setting UNIX directory permissions, you should find that one of the following examples fits your needs. Unless you really need your directory to be world-writable, you should probably use 0755, which allows the world to read your directory but not to write to it.

```
mkdir("testdir", 0777); // global read/write/execute permissions

mkdir("testdir", 0755); // world/group: read/execute; owner: read/write/execute
```

Removing a Directory with `rmdir()`

The `rmdir()` function enables you to remove a directory from the filesystem if the process running your script has the right to do so, and if the directory is empty. The `rmdir()` function requires only a string representing the path to the directory you want to delete.

```
rmdir("testdir");
```

Opening a Directory for Reading with `opendir()`

Before you can read the contents of a directory, you must first obtain a directory resource. You can do so with the `opendir()` function. The `opendir()` function requires a string that represents the path to the directory you want to open. The opendir() function returns a directory handle unless the directory isn't present or readable; in that case, it returns false.

```
$dh = opendir("testdir");
```

In this case, $dh is the directory handle of the open directory.

Reading the Contents of a Directory with readdir()

Just as you use the fgets() function to read a line from a file, you can use readdir() to read a file or directory name from a directory. The readdir() function requires a directory handle and returns a string containing the item name. If the end of the directory is reached, readdir() returns false. Note that readdir() returns only the names of its items, rather than full paths. Listing 13.13 shows the contents of a directory.

LISTING 13.13 Listing the Contents of a Directory with readdir()

```
 1: <?php
 2: $dirname = ".";
 3 : $dh = opendir($dirname) or die("couldn't open directory");
 4:
 5: while (!(($file = readdir($dh)) === false ) ) {
 6:     if (is_dir("$dirname/$file")) {
 7:             echo "(D) ";
 8:     }
 9:     echo $file."<br/>";
10: }
11: closedir($dh);
12: ?>
```

If this code were saved to the document root of your web server as readdir.php and run through your web browser, the output could look something like Figure 13.7.

Listing 13.13 opens the directory for reading with the opendir() function on line 3 and uses a while statement to loop through each of its elements, beginning on line 5. It calls readdir() as part of the while statement's test expression and assigns the result to the $file variable.

Within the body of the while statement, the $dirname variable is used in conjunction with the $file variable to create a full file path, which is then tested on line 6. If the path represents a directory, the code prints (D) to the browser on line 7. Finally, the filename (or directory name) is printed on line 9.

FIGURE 13.7
Output of
readdir.php.

Listing 13.13 uses a cautious construction in the test of the while statement. Most PHP programmers (myself included) would use something like the following:

```
while ($file = readdir($dh)) {
      echo $file."<br/>";
}
```

In this case, the value returned by readdir() is tested and, because any string other than "0" resolves to true, there should be no problem. Imagine, however, a directory that contains four files: 0, 1, 2, and 3. On my system, the output from the preceding code is as follows:

```
.
..
```

When the loop reaches the file named 0, the string returned by readdir() resolves to false, which causes the loop to end. The approach in Listing 13.13 uses === to check that the return value returned by readdir() is not *exactly* equivalent to false. The result 0 only *resolves* to false in the test, so the problem is circumvented.

If you find the ordering of items in a directory listing to be arbitrary, it's because the filesystem determines the order. If you want the items ordered in a specific fashion, you must read the contents into an array, which can then be sorted to your liking and subsequently displayed.

By the Way

Opening Pipes to and from Processes Using popen()

Earlier in this chapter, you learned how to open a file for reading and writing using the fopen() function. Now, you'll see that you can open a pipe to a process using the popen() function.

The popen() function is used like this:

```
$file_pointer = popen("some command", mode)
```

The *mode* is either r (read) or w (write).

Listing 13.14 is designed to produce an error—it attempts to open a nonexistent file for reading.

LISTING 13.14   Using popen() to Read a File

```
1: <?php
2: $file_handle = popen("/path/to/fakefile 2>&1", "r");
3: $read = fread($file_handle, 2096);
4: echo $read;
5: pclose($file_handle);
6: ?>
```

Listing 13.14 first calls the popen() function in line 2, attempting to open a file for reading. In line 3, any error message stored in the $file_handle pointer is read and printed to the screen in line 4. Finally, line 5 closes the file pointer opened in line 2.

If you save this code as test_popen.php, place it in your document root, and access it with your web browser, you will see an error message such as this one:

```
The system cannot find the path specified.
```

Listing 13.15 also uses popen() to read the output of a process; in this case, the output of the UNIX who command.

LISTING 13.15   Using popen() to Read the Output of the UNIX who Command (UNIX Only)

```
1:  <?php
2:  $handle = popen("who", "r");
3:  while (!feof($handle)) {
4:    $line = fgets($handle,1024);
5:    if (strlen($line) >= 1) {
6:        echo $line."<br/>";
7:    }
8:  }
9:  pclose($handle);
10: ?>
```

In line 2, a file pointer is returned when popen() is used for reading. Line 3 begins a while loop that reads each line of output from the process and eventually prints the line—if it contains information—in line 6. The connection is closed in line 9.

If you save this code as popen_who.php, place it in your document root, and access it with your web browser, you see something like the following (with your actual information, not mine, of course):

```
julie pts/0 Mar 14 06:19 (adsl-63-206-120-158.dsl.snfc21.pacbell.net)
```

Listing 13.16 shows how to use popen() in write mode to pass data to an external application. The external application in this case is called column. The goal of the script is to take the elements of a multidimensional array and output them in table format, in an ASCII file.

LISTING 13.16 Using popen() to Pass Data to the UNIX column Command (UNIX Only)

```
1:  <?php
2:  $products = array(
3:            array("HAL 2000", 2, "red"),
4:            array("Tricorder", 3, "blue"),
5:            array("ORAC AI", 1, "pink"),
6:            array("Sonic Screwdriver", 1, "orange")
7:            );
8:
9:  $handle = popen("column -tc 3 -s / > /somepath/purchases.txt", "w");
10: foreach ($products as $p) {
11:    fputs($handle, join('/',$p)."\n");
12: }
13: pclose($handle);
14: echo "done";
15: ?>
```

Lines 2–7 define a multidimensional array called $products and in it place four entries representing products with names, quantities, and colors. In line 9, popen() is used in write format to send a command to the column application. This command sends parameters to the column application telling it to format the input as a three-column table, using / as a field delimiter. The output will be sent to a file called purchases.txt (be sure to change the pathname to one that exists on your system).

Lines 10–12 use foreach to loop through the $products array and send each element to the open file pointer. The join() function is then used to convert the arrays to a string, with the specified delimiter appended to it. The code closes the open file pointer in line 13, and in line 14 prints a status message to the screen.

If you save this code as popen_column.php, place it in your document root, and access it with your web browser, it should create a file in the specified location. Looking at the file created on my machine, I see the following text:

```
HAL 2000            2   red
Tricorder           3   blue
ORAC AI             1   pink
Sonic Screwdriver   1   orange
```

You may or may not have the column program on your system, but this section illustrated the logic and syntax for opening a pipe to an application. Feel free to try out this logic with other programs available to you.

Running Commands with exec()

The exec() function is one of several functions you can use to pass commands to the shell. The exec() function requires a string representing the path to the command you want to run, and optionally accepts an array variable that will contain the output of the command and a scalar variable that will contain the return value (1 or 0). For example:

```
exec("/path/to/somecommand", $output_array, $return_val);
```

Listing 13.17 uses the exec() function to produce a directory listing with the shell-based ls command.

LISTING 13.17   Using exec() and ls to Produce a Directory Listing (UNIX Only)

```
1: <?php
2: exec("ls -al .", $output_array, $return_val);
3: echo "Returned ".$return_val."<br/><pre>";
4: foreach ($output_array as $o) {
5:     echo $o."\n";
6: }
7: echo "</pre>";
8: ?>
```

Line 2 issues the ls command using the exec() function. The output of the command is placed into the $output_array array and the return value in the $return_val variable. Line 3 simply prints the return value, whereas the foreach loop in lines 4–6 prints out each element in $output_array.

By the Way

The string in line 3 includes an opening <pre> tag, and line 7 provides a closing tag. This simply ensures that your directory listing will be readable, using HTML preformatted text.

If you save this code as `exec_ls.php`, place it in your document root, and access it with your web browser, you may see something like Figure 13.8 (with your actual information, not mine, of course).

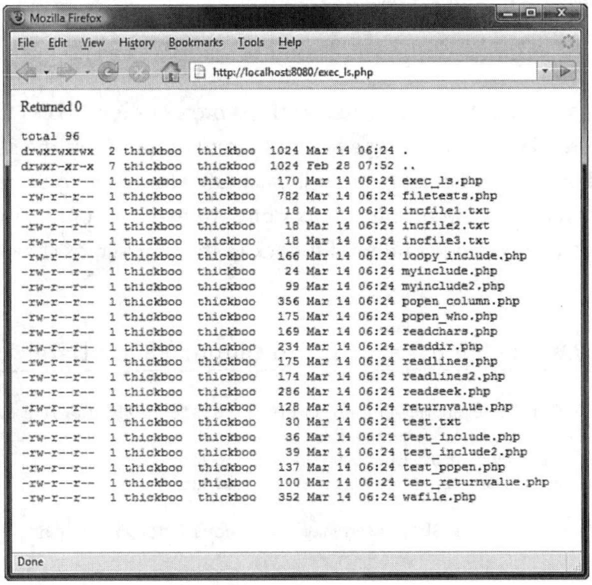

FIGURE 13.8
Output of
`exec_ls.php`.

As wonderful as PHP is, there might come a time when you want to integrate some sort of functionality within your PHP-based application, but someone else has already written code in Perl that does the same thing. In cases like this, there's no need to reinvent the wheel because you can simply use `exec()` to access the existing script and utilize its functionality. However, remember that calling an external process always adds some amount of additional overhead to your script, in terms of both time and memory usage.

Running Commands with `system()` or `passthru()`

The `system()` function is similar to the `exec()` function in that it launches an external application, and it utilizes a scalar variable for storing a return value:

```
system("/path/to/somecommand", $return_val);
```

The `system()` function differs from `exec()` in that it outputs information directly to the browser, without programmatic intervention. The following snippet of code uses

system() to print a man page for the man command, formatted with the
<pre></pre> tag pair:

```
<?php
echo "<pre>";
system("man man | col -b", $return_val);
echo "</pre>";
?>
```

Similarly, the passthru() function follows the syntax of the system() function, but
it behaves differently. When using passthru(), any output from the shell command
is not buffered on its way back to you; this is suitable for running commands that
produce binary data instead of simple text data. An example of this would be to use
shell tools to locate an image and send it back to the browser, as shown in Listing
13.18.

LISTING 13.18   Using passthru() to Output Binary Data

```
1: <?php
2: if ((isset($_GET["imagename"])) && (file_exists($_GET["imagename"]))) {
3:     header("Content-type: image/gif");
4:     passthru("giftopnm ".$_GET["imagename"]." |
5:         pnmscale -xscale .5 -yscale .5 | ppmtogif");
6: } else {
7:     echo "The image ".$_GET["imagename"]." could not be found";
8: }
9: ?>
```

The shell utilities used in this script—giftopnm, pnmscale, and ppmtogif—might
or might not be installed on your system. If they are not, you can probably install
them from your OS distribution CD, but don't worry about it just for this example.
The point is simply to use this listing to understand the concept of using the
passthru() function.

Assuming this file is named getbinary.php, it would be called from HTML like this:

```
<img src="getbinary.php?imagename=<?php echo urlencode("test.gif") ?>">
```

In line 2 of Listing 13.18, the user input is tested to ensure that the file in question
(test.gif, according to the HTML snippet) exists. Because the script will be outputting GIF data to the browser, the appropriate header is set on line 3.

On lines 4 and 5, the passthru() function consecutively executes three different
commands, giftopnm, pnmscale, and ppmtogif, which scales the image to 50% of
its original height and width. The output of the passthru() function—that is, the
new image data—is sent to the browser.

In this and other system-related examples, you could have used the `escapeshellcmd()` or `escapeshellarg()` function to escape elements in the user input. Doing so ensures that the user cannot trick the system into executing arbitrary commands such as deleting important system files or resetting passwords. These functions go around the first instance of the user input, such as

```
$new_input = escapeshellcmd($_GET['someinput']);
```

You would then reference $new_input throughout the remainder of your script, instead of $_GET['someinput']. Using these two commands, plus ensuring that your script is written so as to only perform tasks *you* want it to do, and not commands from your users, is a way to keep your system secure.

By the Way

Summary

In this chapter, you learned how to use the `include()` family of functions (`include_once()`, `require()`, and `require_once()` thrown in for good measure) to incorporate files into your documents and to execute any PHP code contained in include files. You learned how to use some of PHP's file-testing functions and explored functions for reading files by the line, by the character, and in arbitrary chunks. You learned how to write to files, by either replacing or appending to existing content, and you learned how to create, remove, and read directories.

You were also introduced to various methods of communicating with your system and its external applications. Although PHP is a fast and robust language, you might find it more cost- and time-effective to simply utilize preexisting scripts in other languages such as C or Perl. You can access these external applications using the `popen()`, `exec()`, `system()`, and `passthru()` functions.

You learned how to pipe data to a command using `popen()`, which is useful for applications that accept data from standard input and when you want to parse data as it is sent to you by an application. You also learned to use `exec()` and `system()` to pass commands to the shell and acquire user input. You also learned to use the `passthru()` function to accept binary data that is the result of a shell command.

Now that you can work with the filesystem a little more, you can save and access substantial amounts of data. If you need to look up data from large files, however, such scripts begin to slow down considerably. When that occurs, you should look into a database system, which will be coming your way shortly!

Q&A

Q. *Does the `include()` statement slow down my scripts?*

A. Because an included file must be opened and parsed by the engine, it adds some overhead. However, the benefits of reusable code libraries often outweigh the relatively low performance overhead.

Q. *Should I always end script execution if a file cannot be opened for writing or reading?*

A. You should always allow for this possibility. If your script absolutely depends on the file you want to work with, you might want to use the `die()` function, writing an informative error message to the browser. In less critical situations, you still need to allow for the failure, perhaps by adding it to a log file.

Q. *Where can I get more information about security on the Web?*

A. One authoritative introduction to web security is "The World Wide Web Security FAQ" document written by Lincoln Stein, found at http://www.w3.org/Security/Faq/.

Workshop

The workshop is designed to help you anticipate possible questions, review what you've learned, and begin putting your knowledge into practice.

Quiz

1. What functions do you use to add library code to the currently running script?

2. What function do you use to find out whether a file is present on your filesystem?

3. How do you determine the size of a file?

4. What function do you use to open a file for reading or writing?

5. What function do you use to read a line of data from a file?

6. How can you tell when you've reached the end of a file?

7. What function do you use to write a line of data to a file?

8. How do you open a directory for reading?

9. What function do you use to read the name of a directory item after you've opened a directory for reading?

10. Which function do you use to open a pipe to a process?

11. How can you read data from a process after you have opened a connection? What about writing data?

12. How can you escape user input to make it a little safer before passing it to a shell command?

Answers

1. You can use the `require()` or `include()` statement to incorporate PHP files into the current document. You could also use `include_once()` or `require_once()`.

2. You can test for the existence of a file with the `file_exists()` function.

3. The `filesize()` function returns a file's size in bytes.

4. The `fopen()` function opens a file. It accepts the path to a file and a character representing the mode. It returns a file resource.

5. The `fgets()` function reads data up to the buffer size you pass it, the end of the line, or the end of the document, whichever comes first.

6. The `feof()` function returns `true` when the file resource it's passed reaches the end of the file.

7. You can write data to a file with the `fputs()` function.

8. The `opendir()` function enables you to open a directory for reading.

9. The `readdir()` function returns the name of a directory item from an opened directory.

10. The `popen()` function is used to open a pipe to a process.

11. You can read and write to and from a process just as you can with an open file, namely with `feof()` and `fgets()` for reading and `fputs()` for writing.

12. If user input is part of your shell command, you can use the `escapeshell-cmd()` or `escapeshellarg()` function to properly escape it.

Activities

1. Create a form that accepts a user's first and second name. Create a script that saves this data to a file.

2. Create a script that reads the data file you created in the first activity. In addition to writing its contents to the browser (adding a <br /> tag to each line), print a summary that includes the number of lines in the file and the file's size.

14

Working with Images

A standard installation of PHP has many built-in functions for dynamically creating and manipulating images. With a few adjustments, you can expand the functionality even more. In this chapter, you learn the basics of creating and manipulating images using PHP functions:

- ▶ How to modify PHP to increase image-related functionality
- ▶ How to create a new image
- ▶ How to modify existing images

Understanding the Image-Creation Process

Creating an image with PHP is not like creating an image with a drawing program: There's no pointing and clicking or dragging buckets of color into a predefined space to fill your image. Similarly, there's no Save As functionality, in which your drawing program automatically creates a GIF, JPEG, PNG, and so on, just because you ask it to do so.

Instead, *you* have to become the drawing application. As the programmer, you must tell the PHP engine what to do at each step along the way. You are responsible for using the individual PHP functions to define colors, draw and fill shapes, size and resize the image, and save the image as a specific file type. It's not as difficult as it might seem, however, if you understand each step along the way and complete the tasks in order.

By the Way

The examples in this chapter are not the most exciting examples ever, but there are limits to what can be printed in the pages of a book. Rest assured that these examples will give you a good fundamental knowledge of working with the image-related functions in PHP.

A Word About Color

When defining colors in your image-related scripts, you will be using the RGB color system. Using decimal values from 0 to 255 for each of the red, green, and blue (R, G, and B) entries, you can define a specific color. A value of 0 indicates no amount of that specific color whereas a value of 255 indicates the highest amount of that color.

For example, the RGB value for pure red is (255,0,0) or the entire allocation of red values, no green, and no blue. Similarly, pure green has a value of (0,255,0), and pure blue has a value of (0,0,255). White, on the other hand, has an RGB value of (255,255,255), whereas black has an RGB value of (0,0,0). A nice shade of purple has an RGB value of (153,51,153), and a light gray has an RGB value of (204,204,204).

Necessary Modifications to PHP

Current versions of the PHP distribution include a bundled version of Thomas Boutell's GD graphics library. The inclusion of this library eliminates the need to download and install several third-party libraries, but this library needs to be activated at installation time.

By the Way

If you cannot install PHP as directed in Chapter 4, "Installing and Configuring PHP," and are stuck with a version of PHP earlier than 4.3.0, you will have to go to http://www.boutell.com/gd/ and download the source of the GD library. Follow the instructions included with that software and consult its manual for difficulties with installation.

To enable the use of the GD library at installation time, Linux/UNIX users must add the following to the `configure` parameters when preparing to build PHP:

```
--with-gd
```

By the Way

If you download your own version of GD, you must specify the path, as in --with-gd=/path/to/gd.

After running the PHP configure program again, you must go through the make and make install process as you did in Chapter 4. Windows users who want to enable GD simply have to activate php_gd2.dll as an extension in the php.ini file, as you learned in Chapter 4.

When using the GD library, you are limited to working with files in GIF format unless you install additional libraries.

Obtaining Additional Libraries

Working with GIF files might suit your needs perfectly, but if you want to create JPEG or PNG files, you will need to download and install a few libraries and make some modifications to your PHP installation.

▶ JPEG libraries and information can be found at ftp://ftp.uu.net/graphics/jpeg/.

▶ PNG libraries and information can be found at http://www.libpng.org/pub/png/libpng.html.

▶ If you are working with PNG files, you should also install the zlib library, found at http://www.zlib.net/.

Follow the instructions at these sites to install the libraries. After installation, Linux/UNIX users must again reconfigure and rebuild PHP by first adding the following to the PHP configure parameters (assuming that you want to use all three, if not, just add the applicable ones):

```
--with-jpeg-dir=[path to jpeg directory]
--with-png-dir=[path to PNG directory]
--with-zlib=[path to zlib directory]
```

After running the PHP configure program again, you need to go through the make and make install process as you did in Chapter 4. Your libraries should then be activated and ready for use.

Drawing a New Image

The basic PHP function used to create a new image is called ImageCreate(), but creating an image is not as simple as just calling the function. Creating an image is a stepwise process and includes the use of several different PHP functions.

Creating an image begins with the ImageCreate() function, but all this function does is set aside a canvas area for your new image. The following line creates a drawing area that is 150 pixels wide by 150 pixels high:

```
$myImage = ImageCreate(150,150);
```

With a canvas now defined, you should next define a few colors for use in that new image. The following examples define five such colors, using the ImageColorAllocate() function and RGB values:

```
$black = ImageColorAllocate($myImage, 0, 0, 0);

$white = ImageColorAllocate($myImage, 255, 255, 255);

$red  = ImageColorAllocate($myImage, 255, 0, 0);

$green = ImageColorAllocate($myImage, 0, 255, 0);

$blue = ImageColorAllocate($myImage, 0, 0, 255);
```

By the
Way

> In your script, the first color you allocate is used as the background color of the image. In this case, the background color will be black.

Now that you know the basics of setting up your drawing canvas and allocated colors, you can move on to learning to draw shapes and actually output the image to a web browser.

Drawing Shapes and Lines

Several PHP functions can assist you in drawing shapes and lines on your canvas:

▶ ImageEllipse() is used to draw an ellipse.

▶ ImageArc() is used to draw a partial ellipse.

▶ ImagePolygon() is used to draw a polygon.

▶ ImageRectangle() is used to draw a rectangle.

▶ ImageLine() is used to draw a line.

Using these functions requires a bit of thinking ahead because you must set up the points where you want to start and stop the drawing that occurs. Each of these functions uses x-axis and y-axis coordinates as indicators of where to start drawing on the canvas. You must also define how far along the x-axis and y-axis you want the drawing to occur.

For example, the following line draws a rectangle on the canvas beginning at point (15,15) and continuing on for 40 pixels horizontally and 70 pixels vertically, so that the lines end at point (55,85). Additionally, the lines will be drawn with the color red, which has already been defined in the variable $red.

```
ImageRectangle($myImage, 15, 15, 55, 85, $red);
```

If you want to draw another rectangle of the same size but with white lines, beginning at the point where the previous rectangle stopped, you would use this code:

```
ImageRectangle($myImage, 55, 85, 125, 135, $white);
```

Listing 14.1 shows the image-creation script so far, with a few more lines added to output the image to the web browser.

LISTING 14.1   Creating a New Image

```
1:  <?php
2:  //create the canvas
3:  $myImage = ImageCreate(150,150);
4:
5:  //set up some colors
6:  $black = ImageColorAllocate($myImage, 0, 0, 0);
7:  $white = ImageColorAllocate($myImage, 255, 255, 255);
8:  $red  = ImageColorAllocate($myImage, 255, 0, 0);
9:  $green = ImageColorAllocate($myImage, 0, 255, 0);
10: $blue = ImageColorAllocate($myImage, 0, 0, 255);
11:
12: //draw some rectangles
13: ImageRectangle($myImage, 15, 15, 55, 85, $red);
14: ImageRectangle($myImage, 55, 85, 125, 135, $white);
15:
16: //output the image to the browser
17: header ("Content-type: image/png");
18: ImagePng($myImage);
19:
20: //clean up after yourself
21: ImageDestroy($myImage);
22: ?>
```

Lines 17–18 output the stream of image data to the web browser by first sending the appropriate header() function, using the MIME type of the image being created. Then you use the ImageGif(), ImageJpeg(), or ImagePng() function as appropriate to output the data stream; this example outputs a PNG file. In line 21, you use the ImageDestroy() function to clear up the memory used by the ImageCreate() function at the beginning of the script.

Save this listing as imagecreate.php and place it in the document root of your web server. When accessed, it should look something like Figure 14.1, only in color.

FIGURE 14.1
A canvas with
two drawn
rectangles.

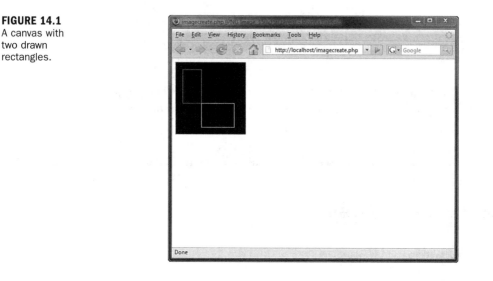

Using a Color Fill

The output of Listing 14.1 produced only outlines of rectangles. PHP has image functions designed to fill areas as well:

- ► `ImageFilledEllipse()` is used to fill an ellipse.

- ► `ImageFilledArc()` is used to fill a partial ellipse.

- ► `ImageFilledPolygon()` is used to fill a polygon.

- ► `ImageFilledRectangle()` is used to fill a rectangle.

You use these functions just like their nonfill counterparts. In Listing 14.2, the nonfill functions are replaced with functions designed to fill an area. In other words, only lines 13 and 14 have changed.

LISTING 14.2   Creating a New Image with Color Fills

```
1:  <?php
2:  //create the canvas
3:  $myImage = ImageCreate(150,150);
4:
5:  //set up some colors
6:  $black = ImageColorAllocate($myImage, 0, 0, 0);
7:  $white = ImageColorAllocate($myImage, 255, 255, 255);
8:  $red   = ImageColorAllocate($myImage, 255, 0, 0);
9:  $green = ImageColorAllocate($myImage, 0, 255, 0);
10: $blue = ImageColorAllocate($myImage, 0, 0, 255);
11:
12: //draw some rectangles
```

LISTING 14.2 **Continued**

```
13: ImageFilledRectangle($myImage, 15, 15, 55, 85, $red);
14: ImageFilledRectangle($myImage, 55, 85, 125, 135, $white);
15:
16: //output the image to the browser
17: header ("Content-type: image/png");
18: ImagePng($myImage);
19:
20: //clean up after yourself
21: ImageDestroy($myImage);
22: ?>
```

Save this listing as imagecreatefill.php and place it in the document root of your web server. When accessed, it should look something like Figure 14.2, but again, in color.

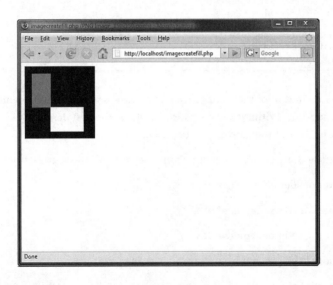

FIGURE 14.2
A canvas with two drawn and filled rectangles.

Getting Fancy with Pie Charts

The previous examples were a little boring, but they introduced you to the process of creating images—define the canvas, define the colors, and then draw and fill. You can use this same sequence of events to expand your scripts to create charts and graphs, using either static or dynamic data for the data points. Listing 14.3 draws a basic pie chart. Lines 1 through 10 will look exactly the same as the previous listings because they just set up the canvas size and colors to be used.

LISTING 14.3   A Basic Pie Chart

```
1:  <?php
2:  //create the canvas
3:  $myImage = ImageCreate(300,300);
4:
5:  //set up some colors
6:  $white = ImageColorAllocate($myImage, 255, 255, 255);
7:  $red   = ImageColorAllocate($myImage, 255, 0, 0);
8:  $green = ImageColorAllocate($myImage, 0, 255, 0);
9:  $blue = ImageColorAllocate($myImage, 0, 0, 255);
10:
11: //draw a pie
12:  ImageFilledArc($myImage, 100, 100, 200, 150, 0, 90, $red, IMG_ARC_PIE);
13:  ImageFilledArc($myImage,100,100,200,150,90,180,$green,IMG_ARC_PIE);
14:  ImageFilledArc($myImage,100,100,200,150,180,360,$blue,IMG_ARC_PIE);
15:
16: //output the image to the browser
17: header ("Content-type: image/png");
18: ImagePng($myImage);
19:
20: //clean up after yourself
21: ImageDestroy($myImage);
22: ?>
```

Okay, so the definition of the color black has been removed from this example, but it's mostly the same. Without the definition of black, the first defined color is white. Therefore, the color of the canvas will be white.

Lines 12–14 use the `ImageFilledArc()` function, which has several attributes:

- ▶ The image identifier
- ▶ The partial ellipse centered at x
- ▶ The partial ellipse centered at y
- ▶ The partial ellipse width
- ▶ The partial ellipse height
- ▶ The partial ellipse start point
- ▶ The partial ellipse end point
- ▶ Color
- ▶ Style

Look at line 14 from Listing 14.3:

```
14:  ImageFilledArc($myImage,100,100,200,150,180,360,$blue,IMG_ARC_PIE);
```

The arc should be filled with the defined color $blue and should use the
IMG_ARC_PIE style. The IMG_ARC_PIE style is one of several built-in styles used in the
display; this one says to create a rounded edge.

> You can learn about all the various styles in the PHP manual, at
> http://www.php.net/image.

By the Way

Save this listing as imagecreatepie.php and place it in the document root of your
web server. When accessed, it should look something like Figure 14.3, but in color.

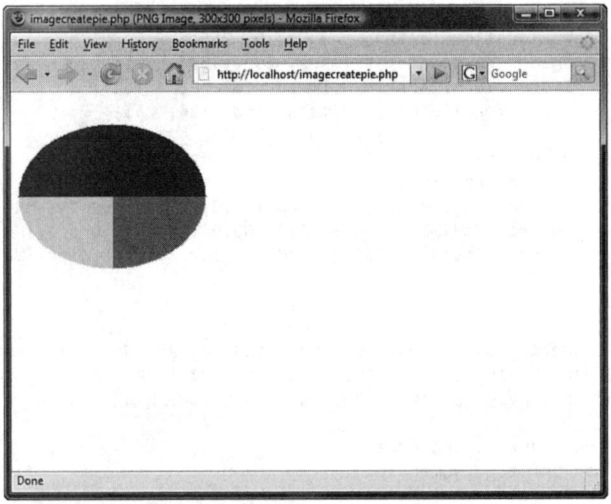

FIGURE 14.3
A simple pie
with slices.

You can extend the code in Listing 14.3 and give your pie a 3D appearance. To do
so, define three more colors for the edge. These colors can be either lighter or darker
than the base colors, as long as they provide some contrast. The following examples
define lighter colors:

```
$lt_red = ImageColorAllocate($myImage, 255, 150, 150);

$lt_green = ImageColorAllocate($myImage, 150, 255, 150);

$lt_blue = ImageColorAllocate($myImage, 150, 150, 255);
```

To create the shading effect, you use a for loop to add a series of small arcs at the
points (100,120) to (100,101), using the lighter colors as fill colors:

```
for ($i = 120;$i > 100;$i--) {
    ImageFilledArc ($myImage,100,$i,200,150,0,90,$lt_red,IMG_ARC_PIE);
    ImageFilledArc ($myImage,100,$i,200,150,90,180,$lt_green,IMG_ARC_PIE);
```

```
        ImageFilledArc ($myImage,100,$i,200,150,180,360,$lt_blue, IMG_ARC_PIE);
}
```

Listing 14.4 shows the code used for a 3D pie.

LISTING 14.4   A 3D Pie Chart

```
1:  <?php
2:  //create the canvas
3:  $myImage = ImageCreate(300,300);
4:
5:  //set up some colors
6:  $white = ImageColorAllocate($myImage, 255, 255, 255);
7:  $red   = ImageColorAllocate($myImage, 255, 0, 0);
8:  $green = ImageColorAllocate($myImage, 0, 255, 0);
9:  $blue = ImageColorAllocate($myImage, 0, 0, 255);
10: $lt_red = ImageColorAllocate($myImage, 255, 150, 150);
11: $lt_green = ImageColorAllocate($myImage, 150, 255, 150);
12: $lt_blue = ImageColorAllocate($myImage, 150, 150, 255);
13:
14: //draw the shaded area
15: for ($i = 120;$i > 100;$i--) {
16:     ImageFilledArc ($myImage,100,$i,200,150,0,90,$lt_red,IMG_ARC_PIE);
17:     ImageFilledArc ($myImage,100,$i,200,150,90,180,$lt_green,IMG_ARC_PIE);
18:     ImageFilledArc ($myImage,100,$i,200,150,180,360,$lt_blue,IMG_ARC_PIE);
19: }
20:
21: //draw a pie
22: ImageFilledArc($myImage, 100, 100, 200, 150, 0, 90, $red, IMG_ARC_PIE);
23: ImageFilledArc($myImage, 100, 100, 200, 150, 90, 180 , $green, IMG_ARC_PIE);
24: ImageFilledArc($myImage, 100, 100, 200, 150, 180, 360 , $blue, IMG_ARC_PIE);
25:
26: //output the image to the browser
27: header ("Content-type: image/png");
28: ImagePng($myImage);
29:
30: //clean up after yourself
31: ImageDestroy($myImage);
32: ?>
```

Save this listing as imagecreate3dpie.php and place it in the document root of your web server. When accessed, it should look something like Figure 14.4, but in color.

These are just basic examples that show the power of some of the image-drawing and filling functions. In the next section, you learn how to manipulate existing images.

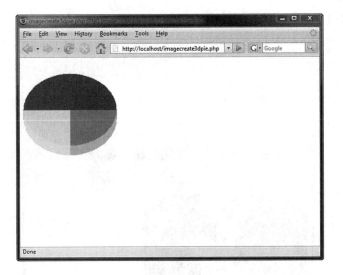

FIGURE 14.4
A 3D pie, with slices.

Modifying Existing Images

The process of creating images from other images follows the same essential steps as creating a new image—the difference lies in what acts as the image canvas. Previously, you created a new canvas using the ImageCreate() function. When creating an image from a new image, you use the ImageCreateFrom*() family of functions.

You can create images from existing GIFs, JPEGs, PNGs, and plenty of other image types. The functions used to create images from these formats are called ImageCreateFromGif(), ImageCreateFromJpg(), ImageCreateFromPng(), and so forth. In the next example, you can see how easy it is to create a new image from an existing one. Figure 14.5 shows the base image.

Listing 14.5 shows how to use an existing image as the canvas, which then has filled ellipses drawn on it.

LISTING 14.5 Creating a New Image from an Existing Image

```
1:  <?php
2:  //use existing image as a canvas
3:  $myImage = ImageCreateFromPng("baseimage.png");
4:
5:  //allocate the color white
6:  $white = ImageColorAllocate($myImage, 255, 255, 255);
7:
8:  //draw on the new canvas
9:  ImageFilledEllipse($myImage, 100, 70, 20, 20, $white);
10: ImageFilledEllipse($myImage, 175, 70, 20, 20, $white);
11: ImageFilledEllipse($myImage, 250, 70, 20, 20, $white);
12:
```

LISTING 14.5   Continued

```
13: //output the image to the browser
14: header ("Content-type: image/png");
15: ImagePng($myImage);
16:
17: //clean up after yourself
18: ImageDestroy($myImage);
19: ?>
```

FIGURE 14.5
The base
image.

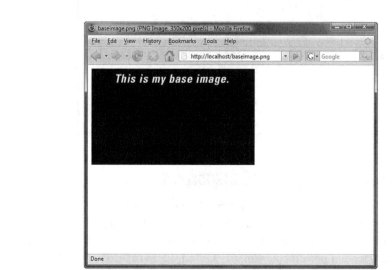

Save this listing as `imagefrombase.php` and place it in the document root of your
web server. When accessed, it should look something like Figure 14.6.

FIGURE 14.6
Drawing on an
existing image.

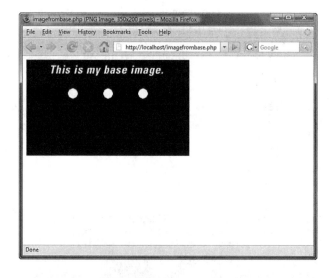

The next example takes this process a few steps forward and utilizes some different image-modification functions. In this case, the existing images are four PNG images, each with a differently colored triangular slice on a gray background. In Listing 14.6, you will stack these images on top of each other and blend them together at each step so that the gray background becomes transparent and the image beneath it shows through.

LISTING 14.6 Stacking Images and Making Them Transparent

```
1:  <?php
2:  //select an image to start with
3:  $baseimage = ImageCreateFromPng("img1.png");
4:
5:  //loop through images #2 through the end
6:  for($i=2; $i <5; $i++) {
7:      //allocate the transparent color, and stack
8:      $myImage = ImageCreateFromPng("img".$i.".png");
9:      $gray = ImageColorAllocate($myImage, 185, 185, 185);
10:     ImageColorTransparent($myImage, $gray);
11:     ImageCopyMerge($baseimage,$myImage,0,0,0,0,150,150,100);
12: }
13:
14: //output the image to the browser
15: header ("Content-type: image/png");
16: ImagePng($baseimage);
17:
18: //clean up after yourself
19: ImageDestroy($baseimage);
20: ?>
```

In line 3, one of the images is selected to be the base image. In this case, it's img1.png. The for loop in lines 8–11 handles the bulk of the work. Knowing that you have four images and that you are already using the first one as the base, that leaves three more images to be stacked and made transparent.

After the new layer is created on line 8, its gray areas are indicated as transparent, and it is merged on top of the base image. As the layers are stacked, the base image contains an increasing number of layers until the total number of four layers is reached. At that point, the image is sent to the browser in lines 15–16.

Save this listing as imagestacker.php and place it in the document root of your web server. When accessed, it should look something like Figure 14.7.

FIGURE 14.7
Stacked trans-
parent images
produce a
composite.

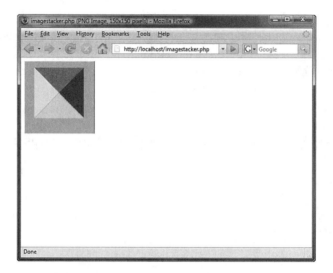

Image Creation from User Input

In addition to creating images from other images and drawing images on your own,
you can also create images based on user input. There's no fundamental difference
in how the scripts are created except for the fact that you'll be gathering values
from a form instead of hard-coding them into your script.

Listing 14.7 creates an all-in-one form and script that asks for user input for a variety of attributes ranging from image size to text and background colors, as well as a
message string. You'll be introduced to the imagestring() function, which is used
to "write" a string onto an image.

Let's get into the script, where lines 2–38 represent the user input form, and the
remaining lines handle the image created per user specifications.

LISTING 14.7   Creating an Image from User Input

```
1:  if (!$_POST) {
2:      //show form
3:      echo "
4:      <html>
5:      <head>
6:      <title>Image Creation Form</title>
7:      </head>
8:      <body>
9:      <h1>Create an Image</h1>
10:     <form method=\"POST\" action=\"\".$_SERVER[\"PHP_SELF\"].\"\">
11:     <p><strong>Image Size:</strong><br/>
12:     W: <input type=\"text\" name=\"w\" size=\"5\" maxlength=\"5\" />
13:     H: <input type=\"text\" name=\"h\" size=\"5\" maxlength=\"5\" /></p>
14:     <p><strong>Background Color:</strong><br />
```

LISTING 14.7 Continued

```
15:    R: <input type=\"text\" name=\"b_r\" size=\"3\" maxlength=\"3\" />
16:    G: <input type=\"text\" name=\"b_g\" size=\"3\" maxlength=\"3\" />
17:    B: <input type=\"text\" name=\"b_b\" size=\"3\" maxlength=\"3\" /></p>
18:    <p><strong>Text Color:</strong><br />
19:    R: <input type=\"text\" name=\"t_r\" size=\"3\" maxlength=\"3\" />
20:    G: <input type=\"text\" name=\"t_g\" size=\"3\" maxlength=\"3\" />
21:    B: <input type=\"text\" name=\"t_b\" size=\"3\" maxlength=\"3\" /></p>
22:    <p><strong>Text String:</strong><br />
23:    <input type=\"text\" name=\"string\" size=35 /></p>
24:    <p><strong>Font Size:</strong><br />
25:    <select name=\"font_size\">
26:    <option value=\"1\">1</option>
27:    <option value=\"2\">2</option>
28:    <option value=\"3\">3</option>
29:    <option value=\"4\">4</option>
30:    <option value=\"5\">5</option>
31:    </select></p>
32:    <p><strong>Text Starting Position:</strong><br />
33:    X: <input type=\"text\" name=\"x\" size=\"3\" maxlength=\"3\" />
34:    Y: <input type=\"text\" name=\"y\" size=\"3\" maxlength=\"3\" /></p>
35:    <p><input type=\"submit\" name=\"submit\" value=\"create image\" /></p>
36:    </form>
37:    </body>
38:    </html>";
```

You see that this basic form uses several fields to obtain image specifications. On lines 12–13 are fields to define the width and the height of the image you want to draw. Next, the code sets up fields to obtain the RGB values for a background color (lines 15–17) and a text color (lines 19–21).

> You could create drop-down list boxes containing values 0 through 255 for the red, green, and blue values. This would ensure that the user input was within the required range.

By the Way

Line 23 contains a form field for the input string. This string will be drawn onto the background of the image in the text color specified. Lines 25–31 represent a drop-down list for the selection of the font size. There are five sizes, 1 through 5, for the default fixed-width font.

> You can specify fonts using the imageloadfont() and imagettftext() functions. Learn more at http://www.php.net/image.

By the Way

Finally, lines 33 and 34 allow you to define the text starting position. The upper-left corner of the image area would be X position 0, Y position 0; 10 increments downward would be Y position 10, 10 increments to the right would be X position 10, and so forth.

If you stopped the script here and closed up the `if...else` statement and PHP block, you would see a form like Figure 14.8 when loaded in your web browser.

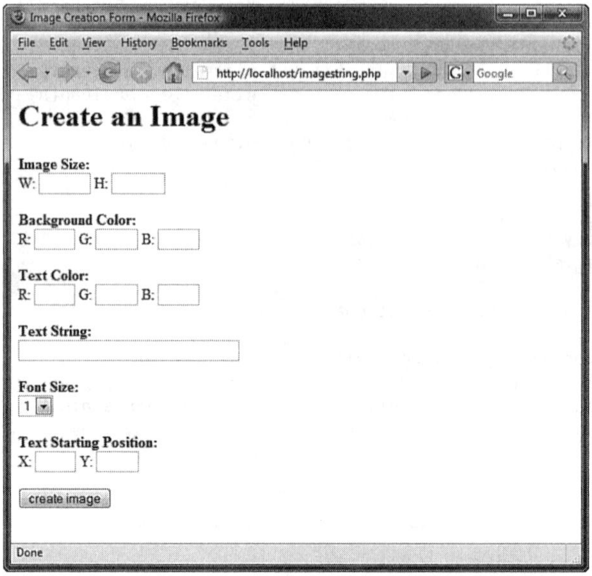

FIGURE 14.8
User input form
for image
creation.

In only 18 more lines, you can finish this script and generate images with text strings, so take a look at the remainder of Listing 14.7.

LISTING 14.7   Creating an Image from User Input (Continued)

```
39: } else {
40:     //create image
41:     //create the canvas
42:     $myImage = ImageCreate($_POST["w"], $_POST["h"]);
43:
44:     //set up some colors
45:     $background = ImageColorAllocate ($myImage, $_POST["b_r"],
46:         $_POST["b_g"], $_POST["b_b"]);
47:     $text = ImageColorAllocate ($myImage, $_POST["t_r"],
48:         $_POST["t_g"], $_POST["t_b"]);
49:
50:     // write the string at the top left
51:     ImageString($myImage, $_POST["font_size"], $_POST["x"],
52;         $_POST["y"], $_POST["string"], $text);
53:
54:     //output the image to the browser
55:     header ("Content-type: image/png");
56:     ImagePNG($myImage);
57:
58:     //clean up after yourself
59:     ImageDestroy($myImage);
60: }
61: ?>
```

The majority of lines 39–61 you've already seen before, only this time it uses extracted elements from the $_POST superglobal to take the place of hard-coded values. Line 42 uses the width and height values from the form to set up the initial image. Lines 45–47 define two colors, $background and $text, using the appropriate RGB values provided by the form.

> The colors weren't given actual color names in this script because there's no way to know what the user input would create—you could call the color $red, but you would look stupid if the user defined it as 0,255,0 because that's the RGB value for green! Instead, simply name the colors after their purpose, not their appearance.

Lines 51–52 represent the only new item in this script, the use of the imagestring() function. The six parameters for this function are the image stream ($myImage), the font size ($_POST["font_size"]), the starting X and Y positions ($_POST["x"] and $_POST["y"]), the string to be drawn ($_POST["string"]), and the color in which to draw it ($text). Lines 55–56 output the image to the browser, and line 59 destroys and cleans up the image creation process.

If you save this file as imagecreate.php, place it in the document root of the web server, and fill out the form, the output could look something like Figure 14.9. But quite likely your results will differ because there are many variables to play with!

FIGURE 14.9
Sample output from image creation form.

Try it yourself, using various sizes, colors, and text strings.

Using Images Created by Scripts

All the earlier scripts produce image output, but you call them as standalone scripts. Using the results of an image created by a script, within your HTML, is as simple as using the name of the script—not an image—in the `src` attribute of the `img` tag. For example:

```
<img src="NameOfScript.php"/>
```

In Listing 14.8, you create a simple script to produce an image. An `img` tag then calls this image and the browser displays it.

To add some new functionality to the mix, this basic script loads and uses a custom font to display a text string as a graphic—much like the user-generated text in the previous section, except the font is fancier. The reasons for this will soon become clear.

First, create the image-generating script. Listing 14.8 shows an example.

LISTING 14.8   Creating an Image with Custom Font and Text

```
 1:  <?php
 2:  //create the canvas
 3:  $myImage = ImageCreate(150,25);
 4:
 5:  //set up some colors
 6:  $white = ImageColorAllocate($myImage, 255, 255, 255);
 7:  $black = ImageColorAllocate($myImage, 0, 0, 0);
 8:
 9:  //load a font
10:  $font = imageloadfont("hootie.gdf");
11:
12:  // write the string
13:  ImageString($myImage, $font, 0, 0, "CAPTCHA!", $black);
14:
15:  //output the image to the browser
16:  header ("Content-type: image/png");
17:  ImagePng($myImage);
18:
19:  //clean up after yourself
20:  ImageDestroy($myImage);
21:  ?>
```

Line 3 creates a canvas that is 150 pixels wide and 25 pixels high. This size is something commonly seen in a CAPTCHA. In fact, that's part of what you're creating here.

By the Way

A *CAPTCHA* is a graphical challenge-response test to determine whether a user is a human. You may have encountered a CAPTCHA when completing a form to leave a comment on a website or to participate in a discussion forum, or when creating a user account. The idea is that only a human can read alphanumeric text in an image. You can read more about CAPTCHAs at http://en.wikipedia.org/wiki/Captcha.

Lines 5–7 set up the colors available to this script: white as the background and black as another color. Line 10 loads a font, using the `imageloadfont()` function. You could also use the `imagettftext()` function if you want to use TrueType fonts. In this example, the hootie.gdf font is a freely available font that comes in a single file placed on the file system and then loaded by the function calling it.

You can find the font used in this example, as well as several other free fonts, at http://www.devtrolls.com/gdf_fonts/. You can also use any GDF or TrueType font found on your web server.

By the Way

Line 13 uses the font loaded in line 10 as part of the `ImageString()` function call. In this example, `$font` is in the second parameter, meaning that the font and font size of the included font package are used in this instance of the function. The starting X and Y positions are hard-coded as "0" in the third and fourth parameters, and the string to be drawn—CAPTCHA!—is also hard-coded. The color in which to draw this string is `$black`, the value in the final parameter.

Lines 16–17 output the stream of image data to the web browser by first sending the appropriate `header()` function and then using `ImagePng()` to output the data stream; this example outputs a PNG file. Line 20 uses the `ImageDestroy()` function to clear up the memory used by the `ImageCreate()` function at the beginning of the script.

If you stopped at this point, sent the script to your web server and simply loaded it in your browser window, it would display the word "CAPTCHA!" in a custom font. But the purpose of this section is to show how to load this image with the `img` tag, and to do that you need a little HTML file. Listing 14.9 contains an `img` tag which does just that.

LISTING 14.9   Creating an Image with Custom Font and Text

```
1: <html>
2: <head>
3: <title>Using Images Created by Scripts</title>
4: </head>
5: </body>
6: <h1>Generated Image Below...</h1>
7: <img src="imagecustomfont.php"/>
8: </body>
9: </html>
```

This little HTML file contains one line of interest: line 7. In line 7, you can see that the value of the `src` attribute of the `img` tag is the name of the script created in Listing 14.8: `imagecustomfont.php`. Name the HTML file something like `useimage.html`, and send both the HTML and the PHP script to your web server.

Open `useimage.html` in your web browser and you will see something like Figure 14.10—namely, the word "CAPTCHA!" in a custom font, which is actually displayed in a graphic.

FIGURE 14.10
Using images created by scripts.

If you were really using this script as part of a CAPTCHA system, you would make at least two additions to it: randomize the string instead of hard-coding it, and saving the randomized string in a database table so that the input matching process can occur.

Summary

This chapter provided a brief introduction to what you can do with images and PHP. The "Image Functions" section of the PHP manual, at http://www.php.net/image, is highly recommended not only for a complete list of image-related functions but also for examples and discussion about their use in your applications.

In this chapter, you learned about installing and using additional libraries for working with images—the examples used PNGs, but you were given instructions for using GIFs and JPGs as well. You learned the basic steps for creating an image canvas and allocating color, and for drawing and filling shapes. You learned that your drawing canvas can consist of an existing image and that you can merge layers so that a final image is a composite of the merged layers. Additionally, you saw how simple it is to use input from users (in this case, from an HTML form) in your image creation scripts, and how to use scripts as image sources in HTML code.

Q&A

Q. *How do I use dynamic data to create the slices of a pie chart?*

A. When creating any image, the start points and drawing lengths do not need to be statically indicated—they can be variables whose values are determined by a database, user input, or calculations within the script. For example, this code creates a red, filled arc of 90°:

```
ImageFilledArc($myImage,50,50,100,50,0,90,$red,IMG_ARC_PIE);
```

You could set this up so that the red-filled arc at the top of the pie holds the percentage of the total for May Sales in a variable called $may_sales_pct. The line then becomes something like this:

```
ImageFilledArc($myImage,50,50,100,50,0,$may_sales_pct,$red,IMG_ARC_PIE);
```

The number then is filled in from the calculations or database queries in your script. Be sure to add code to verify that all your arcs add up to 360.

Workshop

The workshop is designed to help you anticipate possible questions, review what you've learned, and begin putting your knowledge into practice.

Quiz

1. What RGB values would you use for pure black and pure white?

2. How do you create a new, blank canvas that is 300 pixels wide and 200 pixels tall?

3. What function is used to draw a polygon? A filled polygon?

Answers

1. (0,0,0) is pure black, and (255,255,255) is pure white.

2. `$new_image = ImageCreate(300,200);`

3. `ImagePolygon()` and `ImageFilledPolygon()`

Activity

Instead of creating a pie chart, use your drawing skills to create a bar chart with either vertical or horizontal bars, each 30 pixels wide and filled with the same color, but of different lengths. Make sure that there are 10 pixels of space between each bar.

PART IV

PHP and MySQL Integration

15

Understanding the Database Design Process

In this chapter, you'll learn the thought processes behind designing a relational database. After this theory-focused chapter, you'll jump headlong into learning the basic MySQL commands in preparation for integrating MySQL in your own applications.

Topics covered in this chapter are

- ▶ Some advantages to good database design

- ▶ Three types of table relationships

- ▶ How to normalize your database

- ▶ How to implement a good database design process

The Importance of Good Database Design

A good database design is crucial for a high-performance application, just as an aerodynamic body is important to a race car. If the car doesn't have smooth lines, it will produce drag and go slower. Without optimized relationships, your database won't perform as efficiently as possible. Thinking about relationships and database efficiency is part of *normalization*.

Beyond the issue of performance is the issue of maintenance—your database should be easy to maintain. This includes storing only a limited amount (if any) of repetitive data. If you have a lot of repetitive data and one instance of that data undergoes a change (such as a name change), that change has to be made for all occurrences of the data. To eliminate duplication and enhance your ability to maintain the data, you might create a table of possible values and use a key to refer to the value. That way, if the value changes names, the change occurs only once—in the master table. The reference remains the same throughout other tables.

By the Way

Normalization refers to the process of structuring data in order to minimize duplication and inconsistencies.

For example, suppose that you are responsible for maintaining a database of students and the classes in which they're enrolled. If 35 of these students are in the same class, let's call it *Advanced Math*, this class name would appear 35 times in the table. Now, if the instructor decides to change the name of the class to *Mathematics IV*, you must change 35 records to reflect the new name of the class. If the database were designed so that class names appeared in one table and just the class ID number was stored with the student record, you would have to change only 1 record—not 35—to update the name change.

The benefits of a well-planned and designed database are numerous, and it stands to reason that the more work you do up front, the less you'll have to do later. A really bad time for a database redesign is after the public launch of the application using it—although it does happen, and the results are costly.

So, before you even start coding an application, spend a lot of time designing your database. Throughout the rest of this chapter, you'll learn more about relationships and normalization, two important pieces to the design puzzle.

Types of Table Relationships

Table relationships come in several forms:

- ▶ One-to-one relationships
- ▶ One-to-many relationships
- ▶ Many-to-many relationships

For example, suppose that you have a table called `employees` that contains each person's Social Security number, name, and the department in which he or she works. Suppose that you also have a separate table called `departments`, containing the list of all available departments, made up of a Department ID and a name. In the `employees` table, the Department ID field matches an ID found in the `departments` table. You can see this type of relationship in Figure 15.1. The PK next to the field name indicates the primary key for the table.

In the following sections, you will take a closer look at each of the relationship types.

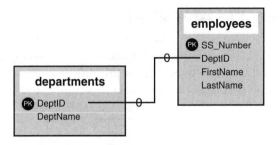

FIGURE 15.1
The employees and depart-ments tables are related through the DeptID key.

One-to-One Relationships

In a one-to-one relationship, a key appears only once in a related table. The employees and departments tables do not have a one-to-one relationship because many employees undoubtedly belong to the same department. A one-to-one relationship exists, for example, if each employee is assigned one computer within a company. Figure 15.2 shows the one-to-one relationship of employees to computers.

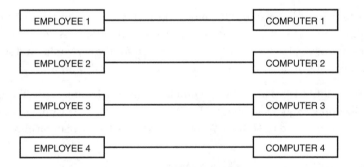

FIGURE 15.2
One computer is assigned to each employee.

The employees and computers tables in your database would look something like Figure 15.3, which represents a one-to-one relationship.

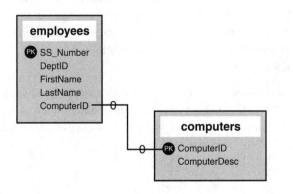

FIGURE 15.3
One-to-one rela-tionship in the data model.

One-to-Many Relationships

In a one-to-many relationship, keys from one table appear multiple times in a related table. The example shown in Figure 15.1, indicating a connection between employees and departments, illustrates a one-to-many relationship. A real-world example would be an organizational chart of the department, as shown in Figure 15.4.

FIGURE 15.4
One department
contains many
employees.

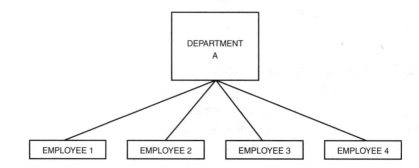

The one-to-many relationship is the most common type of relationship. Another practical example is the use of a state abbreviation in an address database; each state has a unique identifier (CA for California, PA for Pennsylvania, and so on), and each address in the United States has a state associated with it.

If you have eight friends in California and five in Pennsylvania, you will use only two distinct abbreviations in your table. One abbreviation (CA) represents a one-to-eight relationship, and the other (PA) represents a one-to-five relationship.

Many-to-Many Relationships

The many-to-many relationship often causes problems in practical examples of normalized databases, so much so that it is common to simply break many-to-many relationships into a series of one-to-many relationships. In a many-to-many relationship, the key value of one table can appear many times in a related table. So far, it sounds like a one-to-many relationship, but here's the curveball: The opposite is also true, meaning that the primary key from that second table can also appear many times in the first table.

Think of such a relationship this way, using the example of students and classes: A student has an ID and a name. A class has an ID and a name. A student usually takes more than one class at a time, and a class always contains more than one student, as you can see in Figure 15.5.

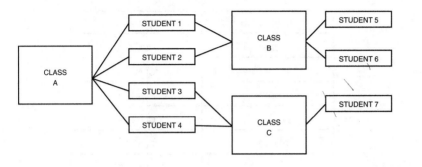

FIGURE 15.5
Students take
classes, and
classes contain
students.

As you can see, this sort of relationship doesn't present an easy method for relating tables. Your tables could look like Figure 15.6, seemingly unrelated.

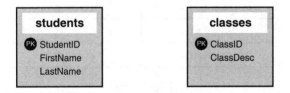

FIGURE 15.6
The students
table and the
classes table,
unrelated.

To make the theoretical many-to-many relationship, you would create an intermediate table, one that sits between the two tables and essentially maps them together. You might build such a table similar to the one in Figure 15.7.

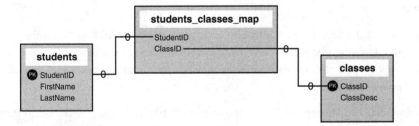

FIGURE 15.7
The students_
classes_map
table acts as an
intermediary.

If you take the information in Figure 15.5 and put it into the intermediate table, you would have something like Figure 15.8.

As you can see, many students and many classes happily coexist within the students_classes_map table.

With this introduction to the types of relationships, learning about normalization should be a snap.

FIGURE 15.8
The students_
classes_map
table populated
with data.

STUDENTID	CLASSID
STUDENT 1	CLASS A
STUDENT 2	CLASS A
STUDENT 3	CLASS A
STUDENT 4	CLASS A
STUDENT 5	CLASS B
STUDENT 6	CLASS B
STUDENT 7	CLASS C
STUDENT 1	CLASS B
STUDENT 2	CLASS B
STUDENT 3	CLASS C
STUDENT 4	CLASS C

Understanding Normalization

Normalization is simply a set of rules that will ultimately make your life easier when you're acting as a database administrator. It's the art of organizing your database in such a way that your tables relate where appropriate and are flexible for future growth.

The sets of rules used in normalization are called *normal forms*. If your database design follows the first set of rules, it's considered in the *first normal form*. If the first three sets of rules of normalization are followed, your database is said to be in the *third normal form*.

Throughout this chapter, you'll learn about each rule in the first, second, and third normal forms and, I hope, will follow them as you create your own applications. You'll be using a sample set of tables for a students-and-courses database and taking it to the third normal form.

Problems with the Flat Table

Before launching into the first normal form, you have to start with something that needs to be fixed. In the case of a database, it's the *flat table*. A flat table is like a spreadsheet—it has many, many columns. There are no relationships between multiple tables; all the data you could possibly want is right there in that flat table. This scenario is inefficient and consumes more physical space on your hard drive than a normalized database.

In your students-and-courses database, assume that you have the following fields in your flat table:

- ▶ **StudentName**—The name of the student.
- ▶ **CourseID1**—The ID of the first course taken by the student.
- ▶ **CourseDescription1**—The description of the first course taken by the student.
- ▶ **CourseInstructor1**—The instructor of the first course taken by the student.
- ▶ **CourseID2**—The ID of the second course taken by the student.
- ▶ **CourseDescription2**—The description of the second course taken by the student.
- ▶ **CourseInstructor2**—The instructor of the second course taken by the student.
- ▶ Repeat `CourseID`, `CourseDescription`, and `CourseInstructor` columns many more times to account for all the classes students can take during their academic career.

With what you've learned so far, you should be able to identify the first problem area: `CourseID`, `CourseDescription`, and `CourseInstructor` columns are repeated groups.

Eliminating redundancy is the first step in normalization, so next you'll take this flat table to first normal form. If your table remained in its flat format, you could have a lot of unclaimed space and a lot of space being used unnecessarily—not an efficient table design.

First Normal Form

The rules for the first normal form are as follows:

- ▶ Eliminate repeating information.
- ▶ Create separate tables for related data.

If you think about the flat table design with many repeated sets of fields for the students-and-courses database, you can identify two distinct topics: students and courses. Taking your students-and-courses database to the first normal form would mean that you create two tables: one for students and one for courses, as shown in Figure 15.9.

FIGURE 15.9
Breaking the
flat table into
two tables.

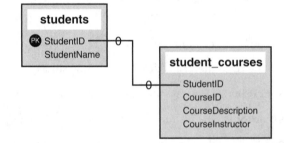

Your two tables now represent a one-to-many relationship of one student to many courses. Students can take as many courses as they want and are not limited to the number of `CourseID`/`CourseDescription`/`CourseInstructor` groupings that existed in the flat table.

The next step is to put the tables into second normal form.

Second Normal Form

The rule for the second normal form is as follows:

▶ No non-key attributes depend on a portion of the primary key.

In plain English, this means that if fields in your table are not entirely related to a primary key, you have more work to do. In the students-and-courses example, you need to break out the courses into their own table and modify the `students_cours-es` table.

`CourseID`, `CourseDescription`, and `CourseInstructor` can become a table called `courses` with a primary key of `CourseID`. The `students_courses` table should then just contain two fields: `StudentID` and `CourseID`. You can see this new design in Figure 15.10.

FIGURE 15.10
Taking your
tables to sec-
ond normal
form.

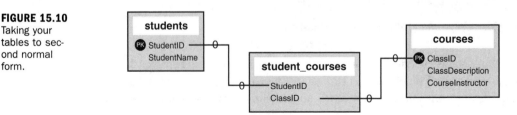

This structure should look familiar to you as a many-to-many relationship using an intermediary mapping table. The third normal form is the last form you'll look at, and you'll find it's just as simple to understand as the first two.

Third Normal Form

The rule for the third normal form is as follows:

▶ No attributes depend on other non-key attributes.

This rule simply means that you need to look at your tables and see whether you have more fields that can be broken down further and that aren't dependent on a key. Think about removing repeated data and you'll find your answer: instructors. Inevitably, an instructor will teach more than one class. However, CourseInstructor is not a key of any sort. So, if you break out this information and create a separate table purely for the sake of efficiency and maintenance (as shown in Figure 15.11), that's the third normal form.

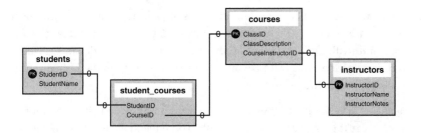

FIGURE 15.11
Taking your tables to third normal form.

Third normal form is usually adequate for removing redundancy and allowing for flexibility and growth. The next section will give you some pointers for the thought process involved in database design and where it fits in the overall design process of your application.

Following the Design Process

The greatest problem in application design is a lack of forethought. As it applies to database-driven applications, the design process must include a thorough evaluation of your database—what it should hold, how data relates to each other, and most importantly, whether it is scalable.

The general steps in the design process are as follows:

▶ Define the objective

▶ Design the data structures (tables, fields)

▶ Discern relationships

▶ Define and implement business rules

▶ Create the application

Creating the application is the last step—not the first! Many developers take an idea for an application, build it, and then go back and try to make a set of database tables fit into it. This approach is completely backward, inefficient, and will cost a lot of time and money.

Before you start any application design process, sit down and talk it out. If you can't describe your application—including the objectives, audience, and target market— you're not ready to build it, let alone model the database.

After you can describe the actions and nuances of your application to other people and have it make sense to them, you can start thinking about the tables you want to create. Start with big flat tables because after you write them down, your new-found normalization skills will take over. You will be able to find your redundancies and visualize your relationships.

The next step is to do the normalization. Go from flat table to first normal form and so on up to the third normal form if possible. Use paper, pencils, sticky notes, or whatever helps you to visualize the tables and relationships. There's no shame in data modeling on sticky notes until you're ready to create the tables themselves. Plus, using sticky notes is a lot cheaper than buying software to do it for you; modeling software ranges from one hundred to several thousands of dollars!

After you have a preliminary data model, look at it from the application's point of view. Or look at it from the point of view of the person using the application you're building. This is the point where you define business rules and see whether your data model will break. An example of a business rule for an online registration application is, "Each user must have one email address, and it must not belong to any other user." If `EmailAddress` wasn't a unique field in your data model, your model would be broken based on the business rule.

After your business rules have been applied to your data model, only then can application programming begin. You can rest assured that your data model is solid and you will not be programming yourself into a brick wall. The latter event is all too common.

Summary

Following proper database design is the only way your application will be efficient, flexible, and easy to manage and maintain. An important aspect of database design is to use relationships between tables instead of throwing all your data into one long flat file. Types of relationships include one-to-one, one-to-many, and many-to-many.

Using relationships to properly organize your data is called *normalization*. There are many levels of normalization, but the primary levels are the first, second, and third normal forms. Each level has a rule or two that you must follow. Following all the rules helps ensure that your database is well organized and flexible.

To take an idea from inception through to fruition, you should follow a design process. This process essentially says, "Think before you act." Discuss rules, requirements, and objectives; then create the final version of your normalized tables.

Q&A

Q. *Are there only three normal forms?*

A. No, there are more than three normal forms. Additional forms are the Boyce-Codd normal form, fourth normal form, and fifth normal form/Join-Projection normal form. These forms are not often followed because the benefits of doing so are outweighed by the cost in man-hours and database efficiency.

Workshop

The workshop is designed to help you anticipate possible questions, review what you've learned, and begin putting your knowledge into practice.

Quiz

1. Name three types of data relationships.

2. Because many-to-many relationships are difficult to represent in an efficient database design, what should you do?

Quiz Answers

1. One-to-one, one-to-many, many-to-many.

2. Create a series of one-to-many relationships using intermediary mapping tables.

Activity

Explain each of the three normal forms to a person who works with spreadsheets and flat tables.

16

Learning Basic SQL Commands

The previous chapter explained the basics of the database design process and this chapter provides a primer on the core SQL syntax, which you will use to create and manipulate your MySQL database tables. This is a hands-on chapter, and it assumes that you are able to issue queries through the MySQL monitor on Windows or Linux/UNIX. Alternatively, if you use a GUI to MySQL, this chapter assumes you know the methods for issuing queries through those interfaces. Please note, this may not be the most exciting chapter in the book, but it will show you many functional examples of elements you'll use throughout the rest of your work.

In this chapter, you will learn

- The basic MySQL data types

- How to use the CREATE TABLE command to create a table

- How to use the INSERT command to enter records

- How to use the SELECT command to retrieve records

- How to use basic functions, the WHERE clause, and the GROUP BY clause in SELECT expressions

- How to select from multiple tables, using JOIN or subselects

- How to use the UPDATE and REPLACE commands to modify existing records

- How to use the DELETE command to remove records

- How to use string functions built into MySQL

- How to use date and time functions built into MySQL

Learning the MySQL Data Types

Properly defining the fields in a table is important to the overall optimization of your database. You should use only the type and size of field you really need to use; don't define a field as 10 characters wide if you know you're only going to use 2 characters—that's 8 extra characters the database has to account for, even if they're unused. These field types are also referred to as *data types*, as in the "type of data" you will be storing in those fields.

MySQL uses many different data types, broken into three categories: numeric, date and time, and string types. Pay close attention because properly defining the data type is more important than any other part of the table-creation process.

Numeric Data Types

MySQL uses all the standard ANSI SQL numeric data types, so if you're coming to MySQL from a different database system, these definitions will look familiar to you. The following list shows the common numeric data types and their descriptions:

By the Way

> The terms *signed* and *unsigned* will be used in the list of numeric data types. If you remember your basic algebra, you'll recall that a signed integer can be a positive or negative integer, whereas an unsigned integer is always a non-negative integer.

- ▶ **INT**—A normal-sized integer that can be signed or unsigned. If signed, the allowable range is from –2147483648 to 2147483647. If unsigned, the allowable range is from 0 to 4294967295. You can specify a width of up to 11 digits.

- ▶ **TINYINT**—A small integer that can be signed or unsigned. If signed, the allowable range is from –128 to 127. If unsigned, the allowable range is from 0 to 255. You can specify a width of up to 4 digits.

- ▶ **SMALLINT**—A small integer that can be signed or unsigned. If signed, the allowable range is from –32768 to 32767. If unsigned, the allowable range is from 0 to 65535. You can specify a width of up to 5 digits.

- ▶ **MEDIUMINT**—A medium-sized integer that can be signed or unsigned. If signed, the allowable range is from –8388608 to 8388607. If unsigned, the allowable range is from 0 to 16777215. You can specify a width of up to 9 digits.

- ▶ **BIGINT**—A large integer that can be signed or unsigned. If signed, the allowable range is from –9223372036854775808 to 9223372036854775807. If unsigned, the allowable range is from 0 to 18446744073709551615. You can specify a width of up to 11 digits.

▶ **FLOAT(M,D)**—A floating-point number that cannot be unsigned. You can define the display length (M) and the number of decimals (D). This is not required and will default to 10,2, where 2 is the number of decimals and 10 is the total number of digits (including decimals). Decimal precision can go to 24 places for a FLOAT.

▶ **DOUBLE(M,D)**—A double-precision floating-point number that cannot be unsigned. You can define the display length (M) and the number of decimals (D). This is not required and will default to 16,4, where 4 is the number of decimals. Decimal precision can go to 53 places for a DOUBLE. REAL is a synonym for DOUBLE.

▶ **DECIMAL(M,D)**—An unpacked floating-point number that cannot be unsigned. In unpacked decimals, each decimal corresponds to one byte. Defining the display length (M) and the number of decimals (D) is required. NUMERIC is a synonym for DECIMAL.

Of all the MySQL numeric data types, you will likely use INT most often. You can run into problems if you define your fields to be smaller than you actually need; for example, if you define an ID field as an unsigned TINYINT, you won't be able to successfully insert that 256th record if ID is a primary key (and thus required).

Date and Time Types

MySQL has several data types available for storing dates and times, and these data types are flexible in their input. In other words, you can enter dates that are not really days, such as February 30—February has only 28 or 29 days, never 30. Also, you can store dates with missing information. For example, if you know that someone was born sometime in November 1980, you can use 1980-11-00, where "00" would have been for the day, if you knew it.

The flexibility of MySQL's date and time types also means that the responsibility for date checking falls on the application developer (that would be you). MySQL checks only two elements for validity: that the month is between 0 and 12 and that the day is between 0 and 31. MySQL does not automatically verify that the thirtieth day of the second month (February 30) is a valid date. Thus, any date validation you want to include in your application should happen in your PHP code before you even attempt to add a record with a bogus date into your database table.

The MySQL date and time data types are

▶ **DATE**—A date in YYYY-MM-DD format, between 1000-01-01 and 9999-12-31. For example, December 30th, 1973, would be stored as 1973-12-30.

▶ **DATETIME**—A date and time combination in YYYY-MM-DD HH:MM:SS format, between 1000-01-01 00:00:00 and 9999-12-31 23:59:59. For example, 3:30 in the afternoon on December 30th, 1973, would be stored as 1973-12-30 15:30:00.

▶ **TIMESTAMP**—A time stamp between midnight, January 1, 1970, and sometime in 2037. You can define multiple lengths to the TIMESTAMP field, which directly correlates to what is stored in it. The default length for TIMESTAMP is 14, which stores YYYYMMDDHHMMSS. This looks like the previous DATETIME format, only without the hyphens between numbers; 3:30 in the afternoon on December 30th, 1973, would be stored as 19731230153000. Other definitions of TIMESTAMP are 12 (YYMMDDHHMMSS), 8 (YYYYMMDD), and 6 (YYMMDD).

▶ **TIME**—Stores the time in HH:MM:SS format.

▶ **YEAR(M)**—Stores a year in 2-digit or 4-digit format. If the length is specified as 2 (for example, YEAR(2)), YEAR can be 1970 to 2069 (70 to 69). If the length is specified as 4, YEAR can be 1901 to 2155. The default length is 4.

You will likely use DATETIME or DATE more often than any other date- or time-related data type.

String Types

Although numeric and date types are fun, most data you'll store will be in string format. This list describes the common string data types in MySQL:

▶ **CHAR(M)**—A fixed-length string between 1 and 255 characters in length (for example, CHAR(5)), right-padded with spaces to the specified length when stored. Defining a length is not required, but the default is 1.

▶ **VARCHAR(M)**—A variable-length string between 1 and 255 characters in length; for example, VARCHAR(25). You must define a length when creating a VARCHAR field.

▶ **BLOB** or **TEXT**—A field with a maximum length of 65,535 characters. BLOBs are "Binary Large Objects" and are used to store large amounts of binary data, such as images or other types of files. Fields defined as TEXT also hold large amounts of data; the difference between the two is that sorts and comparisons on stored data are case sensitive on BLOBs and are not case sensitive in TEXT fields. You do not specify a length with BLOB or TEXT.

▶ **TINYBLOB** or **TINYTEXT**—A BLOB or TEXT column with a maximum length of 255 characters. You do not specify a length with TINYBLOB or TINYTEXT.

▶ **MEDIUMBLOB** or **MEDIUMTEXT**—A BLOB or TEXT column with a maximum length of 16,777,215 characters. You do not specify a length with MEDIUMBLOB or MEDIUMTEXT.

▶ **LONGBLOB** or **LONGTEXT**—A BLOB or TEXT column with a maximum length of 4,294,967,295 characters. You do not specify a length with LONGBLOB or LONGTEXT.

▶ **ENUM**—An enumeration, which is a fancy term for *list*. When defining an ENUM, you are creating a list of items from which the value must be selected (or it can be NULL). For example, if you wanted your field to contain "A" or "B" or "C", you would define your ENUM as ENUM ('A', 'B', 'C'), and only those values (or NULL) could ever populate that field. ENUMs can have 65,535 different values. ENUMs use an index for storing items.

> The SET type is similar to ENUM in that it is defined as a list. However, the SET type is stored as a full value rather than an index of a value, as with ENUMs.

By the Way

You will probably use VARCHAR and TEXT fields more often than other field types, and ENUMs are useful as well.

Learning the Table Creation Syntax

The table creation command requires

▶ Name of the table

▶ Names of fields

▶ Definitions for each field

The generic table creation syntax is

```
CREATE TABLE table_name (column_name column_type);
```

The table name is up to you of course, but should be a name that reflects the usage of the table. For example, if you have a table that holds the inventory of a grocery

store, you wouldn't name the table s. You would probably name it something like
grocery_inventory. Similarly, the field names you select should be as concise as
possible and relevant to the function they serve and the data they hold. For example, you might call a field holding the name of an item item_name, not n.

The following table creation example creates a generic grocery_inventory table
with fields for ID, item name, item description, item price, and quantity. Each of the
fields are a different type; the ID and quantity fields will hold integers, the item
name field will hold up to 50 characters, the item description field will hold up to
65,535 characters of text, and the item price field will contain a float:

```
mysql> CREATE TABLE grocery_inventory (
    -> id INT NOT NULL PRIMARY KEY AUTO_INCREMENT,
    -> item_name VARCHAR (50) NOT NULL,
    -> item_desc TEXT,
    -> item_price FLOAT NOT NULL,
    -> curr_qty INT NOT NULL
    -> );
Query OK, 0 rows affected (0.02 sec)
```

By the Way

> The id field is defined as a *primary key*. You will learn more about keys in later
> chapters, in the context of creating specific tables as parts of sample applica-
> tions. Additionally, by using auto_increment as an attribute of the field in the
> example here, you are telling MySQL to go ahead and add the next available num-
> ber to the id field for you when a record is inserted.

The MySQL server responds with Query OK each time a command, regardless of
type, is successful. Otherwise, an error message displays, telling you where your
query went awry.

Using the INSERT Command

After you have created some tables, you'll use the SQL command INSERT for adding
new records to these tables. The basic syntax of INSERT is

```
INSERT INTO table_name (column list) VALUES (column values);
```

Within the parenthetical list of values, you must enclose strings within quotation
marks. The SQL standard is single quotes, but MySQL enables the usage of either
single or double quotes. Remember to escape the type of quotation mark used, if it's
within the string itself.

By the Way

Integers do not require quotation marks around them.

Here is an example of a string where escaping is necessary:

```
O'Connor said "Boo"
```

If you enclose your strings in double quotes, the `INSERT` statement would look like this:

```
INSERT INTO table_name (column_name) VALUES ("O'Connor said \"Boo\"");
```

If you enclose your strings in single quotes instead, the `INSERT` statement would look like this:

```
INSERT INTO table_name (column_name) VALUES ('O\'Connor said "Boo"');
```

A Closer Look at `INSERT`

Besides the table name, there are two main parts of the `INSERT` statement: the column list and the value list. Only the value list is actually required, but if you omit the column list, you must specifically provide for each column in your value list—in the exact order.

Using the `grocery_inventory` table as an example, you have five fields: id, item_name, item_desc, item_price, and curr_qty. To insert a complete record, you could use either of these statements:

▶ A statement with all columns named:

```
INSERT INTO grocery_inventory
(id, item_name, item_desc, item_price, curr_qty)
VALUES ('1', 'Apples', 'Ripe apples.', '0.25', 1000);
```

▶ A statement that uses all columns but does not explicitly name them:

```
INSERT INTO grocery_inventory VALUES ('2', 'Bunches of Grapes',
'Seedless grapes.', '2.99', 500);
```

Give both of them a try and see what happens. You should get a "Query OK" result for both commands.

Now for some more interesting methods of using INSERT. Because id is an auto-incrementing integer in the `grocery_inventory` table, you don't have to put it in your value list. However, if there's a value you specifically *don't* want to list (such as id), you then must list the remaining columns in use. For example, the following statement does not list the columns, does not give a value for id, and it produces an error:

```
mysql> INSERT INTO grocery_inventory VALUES
    -> ('Bottled Water (6-pack)', '500ml spring water.', 2.29, 250);
ERROR 1136: Column count doesn't match value count at row 1
```

Because you didn't list any columns, MySQL expects all of them to be in the value list, causing an error on the previous statement. If the goal was to let MySQL do the work for you by auto-incrementing the id field, you could use either of these statements:

- ▶ A statement with all columns named except id:

  ```
  INSERT INTO grocery_inventory (item_name, item_desc, item_price, curr_qty)
  VALUES ('Bottled Water (6-pack)', '500ml spring water.', '2.29', 250);
  ```

- ▶ A statement that uses all columns, but does not explicitly name them *and* indicates a NULL entry for id (so one is filled in for you):

  ```
  INSERT INTO grocery_inventory VALUES ('NULL', 'Bottled Water (12-pack)',
  '500ml spring water.', 4.49, 500);
  ```

Go ahead and try both so that your grocery_inventory table has four records in total. It makes no difference to MySQL which one you use, but as with everything based on your own preferences, be consistent in your application development. Consistent structures will be easier for you to debug later, because you'll know what to expect.

Using the SELECT Command

SELECT is the SQL command used to retrieve records from your tables. This command syntax can be totally simplistic or very complicated, depending on which fields you want to select, whether you want to select from multiple tables, and what conditions you plan to impose. As you become more comfortable with database programming, you will learn to enhance your SELECT statements, ultimately making your database do as much work as possible and not overworking your programming language.

The most basic SELECT syntax looks like this:

```
SELECT expressions_and_columns FROM table_name
[WHERE some_condition_is_true]
[ORDER BY some_column [ASC ¦ DESC]]
[LIMIT offset, rows]
```

Look at the first line:

```
SELECT expressions_and_columns FROM table_name
```

One handy expression is the * symbol, which stands for *everything*. So, to select everything (all rows, all columns) from the grocery_inventory table, your SQL statement would be

```
SELECT * FROM grocery_inventory;
```

Depending on how much data is in the grocery_inventory table, your results will vary, but the results might look something like this:

```
mysql> SELECT * FROM grocery_inventory;
+----+-----------------------+---------------------+------------+----------+
| id | item_name             | item_desc           | item_price | curr_qty |
+----+-----------------------+---------------------+------------+----------+
| 1  | Apples                | Ripe apples.        | 0.25       | 1000     |
| 2  | Bunches of Grapes     | Seedless grapes.    | 2.99       | 500      |
| 3  | Bottled Water (6-pack)| 500ml spring water. | 2.29       | 250      |
| 4  | Bottled Water (12-pack)| 500ml spring water.| 4.49       | 500      |
+----+-----------------------+---------------------+------------+----------+
4 rows in set (0.00 sec)
```

As you can see, MySQL creates a lovely, formatted table with the names of the columns along the first row as part of the resultset. If you only want to select specific columns, replace the * with the names of the columns, separated by commas. The following statement selects just the id, item_name, and curr_qty fields from the grocery_inventory table:

```
mysql> SELECT id, item_name, curr_qty FROM grocery_inventory;
+----+-----------------------+----------+
| id | item_name             | curr_qty |
+----+-----------------------+----------+
| 1  | Apples                | 1000     |
| 2  | Bunches of Grapes     | 500      |
| 3  | Bottled Water (6-pack)| 250      |
| 4  | Bottled Water (12-pack)| 500     |
+----+-----------------------+----------+
4 rows in set (0.00 sec)
```

Ordering SELECT Results

Results of SELECT queries are ordered as they were inserted into the table and shouldn't be relied on as a meaningful ordering system. If you want to order results a specific way, such as by date, ID, name, and so on, specify your requirements using the ORDER BY clause. In the following statement, results are ordered alphanumerically by item_name:

```
mysql> SELECT id, item_name, curr_qty FROM grocery_inventory
    -> ORDER BY item_name;
+----+-------------------------+----------+
| id | item_name               | curr_qty |
+----+-------------------------+----------+
| 1  | Apples                  | 1000     |
| 4  | Bottled Water (12-pack) | 500      |
| 3  | Bottled Water (6-pack)  | 250      |
| 2  | Bunches of Grapes        | 500      |
+----+-------------------------+----------+
4 rows in set (0.03 sec)
```

When selecting results from a table without specifying a sort order, the results may or may not be ordered by their key value. This occurs because MySQL reuses the space taken up by previously deleted rows. In other words, if you add records with ID values of 1 through 5, delete the record with ID number 4, and then add another record (ID number 6), the records might appear in the table in this order: 1, 2, 3, 6, 5.

The default sorting of ORDER BY results ascending (ASC); strings sort from A to Z, integers start at 0, dates sort from oldest to newest. You can also specify a descending sort, using DESC:

```
mysql> SELECT id, item_name, curr_qty FROM grocery_inventory
    -> ORDER BY item_name DESC;
+----+-------------------------+----------+
| id | item_name               | curr_qty |
+----+-------------------------+----------+
| 2  | Bunches of Grapes        | 500      |
| 3  | Bottled Water (6-pack)  | 250      |
| 4  | Bottled Water (12-pack) | 500      |
| 1  | Apples                  | 1000     |
+----+-------------------------+----------+
4 rows in set (0.00 sec)
```

You're not limited to sorting by just one field—you can specify as many fields as you want as long as they are separated by commas. The sorting priority is the order in which you list the fields.

Limiting Your Results

You can use the LIMIT clause to return only a certain number of records from your SELECT query result. There are two requirements when using the LIMIT clause: the offset and the number of rows. The offset is the starting position, and the number of rows should be self-explanatory.

Suppose that you had more than two or three records in the grocery_inventory table, and you wanted to select the ID, name, and quantity of the first two, ordered by curr_qty. In other words, you want to select the two items with the least inventory. The following single-parameter limit will start at the 0 position and go to the second record:

```
mysql> SELECT id, item_name, curr_qty FROM grocery_inventory
    -> ORDER BY curr_qty LIMIT 2;
+----+-----------------------+----------+
| id | item_name             | curr_qty |
+----+-----------------------+----------+
| 3  | Bottled Water (6-pack)| 250      |
| 2  | Bunches of Grapes     | 500      |
+----+-----------------------+----------+
2 rows in set (0.00 sec)
```

The LIMIT clause can be useful in an actual application. For example, you can use the LIMIT clause within a series of SELECT statements to travel through results in steps (first two items, next two items, next two items after that):

1. `SELECT * FROM grocery_inventory ORDER BY curr_qty LIMIT 0, 2;`

2. `SELECT * FROM grocery_inventory ORDER BY curr_qty LIMIT 2, 2;`

3. `SELECT * FROM grocery_inventory ORDER BY curr_qty LIMIT 4, 2;`

If you specify an offset and number of rows in your query, and no results are found, you won't see an error—just an empty resultset. For example, if the grocery_inventory table contains only six records, a query with a LIMIT offset of 6 will produce no results:

```
mysql> SELECT id, item_name, curr_qty FROM grocery_inventory
    -> ORDER BY curr_qty LIMIT 6, 2;
Empty set (0.00 sec)
```

In web-based applications, when you see lists of data display with links such as "previous 10" and "next 10," it's a safe bet that a LIMIT clause is at work.

Using WHERE in Your Queries

You have learned numerous ways to retrieve particular columns from your tables but not specific rows. This is when the WHERE clause comes in to play. From the example SELECT syntax, you see that WHERE is used to specify a particular condition:

```
SELECT expressions_and_columns FROM table_name
[WHERE some_condition_is_true]
```

An example would be to retrieve all the records for items with a quantity of 500:

```
mysql> SELECT * FROM grocery_inventory WHERE curr_qty = 500;
+----+----------------------+----------------------+------------+----------+
| id | item_name            | item_desc            | item_price | curr_qty |
+----+----------------------+----------------------+------------+----------+
| 2  | Bunches of Grapes    | Seedless grapes.     | 2.99       | 500      |
| 4  | Bottled Water (12-pack) | 500ml spring water. | 4.49     | 500      |
+----+----------------------+----------------------+------------+----------+
2 rows in set (0.00 sec)
```

As shown previously, if you use an integer as part of your WHERE clause, quotation marks are not required. Quotation marks are required around strings, however, and the same rules apply with regard to escaping characters as you learned in the section on INSERT.

Using Operators in WHERE Clauses

You've used the equal sign (=) in your WHERE clauses to determine the truth of a condition—that is, whether one thing is equal to another. You can use many types of operators, with comparison operators and logical operators being the most popular types. Table 16.1 lists the comparison operators and their meanings.

TABLE 16.1   Basic Comparison Operators and Their Meanings

Operator	Meaning
=	Equal to
!=	Not equal to
<=	Less than or equal to
<	Less than
>=	Greater than or equal to
>	Greater than

There's also a handy operator called BETWEEN, which is useful with integer or date comparisons because it searches for results between a minimum and maximum value. For example:

```
mysql> SELECT * FROM grocery_inventory WHERE
    -> item_price BETWEEN 1.50 AND 3.00;
+----+----------------------+----------------------+------------+----------+
| id | item_name            | item_desc            | item_price | curr_qty |
+----+----------------------+----------------------+------------+----------+
| 2  | Bunches of Grapes    | Seedless grapes.     | 2.99       | 500      |
| 3  | Bottled Water (6-pack) | 500ml spring water. | 2.29      | 250      |
+----+----------------------+----------------------+------------+----------+
2 rows in set (0.00 sec)
```

Other operators include logical operators, which enable you to use multiple comparisons within your WHERE clause. The basic logical operators are AND and OR. When using AND, all comparisons in the clause must be true to retrieve results, whereas using OR allows a minimum of one comparison to be true. Also, you can use the IN operator to specify a list of items that you want to match.

String Comparison Using LIKE

You were introduced to matching strings within a WHERE clause by using = or !=, but there's another useful operator for the WHERE clause when comparing strings: the LIKE operator. This operator uses two characters as wildcards in pattern matching:

▶ %—Matches multiple characters

▶ _—Matches exactly one character

For example, if you want to find records in the grocery_inventory table where the first name of the item starts with the letter A, you would use

```
mysql> SELECT * FROM grocery_inventory WHERE item_name LIKE 'A%';
+----+-----------+----------------+------------+----------+
| id | item_name | item_desc      | item_price | curr_qty |
+----+-----------+----------------+------------+----------+
|  1 | Apples    | Ripe apples.   |       0.25 |     1000 |
+----+-----------+----------------+------------+----------+
```

> Unless performing a LIKE comparison on a binary string, the comparison is not case sensitive. You can force a case-sensitive comparison using the BINARY keyword.

By the Way

Selecting from Multiple Tables

You're not limited to selecting only one table at a time. That would certainly make application programming a long and tedious task! When you select from more than one table in one SELECT statement, you are really joining the tables together.

Suppose that you have two tables: fruit and color. You can select all rows from each of the two tables by using two separate SELECT statements:

```
mysql> SELECT * FROM fruit;
+----+-----------+
| id | fruitname |
+----+-----------+
|  1 | apple     |
|  2 | orange    |
|  3 | grape     |
|  4 | banana    |
+----+-----------+
4 rows in set (0.00 sec)

mysql> SELECT * FROM color;
+----+-----------+
| id | colorname |
+----+-----------+
|  1 | red       |
|  2 | orange    |
|  3 | purple    |
|  4 | yellow    |
+----+-----------+
4 rows in set (0.00 sec)
```

When you want to select from both tables at once, there are a few differences in the syntax of the SELECT statement. First, you must ensure that all the tables you're using in your query appear in the FROM clause of the SELECT statement. Using the fruit and color example, if you simply want to select all columns and rows from both tables, you might think you would use the following SELECT statement:

```
mysql> SELECT * FROM fruit, color;
+----+-----------+----+-----------+
| id | fruitname | id | colorname |
+----+-----------+----+-----------+
|  1 | apple     |  1 | red       |
|  2 | orange    |  1 | red       |
|  3 | grape     |  1 | red       |
|  4 | banana    |  1 | red       |
|  1 | apple     |  2 | orange    |
|  2 | orange    |  2 | orange    |
|  3 | grape     |  2 | orange    |
|  4 | banana    |  2 | orange    |
|  1 | apple     |  3 | purple    |
|  2 | orange    |  3 | purple    |
|  3 | grape     |  3 | purple    |
|  4 | banana    |  3 | purple    |
|  1 | apple     |  4 | yellow    |
|  2 | orange    |  4 | yellow    |
|  3 | grape     |  4 | yellow    |
|  4 | banana    |  4 | yellow    |
+----+-----------+----+-----------+
16 rows in set (0.00 sec)
```

Sixteen rows of repeated information are probably not what you were looking for! What this query did is *literally* join a row in the color table to each row in the fruit table. Because there are four records in the fruit table and four entries in the color table, that's 16 records returned to you.

When you select from multiple tables, you must build proper WHERE clauses to ensure that you really get what you want. In the case of the fruit and color tables, what you really want is to see the fruitname and colorname records from these two tables where the IDs of each match up. This brings us to the next nuance of the query—how to indicate exactly which field you want when the fields are named the same in both tables.

Simply, you append the table name to the field name, like this:

```
tablename.fieldname
```

So, the query for selecting fruitname and colorname from both tables where the IDs match would be

```
mysql> SELECT fruitname, colorname FROM fruit, color WHERE fruit.id = color.id;
+-----------+-----------+
| fruitname | colorname |
+-----------+-----------+
| apple     | red       |
| orange    | orange    |
| grape     | purple    |
| banana    | yellow    |
+-----------+-----------+
4 rows in set (0.00 sec)
```

However, if you attempt to select a column that appears in both tables with the same name, you will get an ambiguity error:

```
mysql> SELECT id, fruitname, colorname FROM fruit, color
    -> WHERE fruit.id = color.id;
ERROR 1052: Column: 'id' in field list is ambiguous
```

If you mean to select the ID from the fruit table, you would use

```
mysql> SELECT fruit.id, fruitname, colorname FROM fruit,
    -> color WHERE fruit.id = color.id;
+------+-----------+-----------+
| id   | fruitname | colorname |
+------+-----------+-----------+
|    1 | apple     | red       |
|    2 | orange    | orange    |
|    3 | grape     | purple    |
|    4 | banana    | yellow    |
+------+-----------+-----------+
4 rows in set (0.00 sec)
```

This was a basic example of joining two tables together for use in a single SELECT query. The JOIN keyword is an actual part of SQL, which enables you to build more complex queries.

Using JOIN

Several types of JOINs can be used in MySQL, all of which refer to the order in which the tables are put together and the results are displayed. The type of JOIN used with the fruit and color tables is an INNER JOIN, although it wasn't written explicitly as such. To rewrite the SQL statement using the proper INNER JOIN syntax, you would use

```
mysql> SELECT fruitname, colorname FROM fruit
    -> INNER JOIN color ON fruit.id = color.id;
+-----------+-----------+
| fruitname | colorname |
+-----------+-----------+
| apple     | red       |
| orange    | orange    |
| grape     | purple    |
| banana    | yellow    |
+-----------+-----------+
4 rows in set (0.00 sec)
```

The ON clause replaces the WHERE clause you've seen before; in this instance it tells MySQL to join together the rows in the tables where the IDs match each other. When joining tables using ON clauses, you can use any conditions that you would use in a WHERE clause, including all the various logical and arithmetic operators.

Another common type of JOIN is the LEFT JOIN. When joining two tables with LEFT JOIN, all rows from the first table will be returned, no matter whether there are matches in the second table or not. Suppose that you have two tables in an address book, one called master_name, containing basic records, and one called email, containing email records. Any records in the email table would be tied to a particular ID of a record in the master_name table. For example, look at these two tables:

```
mysql> SELECT name_id, firstname, lastname FROM master_name;
+---------+-----------+----------+
| name_id | firstname | lastname |
+---------+-----------+----------+
| 1       | John      | Smith    |
| 2       | Jane      | Smith    |
| 3       | Jimbo     | Jones    |
| 4       | Andy      | Smith    |
| 5       | Chris     | Jones    |
| 6       | Anna      | Bell     |
| 7       | Jimmy     | Carr     |
| 8       | Albert    | Smith    |
| 9       | John      | Doe      |
+---------+-----------+----------+
9 rows in set (0.00 sec)
```

```
mysql> select name_id, email from email;
+---------+--------------------+
| name_id | email              |
+---------+--------------------+
| 2       | jsmith@jsmith.com  |
| 6       | annabell@aol.com   |
| 9       | jdoe@yahoo.com     |
+---------+--------------------+
3 rows in set (0.00 sec)
```

Using LEFT JOIN on these two tables, you can see that if a value from the email table doesn't exist, an empty value will appear in place of an email address:

```
mysql> SELECT firstname, lastname, email FROM master_name
    -> LEFT JOIN email ON master_name.name_id = email.name_id;
+-----------+----------+--------------------+
| firstname | lastname | email              |
+-----------+----------+--------------------+
| John      | Smith    |                    |
| Jane      | Smith    | jsmith@jsmith.com  |
| Jimbo     | Jones    |                    |
| Andy      | Smith    |                    |
| Chris     | Jones    |                    |
| Anna      | Bell     | annabell@aol.com   |
| Jimmy     | Carr     |                    |
| Albert    | Smith    |                    |
| John      | Doe      | jdoe@yahoo.com     |
+-----------+----------+--------------------+
9 rows in set (0.00 sec)
```

A RIGHT JOIN works like LEFT JOIN but with the table order reversed. In other words, when using a RIGHT JOIN, all rows from the second table will be returned, no matter whether there are matches in the first table. However, in the case of the master_name and email tables, there are only three rows in the email table, whereas there are nine rows in the master_name table. This means that only three of the nine rows will be returned:

```
mysql> SELECT firstname, lastname, email FROM master_name
    -> RIGHT JOIN email ON master_name.name_id = email.name_id;
+-----------+----------+--------------------+
| firstname | lastname | email              |
+-----------+----------+--------------------+
| Jane      | Smith    | jsmith@jsmith.com  |
| Anna      | Bell     | annabell@aol.com   |
| John      | Doe      | jdoe@yahoo.com     |
+-----------+----------+--------------------+
3 rows in set (0.00 sec)
```

Several different types of JOINs are available in MySQL, and you've learned about the most common types. To learn more about JOINs such as CROSS JOIN, STRAIGHT JOIN, and NATURAL JOIN, visit the MySQL Manual at http://dev.mysql.com/doc/refman/5.0/en/join.html.

Using Subqueries

Simply stated, a subquery is a SELECT statement that appears within another SQL statement. Such queries are useful because they often eliminate the need for bulky JOIN queries, and in the case of application programming, subqueries can eliminate the need for multiple queries within loops.

An example of the basic subquery syntax is shown here:

```
SELECT expressions_and_columns FROM table_name WHERE somecolumn = (SUBQUERY);
```

You can also use subqueries with UPDATE and DELETE statements, as shown here:

```
DELETE FROM table_name WHERE somecolumn = (SUBQUERY);
```

or

```
UPDATE table_name SET somecolumn = 'something' WHERE somecolumn = (SUBQUERY);
```

By the Way

> The outer statement of a subquery can be SELECT, INSERT, UPDATE, DELETE, SET, or DO.

The subquery must always appear in parentheses—no exceptions!

When using subqueries, the WHERE portion of the outer statement does not have to use the = comparison operator. In addition to =, you can use any of the basic comparison operators as well as keywords such as IN.

The following example uses a subquery to obtain records from users in the master_name table who have an email address in the email table:

```
mysql> SELECT firstname, lastname FROM master_name
    -> WHERE name_id IN (SELECT name_id FROM email);
+-----------+----------+
| firstname | lastname |
+-----------+----------+
| Jane      | Smith    |
| Anna      | Bell     |
| John      | Doe      |
+-----------+----------+
3 rows in set (0.00 sec)
```

For a more detailed discussion of subqueries, including limitations, see the Subqueries section of the MySQL Manual at http://dev.mysql.com/doc/refman/5.0/en/subqueries.html.

Using the UPDATE **Command to Modify Records**

UPDATE is the SQL command used to modify the contents of one or more columns in an existing record or set of records. The most basic UPDATE syntax looks like this:

```
UPDATE table_name
SET column1='new value',
column2='new value2'
[WHERE some_condition_is_true]
```

The guidelines for updating a record are similar to those used when inserting a record: The data you're entering must be appropriate to the data type of the field, and you must enclose your strings in single or double quotes, escaping where necessary.

For example, assume that you have a table called fruit containing an ID, a fruit name, and the status of the fruit (ripe or rotten):

```
mysql> SELECT * FROM fruit;
+----+------------+--------+
| id | fruit_name | status |
+----+------------+--------+
|  1 | apple      | ripe   |
|  2 | orange     | rotten |
|  3 | grape      | ripe   |
|  4 | banana     | rotten |
+----+------------+--------+
4 rows in set (0.00 sec)
```

To update the status of the fruit to ripe, use

```
mysql> UPDATE fruit SET status = 'ripe';
Query OK, 2 rows affected (0.00 sec)
Rows matched: 4  Changed: 2  Warnings: 0
```

Take a look at the result of the query. It was successful, as you can tell from the Query OK message. Also note that only two rows were affected—if you try to set the value of a column to the value it already is, the update won't occur for that column.

The second line of the response shows that four rows were matched, and only two were changed. If you're wondering what matched, the answer is simple: Because you did not specify a particular condition for matching, the match would be all rows.

You must be careful and use a condition when updating a table, unless you really intend to change all the columns for all records to the same value. For the sake of argument, assume that "grape" is spelled incorrectly in its row in the table, and you want to use UPDATE to correct this mistake. This query would have horrible results:

```
mysql> UPDATE fruit SET fruit_name = 'grape';
Query OK, 4 rows affected (0.00 sec)
Rows matched: 4  Changed: 4  Warnings: 0
```

When you read the result, you should be filled with dread: 4 of 4 records were changed, instead of only the one you intended, meaning your fruit table now looks like this:

```
mysql> SELECT * FROM fruit;
+----+------------+--------+
| id | fruit_name | status |
+----+------------+--------+
|  1 | grape      | ripe   |
|  2 | grape      | ripe   |
|  3 | grape      | ripe   |
|  4 | grape      | ripe   |
+----+------------+--------+
4 rows in set (0.00 sec)
```

All your fruit records are now grapes. While attempting to correct the spelling of one field, all fields were changed because no condition was specified! When doling out UPDATE privileges to your users, think about the responsibility you're giving to someone—one wrong move and your entire table could be grapes. In the preceding example, you could have used the id or fruit_name field in your WHERE clause, as you will see in the following section.

Conditional UPDATEs

Making a conditional UPDATE means that you are using WHERE clauses to match specific records. Using a WHERE clause in an UPDATE statement is just like using a WHERE clause in a SELECT statement. All the same comparison and logical operators can be used, such as equal to, greater than, OR, and AND.

Assume that your fruit table has not been completely filled with grapes but instead contains four records, one with a spelling mistake (grappe instead of grape). The UPDATE statement to fix the spelling mistake would be

```
mysql> UPDATE fruit SET fruit_name = 'grape' WHERE fruit_name = 'grappe';
Query OK, 1 row affected (0.00 sec)
Rows matched: 1  Changed: 1  Warnings: 0
```

In this case, only one row was matched and one row was changed. Your fruit table should be intact, and all fruit names should be spelled properly:

```
mysql> SELECT * FROM fruit;
+----+------------+--------+
| id | fruit_name | status |
+----+------------+--------+
|  1 | apple      | ripe   |
|  2 | pear       | ripe   |
|  3 | banana     | ripe   |
|  4 | grape      | ripe   |
+----+------------+--------+
4 rows in set (0.00 sec)
```

Using Existing Column Values with UPDATE

Another feature of UPDATE is the capability to use the current value in the record as the base value. For example, go back to the grocery_inventory table example:

```
mysql> SELECT * FROM grocery_inventory;
+----+------------------------+-------------------------+------------+----------+
| id | item_name              | item_desc               | item_price | curr_qty |
+----+------------------------+-------------------------+------------+----------+
| 1  | Apples                 | Ripe apples.            | 0.25       | 1000     |
| 2  | Bunches of Grapes      | Seedless grapes.        | 2.99       | 500      |
| 3  | Bottled Water (6-pack) | 500ml spring water.     | 2.29       | 250      |
| 4  | Bottled Water (12-pack)| 500ml spring water.     | 4.49       | 500      |
| 5  | Bananas                | Bunches, green.         | 1.99       | 150      |
| 6  | Pears                  | Anjou, nice and sweet.  | 0.5        | 500      |
| 7  | Avocado                | Large Haas variety.     | 0.99       | 750      |
+----+------------------------+-------------------------+------------+----------+
7 rows in set (0.00 sec)
```

When someone purchases a product, such as an apple (id = 1), the inventory table should be updated accordingly. However, you won't know exactly what number to enter in the curr_qty column, just that you sold one. In this case, use the current value of the column and subtract 1:

```
mysql> UPDATE grocery_inventory SET curr_qty = curr_qty - 1 WHERE id = 1;
Query OK, 1 row affected (0.00 sec)
Rows matched: 1  Changed: 1  Warnings: 0
```

This should give you a new value of 999 in the curr_qty column, and indeed it does:

```
mysql> SELECT * FROM grocery_inventory;
+----+------------------------+-------------------------+------------+----------+
| id | item_name              | item_desc               | item_price | curr_qty |
+----+------------------------+-------------------------+------------+----------+
| 1  | Apples                 | Ripe apples.            | 0.25       | 999      |
| 2  | Bunches of Grapes      | Seedless grapes.        | 2.99       | 500      |
| 3  | Bottled Water (6-pack) | 500ml spring water.     | 2.29       | 250      |
| 4  | Bottled Water (12-pack)| 500ml spring water.     | 4.49       | 500      |
| 5  | Bananas                | Bunches, green.         | 1.99       | 150      |
| 6  | Pears                  | Anjou, nice and sweet.  | 0.5        | 500      |
| 7  | Avocado                | Large Haas variety.     | 0.99       | 750      |
+----+------------------------+-------------------------+------------+----------+
7 rows in set (0.00 sec)
```

Using the REPLACE Command

Another method for modifying records is to use the REPLACE command, which is remarkably similar to the INSERT command.

```
REPLACE INTO table_name (column list) VALUES (column values);
```

The REPLACE statement works like this: If the record you are inserting into the table contains a primary key value that matches a record already in the table, the record in the table will be deleted and the new record inserted in its place.

By the Way

> The REPLACE command is a MySQL-specific extension to ANSI SQL. This command mimics the action of a DELETE and re-INSERT of a particular record. In other words, you get two commands for the price of one.

Using the grocery_inventory table, the following command replaces the entry for Apples:

```
mysql> REPLACE INTO grocery_inventory VALUES
    -> (1, 'Granny Smith Apples', 'Sweet!', '0.50', 1000);
Query OK, 2 rows affected (0.00 sec)
```

In the query result, notice that the result states 2 rows affected. In this case, because id is a primary key that had a matching value in the grocery_inventory table, the original row was deleted and the new row was inserted: 2 rows affected.

Select the records to verify that the entry is correct, which it is:

```
mysql> SELECT * FROM grocery_inventory;
+----+-----------------------+------------------------+------------+----------+
| id | item_name             | item_desc              | item_price | curr_qty |
+----+-----------------------+------------------------+------------+----------+
| 1  | Granny Smith Apples   | Sweet!                 | 0.50       | 1000     |
| 2  | Bunches of Grapes     | Seedless grapes.       | 2.99       | 500      |
| 3  | Bottled Water (6-pack)| 500ml spring water.    | 2.29       | 250      |
| 4  | Bottled Water (12-pack)| 500ml spring water.   | 4.49       | 500      |
| 5  | Bananas               | Bunches, green.        | 1.99       | 150      |
| 6  | Pears                 | Anjou, nice and sweet. | 0.5        | 500      |
| 7  | Avocado               | Large Haas variety.    | 0.99       | 750      |
+----+-----------------------+------------------------+------------+----------+
7 rows in set (0.00 sec)
```

If you use a REPLACE statement, and the value of the primary key in the new record does not match a value for a primary key already in the table, the record would simply be inserted, and only one row would be affected.

Using the DELETE Command

The basic DELETE syntax is

```
DELETE FROM table_name
[WHERE some_condition_is_true]
[LIMIT rows]
```

Notice there is no column specification used in the DELETE command—when you use DELETE, the entire record is removed. You might recall the fiasco earlier in this chapter, regarding grapes in the `fruit` table, when updating a table without specifying a condition caused an update of all records. You must be similarly careful when using DELETE.

Assuming the following structure and data in a table called `fruit`:

```
mysql> SELECT * FROM fruit;
+----+------------+--------+
| id | fruit_name | status |
+----+------------+--------+
|  1 | apple      | ripe   |
|  2 | pear       | rotten |
|  3 | banana     | ripe   |
|  4 | grape      | rotten |
+----+------------+--------+
4 rows in set (0.00 sec)
```

The following statement removes all records in the table:

```
mysql> DELETE FROM fruit;
Query OK, 0 rows affected (0.00 sec)
```

You can always verify the deletion by attempting to SELECT data from the table. If you issued this command after removing all the records:

```
mysql> SELECT * FROM fruit;
Empty set (0.00 sec)
```

You would see that all your fruit is gone.

Conditional DELETE

A conditional DELETE statement, just like a conditional SELECT or UPDATE statement, means you are using WHERE clauses to match specific records. You have the full range of comparison and logical operators available to you, so you can pick and choose which records you want to delete.

A prime example would be to remove all records for rotten fruit from the `fruit` table:

```
mysql> DELETE FROM fruit WHERE status = 'rotten';
Query OK, 2 rows affected (0.00 sec)
```

Two records were deleted, and only ripe fruit remains:

```
mysql> SELECT * FROM fruit;
+----+------------+--------+
| id | fruit_name | status |
+----+------------+--------+
|  1 | apple      | ripe   |
|  3 | banana     | ripe   |
+----+------------+--------+
2 rows in set (0.00 sec)
```

You can also use ORDER BY clauses in your DELETE statements; look at the basic DELETE syntax with the ORDER BY clause added to its structure:

```
DELETE FROM table_name
[WHERE some_condition_is_true]
[ORDER BY some_column [ASC | DESC]]
[LIMIT rows]
```

At first glance, you might wonder, "Why does it matter in what order I delete records?" The ORDER BY clause isn't for the deletion order; it's for the sorting order of records.

In this example, a table called access_log shows access time and username:

```
mysql> SELECT * FROM access_log;
+----+---------------------+----------+
| id | date_accessed       | username |
+----+---------------------+----------+
|  1 | 2008-01-06 06:09:13 | johndoe  |
|  2 | 2008-01-06 06:09:22 | janedoe  |
|  3 | 2008-01-06 06:09:39 | jsmith   |
|  4 | 2008-01-06 06:09:44 | mikew    |
+----+---------------------+----------+
4 rows in set (0.00 sec)
```

To remove the oldest record, first use ORDER BY to sort the results appropriately, and then use LIMIT to remove just one record:

```
mysql> DELETE FROM access_log ORDER BY date_accessed DESC LIMIT 1;
Query OK, 1 row affected (0.01 sec)
```

Select the record from access_log and verify that only three records exist:

```
mysql> SELECT * FROM access_log;
+----+---------------------+----------+
| id | date_accessed       | username |
+----+---------------------+----------+
|  2 | 2008-01-06 06:09:22 | janedoe  |
|  3 | 2008-01-06 06:09:39 | jsmith   |
|  4 | 2008-01-06 06:09:44 | mikew    |
+----+---------------------+----------+
3 rows in set (0.00 sec)
```

Frequently Used String Functions in MySQL

MySQL's built-in string-related functions can be used several ways. You can use functions in SELECT statements without specifying a table to retrieve a result of the function. Or you can use functions to enhance your SELECT results by concatenating two fields to form a new string. The following examples are by no means a complete library of MySQL string-related functions. For more, see the MySQL Manual at http://dev.mysql.com/doc/refman/5.0/en/string-functions.html.

Length and Concatenation Functions

The group of length and concatenation functions focuses on the length of strings and concatenating strings together. Length-related functions include `LENGTH()`, `OCTET_LENGTH()`, `CHAR_LENGTH()`, and `CHARACTER_LENGTH()`, which do virtually the same thing: count characters in a string.

```
mysql> SELECT LENGTH('This is cool!');
+-----------------------+
| LENGTH('This is cool!') |
+-----------------------+
|                    13 |
+-----------------------+
1 row in set (0.00 sec)
```

The fun begins with the `CONCAT()` function, which concatenates two or more strings:

```
mysql> SELECT CONCAT('My', 'S', 'QL');
+-----------------------+
| CONCAT('My', 'S', 'QL') |
+-----------------------+
| MySQL                 |
+-----------------------+
1 row in set (0.00 sec)
```

Imagine using this function with a table containing names, split into `firstname` and `lastname` fields. Instead of using two strings, use two field names to concatenate the `firstname` and the `lastname` fields. By concatenating the fields, you reduce the lines of code necessary to achieve the same result in your application:

```
mysql> SELECT CONCAT(firstname, lastname) FROM master_name;
+-----------------------------+
| CONCAT(firstname, lastname) |
+-----------------------------+
| JohnSmith                   |
| JaneSmith                   |
| JimboJones                  |
| AndySmith                   |
| ChrisJones                  |
| AnnaBell                    |
| JimmyCarr                   |
| AlbertSmith                 |
| JohnDoe                     |
+-----------------------------+
9 rows in set (0.00 sec)
```

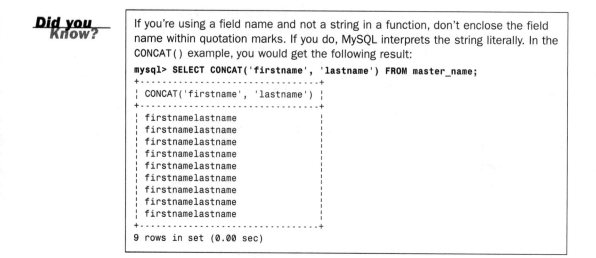

Did you Know?

If you're using a field name and not a string in a function, don't enclose the field name within quotation marks. If you do, MySQL interprets the string literally. In the CONCAT() example, you would get the following result:

```
mysql> SELECT CONCAT('firstname', 'lastname') FROM master_name;
+-------------------------------+
| CONCAT('firstname', 'lastname') |
+-------------------------------+
| firstnamelastname             |
| firstnamelastname             |
| firstnamelastname             |
| firstnamelastname             |
| firstnamelastname             |
| firstnamelastname             |
| firstnamelastname             |
| firstnamelastname             |
| firstnamelastname             |
+-------------------------------+
9 rows in set (0.00 sec)
```

The CONCAT() function would be useful if there were some sort of separator between the names, and that's where the next function comes in: CONCAT_WS().

As you may have figured out, CONTACT_WS() stands for *concatenate with separator*. The separator can be anything you choose, but the following example uses whitespace:

```
mysql> SELECT CONCAT_WS(' ', firstname, lastname) FROM master_name;
+-----------------------------------+
| CONCAT_WS(' ', firstname, lastname) |
+-----------------------------------+
| John Smith                        |
| Jane Smith                        |
| Jimbo Jones                       |
| Andy Smith                        |
| Chris Jones                       |
| Anna Bell                         |
| Jimmy Carr                        |
| Albert Smith                      |
| John Doe                          |
+-----------------------------------+
9 rows in set (0.00 sec)
```

If you want to shorten the width of your result table, you can use AS to name the custom result field:

```
mysql> SELECT CONCAT_WS(' ', firstname, lastname) AS fullname FROM master_name;
+--------------+
| fullname     |
+--------------+
| John Smith   |
| Jane Smith   |
| Jimbo Jones  |
| Andy Smith   |
| Chris Jones  |
| Anna Bell    |
| Jimmy Carr   |
| Albert Smith |
| John Doe     |
+--------------+
9 rows in set (0.00 sec)
```

Trimming and Padding Functions

MySQL provides several functions for adding and removing extra characters (including whitespace) from strings. The RTRIM() and LTRIM() functions remove whitespace from either the right or left side of a string:

```
mysql> SELECT RTRIM('stringstring   ');
+-----------------------+
| RTRIM('stringstring   ') |
+-----------------------+
| stringstring          |
+-----------------------+
1 row in set (0.00 sec)

mysql> SELECT LTRIM('   stringstring');
+----------------------+
| LTRIM('   stringstring') |
+----------------------+
| stringstring         |
+----------------------+
1 row in set (0.00 sec)
```

You may have padded strings to trim if the string is coming out of a fixed-width field and either doesn't need to carry along the additional padding or is being inserted into a varchar or other non–fixed-width field. If your strings are padded with a character besides whitespace, use the TRIM() function to name the characters you want to remove. For example, to remove the leading X characters from the string XXXneedleXXX, use

```
mysql> SELECT TRIM(LEADING 'X' FROM 'XXXneedleXXX');
+------------------------------------+
| TRIM(LEADING 'X' FROM 'XXXneedleXXX') |
+------------------------------------+
| needleXXX                          |
+------------------------------------+
1 row in set (0.00 sec)
```

Use TRAILING to remove the characters from the end of the string:

```
mysql> SELECT TRIM(TRAILING 'X' FROM 'XXXneedleXXX');
+------------------------------------------+
| TRIM(TRAILING 'X' FROM 'XXXneedleXXX')   |
+------------------------------------------+
| XXXneedle                                |
+------------------------------------------+
1 row in set (0.00 sec)
```

If neither LEADING nor TRAILING is indicated, both are assumed:

```
mysql> SELECT TRIM('X' FROM 'XXXneedleXXX');
+-------------------------------+
| TRIM('X' FROM 'XXXneedleXXX') |
+-------------------------------+
| needle                        |
+-------------------------------+
1 row in set (0.00 sec)
```

Just as RTRIM() and LTRIM() remove padding characters, RPAD() and LPAD() add characters to a string. For example, you may want to add specific identification characters to a string that is part of an order number, in a database used for sales. When you use the padding functions, the required elements are the string, the target length, and the padding character. For example, pad the string needle with the X character until the string is 10 characters long:

```
mysql> SELECT RPAD('needle', 10, 'X');
+-------------------------+
| RPAD('needle', 10, 'X') |
+-------------------------+
| needleXXXX              |
+-------------------------+
1 row in set (0.00 sec)
```

```
mysql> SELECT LPAD('needle', 10, 'X');
+-------------------------+
| LPAD('needle', 10, 'X') |
+-------------------------+
| XXXXneedle              |
+-------------------------+
1 row in set (0.00 sec)
```

Location and Position Functions

The group of location and position functions is useful for finding parts of strings within other strings. The LOCATE() function returns the position of the first occurrence of a given substring within the target string. For example, you can look for a needle in a haystack:

```
mysql> SELECT LOCATE('needle', 'haystackneedlehaystack');
+----------------------------------------+
| LOCATE('needle', 'haystackneedlehaystack') |
+----------------------------------------+
|                                      9 |
+----------------------------------------+
1 row in set (0.00 sec)
```

The substring `needle` begins at position 9 in the target string. If the substring cannot be found in the target string, MySQL returns 0 as a result.

> Unlike position counting within most programming languages, which start at 0, position counting using MySQL starts at 1.

By the Way

An extension of the `LOCATE()` function is to use a third argument for starting position. If you start looking for `needle` in `haystack` before position 9, you'll receive a result. Otherwise, because `needle` starts at position 9, you'll receive a 0 result if you specify a greater starting position:

```
mysql> SELECT LOCATE('needle', 'haystackneedlehaystack',6);
+------------------------------------------+
| LOCATE('needle', 'haystackneedlehaystack',9) |
+------------------------------------------+
|                                        9 |
+------------------------------------------+
1 row in set (0.00 sec)
```

```
mysql> SELECT LOCATE('needle', 'haystackneedlehaystack',12);
+-------------------------------------------+
| LOCATE('needle', 'haystackneedlehaystack',12) |
+-------------------------------------------+
|                                         0 |
+-------------------------------------------+
1 row in set (0.00 sec)
```

Substring Functions

If your goal is to extract a substring from a target string, several functions fit the bill. Given a string, starting position, and length, you can use the `SUBSTRING()` function. This example gets three characters from the string MySQL, starting at position 2:

```
mysql> SELECT SUBSTRING("MySQL", 2, 3);
+------------------------+
| SUBSTRING("MySQL", 2, 3) |
+------------------------+
| ySQ                    |
+------------------------+
1 row in set (0.00 sec)
```

If you just want a few characters from the left or right ends of a string, use the
`LEFT()` and `RIGHT()` functions:

```
mysql> SELECT LEFT("MySQL", 2);
+------------------+
| LEFT("MySQL", 2) |
+------------------+
| My               |
+------------------+
1 row in set (0.00 sec)
```

```
mysql> SELECT RIGHT("MySQL", 3);
+-------------------+
| RIGHT("MySQL", 3) |
+-------------------+
| SQL               |
+-------------------+
1 row in set (0.00 sec)
```

One of the many common uses of substring functions is to extract parts of order
numbers to find out who placed the order. In some applications, the system is
designed to automatically generate an order number containing a date, customer
identification, and other information. If this order number always follows a particular pattern, such as XXXX-YYYYY-ZZ, you can use substring functions to extract the
individual parts of the whole. For example, if ZZ always represents the state to
which the order was shipped, you can use the `RIGHT()` function to extract these
characters and report the number of orders shipped to a particular state.

String Modification Functions

PHP has numerous functions to modify the appearance of strings, but if you can
perform the task as part of the SQL statement, all the better.

The MySQL `LCASE()` and `UCASE()` functions transform a string into lowercase or
uppercase:

```
mysql> SELECT LCASE('MYSQL');
+----------------+
| LCASE('MYSQL') |
+----------------+
| mysql          |
+----------------+
1 row in set (0.00 sec)
```

```
mysql> SELECT UCASE('mysql');
+----------------+
| UCASE('mysql') |
+----------------+
| MYSQL          |
+----------------+
1 row in set (0.00 sec)
```

A practical use of the LCASE() and UCASE() functions is when you are validating user input against data stored in MySQL—such as in the case of a user login form. If you want the login process to appear not case sensitive, you could attempt to match the uppercase (or lowercase) version of the user input against the uppercase (or lowercase) version of the data stored in the table.

Did you Know?

Remember, if you use the functions with field names, don't use quotation marks:

```
mysql> SELECT UCASE(lastname) FROM master_name;
+-----------------+
| UCASE(lastname) |
+-----------------+
| BELL            |
| CARR            |
| DOE             |
| JONES           |
| JONES           |
| SMITH           |
| SMITH           |
| SMITH           |
| SMITH           |
+-----------------+
9 rows in set (0.00 sec)
```

Another fun string-manipulation function is REPEAT(), which does just what it sounds like—repeats a string for a given number of times:

```
mysql> SELECT REPEAT("bowwow", 4);
+--------------------------+
| REPEAT("bowwow", 4)      |
+--------------------------+
| bowwowbowwowbowwowbowwow |
+--------------------------+
1 row in set (0.00 sec)
```

The REPLACE() function replaces all occurrences of a given string with another string:

```
mysql> SELECT REPLACE('bowwowbowwowbowwowbowwow', 'wow', 'WOW');
+---------------------------------------------------+
| REPLACE('bowwowbowwowbowwowbowwow', 'wow', 'WOW') |
+---------------------------------------------------+
| bowWOWbowWOWbowWOWbowWOW                           |
+---------------------------------------------------+
1 row in set (0.00 sec)
```

Using Date and Time Functions in MySQL

MySQL's built-in date-related functions can be used in SELECT statements, with or without specifying a table, to retrieve a result of the function. Or you can use the functions with any type of date field: date, datetime, timestamp, and year. Depending on the type of field in use, the results of the date-related functions are more or less useful. The following examples are by no means a complete library of MySQL date and time-related functions. For more, see the MySQL Manual at http://dev.mysql.com/doc/refman/5.0/en/date-and-time-functions.html.

Working with Days

The DAYOFWEEK() and WEEKDAY() functions do similar things with slightly different results. Both functions find the weekday index of a date, but the difference lies in the starting day and position.

If you use DAYOFWEEK(), the first day of the week is Sunday, at position 1, and the last day of the week is Saturday, at position 7. For example:

```
mysql> SELECT DAYOFWEEK('2008-01-28');
+-------------------------+
| DAYOFWEEK('2008-01-28') |
+-------------------------+
|                       2 |
+-------------------------+
1 row in set (0.00 sec)
```

The result shows that January 28, 2008, was weekday index 2, or Monday. Using the same date with WEEKDAY() gives you a different result with the same meaning:

```
mysql> SELECT WEEKDAY('2008-01-28');
+-----------------------+
| WEEKDAY('2008-01-28') |
+-----------------------+
|                     0 |
+-----------------------+
1 row in set (0.00 sec)
```

The result shows that January 28, 2008, was weekday index 0. Because WEEKDAY() uses Monday as the first day of the week at position 0 and Sunday as the last day at position 6, 0 is accurate: Monday.

The DAYOFMONTH() and DAYOFYEAR() functions are more straightforward, with only one result and a range that starts at 1 and ends at 31 for DAYOFMONTH() and 366 for DAYOFYEAR(). Some examples follow:

```
mysql> SELECT DAYOFMONTH('2008-01-28');
+--------------------------+
| DAYOFMONTH('2008-01-28') |
+--------------------------+
|                       28 |
+--------------------------+
1 row in set (0.00 sec)

mysql> SELECT DAYOFYEAR('2008-01-28');
+-------------------------+
| DAYOFYEAR('2008-01-28') |
+-------------------------+
|                      28 |
+-------------------------+
1 row in set (0.00 sec)
```

It might seem odd to have a function that returns the day of the month on a particular date because the day is right there in the string. But think about using these types of functions in WHERE clauses to perform comparisons on records. If you have a table that holds online orders with a field containing the date the order was placed, you can quickly get a count of the orders placed on any given day of the week, or see how many orders were placed during the first half of the month versus the second half.

The following two queries show how many orders were placed during the first three days of the week (throughout all months) and then the remaining days of the week:

```
mysql> SELECT COUNT(id) FROM orders WHERE DAYOFWEEK(date_ordered) < 4;
+-----------+
| COUNT(id) |
+-----------+
|         3 |
+-----------+
1 row in set (0.00 sec)

mysql> SELECT COUNT(id) FROM orders WHERE DAYOFWEEK(date_ordered) > 3;
+-----------+
| COUNT(id) |
+-----------+
|         5 |
+-----------+
1 row in set (0.00 sec)
```

Using DAYOFMONTH(), the following examples show the number of orders placed during the first half of any month versus the second half:

```
mysql> SELECT COUNT(id) FROM orders WHERE DAYOFMONTH(date_ordered) < 16;
+-----------+
| COUNT(id) |
+-----------+
|         6 |
+-----------+
1 row in set (0.00 sec)
```

```
mysql> SELECT COUNT(id) FROM orders WHERE DAYOFMONTH(date_ordered) > 15;
+-----------+
| COUNT(id) |
+-----------+
|         2 |
+-----------+
1 row in set (0.00 sec)
```

You can use the DAYNAME() function to add more life to your results because it returns the name of the weekday for any given date:

```
mysql> SELECT DAYNAME(date_ordered) FROM orders;
+-----------------------+
| DAYNAME(date_ordered) |
+-----------------------+
| Thursday              |
| Monday                |
| Thursday              |
| Thursday              |
| Wednesday             |
| Thursday              |
| Sunday                |
| Sunday                |
+-----------------------+
8 rows in set (0.00 sec)
```

Functions aren't limited to WHERE clauses—you can use them in ORDER BY clauses as well:

```
mysql> SELECT DAYNAME(date_ordered) FROM orders
    -> ORDER BY DAYOFWEEK(date_ordered);
+-----------------------+
| DAYNAME(date_ordered) |
+-----------------------+
| Sunday                |
| Sunday                |
| Monday                |
| Wednesday             |
| Thursday              |
| Thursday              |
| Thursday              |
| Thursday              |
+-----------------------+
8 rows in set (0.00 sec)
```

Working with Months and Years

Days of the week aren't the only parts of the calendar, and MySQL has functions specifically for months and years as well. Just like the DAYOFWEEK() and DAYNAME() functions, MONTH() and MONTHNAME() return the number of the month in a year and the name of the month for a given date. For example:

```
mysql> SELECT MONTH('2008-01-28'), MONTHNAME('2008-01-28');
+---------------------+-------------------------+
| MONTH('2008-01-28') | MONTHNAME('2008-01-28') |
+---------------------+-------------------------+
| 1                   | January                 |
+---------------------+-------------------------+
1 row in set (0.00 sec)
```

Using MONTHNAME() on the orders table shows the proper results but a lot of repeated data:

```
mysql> SELECT MONTHNAME(date_ordered) FROM orders;
+------------------------+
| MONTHNAME(date_ordered) |
+------------------------+
| November               |
| November               |
| November               |
| November               |
| November               |
| November               |
| November               |
| October                |
+------------------------+
8 rows in set (0.00 sec)
```

You can use DISTINCT to get nonrepetitive results:

```
mysql> SELECT DISTINCT MONTHNAME(date_ordered) FROM orders;
+------------------------+
| MONTHNAME(date_ordered) |
+------------------------+
| November               |
| October                |
+------------------------+
2 rows in set (0.00 sec)
```

For work with years, the YEAR() function returns the year of a given date:

```
mysql> SELECT DISTINCT YEAR(date_ordered) FROM orders;
+-------------------+
| YEAR(date_ordered) |
+-------------------+
|              2007 |
|              2008 |
+-------------------+
1 row in set (0.00 sec)
```

Working with Weeks

Weeks can be tricky things—there can be 53 weeks in a year if Sunday is the first day of the week and December hasn't ended. For example, December 30th of 2001 was a Sunday:

```
mysql> SELECT DAYNAME('2001-12-30');
+-----------------------+
| DAYNAME('2001-12-30') |
+-----------------------+
| Sunday                |
+-----------------------+
1 row in set (0.00 sec)
```

That fact made December 30 of 2001 part of the 53rd week of the year:

```
mysql> SELECT WEEK('2001-12-30');
+--------------------+
| WEEK('2001-12-30') |
+--------------------+
|                 53 |
+--------------------+
1 row in set (0.00 sec)
```

The 53rd week contained December 30 and 31 and was only two days long; the first week of 2002 began with January 1.

If you want your weeks to start on Mondays but still want to find the week of the year, the optional second argument enables you to change the start day. A 1 indicates a week that starts on Monday. In the following examples, a Monday start day makes December 30 part of the 52nd week of 2001, but December 31 is still part of the 53rd week of 2001.

```
mysql> SELECT WEEK('2001-12-30',1);
+----------------------+
| WEEK('2001-12-30',1) |
+----------------------+
|                   52 |
+----------------------+
1 row in set (0.00 sec)
```

```
mysql> SELECT WEEK('2001-12-31',1);
+----------------------+
| WEEK('2001-12-31',1) |
+----------------------+
|                   53 |
+----------------------+
1 row in set (0.00 sec)
```

Working with Hours, Minutes, and Seconds

If you're using a date that includes the exact time, such as datetime or timestamp, or even just a time field, there are functions to find the hours, minutes, and seconds from that string. Not surprisingly, these functions are called HOUR(), MINUTE(), and SECOND(). HOUR() returns the hour in a given time, which is between 0 and 23. The range for MINUTE() and SECOND() is 0 to 59.

Here are some examples:

```
mysql> SELECT HOUR('2008-01-28 07:27:49') AS hour,
    -> MINUTE('2008-01-28 07:27:49') AS minute,
    -> SECOND('2008-01-28 07:27:49') AS second;
''''''
+------+--------+--------+
| hour | minute | second |
+------+--------+--------+
|    7 |     27 |     49 |
+------+--------+--------+
1 row in set (0.00 sec)
```

That's a lot of queries to get at one time from a datetime field—you can put the hour and minute together and even use CONCAT_WS() to put the : between the results and get a representation of the time:

```
mysql> SELECT CONCAT_WS(':',HOUR('2008-01-28 07:27:49'),
    -> MINUTE('2008-01-28 07:27:49')) AS sample_time;
+-------------+
| sample_time |
+-------------+
| 7:27        |
+-------------+
1 row in set (0.00 sec)
```

If you use field names instead of strings, remember not to use quotation marks. Here's an example that uses the dateadded field from the sometable table:

```
mysql> SELECT CONCAT_WS(':',HOUR(dateadded), MINUTE(dateadded))
    -> AS sample_time FROM sometable;
+-------------+
| sample_time |
+-------------+
| 13:11       |
| 13:11       |
| 13:11       |
| 13:11       |
| 14:16       |
| 10:12       |
| 10:12       |
| 10:12       |
| 10:12       |
+-------------+
9 rows in set (0.00 sec)
```

This is cheating because it's not the actual time—it's just two numbers stuck together to look like a time. If you used the concatenation trick on a time such as 02:02, the result would be 2:2, as shown here:

```
mysql> SELECT CONCAT_WS(':',HOUR('02:02'), MINUTE('02:02')) AS sample_time;
+-------------+
| sample_time |
+-------------+
| 2:2         |
+-------------+
1 row in set (0.00 sec)
```

This result is obviously not the intended result. In the next section, you learn how to use the DATE_FORMAT() function to properly format dates and times.

Formatting Dates and Times with MySQL

The DATE_FORMAT() function formats a date, datetime, or timestamp field into a string by using options that tell it exactly how to display the results. The syntax of DATE_FORMAT() is

```
DATE_FORMAT(date,format)
```

Table 16.2 lists many formatting options.

TABLE 16.2   DATE_FORMAT() **Format String Options**

Option	Result
%M	Month name (January through December)
%b	Abbreviated month name (Jan through Dec)
%m	Month, padded digits (01 through 12)
%c	Month (1 through 12)
%W	Weekday name (Sunday through Saturday)
%a	Abbreviated weekday name (Sun through Sat)
%D	Day of the month using the English suffix, such as first, second, third, and so on
%d	Day of the month, padded digits (00 through 31)
%e	Day of the month (0 through 31)
%j	Day of the year, padded digits (001 through 366)
%Y	Year, four digits
%y	Year, two digits
%X	Four-digit year for the week where Sunday is the first day; used with %V
%x	Four-digit year for the week where Monday is the first day; used with %v
%w	Day of the week (0=Sunday...6=Saturday)
%U	Week (0 through 53) where Sunday is the first day of the week
%u	Week (0 through 53) where Monday is the first day of the week
%V	Week (1 through 53) where Sunday is the first day of the week; used with %X
%v	Week (1 through 53) where Monday is the first day of the week; used with %x
%H	Hour, padded digits (00 through 23)
%k	Hour (0 through 23)
%h	Hour, padded digits (01 through 12)

TABLE 16.2   Continued

Option	Result
%l	Hour (1 through 12)
%i	Minutes, padded digits (00 through 59)
%S	Seconds, padded digits (00 through 59)
%s	Seconds, padded digits (00 through 59)
%r	Time, 12-hour clock (hh:mm:ss [AP]M)
%T	Time, 24-hour clock (hh:mm:ss)
%p	AM or PM

> Any other characters used in the DATE_FORMAT() option string appear literally.

By the Way

To display the 02:02 result that we rigged in the previous section, you use the %h and %i options to return the hour and minute from the date with a : between the two options. For example:

```
mysql> SELECT DATE_FORMAT('2008-01-28 02:02:00', '%h:%i') AS sample_time;
+-------------+
| sample_time |
+-------------+
| 02:02       |
+-------------+
1 row in set (0.00 sec)
```

The following are just a few more examples of the DATE_FORMAT() function in use, but this function is best understood by practicing it yourself.

```
mysql> SELECT DATE_FORMAT('2008-01-28', '%W, %M %D, %Y') AS sample_time;
+---------------------------+
| sample_time               |
+---------------------------+
| Monday, January 28th, 2008 |
+---------------------------+
1 row in set (0.00 sec)
```

```
mysql> SELECT DATE_FORMAT(NOW(),'%W the %D of %M, %Y
    -> around %l o\'clock %p') AS sample_time;
+-------------------------------------------------------+
| sample_time                                           |
+-------------------------------------------------------+
| Sunday the 3rd of February, 2008 around 3 o'clock PM  |
+-------------------------------------------------------+
1 row in set (0.03 sec)
```

If you're working specifically with time fields, the TIME_FORMAT() function works just like the DATE_FORMAT() function. Only the format options for hours, minutes, and seconds are allowed:

```
mysql> SELECT TIME_FORMAT('02:02:00', '%h:%i') AS sample_time;
+-------------+
| sample_time |
+-------------+
| 02:02       |
+-------------+
1 row in set (0.00 sec)
```

Performing Date Arithmetic with MySQL

MySQL has several functions to help perform date arithmetic, and this is one of the areas where it might be quicker to allow MySQL to do the math than your PHP script. The DATE_ADD() and DATE_SUB() functions return a result given a starting date and an interval. The syntax for both functions is

```
DATE_ADD(date,INTERVAL value type)
```

```
DATE_SUB(date,INTERVAL value type)
```

Table 16.3 shows the possible types and their expected value format.

TABLE 16.3   Values and Types in Date Arithmetic

Value	Type
Number of seconds	SECOND
Number of minutes	MINUTE
Number of hours	HOUR
Number of days	DAY
Number of months	MONTH
Number of years	YEAR
"minutes:seconds"	MINUTE_SECOND
"hours:minutes"	HOUR_MINUTE
"days hours"	DAY_HOUR
"years-months"	YEAR_MONTH
"hours:minutes:seconds"	HOUR_SECOND
"days hours:minutes"	DAY_MINUTE
"days hours:minutes:seconds"	DAY_SECOND

For example, to find the date of the current day plus 21 days, use the following:

```
mysql> SELECT DATE_ADD(NOW(), INTERVAL 21 DAY);
+----------------------------------+
| DATE_ADD(NOW(), INTERVAL 21 DAY) |
+----------------------------------+
| 2008-02-24 15:21:21              |
+----------------------------------+
1 row in set (0.03 sec)
```

To subtract 21 days, use the following:

```
mysql> SELECT DATE_SUB(now(), INTERVAL 21 DAY);
+----------------------------------+
| DATE_SUB(NOW(), INTERVAL 21 DAY) |
+----------------------------------+
| 2008-01-13 15:21:44              |
+----------------------------------+
1 row in set (0.00 sec)
```

Use the expression as it's shown in Table 16.3, despite what might be a natural tendency to use DAYS instead of DAY. Using DAYS results in an error:

```
mysql> SELECT DATE_ADD(NOW(), INTERVAL 21 DAYS);
ERROR 1064: You have an error in your SQL syntax near 'DAYS)' at line 1
```

If you're using DATE_ADD() or DATE_SUB() with a date value instead of a datetime value, the result will be shown as a date value unless you use expressions related to hours, minutes, and seconds. In that case, your result will be a datetime result.

For example, the result of the first query remains a date field, whereas the second becomes a datetime:

```
mysql> SELECT DATE_ADD("2007-12-31", INTERVAL 1 DAY);
+----------------------------------------+
| DATE_ADD("2007-12-31", INTERVAL 1 DAY) |
+----------------------------------------+
| 2008-01-01                             |
+----------------------------------------+
1 row in set (0.00 sec)
```

```
mysql> SELECT DATE_ADD("2007-12-31", INTERVAL 12 HOUR);
+------------------------------------------+
| DATE_ADD("2007-12-31", INTERVAL 12 HOUR) |
+------------------------------------------+
| 2007-12-31 12:00:00                      |
+------------------------------------------+
1 row in set (0.00 sec)
```

You can also perform date arithmetic using the + and - operators instead of DATE_ADD() and DATE_SUB() functions:

```
mysql> SELECT "2007-12-31" + INTERVAL 1 DAY;
+-------------------------------+
| "2007-12-31" + INTERVAL 1 DAY |
+-------------------------------+
| 2008-01-01                    |
+-------------------------------+
1 row in set (0.00 sec)
```

```
mysql> SELECT "2007-12-31" - INTERVAL 14 HOUR;
+---------------------------------+
| "2007-12-31" - INTERVAL 14 HOUR |
+---------------------------------+
| 2007-12-30 10:00:00             |
+---------------------------------+
1 row in set (0.00 sec)
```

Special Functions and Conversion Features

The MySQL NOW() function returns a current datetime result and is useful for time-stamping login or access times, as well as numerous other tasks. MySQL has a few other functions that perform similarly.

The CURDATE() and CURRENT_DATE() functions are synonymous, and each returns the current date in YYYY-MM-DD format:

```
mysql> SELECT CURDATE(), CURRENT_DATE();
+------------+----------------+
| CURDATE()  | CURRENT_DATE() |
+------------+----------------+
| 2008-02-03 | 2008-02-03     |
+------------+----------------+
1 row in set (0.01 sec)
```

Similarly, the CURTIME() and CURRENT_TIME() functions return the current time in HH:MM:SS format:

```
mysql> SELECT CURTIME(), CURRENT_TIME();
+-----------+----------------+
| CURTIME() | CURRENT_TIME() |
+-----------+----------------+
| 09:14:26  | 09:14:26       |
+-----------+----------------+
1 row in set (0.00 sec)
```

The NOW(), SYSDATE(), and CURRENT_TIMESTAMP() functions return values in full datetime format (YYYY-MM-DD HH:MM:SS):

```
mysql> SELECT NOW(), SYSDATE(), CURRENT_TIMESTAMP();
+---------------------+---------------------+---------------------+
| NOW()               | SYSDATE()           | CURRENT_TIMESTAMP() |
+---------------------+---------------------+---------------------+
| 2008-02-03 15:23:52 | 2008-02-03 15:23:52 | 2008-02-03 15:23:52 |
+---------------------+---------------------+---------------------+
1 row in set (0.00 sec)
```

The UNIX_TIMESTAMP() function returns the current date in—or converts a given date to—UNIX time stamp format. UNIX time stamp format is in seconds since the epoch, or seconds since midnight, January 1, 1970. For example:

```
mysql> SELECT UNIX_TIMESTAMP();
+------------------+
| UNIX_TIMESTAMP() |
+------------------+
|       1202073856 |
+------------------+
1 row in set (0.00 sec)
```

```
mysql> SELECT UNIX_TIMESTAMP('1973-12-30');
+------------------------------+
| UNIX_TIMESTAMP('1973-12-30') |
+------------------------------+
|                    126086400 |
+------------------------------+
1 row in set (0.00 sec)
```

The FROM_UNIXTIME() function performs a conversion of a UNIX time stamp to a full datetime format when used without any options:

```
mysql> SELECT FROM_UNIXTIME('1202073856');
+-----------------------------+
| FROM_UNIXTIME('1202073856') |
+-----------------------------+
| 2008-02-03 15:24:16         |
+-----------------------------+
1 row in set (0.00 sec)
```

You can use the format options from the DATE_FORMAT() functions to display a time stamp in a more appealing manner:

```
mysql> SELECT FROM_UNIXTIME(UNIX_TIMESTAMP(), '%D %M %Y at %h:%i:%s');
+--------------------------------------------------------+
| FROM_UNIXTIME(UNIX_TIMESTAMP(), '%D %M %Y at %h:%i:%s') |
+--------------------------------------------------------+
| 3rd February 2008 at 03:26:41                          |
+--------------------------------------------------------+
1 row in set (0.00 sec)
```

If you're working with a number of seconds and want to convert the seconds to a time-formatted result, you can use SEC_TO_TIME() and TIME_TO_SEC() to convert values back and forth.

For example, 1440 seconds is equal to 24 minutes and vice versa:

```
mysql> SELECT SEC_TO_TIME('1440'), TIME_TO_SEC('00:24:00');
+---------------------+-------------------------+
| SEC_TO_TIME('1440') | TIME_TO_SEC('00:24:00') |
+---------------------+-------------------------+
| 00:24:00            |                    1440 |
+---------------------+-------------------------+
1 row in set (0.01 sec)
```

Summary

In this chapter, you learned the basics of SQL from table creation to manipulating records. The table creation command requires three important pieces of information: the table name, the field name, and the field definitions. Field definitions are important because a well-designed table will help speed along your database. MySQL has three different categories of data types: numeric, date and time, and string.

The INSERT command, used to add records to a table, names the table and columns you want to populate and then defines the values. When placing values in the INSERT statement, strings must be enclosed with single or double quotes. The SELECT SQL command is used to retrieve records from specific tables. The * character enables you to easily select all fields for all records in a table, but you can also specify particular column names. If the resultset is too long, the LIMIT clause provides a simple method for extracting slices of results if you indicate a starting position and the number of records to return. To order the results, use the ORDER BY clause to select the columns to sort. Sorts can be performed on integers, dates, and strings, in either ascending or descending order. The default order is ascending. Without specifying an order, results display in the order they appear in the table.

You can pick and choose which records you want to return using WHERE clauses to test for the validity of conditions. Comparison or logical operators are used in WHERE clauses, and sometimes both types are used for compound statements. Selecting records from multiple tables within one statement is as advanced as it gets because this type of statement—called JOIN—requires forethought and planning to produce correct results. Common types of JOIN are INNER JOIN, LEFT JOIN, and RIGHT JOIN, although MySQL supports many different kinds of JOIN. You also learned that you can use subqueries instead of JOINs when working with multiple tables.

The UPDATE and REPLACE commands modify existing data in your MySQL tables. UPDATE is good for changing values in specific columns and for changing values in multiple records based on specific conditions. REPLACE is a variation of INSERT that deletes and then reinserts a record with a matching primary key. Be careful when using UPDATE to change values in a column because failure to add a condition results in the given column being updated throughout all records in the table.

The DELETE command is simple—it removes whole records from tables. This also makes it dangerous, so be sure you give DELETE privileges only to users who can handle the responsibility. You can specify conditions when using DELETE so that records are removed only if a particular expression in a WHERE clause is true. Also, you can delete smaller sets of records in your table using a LIMIT clause. If you have an exceptionally large table, deleting portions is less resource-intensive than deleting each record in a huge table.

You were introduced to MySQL functions that perform actions on strings, dates, and times. If you have strings in MySQL that you want to concatenate or for which you want to count characters, you can use functions such as CONCAT(), CONCAT_WS(), and LENGTH(). To pad or remove padding from strings, use RPAD(), LPAD(), TRIM(), LTRIM(), and RRIM() to get just the strings you want. You can also find the location of a string within another string, or return a part of a given string using the LOCATE(), SUBSTRING(), LEFT(), and RIGHT() functions. Functions such as LCASE(), UCASE(), REPEAT(), and REPLACE() also return variations of the original strings. MySQL's built-in date and time functions can definitely take some of the load off your application by internally formatting dates and times and performing the date and time arithmetic. The formatting options used for the DATE_FORMAT() function provide a simple method to produce a custom display string from any sort of date field. The DATE_ADD() and DATE_SUB() functions and their numerous available interval types help you determine dates and times in the past or future. Additionally, functions such as DAY(), WEEK(), MONTH(), and YEAR() are useful for extracting parts of dates for use in WHERE or ORDER BY clauses.

Q&A

Q. *What characters can I use to name my tables and fields, and what is the character limit?*

A. The maximum length of database, table, or field names is 64 characters. Any character you can use in a directory name or filename, you can use in database and table names—except / and .. These limitations are in place because MySQL creates directories and files in your file system, which correspond to database and table names. There are no character limitations (besides length) in field names.

Q. *Can I use multiple functions in one statement, such as making a concatenated string all uppercase?*

A. Sure—just be mindful of your opening and closing parentheses. This example shows how to uppercase the concatenated first and last names from the master name table:

```
mysql> SELECT UCASE(CONCAT_WS(' ', firstname, lastname)) FROM master_name;
+--------------------------------------------+
| UCASE(CONCAT_WS(' ', firstname, lastname)) |
+--------------------------------------------+
| JOHN SMITH                                 |
| JANE SMITH                                 |
| JIMBO JONES                                |
| ANDY SMITH                                 |
| CHRIS JONES                                |
| ANNA BELL                                  |
| JIMMY CARR                                 |
| ALBERT SMITH                               |
| JOHN DOE                                   |
+--------------------------------------------+
9 rows in set (0.00 sec)
```

If you want to uppercase just the last name, use

```
mysql> SELECT CONCAT_WS(' ', firstname, UCASE(lastname)) FROM master_name;
+--------------------------------------------+
| CONCAT_WS(' ', firstname, UCASE(lastname)) |
+--------------------------------------------+
| John SMITH                                 |
| Jane SMITH                                 |
| Jimbo JONES                                |
| Andy SMITH                                 |
| Chris JONES                                |
| Anna BELL                                  |
| Jimmy CARR                                 |
| Albert SMITH                               |
| John DOE                                   |
+--------------------------------------------+
9 rows in set (0.00 sec)
```

Workshop

The workshop is designed to help you anticipate possible questions, review what you've learned, and begin putting your knowledge into practice.

Quiz

1. The integer 56678685 could be which data type(s)?

2. How would you define a field that could contain only the following strings: apple, pear, banana, cherry?

3. What would be the LIMIT clauses for selecting the first 25 records of a table? Then the next 25?

4. How would you formulate a string comparison using LIKE to match first names of "John" or "Joseph"?

5. How would you explicitly refer to a field called id in a table called table1?

6. Write an SQL statement that joins two tables, orders and items_ordered, each of which has a primary key of order_id. From the orders table, select the following fields: order_name and order_date. From the items_ordered table, select the item_description field.

7. Write an SQL query to find the starting position of a substring "grape" in a string "applepearbananagrape".

8. Write a query that selects the last five characters from the string "applepear-bananagrape".

Answers

1. MEDIUMINT, INT, or BIGINT.

2. ENUM ('apple', 'pear', 'banana', 'cherry')

   or

   SET ('apple', 'pear', 'banana', 'cherry')

3. LIMIT 0, 25 and LIMIT 25, 25

4. LIKE 'Jo%'

5. Use table1.id instead of id in your query.

6. SELECT orders.order_name, orders.order_date,
   items_ordered.item_description FROM orders LEFT JOIN
   items_ordered ON orders.order_id = items_ordered.id;

7. SELECT LOCATE('grape', 'applepearbananagrape');

8. SELECT RIGHT("applepearbananagrape", 5);

Activity

Take the time to create some sample tables and practice using basic INSERT and SELECT commands.

17

Using Transactions and Stored Procedures in MySQL

In the previous chapter, you learned the basics of SQL and how to use the MySQL command-line interface to issue queries and retrieve the results. Armed with only that knowledge, you can successfully complete the projects found in the remaining chapters of this book. However, when you move forward with your knowledge and think about building applications suitable for use in an enterprise environment, you might require more advanced tactics to maintain the integrity of your data and enhance your application's communication with MySQL.

Although the remaining chapters in this book will not contain elements from this chapter, you can easily update the code on your own to include the information you learn in this chapter. In this chapter you will learn

- ▶ The basics of transactions and how to use them in MySQL
- ▶ The basics of stored procedures and how to create and access them in MySQL

What Are Transactions?

Database transactions are simply sets of queries that must execute in such a way so that if one query fails to execute completely, they all fail. For instance, say that you have a set of three queries, the second dependent on the results of the first, and the third dependent on the results of the second. If the second query fails, you need to have a way to negate the results of the first query; similarly, if the third query fails, you need to negate the results of the first and second queries as well.

By instituting transactional processing in your database-driven applications, you ensure the integrity of the data stored in your database. The following sections describe the process of using transactions both through the command-line interface and PHP functions.

Basic Syntax Used in Transactions

You will need to understand the following key terms when thinking about using transactions with MySQL:

▶ **COMMIT**—This command occurs at the end of the series of queries in your transaction and is issued only if all the required queries have executed successfully.

▶ **ROLLBACK**—This command is used when one or more of the series of queries in your transaction fails and resets the affected tables to their pretransaction state.

Going back to the example used previously, of three queries dependent on each other, a sequence of events in the MySQL command-line interface might look something like this:

1. Issue the BEGIN command to begin a new transaction.

2. Select a value from table1 to insert into table2.

3. If a value cannot be selected from table1, issue a ROLLBACK command to ensure that the transaction ends and that the tables return to their previous state.

4. If a value can be selected from table1, insert a value into table2.

5. If the insertion of a record into table2 fails, issue a ROLLBACK command to ensure that the transaction ends and that the tables return to their previous state.

6. If a value can be inserted into table1, insert a value into table2.

7. If the insertion of a record into table3 fails, issue a ROLLBACK command to ensure that the transaction ends and that the tables return to their previous state.

8. However, if the insertion of a record into table3 is successful, issue a COMMIT command to ensure that the transaction ends and that the tables update appropriately.

For more information on the inner workings of transactions in MySQL, see the MySQL Manual at http://dev.mysql.com/doc/refman/5.0/en/transactional-statements.html.

In the next section, you'll see an example of transactions as used with tables concerning inventory and sales records.

Working Example Using Transactions

For the purposes of this example, imagine that you've created an online storefront with database tables that hold inventory, sales records, and the line items for the sales records:

```
mysql> DESC store_inventory;
+------------+-------------+------+-----+---------+----------------+
| Field      | Type        | Null | Key | Default | Extra          |
+------------+-------------+------+-----+---------+----------------+
| id         | int(11)     | NO   | PRI |         | auto_increment |
| item_name  | varchar(25) | YES  |     |         |                |
| item_price | float(6,2)  | YES  |     |         |                |
| item_qty   | int(11)     | YES  |     |         |                |
+------------+-------------+------+-----+---------+----------------+
4 rows in set (0.02 sec)

mysql> DESC store_orders;
+---------------+-------------+------+-----+---------+----------------+
| Field         | Type        | Null | Key | Default | Extra          |
+---------------+-------------+------+-----+---------+----------------+
| id            | int(11)     | NO   | PRI |         | auto_increment |
| purchaser_name| varchar(50) | YES  |     |         |                |
| purchase_date | datetime    | YES  |     |         |                |
+---------------+-------------+------+-----+---------+----------------+
3 rows in set (0.00 sec)

mysql> DESC store_orders_lineitems;
+--------------+---------+------+-----+---------+----------------+
| Field        | Type    | Null | Key | Default | Extra          |
+--------------+---------+------+-----+---------+----------------+
| id           | int(11) | NO   | PRI |         | auto_increment |
| order_id     | int(11) | YES  |     |         |                |
| inventory_id | int(11) | YES  |     |         |                |
| item_qty     | int(11) | YES  |     |         |                |
+--------------+---------+------+-----+---------+----------------+
4 rows in set (0.00 sec)
```

In the store_inventory table for this example, you can find two records:

```
mysql> SELECT * FROM store_inventory;
+----+------------+------------+----------+
| id | item_name  | item_price | item_qty |
+----+------------+------------+----------+
| 1  | Great Book | 19.99      | 10       |
| 2  | Awesome CD | 9.99       | 20       |
+----+------------+------------+----------+
2 rows in set (0.00 sec)
```

If a shopper wants to purchase two Great Books and one Awesome CD through your online store, the process would go something like this:

1. The user completes an online form and attempts to pay for the purchases, so issue a BEGIN command for the transaction that would be part of the checkout script:

```
BEGIN;
```

2. Decrement the quantity of items in the store_inventory table:

```
UPDATE store_inventory SET item_qty = item_qty - 2 WHERE id = 1;
UPDATE store_inventory SET item_qty = item_qty - 1 WHERE id = 2;
```

3. Add a record to the store_orders table:

```
INSERT INTO store_orders (purchaser_name, purchase_date)
        VALUES ('John Smith', now());
```

4. If adding the record fails, issue a ROLLBACK command to reset the available quantity of the items:

```
ROLLBACK;
```

5. If adding the record succeeds, get the ID of the record just added and use it in your query to add line items to the sales record by inserting records in the store_orders_lineitems table:

```
INSERT INTO store_orders_lineitems (order_id, inventory_id, item_qty)
        VALUES ('1', '1', '2');
INSERT INTO store_orders_lineitems (order_id, inventory_id, item_qty)
        VALUES ('1', '2', '1');
```

6. If adding the records fails, issue a ROLLBACK command to reset the available quantity of the items and remove the record in store_orders:

```
ROLLBACK;
```

7. If adding the records succeeds but the subsequent charging of a credit card or other payment method fails, issue a ROLLBACK command to reset the available quantity of the items, remove the record in store_orders, and remove the records in store_orders_lineitems:

```
ROLLBACK;
```

8. If adding the records succeeds and the subsequent charging of a credit card or other payment method succeeds, issue a COMMIT command to ensure that all the changes are stored and the transaction ends:

```
COMMIT;
```

Of course, an online storefront would not directly interface with MySQL via the command-line interface but rather through a scripting language such as PHP. But if you understand the processes behind the transaction, plugging it into PHP is simple—issuing the queries and commands listed previously is no different from any other PHP-to-MySQL communication, which you will learn about in Chapter 18, "Interacting with MySQL Using PHP."

In addition to the information you'll learn in Chapter 18, be sure to review these function definitions in the PHP Manual if you intend to use transactions in your scripts:

- `mysqli_autocommit()`—http://www.php.net/mysqli_autocommit
- `mysqli_commit()`—http://www.php.net/mysqli_commit
- `mysqli_rollback()`—http://www.php.net/mysqli_rollback

What Are Stored Procedures?

Simply put, a stored procedure is a procedure in SQL that is stored in the database server rather than the web server. You might be thinking that you don't store any procedures on the web server, but in fact you do—any script that contains SQL queries counts as a procedure stored on the web server. For example, every query in your application that selects, deletes, updates, or inserts data into tables—which you will have painstakingly coded in your scripts—could be stored in the database as a stored procedure and referenced as such in your scripts.

Proponents of using stored procedures in code point to performance and maintenance as key reasons for doing so:

- **Better performance**—Stored procedures exist as precompiled SQL in the database, so a typical two-step process (compile and execute) becomes a single-step process (execute).

- **Ease of maintenance**—Maintaining one statement in one place (the database) is significantly less time-consuming than maintaining one statement in numerous places, such as all through scripts on your web server. Additionally, storing all your statements in the database as opposed to actual text files in your web server document root is one more line of defense should someone gain access to the files on your web server—all that person has are queries that call stored procedures instead of the logic of the procedure itself.

An example of a useful stored procedure would be the SQL query used to generate a report of some sort—be it financial data, sales inventory, or otherwise—just imagine a complex query that involves a lot of processing. Creating a stored procedure out of this type of query goes along with the performance benefits of stored procedures. If you had a simple query used frequently throughout your application, creating a stored procedure for it would go along with the maintenance benefits of stored procedures. Regardless of the simplicity or complexity of the stored procedure, creating and using it follows the same basic process.

This stored procedure example uses the following table:

```
mysql> DESC testSP;
+------------+-------------+------+-----+---------+----------------+
| Field      | Type        | Null | Key | Default | Extra          |
+------------+-------------+------+-----+---------+----------------+
| id         | int(11)     | NO   | PRI |         | auto_increment |
| field_name | varchar(25) | YES  |     |         |                |
+------------+-------------+------+-----+---------+----------------+
2 rows in set (0.00 sec)
```

Next, you must ensure that MySQL knows the delimiter character you'll be using in your stored procedures. This example uses "//" as the delimiter, so you issue the following query:

```
mysql> DELIMITER //
```

The syntax for creating a basic stored procedure is

```
CREATE PROCEDURE procedure_name () query //
```

For this example, the stored procedure simply selects all data from the testSP table, and you name the stored procedure sp1:

```
mysql> CREATE PROCEDURE sp1 () SELECT * FROM testSP //
Query OK, 0 rows affected (0.11 sec)
```

To call the stored procedure, use the CALL command:

```
mysql> CALL sp1 ()//
+----+------------+
| id | field_name |
+----+------------+
| 1  | test1      |
| 2  | test2      |
| 3  | test3      |
+----+------------+
3 rows in set (0.44 sec)
Query OK, 0 rows affected (0.44 sec)
```

In Chapter 18, you'll learn the process for issuing these SQL queries using PHP.

Clearly, these few pages do not even begin to scratch the surface of working with stored procedures; this section intends only to introduce you to the concept. Additional recommended reading includes the MySQL AB informational publication (70 pages) at http://dev.mysql.com/tech-resources/articles/mysql-storedprocedures.html.

Summary

This short chapter provided a brief introduction to the concepts of transactional processing and the use of stored procedures in MySQL. In addition to a brief overview of both topics, real-life examples described each of these advanced topics. The overall purpose of this chapter was to introduce you to some concepts and keywords you should understand by the time you're developing enterprise applications on your own.

Q&A

Q. *Do I have to use transactions all the time now that MySQL supports them?*

A. No, especially not if the dynamic aspect of your application or site is for dynamic *display* of data and not for dynamic *insertion* of data. Additionally, if the insertion of data is not necessarily related to any financial or inventory related actions, you could get away with not using transactions. In other words, if you don't use transactions and an insert or update query fails, be sure that you can live with the failure—either because no money or crucial customer data would be lost.

Workshop

The workshop is designed to help you anticipate possible questions, review what you've learned, and begin putting your knowledge into practice.

Quiz

1. If step two of a three-step transaction fails, what command would you issue?

2. What are two advantages of using stored procedures?

Answers

1. ROLLBACK

2. Better performance and ease of maintenance

18

Interacting with MySQL Using PHP

Now that you've learned the basics of PHP as well as the basics of working with MySQL, you're ready to make the two interact. Think of PHP as a conduit to MySQL—the commands you learned in the previous chapter are the same commands that you will send to MySQL in this chapter, only this time you'll send them with PHP. In this chapter, you will learn

- ▶ How to connect to MySQL using PHP

- ▶ How to insert and select data through PHP scripts

MySQL Versus MySQLi Functions

If you have used previous versions of PHP, or current versions of PHP with older versions of MySQL, you likely are familiar with the mysql_* family of functions. However, MySQL 4.1.3 (and subsequent versions) have new functionality and thus new communication methods are present in PHP: the mysqli_* family of functions. All code in this chapter, and throughout the rest of this book, uses the mysqli_* family of functions. For more information, see the PHP Manual chapter, "MySQL Improved Extension," at http://www.php.net/mysqli.

Connecting to MySQL with PHP

To successfully use the PHP functions to talk to MySQL, you must have MySQL running at a location to which your web server can connect (not necessarily the same machine as your web server). You also must have created a user (with a password), and you must know the name of the database to which you want to connect. If you followed the instructions in Chapter 2, "Installing and Configuring MySQL," and Chapter 4, "Installing and Configuring PHP," you should already have taken care of this. If you are using PHP and MySQL as part of a hosting package at an Internet service provider, make sure that you have the correct username, password, and database name from your system administrator before proceeding.

In all sample scripts in this chapter, the sample database name is testDB, the sample user is joeuser, and the sample password is somepass. Substitute your own information when you use these scripts.

By the
~~Way~~

> All code in this chapter, as well as other chapters moving forward, reflects the procedural use of the mysqli_* family of functions. You can also use these functions in an object-oriented way; for more information on that, visit the PHP Manual at http://www.php.net/mysqli.

Making a Connection

The basic syntax for a connection to MySQL is

```
$mysqli = mysqli_connect("hostname", "username", "password", "database");
```

Using actual sample values, the connection code looks like this:

```
$mysqli = mysqli_connect("localhost", "joeuser", "somepass", "testDB");
```

Listing 18.1 is a working example of a connection script. It creates a new connection in line 2 and then tests to see whether an error occurred. If an error occurred, line 5 prints an error message and uses the mysqli_connect_error() function to print the message. If no error occurs, line 8 prints a message including host information resulting from calling the mysqli_get_host_info() function.

LISTING 18.1   A Simple Connection Script

```
1:  <?php
2:  $mysqli = new mysqli("localhost", "joeuser", "somepass", "testDB");
3:
4:  if (mysqli_connect_errno()) {
5:      printf("Connect failed: %s\n", mysqli_connect_error());
6:      exit();
7:  } else {
8:      printf("Host information: %s\n", mysqli_get_host_info($mysqli));
9:  }
10: ?>
```

Save this script as mysqlconnect.php and place it in the document area of your web server. Access the script with your web browser and you will see something like the following, if the connection was successful:

```
Host information: localhost via TCP/IP
```

You might also see this:

```
Host information: Localhost via UNIX socket
```

If the connection fails, an error message is printed. Line 5 generates an error via the `mysqli_connect_error()` function; an example is shown here:

```
Connect failed: Access denied for user 'joeuser'@'localhost' (using password:
YES)
```

However, if the connection is successful, line 8 prints the output of `mysqli_get_host_info()`, such as:

```
Host information: localhost via TCP/IP
```

Although the connection closes when the script finishes its execution, it's a good idea to close the connection explicitly. You can see how to do this in line 9 of Listing 18.2, using the `mysqli_close()` function.

LISTING 18.2   The Modified Simple Connection Script

```
1:  <?php
2:  $mysqli = new mysqli("localhost", "joeuser", "somepass", "testDB");
3:
4:  if (mysqli_connect_errno()) {
5:      printf("Connect failed: %s\n", mysqli_connect_error());
6:      exit();
7:  } else {
8:      printf("Host information: %s\n", mysqli_get_host_info($mysqli));
9:      mysqli_close($mysqli);
10: }
11: ?>
```

That's all there is to it. The next section covers the query execution functions, which are far more interesting than simply opening a connection and letting it sit there!

Executing Queries

Half the battle in executing MySQL queries using PHP is knowing how to write the SQL—and you've already learned the basics of this in previous chapters. The `mysqli_query()` function in PHP is used to send your SQL query to MySQL.

In your script, first make the connection and then execute a query. The script in Listing 18.3 creates a simple table called `testTable`.

LISTING 18.3   A Script to Create a Table

```
1:   <?php
2:   $mysqli = mysqli_connect("localhost", "joeuser", "somepass", "testDB");
3:
4:   if (mysqli_connect_errno()) {
5:       printf("Connect failed: %s\n", mysqli_connect_error());
6:       exit();
7:   } else {
8:       $sql = "CREATE TABLE testTable
9:               (id INT NOT NULL PRIMARY KEY AUTO_INCREMENT,
10:              testField VARCHAR(75))";
11:      $res = mysqli_query($mysqli, $sql);
12:
13:      if ($res === TRUE) {
14:          echo "Table testTable successfully created.";
15:      } else {
16:          printf("Could not create table: %s\n", mysqli_error($mysqli));
17:      }
18:
19:      mysqli_close($mysqli);
20:  }
21:  ?>
```

By the Way

> When issuing queries via a script, the semicolon at the end of the SQL statement is not required.

In lines 8–10, the text that makes up the SQL statement is assigned to the variable $sql. This is arbitrary, and you don't even need to place the content of your SQL query in a separate variable—it appears as such in the example so that the different parts of this process are clear.

The mysqli_query function returns a value of true or false, and this value is checked in the if...else statement beginning in line 13. If the value of $res is true, a success message is printed to the screen. If you access MySQL through the command-line interface to verify the creation of the testTable table, you will see:

```
mysql> DESCRIBE testTable;
+-----------+-------------+------+-----+---------+----------------+
| Field     | Type        | Null | Key | Default | Extra          |
+-----------+-------------+------+-----+---------+----------------+
| id        | int(11)     |      | PRI | NULL    | auto_increment |
| testField | varchar(75) | YES  |     | NULL    |                |
+-----------+-------------+------+-----+---------+----------------+
2 rows in set (0.00 sec)
```

If this is the case, congratulations—you have successfully created a table in your MySQL database using PHP!

However, if the value of $res is not true and the table was not created, an error message will appear, generated by the mysqli_error() function.

Retrieving Error Messages

Take some time to familiarize yourself with the `mysqli_error()` function—it will become your friend. When used in conjunction with the PHP `die()` function, which simply exits the script at the point at which it appears, the `mysqli_error()` function will return a helpful error message when you make a mistake.

For example, now that you have created a table called `testTable`, you won't be able to execute that script again without an error. Try to execute the script again; when you execute the script, you should see something like the following in your web browser:

```
Could not create table: Table 'testtable' already exists
```

How exciting! Move on to the next section to start inserting data into your table, and soon you'll be retrieving and formatting it via PHP.

Working with MySQL Data

Inserting, updating, deleting, and retrieving data all revolve around the use of the `mysqli_query()` function to execute the basic SQL queries you learned about in Chapter 16, "Learning Basic SQL Commands." For INSERT, UPDATE, and DELETE queries, no additional scripting is required after the query has been executed because you're not displaying any results (unless you want to). When using SELECT queries, you have a few options for displaying the data retrieved by your query. Let's start with the basics and insert some data, so you'll have something to retrieve later.

Inserting Data with PHP

The easiest method for inserting data at this stage in the game is to simply hard-code the INSERT statement, as shown in Listing 18.4.

LISTING 18.4 A Script to Insert a Record

```
1:  <?php
2:  $mysqli = mysqli_connect("localhost", "joeuser", "somepass", "testDB");
3:
4:  if (mysqli_connect_errno()) {
5:      printf("Connect failed: %s\n", mysqli_connect_error());
6:      exit();
7:  } else {
8:      $sql = "INSERT INTO testTable (testField) VALUES ('some value')";
9:      $res = mysqli_query($mysqli, $sql);
10:
11:     if ($res === TRUE) {
12:         echo "A record has been inserted.";
13:     } else {
14:         printf("Could not insert record: %s\n", mysqli_error($mysqli));
```

LISTING 18.4   Continued

```
15:     }
16:
17:     mysqli_close($mysqli);
18: }
19: ?>
```

The only change between this script—for record insertion—and the script in Listing 18.3 for table creation is the SQL query stored in the $sql variable on line 8, and text modifications on lines 12 and 14. The connection code and the structure for issuing a query remain the same—in fact, most procedural code for accessing MySQL will fall into this same type of code template.

Call this script mysqlinsert.php and place it on your web server. Running this script will result in the addition of a row to the testTable table. To enter more records than the one shown in the script, you can either make a long list of hard-coded SQL statements and use mysqli_query() multiple times to execute these statements, or you can create a form-based interface to the record addition script.

To create the form for this script, you need only one field because the id field can automatically increment. The action of the form is the name of the record-addition script; let's call it insert.php. Your HTML form might look something like Listing 18.5.

LISTING 18.5   An Insert Form

```
1:  <html>
2:  <head>
3:  <title>Record Insertion Form</title>
4:  </head>
5:  <body>
6:  <form action="insert.php" method="POST">
7:  <p>Text to Add:<br>
8:  <input type="text" name="testfield" size="30">
9:  <p><input type="submit" name="submit" value="insert record"></p>
10: </form>
11: </body>
12: </html>
```

Save this file as insert_form.html and put it in the document root of your web server. Next, create the insert.php script shown in Listing 18.6. The value entered in the form will replace the hard-coded values in the SQL query with a variable called $_POST["testfield"].

LISTING 18.6   An Insert Script Used with the Form

```
1:  <?php
2:  $mysqli = mysqli_connect("localhost", "joeuser", "somepass", "testDB");
3:
4:  if (mysqli_connect_errno()) {
```

LISTING 18.6   Continued

```
5:      printf("Connect failed: %s\n", mysqli_connect_error());
6:      exit();
7:  } else {
8:      $sql = "INSERT INTO testTable (testField)
9:            VALUES ('".$_POST["testfield"]."')";
10:     $res = mysqli_query($mysqli, $sql);
11:
12:      if ($res === TRUE) {
13:            echo "A record has been inserted.";
14:      } else {
15:          printf("Could not insert record: %s\n", mysqli_error($mysqli));
16:      }
17:
18:      mysqli_close($mysqli);
19:  }
20:  ?>
```

The only change between this script and the script in Listing 18.4 is the use of $_POST["testfield"] in place of the hard-coded text string. Save the script as insert.php and put it in the document root of your web server. In your web browser, access the HTML form that you created. It should look something like Figure 18.1.

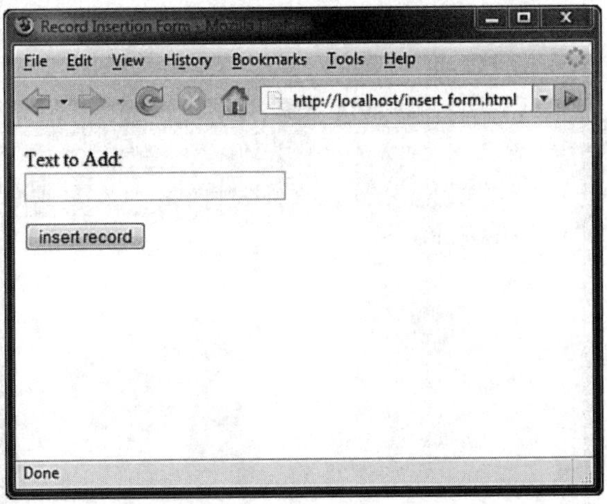

FIGURE 18.1
The HTML form for adding a record.

Enter a string in the Text to Add field, as shown in Figure 18.2.

Finally, click the Insert Record button to execute the insert.php script and insert the record. If successful, you will see results similar to Figure 18.3.

To verify your work, you can use the MySQL command-line interface to view the records in the table:

```
mysql> SELECT * FROM testTable;
+----+--------------------+
| id | testField          |
+----+--------------------+
|  1 | some value         |
|  2 | this is some text! |
+----+--------------------+
2 rows in set (0.00 sec)
```

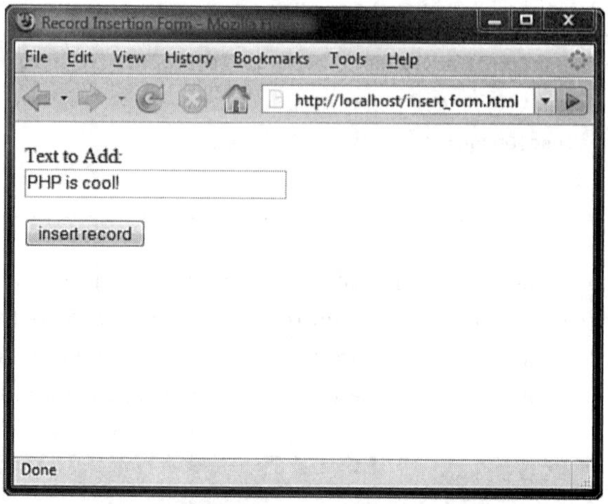

FIGURE 18.2
Text typed in
the form field.

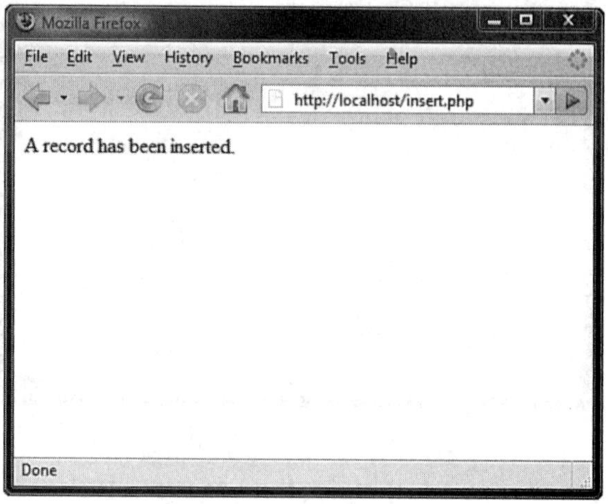

FIGURE 18.3
The record has
been success-
fully added.

Next, you'll learn how to retrieve and format results with PHP.

Retrieving Data with PHP

Because you have a few rows in your testTable table, you can write a PHP script to retrieve that data. Starting with the basics, write a script that issues a SELECT query but doesn't overwhelm you with result data; let's just get the number of rows. To do this, use the mysqli_num_rows() function (see line 12 of Listing 18.7).

LISTING 18.7   A Script to Retrieve Data

```
1:  <?php
2:  $mysqli = mysqli_connect("localhost", "joeuser", "somepass", "testDB");
3:
4:  if (mysqli_connect_errno()) {
5:      printf("Connect failed: %s\n", mysqli_connect_error());
6:      exit();
7:  } else {
8:      $sql = "SELECT * FROM testTable";
9:      $res = mysqli_query($mysqli, $sql);
10:
11:     if ($res) {
12:         $number_of_rows = mysqli_num_rows($res);
13:         printf("Result set has %d rows.\n", $number_of_rows);
14:     } else {
15:         printf("Could not retrieve records: %s\n", mysqli_error($mysqli));
16:     }
17:
18:     mysqli_free_result($res);
19:     mysqli_close($mysqli);
20: }
21: ?>
```

Save this script as count.php, place it in your web server document directory, and access it through your web browser. You should see a message like this (the actual number will vary depending on how many records you inserted into the table):

```
Result set has 6 rows.
```

Line 12 uses the mysqli_num_rows() function to retrieve the number of rows in the resultset ($res), and it places the value in a variable called $number_of_rows. Line 13 prints this number to your browser. The number should be equal to the number of records you inserted during testing.

> The use of mysqli_free_result() before closing the connection with mysqli_close() ensures that all memory associated with the query and result is freed for use by other scripts.

By the Way

Now that you know there are some records in the table, you can get fancy and fetch the actual contents of those records. You can do this in a few ways, but the easiest method is to retrieve each row as an array.

You'll use a while statement to go through each record in the resultset, placing the values of each field into a specific variable, and then displaying the results onscreen. The syntax of `mysqli_fetch_array()` is

```
$newArray = mysqli_fetch_array($result_set);
```

Follow along using the sample script in Listing 18.8.

LISTING 18.8   A Script to Retrieve Data and Display Results

```
 1:  <?php
 2:  $mysqli = mysqli_connect("localhost", "joeuser", "somepass", "testDB");
 3:
 4:  if (mysqli_connect_errno()) {
 5:      printf("Connect failed: %s\n", mysqli_connect_error());
 6:      exit();
 7:  } else {
 8:      $sql = "SELECT * FROM testTable";
 9:      $res = mysqli_query($mysqli, $sql);
10:
11:      if ($res) {
12:          while ($newArray = mysqli_fetch_array($res, MYSQLI_ASSOC)) {
13:              $id   = $newArray['id'];
14:              $testField = $newArray['testField'];
15:              echo "The ID is ".$id." and the text is ".$testField."<br/>";
16:          }
17:      } else {
18:          printf("Could not retrieve records: %s\n", mysqli_error($mysqli));
19:      }
20:
21:      mysqli_free_result($res);
22:      mysqli_close($mysqli);
23:  }
24:  ?>
```

Save this script as `select.php`, place it in your web server document directory, and access it through your web browser. You should see a message for each record entered into `testTable`, as shown in Figure 18.4. This message is created in the while loop in lines 12 through 15.

Essentially, you can create an entire database-driven application using just four or five MySQLi functions. This chapter barely scratched the surface of using PHP with MySQL; there are many more MySQLi functions in PHP.

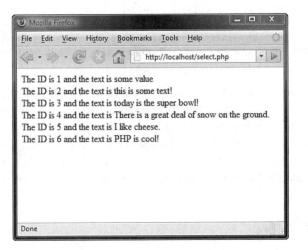

FIGURE 18.4
Selecting records from MySQL.

Additional MySQL Functions in PHP

More than 100 MySQL-specific functions are available through the MySQLi interface in PHP. Most of these functions are simply alternative methods of retrieving data or are used to gather information about the table structure in question. Throughout this book, especially in the project-related chapters a little later, you'll gradually be introduced to more of the MySQL-specific functions in PHP. However, for a complete list of functions, with practical examples, visit the MySQLi section of the PHP Manual at http://www.php.net/mysqli.

Summary

Using PHP and MySQL to create dynamic, database-driven websites is a breeze. Just remember that the PHP functions are essentially a gateway to the database server; anything you'd enter using the MySQL command-line interface, you can use with the `mysqli_query()` function.

To connect to MySQL with PHP, you need to know your MySQL username, password, and database name. When connected, you can issue standard SQL commands with the `mysqli_query()` function. If you have issued a SELECT command, you can use `mysqli_num_rows()` to count the records returned in the resultset. If you want to display the data found, you can use `mysqli_fetch_array()` to get all the results during a loop and display them onscreen.

Q&A

Q. *Is it possible to use both `mysql_*` and `mysqli_*` functions in one application?*

A. If PHP was built with both libraries enabled, you can use either set of functions to talk to MySQL. However, be aware that if you use the `mysql_*` set of functions with a version of MySQL greater than 4.1.3, you will not be able to access certain new functionality. Additionally, if you are inconsistent with your usage throughout your application, maintenance and upkeep of your application will be time-consuming and produce less than optimal results.

Workshop

The workshop is designed to help you anticipate possible questions, review what you've learned, and begin putting your knowledge into practice.

Quiz

1. What is the primary function used to make the connection between PHP and MySQL, and what information is necessary?

2. Which PHP function retrieves the text of a MySQL error message?

3. Which PHP function counts the number of records in a resultset?

Answers

1. The `mysqli_connect()` function creates a connection to MySQL and requires the hostname, username, and password.

2. The `mysqli_error()` function returns a MySQL error message.

3. The `mysqli_num_rows()` function counts the number of records in a resultset.

PART V

Basic Projects

19

Managing a Simple Mailing List

This chapter provides the first of several hands-on, small projects designed to pull together your PHP and MySQL knowledge. In this chapter, you'll learn the methods for creating a managed distribution list that you can use to send out newsletters or anything else you want to send to a list of email addresses in a database.

The mailing mechanism you'll use in this chapter is not meant to be a replacement for mailing list software, which is specifically designed for bulk messages. You should use the type of system you'll build in this lesson only for small lists, fewer than a few hundred email addresses.

In this chapter, you will learn

▶ How to create a subscribe/unsubscribe form and script

▶ How to create a front end for sending your message

▶ How to create the script that sends your message

Developing the Subscription Mechanism

You learned in earlier chapters that planning is the most important aspect of creating any product. In this case, think of the elements you will need for your subscription mechanism:

▶ A table to hold email addresses

▶ A way for users to add or remove their email addresses

▶ A form and script for sending the message

The following sections describe each item individually.

Creating the subscribers Table

You really need only one field in the subscribers table: to hold the email address of the user. However, you should have an ID field just for consistency among your tables, and because referencing an ID is much simpler than referencing a long email address in where clauses. So, in this case, your MySQL query would look something like

```
mysql> CREATE TABLE subscribers (
    -> id INT NOT NULL PRIMARY KEY AUTO_INCREMENT,
    -> email VARCHAR (150) UNIQUE NOT NULL
    -> );
Query OK, 0 rows affected (0.00 sec)
```

Note the use of UNIQUE in the field definition for email. This means that although id is the primary key, duplicates should not be allowed in the email field either. The email field is a unique key, and id is the primary key.

Log in to MySQL via the command line and issue this query. After creating the table, issue a DESC or DESCRIBE query to verify that the table has been created to your specifications, such as

```
mysql> DESC subscribers;
+--------+--------------+------+-----+---------+----------------+
| Field  | Type         | Null | Key | Default | Extra          |
+--------+--------------+------+-----+---------+----------------+
| id     | int(11)      | NO   | PRI | NULL    | auto_increment |
| email  | varchar(150) | NO   | UNI |         |                |
+--------+--------------+------+-----+---------+----------------+
2 rows in set (0.00 sec)
```

Now that you have a table in your database, you can create the form and script that place values in there.

Creating an Include File for Common Functions

Although there are only two scripts in this process, there are some common functions between them—namely, the database connection information. To make your scripts more concise in situations like this, take the common functions or code snippets and put them in a file to be included in your other scripts via the include() function that you learned about in Chapter 13, "Working with Files and Directories." Listing 19.1 contains the code shared by the scripts in this chapter.

LISTING 19.1   Common Functions in an Included File

```
1:   <?php
2:
3:   function doDB() {
4:       global $mysqli;
5:
6:       //connect to server and select database; you may need it
7:       $mysqli = mysqli_connect("localhost", "joeuser",
8:           "somepass", "testDB");
9:
10:      //if connection fails, stop script execution
11:      if (mysqli_connect_errno()) {
12:          printf("Connect failed: %s\n", mysqli_connect_error());
13:          exit();
14:      }
15:  }
16:
17:  function emailChecker($email) {
18:      global $mysqli, $check_res;
19:
20:      //check that email is not already in list
21:      $check_sql = "SELECT id FROM SUBSCRIBERS
22:          WHERE email = '".$email."'";
23:      $check_res = mysqli_query($mysqli, $check_sql)
24:          or die(mysqli_error($mysqli));
25:  }
26:  ?>
```

Lines 3–15 set up the first function, doDB(), which is simply the database connection function. If the connection cannot be made, the script will exit when this function is called; otherwise, it will make the value of $mysqli available to other parts of your script.

Lines 17–25 define a function called emailChecker(), which takes an input and returns an output—like most functions do. We'll look at this one in the context of the script, as we get to it in Listing 19.2.

Save this file as ch19_include.php and place it on your web server. In Listing 19.2, you will see how to include this file when necessary in your scripts.

Creating the Subscription Form

The subscription form will actually be an all-in-one form and script called manage.php, which will handle both subscribe and unsubscribe requests. Listing 19.2 shows the code for manage.php, which uses a few user-defined functions to eliminate repetitive code and to start you thinking about creating functions on your own. The code looks long, but a line-by-line description follows, and the majority of the code is an HTML form, so no worries!

LISTING 19.2   Subscribe and Unsubscribe with `manage.php`

```
1:   <?php
2:   include("ch19_include.php");
3:   //determine if they need to see the form or not
4:   if (!$_POST) {
5:        //they need to see the form, so create form block
6:        $display_block = "
7:        <form method=\"POST\" action=\"".$_SERVER["PHP_SELF"]."\">
8:
9:        <p><strong>Your E-Mail Address:</strong><br/>
10:       <input type=\"text\" name=\"email\" size=\"40\">
11:
12:       <p><strong>Action:</strong><br/>
13:       <input type=\"radio\" name=\"action\"
14:          value=\"sub\" checked> subscribe
15:       <input type=\"radio\" name=\"action\"
16:          value=\"unsub\"> unsubscribe
17:
18:       <p><input type=\"submit\" name=\"submit\"
19:          value=\"Submit Form\"></p>
20:       </form>";
21:
22:  } else if (($_POST) && ($_POST["action"] == "sub")) {
23:       //trying to subscribe; validate email address
24:       if ($_POST["email"] == "") {
25:            header("Location: manage.php");
26:            exit;
27:       } else {
28:            //connect to database
29:            doDB();
30:
31:            //check that email is in list
32:            emailChecker($_POST["email"]);
33:
34:            //get number of results and do action
35:            if (mysqli_num_rows($check_res) < 1) {
36:                //free result
37:                mysqli_free_result($check_res);
38:
39:                //add record
40:                $add_sql = "INSERT INTO subscribers (email)
41:                        VALUES('".$_POST["email"]."')";
42:                $add_res = mysqli_query($mysqli, $add_sql)
43:                        or die(mysqli_error($mysqli));
44:                $display_block = "<p>Thanks for signing up!</p>";
45:
46:                //close connection to MySQL
47:                mysqli_close($mysqli);
48:            } else {
49:                //print failure message
50:                $display_block = "<p>You're already subscribed!</p>";
51:            }
52:       }
53:  } else if (($_POST) && ($_POST["action"] == "unsub")) {
54:       //trying to unsubscribe; validate email address
55:       if ($_POST["email"] == "") {
56:            header("Location: manage.php");
57:            exit;
```

LISTING 19.2 Continued

```
58:        } else {
59:            //connect to database
60:            doDB();
61:
62:            //check that email is in list
63:            emailChecker($_POST["email"]);
64:
65:            //get number of results and do action
66:            if (mysqli_num_rows($check_res) < 1) {
67:                //free result
68:                mysqli_free_result($check_res);
69:
70:                //print failure message
71:                $display_block = "<p>Couldn't find your address!</p>
72:                <p>No action was taken.</p>";
73:            } else {
74:                //get value of ID from result
75:                while ($row = mysqli_fetch_array($check_res)) {
76:                    $id = $row["id"];
77:                }
78:
79:                //unsubscribe the address
80:                $del_sql = "DELETE FROM subscribers
81:                            WHERE id = '".$id."'";
82:                $del_res = mysqli_query($mysqli, $del_sql)
83:                            or die(mysqli_error($mysqli));
84:                $display_block = "<P>You're unsubscribed!</p>";
85:            }
86:            mysqli_close($mysqli);
87:        }
88:    }
89:    ?>
90:    <html>
91:    <head>
92:    <title>Subscribe/Unsubscribe to a Mailing List</title>
93:    </head>
94:    <body>
95:    <h1>Subscribe/Unsubscribe to a Mailing List</h1>
96:    <?php echo "$display_block"; ?>
97:    </body>
98:    </html>
```

Listing 19.2 might be long, but it's not complicated. In fact, it could be longer were it not for the user-defined functions placed in ch19_include.php and included on line 2 of this script.

Line 4 starts the main logic of the script. Because this script performs several actions, you need to determine which action it is currently attempting. If the presence of $_POST is false, you know that the user has not submitted the form; therefore, you must show the form to the user.

Lines 5–20 create the subscribe/unsubscribe form, using $_SERVER["PHP_SELF"] as the action (line 7), creating a text field called email for the user's email address and setting up a set of radio buttons (lines 12–16) to find the desired task. At this point, the script breaks out of the if...else construct, skips down to line 96, and proceeds to print the HTML, which is stored in the $display_block variable. The form displays as shown in Figure 19.1.

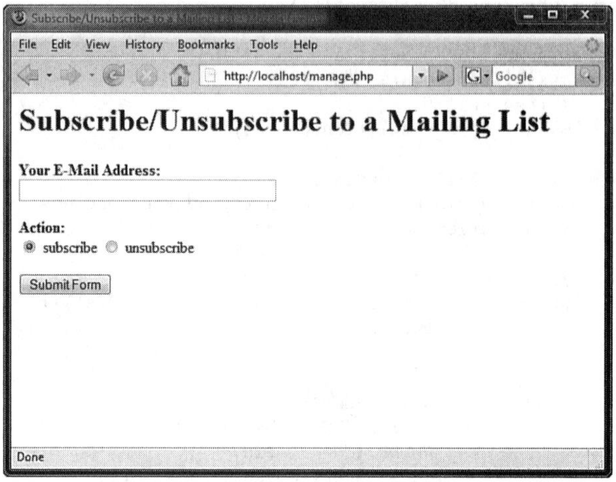

FIGURE 19.1
The subscribe/
unsubscribe
form.

Back inside the if...else construct, if the presence of $_POST is true, you need to do something. There are two possibilities: the subscribing and unsubscribing actions for the email address provided in the form. You determine which action to take by looking at the value of $_POST["action"] from the radio button group.

In line 22, if the presence of $_POST is true and the value of $_POST["action"] is "sub", you know the user is trying to subscribe. To subscribe, the user needs an email address, so check for one in lines 24–26. If no address is present, redirect the user back to the form.

However, if an address is present, call the doDB() function (stored in ch19_include.php) in line 29 to connect to the database so that you can issue queries. In line 32, you call the second of our user-defined functions: emailChecker(). This function takes an input ($_POST["email"], in this case) and processes it. If you look back to lines 21–24 of Listing 19.1, you'll see code within the emailChecker() function that issues a query in an attempt to find an id value in the subscribers table for the record containing the email address passed to the function. The function then returns the resultset, called $check_res, for use within the larger script.

By the Way

Note the definition of global variables at the beginning of both user-defined functions in Listing 19.1. These variables need to be shared with the entire script, and so are declared global.

Jump down to line 35 to see how the $check_res variable is used: The number of records referred to by the $check_res variable is counted to determine whether the email address already exists in the table. If the number of rows is less than 1, the address is not in the list, and it can be added. The record is added, the response is stored in lines 40–44, and the failure message (if the address is already in the table) is stored in line 50. At that point, the script breaks out of the if...else construct, skips down to line 96, and proceeds to print the HTML. You'll test this functionality later.

The last combination of inputs occurs if the presence of $_POST is true and the value of the $_POST["action"] variable is "unsub". In this case, the user is trying to unsubscribe. To unsubscribe, an existing email address is required, so check for one in lines 55–57. If no address is present, send the user back to the form.

If an address is present, call the doDB() function in line 60 to connect to the database. Then, in line 63, you call emailChecker(), which again will return the resultset, $check_res. Line 66 counts the number of records in the resultset to determine whether the email address already exists in the table. If the number of rows is less than 1, the address is not in the list and it cannot be unsubscribed.

In this case, the response message is stored in lines 71–72. However, if the number of rows is not less than 1, the user is unsubscribed (the record deleted) and the response is stored in lines 80–84. At that point, the script breaks out of the if...else construct, skips down to line 96, and proceeds to print the HTML.

Figures 19.2 through 19.5 show the various results of the script, depending on the actions selected and the status of email addresses in the database.

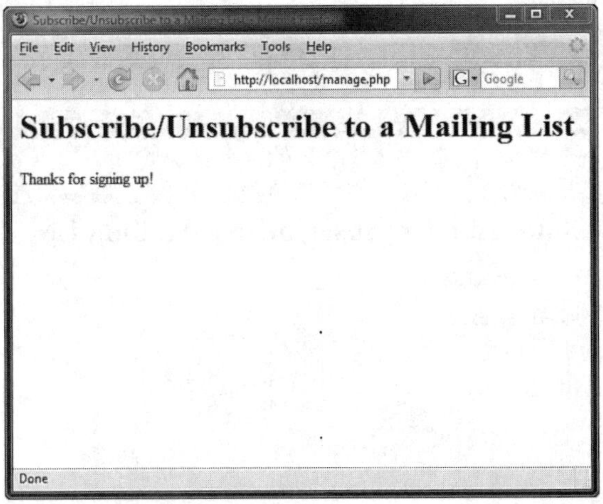

FIGURE 19.2
Successful subscription.

FIGURE 19.3
Subscription
failure.

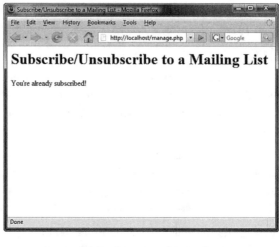

FIGURE 19.4
Successful
unsubscribe
action.

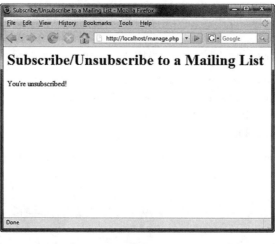

FIGURE 19.5
Unsuccessful
unsubscribe
action.

Next, you'll create the form and script that sends along mail to each of your subscribers.

Developing the Mailing Mechanism

With the subscription mechanism in place, you can create a basic form interface for a script that takes the content of your form and sends it to every address in your subscribers table. This is another one of those all-in-one scripts, called sendmymail.php, and it is shown in Listing 19.3.

> Before attempting to use the script in this section, make sure that you have read the section in Chapter 11, "Working with Forms," regarding the configuration in your php.ini file. The php.ini file is required to send mail.
>
> **By the Way**

LISTING 19.3 Send Mail to Your List of Subscribers

```
1: <?php
2: include("ch19_include.php");
3: if (!$_POST) {
4:     //haven't seen the form, so display it
5:     echo "<html>
6:     <head>
7:     <title>Send a Newsletter</title>
8:     </head>
9:     <body>
10:    <h1>Send a Newsletter</h1>
11:    <form method=\"post\" action=\"".$_SERVER["PHP_SELF"]."\">
12:    <p><strong>Subject:</strong><br/>
13:    <input type=\"text\" name=\"subject\" size=\"30\"></p>
14:    <p><strong>Mail Body:</strong><br/>
15:    <textarea name=\"message\" cols=\"50\" rows=\"10\"
16:         wrap=\"virtual\"></textarea>
17:    <p><input type=\"submit\" name=\"submit\" value=\"Send It\"></p>
18:    </form>
19:    </body>
20:    </html>";
21: } else if ($_POST) {
22:    //want to send form, so check for required fields
23:    if (($_POST["subject"] == "") || ($_POST["message"] == "")) {
24:        header("Location: sendmymail.php");
25:        exit;
26:    }
27:
28:    //connect to database
29:    doDB();
30:
31:    if (mysqli_connect_errno()) {
32:        //if connection fails, stop script execution
33:        printf("Connect failed: %s\n", mysqli_connect_error());
34:        exit();
35:    } else {
```

LISTING 19.3   Continued

```
36:          //otherwise, get emails from subscribers list
37:          $sql = "SELECT email FROM subscribers";
38:          $result = mysqli_query($mysqli, $sql)
39:                  or die(mysqli_error($mysqli));
40:
41:          //create a From: mailheader
42:          $mailheaders = "From: Your Mailing List
43:              <you@yourdomain.com>";
44:          //loop through results and send mail
45:          while ($row = mysqli_fetch_array($result)) {
46:              set_time_limit(0);
47:              $email = $row["email"];
48:              mail("$email", stripslashes($_POST["subject"]),
49:                  stripslashes($_POST["message"]), $mailheaders);
50:              echo "newsletter sent to: ".$email."<br/>";
51:          }
52:          mysqli_free_result($result);
53:          mysqli_close($mysqli);
54:      }
55: }
56: ?>
```

As in Listing 19.2, the file of user-defined functions is included on line 2. Although only the database connection function will be used in this file, there's no harm in having the other function in the file as well.

The main logic of the script starts at line 3, where you determine whether the user has seen the form yet. If the presence of the $_POST variable is false, you know the user has not submitted the form; therefore, you must show the form.

Lines 5–20 create the form for sending the newsletter to your subscriber list, which uses $_SERVER["PHP_SELF"] as the action (line 11), creates a text field called subject for the subject of the mail, and creates a textarea called message for the body of the mail to be sent.

At this point, the script breaks out of the if...else construct, and the HTML is printed. The form displays as shown in Figure 19.6.

If the presence of $_POST is not false, the script should send the form to the email addresses in the subscribers table. Before sending the message, you must check for the two required items from the form in lines 23–25: $_POST["subject"] and $_POST["message"]. If either of these items is not present, redirect the user to the form again.

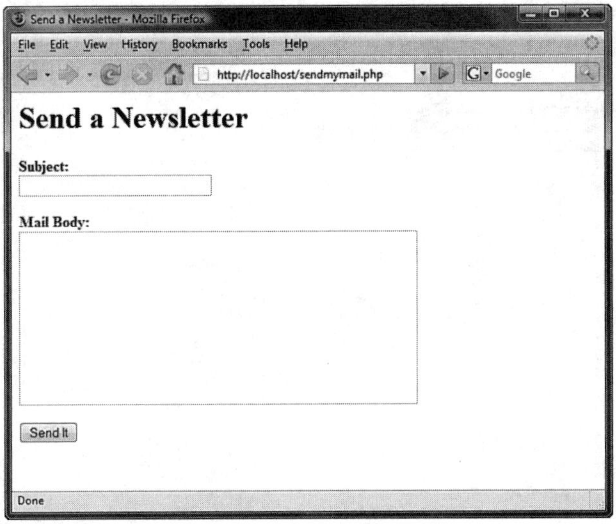

FIGURE 19.6
Form for sending the bulk mail.

If the required items are present, the script moves on to line 29, which calls the database connection function. A query is issued in line 38, which grabs all the email addresses from the subscribers table. There is no order to these results, although you could throw an order by clause in there if you want to send them out in alphabetical order for whatever reason.

Lines 42–43 create a From: mail header, which is used inside the upcoming while loop, when the mail is sent. This header ensures that the mail looks like it is from a person and not a machine because you've specifically provided a value in this string. The while loop, which begins on line 45, extracts the email addresses from the resultset one at a time. On line 46, you use the set_time_limit() function to set the time limit to 0, or "no limit." Doing so allows the script to run for as long as it needs to.

> Because the script in Listing 19.3 simply executes the mail() function numerous times, it does not take into account the queuing factors in actual mailing list software, which are designed to ease the burden on your outgoing mail server. Using set_time_limit() does not ease its burden; it just allows the script to continue to run when it might have timed out before.

By the Way

In lines 48–49, the mail is sent using the mail() function, inserting the values from the form where appropriate. Line 50 prints a message to the screen for you to show who should have received the mail. In Figures 19.7 and 19.8, you can see the outcome of the script.

FIGURE 19.7
Mail has been
sent!

FIGURE 19.8
The mail arrived
safely.

Summary

In this chapter, you applied your basic PHP and MySQL knowledge to the creation of a personal mailing list. Included were the database table creation, the subscribe and unsubscribe mechanisms, and the form and script for sending the mail.

Q&A

Q. *How can I ease the burden on my mail server?*

A. Besides looking into package mailing list software, you can bypass the `mail()` function and talk directly to your SMTP server via a socket connection. Such an example is shown in the PHP manual for the `fsockopen()` function (http://www.php.net/fsockopen), as well as in other developer resource sites.

Q. *Where do bounced messages go?*

A. Bounces go to whatever address you specify in your `From:` or `Reply-to:` mail headers.

Workshop

The workshop is designed to help you anticipate possible questions, review what you've learned, and begin putting your knowledge into practice.

Quiz

1. What function sends mail?

2. What function call causes the script to execute for as long as it needs to run?

Answers

1. This is not a trick question. It's the `mail()` function!

2. `set_time_limit(0)`

## 20

Creating an Online Address Book

In this hands-on lesson, your project will be to create a manageable online address book. You will learn the methods for creating the relevant database tables, as well as the forms and scripts for adding, deleting, and viewing database records.

In this chapter, you will learn

▶ How to create relational tables for an online address book

▶ How to create the forms and scripts for adding and deleting records in the address book

▶ How to create the forms and scripts for viewing records

Planning and Creating the Database Tables

When you think of an address book, the obvious fields come to mind: name, address, telephone number, email address. However, if you look at your own paper-based address book, you might note that you have several entries for one person. Maybe that person has three telephone numbers, or two email addresses, and so forth. In your online address book, a set of related tables will help alleviate the redundancy and repetition of information.

Table 20.1 shows sample table and field names to use for your online address book. In a minute, you'll use actual SQL statements to create the tables, but first you should look at this information and try to see the relationships appear. Ask yourself which of the fields should be primary or unique keys.

TABLE 20.1   Address Book Table and Field Names

Table Name	Field Names
master_name	id, date_added, date_modified, f_name, l_name
address	id, master_id, date_added, date_modified, address, city, state, zipcode, type
telephone	id, master_id, date_added, date_modified, tel_number, type
fax	id, master_id, date_added, date_modified, fax_number, type
email	id, master_id, date_added, date_modified, email, type
personal_notes	id, master_id, date_added, date_modified, note

Notice the use of date-related fields; each table has a date_added and date_modi-fied field in it. The fields will help maintain your data; you might at some point want to issue a query that removes all records older than a certain number of months or years, or removes all records that haven't been updated within a certain period.

As you can see in the following SQL statements, the master_name table has two fields besides the ID and date-related fields: f_name and l_name, for first name and last name. The id field is the primary key. No other keys need to be primary or unique unless you really want to limit your address book to one John Smith, one Mary Jones, and so forth.

By the Way

> The field lengths for the text fields in the following statements are arbitrary; you can make them as long or as short as you want, within the allowable definition of the field type.

The following SQL statement creates the master_name table:

```
mysql> CREATE TABLE master_name (
    -> id INT NOT NULL PRIMARY KEY AUTO_INCREMENT,
    -> date_added DATETIME,
    -> date_modified DATETIME,
    -> f_name VARCHAR (75),
    -> l_name VARCHAR (75)
    -> );
Query OK, 0 rows affected (0.01 sec)
```

Next, you'll create the supplementary tables, which all relate back to the master_name table. For instance, the address table has the basic primary key id field, the date_added field, and the date_modified field, plus the field through which the relationship will be made—the master_id field.

The master_id will be equal to the id field in the master_name table, matching the person whose address this is. The master_id field is not a unique key because it is a perfectly valid assumption that one person may have several address entries. You see this in the type field, defined as an enumerated list containing three options: home, work, or other. A person may have one or more of all three types, so no other keys are present in this table besides the primary key id. Assuming that this particular address book contains only United States addresses, round out the table with address, city, state, and zipcode fields:

```
mysql> CREATE TABLE address (
    -> id INT NOT NULL PRIMARY KEY AUTO_INCREMENT,
    -> master_id INT NOT NULL,
    -> date_added DATETIME,
    -> date_modified DATETIME,
    -> address VARCHAR (255),
    -> city VARCHAR (30),
    -> state CHAR (2),
    -> zipcode VARCHAR (10),
    -> type ENUM ('home', 'work', 'other')
    -> );
Query OK, 0 rows affected (0.01 sec)
```

The telephone, fax, and email tables are all variations on the same theme:

```
mysql> CREATE TABLE telephone (
    -> id INT NOT NULL PRIMARY KEY AUTO_INCREMENT,
    -> master_id INT NOT NULL,
    -> date_added DATETIME,
    -> date_modified DATETIME,
    -> tel_number VARCHAR (25),
    -> type ENUM ('home', 'work', 'other')
    -> );
Query OK, 0 rows affected (0.01 sec)
```

```
mysql> CREATE TABLE fax (
    -> id INT NOT NULL PRIMARY KEY AUTO_INCREMENT,
    -> master_id INT NOT NULL,
    -> date_added DATETIME,
    -> date_modified DATETIME,
    -> fax_number VARCHAR (25),
    -> type ENUM ('home', 'work', 'other')
    -> );
Query OK, 0 rows affected (0.00 sec)
```

```
mysql> CREATE TABLE email (
    -> id INT NOT NULL PRIMARY KEY AUTO_INCREMENT,
    -> master_id INT NOT NULL,
    -> date_added DATETIME,
    -> date_modified DATETIME,
    -> email VARCHAR (150),
    -> type ENUM ('home', 'work', 'other')
    -> );
Query OK, 0 rows affected (0.00 sec)
```

The personal_notes table also follows the same sort of pattern, except that master_id is a unique key and allows only one notes record per person:

```
mysql> CREATE TABLE personal_notes (
    -> id int NOT NULL PRIMARY KEY AUTO_INCREMENT,
    -> master_id INT NOT NULL UNIQUE,
    -> date_added DATETIME,
    -> date_modified DATETIME,
    -> note TEXT
    -> );
Query OK, 0 rows affected (0.00 sec)
```

Now that your tables are created, you can work through the forms and scripts for managing and viewing your records.

Creating an Include File for Common Functions

In Chapter 19, "Managing a Simple Mailing List," an included file of common functions was used to make your scripts more concise. The same thing is true in this chapter. Although the only content in the common functions file is the database connection function, this process serves two purposes: to make your scripts more concise and to eliminate the need to modify the database connection information throughout multiple files should that information change. Listing 20.1 contains the code shared by the scripts in this chapter.

LISTING 20.1   Common Functions in an Included File

```
1:   <?php
2:
3:   function doDB() {
4:       global $mysqli;
5:
6:       //connect to server and select database; you may need it
7:       $mysqli = mysqli_connect("localhost", "joeuser",
8:           "somepass", "testDB");
9:
10:      //if connection fails, stop script execution
11:      if (mysqli_connect_errno()) {
12:          printf("Connect failed: %s\n", mysqli_connect_error());
13:          exit();
14:      }
15:  }
16:  ?>
```

Lines 3–15 set up the database connection function, doDB. If the connection cannot be made, the script will exit when this function is called; otherwise, it will make the value of $mysqli available to other parts of your script.

Save this file as ch20_include.php and place it on your web server. The other code listings in this chapter will include this file within the first few lines of the script.

Creating a Menu

Your online address book will contain several actions, so it makes sense to create a menu for your links. Listing 20.2 creates a simple menu for all the scripts you will create in this chapter, called mymenu.html.

LISTING 20.2   Address Book Menu

```
 1: <html>
 2: <head>
 3: <title>My Address Book</title>
 4: </head>
 5: <body>
 6: <h1>My Address Book</h1>
 7:
 8: <p><strong>Management</strong></p>
 9: <ul>
10: <li><a href="addentry.php">Add an Entry</a></li>
11: <li><a href="delentry.php">Delete an Entry</a></li>
12: </ul>
13:
14: <p><strong>Viewing</strong></p>
15: <ul>
16: <li><a href="selentry.php">Select a Record</a></li>
17: </ul>
18: </body>
19: </html>
```

Figure 20.1 shows the output of Listing 20.2. You'll tackle each of these items in order, starting with "Add an Entry" in the next section.

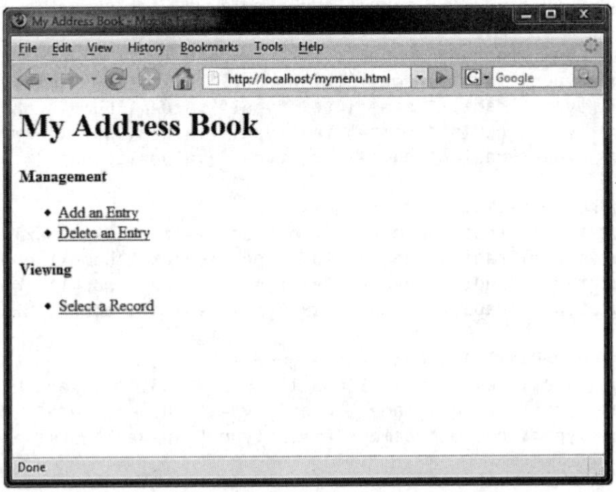

FIGURE 20.1
Address book menu.

Creating the Record Addition Mechanism

Just because you'll potentially be adding information to six different tables doesn't mean your form or script will be monstrous. In fact, your scripts won't look much different from any of the ones you created in previous lessons. With practice, you will be able to make these verbose scripts much more streamlined and efficient.

Listing 20.3 shows a basic record addition script, called addentry.php, which has two parts: what to do if the form should be displayed (lines 3–46) and what actions to take if the form is being submitted (lines 48–134). Lines 3–46 simply place the contents of the HTML form into a string called $display_block.

LISTING 20.3 Basic Record Addition Script Called addentry.php

```
1:   <?php
2:   include("ch20_include.php");
3:   if (!$_POST) {
4:       $display_block = "
5:       <form method=\"post\" action=\"".$_SERVER["PHP_SELF"]."\">
6:       <p><strong>First/Last Names:</strong><br/>
7:       <input type=\"text\" name=\"f_name\" size=\"30\" maxlength=\"75\">
8:       <input type=\"text\" name=\"l_name\" size=\"30\" maxlength=\"75\"></p>
9:
10:      <p><strong>Address:</strong><br/>
11:      <input type=\"text\" name=\"address\" size=\"30\"></p>
12:
13:      <p><strong>City/State/Zip:</strong><br/>
14:      <input type=\"text\" name=\"city\" size=\"30\" maxlength=\"50\">
15:      <input type=\"text\" name=\"state\" size=\"5\" maxlength=\"2\">
16:      <input type=\"text\" name=\"zipcode\" size=\"10\" maxlength=\"10\"></p>
17:
18:      <p><strong>Address Type:</strong><br/>
19:      <input type=\"radio\" name=\"add_type\" value=\"home\" checked> home
20:      <input type=\"radio\" name=\"add_type\" value=\"work\"> work
21:      <input type=\"radio\" name=\"add_type\" value=\"other\"> other</p>
22:
23:      <p><strong>Telephone Number:</strong><br/>
24:      <input type=\"text\" name=\"tel_number\" size=\"30\" maxlength=\"25\">
25:      <input type=\"radio\" name=\"tel_type\" value=\"home\" checked> home
26:      <input type=\"radio\" name=\"tel_type\" value=\"work\"> work
27:      <input type=\"radio\" name=\"tel_type\" value=\"other\"> other</p>
28:
29:      <p><strong>Fax Number:</strong><br/>
30:      <input type=\"text\" name=\"fax_number\" size=\"30\" maxlength=\"25\">
31:      <input type=\"radio\" name=\"fax_type\" value=\"home\" checked> home
32:      <input type=\"radio\" name=\"fax_type\" value=\"work\"> work
33:      <input type=\"radio\" name=\"fax_type\" value=\"other\"> other</p>
34:
35:      <p><strong>Email Address:</strong><br/>
36:      <input type=\"text\" name=\"email\" size=\"30\" maxlength=\"150\">
37:      <input type=\"radio\" name=\"email_type\" value=\"home\" checked> home
38:      <input type=\"radio\" name=\"email_type\" value=\"work\"> work
```

LISTING 20.3   Continued

```
39:        <input type=\"radio\" name=\"email_type\" value=\"other\"> other</p>
40:
41:        <p><strong>Personal Note:</strong><br/>
42:        <textarea name=\"note\" cols=\"35\" rows=\"3\"
43:        wrap=\"virtual\"></textarea></p>
44:
45:        <p><input type=\"submit\" name=\"submit\" value=\"Add Entry\"></p>
46:        </form>";
47:
48:    } else if ($_POST) {
49:        //time to add to tables, so check for required fields
50:        if (($_POST["f_name"] == "") || ($_POST["l_name"] == "")) {
51:            header("Location: addentry.php");
52:            exit;
53:        }
54:
55:        //connect to database
56:        doDB();
57:
58:        //add to master_name table
59:        $add_master_sql = "INSERT INTO master_name (date_added, date_modified,
60:                           f_name, l_name) VALUES (now(), now(),
61:                           '".$_POST["f_name"]."', '".$_POST["l_name"]."')";
62:        $add_master_res = mysqli_query($mysqli, $add_master_sql)
63:                          or die(mysqli_error($mysqli));
64:
65:        //get master_id for use with other tables
66:        $master_id = mysqli_insert_id($mysqli);
67:
68:        if (($_POST["address"]) || ($_POST["city"]) || ($_POST["state"])
69:            || ($_POST["zipcode"])) {
70:            //something relevant, so add to address table
80:            $add_address_sql = "INSERT INTO address (master_id, date_added,
81:                               date_modified, address, city, state, zipcode,
82:                               type)  VALUES ('".$master_id."', now(), now(),
83:                               '".$_POST["address"]."', '".$_POST["city"]."',
84:                               '".$_POST["state"]."' , '".$_POST["zipcode"]."',
85:                               '".$_POST["add_type"]."')";
86:            $add_address_res = mysqli_query($mysqli, $add_address_sql)
87:                               or die(mysqli_error($mysqli));
88:        }
89:
90:        if ($_POST["tel_number"]) {
91:            //something relevant, so add to telephone table
92:            $add_tel_sql = "INSERT INTO telephone (master_id, date_added,
93:                           date_modified, tel_number, type) VALUES
94:                           ('".$master_id."', now(), now(),
95:                           '".$_POST["tel_number"]."',
96:                           '".$_POST["tel_type"]."')";
97:            $add_tel_res = mysqli_query($mysqli, $add_tel_sql)
98:                           or die(mysqli_error($mysqli));
99:        }
100:
101:        if ($_POST["fax_number"]) {
102:            //something relevant, so add to fax table
103:            $add_fax_sql = "INSERT INTO fax (master_id, date_added,
```

LISTING 20.3   Continued

```
104:                              date_modified, fax_number, type)   VALUES
105:                              ('".$master_id."', now(), now(),
106:                              '".$_POST["fax_number"]."',
107:                              '".$_POST["fax_type"]."')";
108:          $add_fax_res = mysqli_query($mysqli, $add_fax_sql)
109:                              or die(mysqli_error($mysqli));
110:      }
111:
112:      if ($_POST["email"]) {
113:          //something relevant, so add to email table
114:          $add_email_sql = "INSERT INTO email (master_id, date_added,
115:                              date_modified, email, type)   VALUES
116:                              ('".$master_id."', now(), now(),
117:                              '".$_POST["email"]."',
118:                              '".$_POST["email_type"]."')";
119:          $add_email_res = mysqli_query($mysqli, $add_email_sql)
120:                              or die(mysqli_error($mysqli));
121:      }
122:
123:      if ($_POST["note"]) {
124:          //something relevant, so add to notes table
125:          $add_notes_sql = "INSERT INTO personal_notes (master_id,
126:              date_added, date_modified, note)   VALUES
127:              ('".$master_id."',now(),now(),'".$_POST["note"]."')";
128:          $add_notes_res = mysqli_query($mysqli, $add_notes_sql)
129:                              or die(mysqli_error($mysqli));
130:      }
131:      mysqli_close($mysqli);
132:      $display_block = "<p>Your entry has been added.
133:      Would you like to <a href=\"addentry.php\">add another</a>?</p>";
134: }
135: ?>
136: <html>
137: <head>
138: <title>Add an Entry</title>
139: </head>
140: <body>
141: <h1>Add an Entry</h1>
142: <?php echo $display_block; ?>
143: </body>
144: </html>
```

Before any other code, note that the file of user-defined functions is included on line 2. After that, as already noted, this script performs one of two tasks at any given time: it either shows the record addition form, or it performs the SQL queries related to adding a new record. The logic that determines the task begins at line 3, with a test for the value of $_POST. If there is no value in the $_POST superglobal, the user has not submitted the form and therefore needs to see the form. The HTML for the form is placed in a string called $display_block, from lines 4–46. The script then breaks out of the if...else construct and jumps down to line 136, which outputs the HTML and prints the value of $display_block, in this case the form. Figure 20.2 displays the outcome.

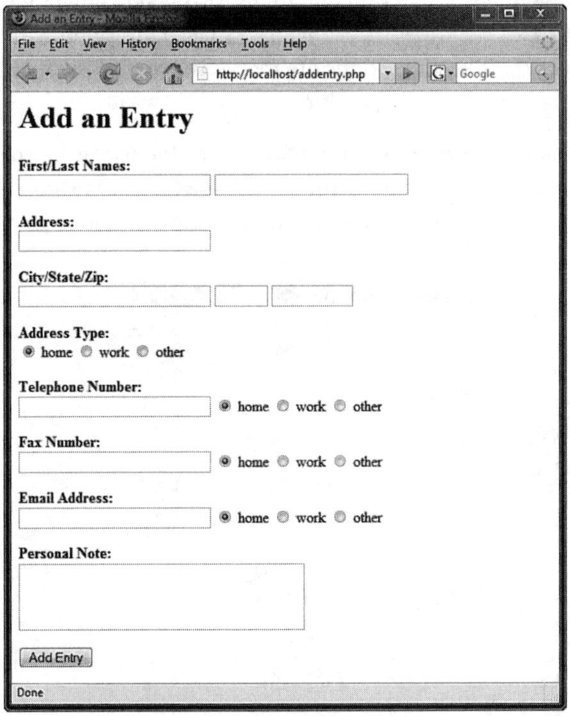

FIGURE 20.2
The record addition form.

The else condition on Line 48 is invoked if there is a value in $_POST, meaning that the user has submitted the form. In this simple example, you designate two fields as required fields: the first name and last name of the person. So, lines 59–62 check for values in $_POST["f_name"] and $_POST["l_name"] and redirect the user back to the form if either value is missing.

After making it through the check for required fields, the code connects to the database in line 65. Next comes the multitude of insertion statements, only one of which is required—the insertion of a record into the master_name table. This occurs on lines 68–72. After the insertion is made, the id of this record is extracted using mysqli_insert_id() on line 75. You use this value, now referred to as $master_id, in your remaining SQL queries.

The SQL queries for inserting records into the remaining tables are all conditional, meaning they will occur only if some condition is true. In lines 77–78, you see that the condition that must be met is that a value exists for any of the following variables: $_POST["address"], $_POST["city"], $_POST["state"], $_POST["zip-code"]. Lines 80–87 create and issue the query if this condition is met.

The same principle holds true for adding to the telephone table (lines 90–99), the fax table (lines 101–110), the email table (lines 112–121), and the personal_notes table (lines 123–130). If the conditions are met, records are inserted into those tables.

Once through this set of conditions, the message for the user is placed in the $display_block variable, and the script exits this if...else construct and prints HTML from lines 136–145. Figure 20.3 shows an output of the record addition script.

FIGURE 20.3
A record has been added.

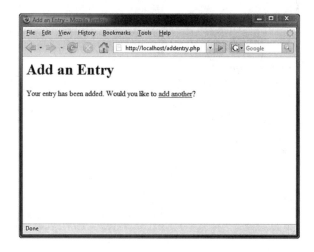

Add a few records using this form so that you have some values to play with in the following sections. On your own, try to modify this script in such a way that the values entered in the form print to the screen after successful record insertion.

Viewing Records

If you verified your work in the preceding section by issuing queries through the MySQL monitor or other interface, you probably became tired of typing SELECT * FROM... for every table. In this section, you'll create the two-part script that shows you how to select and view records in your database.

Listing 20.4 shows the select-and-view script called selentry.php, which has two parts: the record selection form (lines 5–40) and the code to display the record contents (lines 51–163). Because this code is longer than the other code you've seen so far, it is broken into smaller chunks for discussion.

LISTING 20.4   Script Called `selentry.php` for Selecting and Viewing a Record

```
 1:  <?php
 2:  include("ch20_include.php");
 3:  doDB();
 4:
 5:  if (!$_POST)  {
 6:        //haven't seen the selection form, so show it
 7:        $display_block = "<h1>Select an Entry</h1>";
 8:
 9:        //get parts of records
10:        $get_list_sql = "SELECT id,
11:                    CONCAT_WS(', ', l_name, f_name) AS display_name
12:                    FROM master_name ORDER BY l_name, f_name";
13:        $get_list_res = mysqli_query($mysqli, $get_list_sql)
14:                    or die(mysqli_error($mysqli));
15:
16:        if (mysqli_num_rows($get_list_res) < 1) {
17:              //no records
18:              $display_block .= "<p><em>Sorry, no records to select!</em></p>";
19:
20:        } else {
21:              //has records, so get results and print in a form
22:              $display_block .= "
23:              <form method=\"post\" action=\"".$_SERVER["PHP_SELF"]."\">
24:              <p><strong>Select a Record to View:</strong><br/>
25:              <select name=\"sel_id\">
26:              <option value=\"\">-- Select One --</option>";
27:
28:              while ($recs = mysqli_fetch_array($get_list_res)) {
29:                    $id = $recs['id'];
30:                    $display_name = stripslashes($recs["display_name"]);
31:                    $display_block .= "<option value=\"".$id."\">".
32:                    $display_name."</option>";
33:              }
34:
35:              $display_block .= "
36:              </select>
37:              <p><input type=\"submit\" name=\"submit\"
38:                    value=\"View Selected Entry\"></p>
39:              </form>";
40:        }
41:        //free result
42:        mysqli_free_result($get_list_res);
```

As with the addentry.php script, the selentry.php script performs one of two tasks at any given time: It either shows the selection form, or it performs all the SQL queries related to viewing the record. No matter which of the two tasks the script performs, the database still comes into play. Given that, include the file with the connection function on line 2, and call that function on line 3.

The logic that determines the task begins at line 5, with a test for the value of the $_POST superglobal. If $_POST has no value, the user is not coming from the selection form and therefore needs to see it. A string called $display_block is started in line 7, and this string will ultimately hold the HTML that makes up the record selection form.

Lines 10–12 select specific fields from the records in the master_name table to build the selection drop-down options in the form. For this step, you need only the name and ID of the person whose record you want to select. Line 16 tests for results of the query; if the query has no results, you can't build a form. If this were the case, the value of $display_block would be filled with an error message and the script would end, printing the resulting HTML to the screen.

However, assume that you have a few records in the master_name table. In this case, you have to extract the information from the query results to be able to build the form. This is done in lines 28–33, with form elements written to the $display_block string both above and below it.

This listing stops at line 42, but you'll soon see lines 43 through the end of the script. If you were to close up the if statement and the PHP block and print the value of $display_block to the screen at this point, you would see a form something like that shown in Figure 20.4 (with different entries).

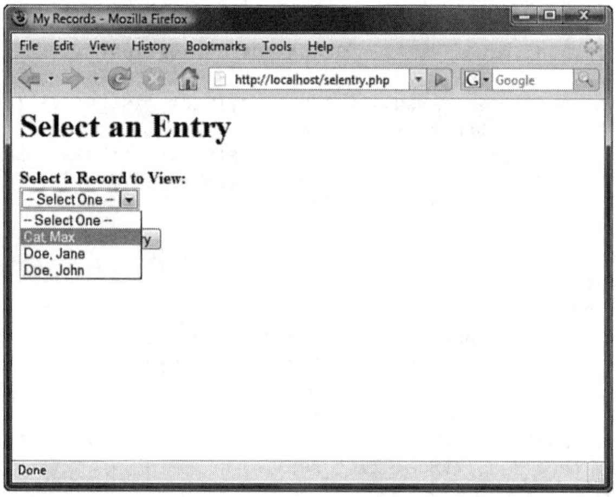

FIGURE 20.4
The record
selection form.

However, you must finish the selentry.php script, so continue Listing 20.4 at line 43, which begins the else portion of the if...else statement:

LISTING 20.4 (continued)

```
43:  } else if ($_POST) {
44:      //check for required fields
45:      if ($_POST["sel_id"] == "")  {
46:            header("Location: selentry.php");
47:            exit;
48:      }
49:
50:      //get master_info
51:      $get_master_sql = "SELECT concat_ws(' ',f_name,l_name) as display_name
52:                        FROM master_name WHERE id = '".$_POST["sel_id"]."'";
53:      $get_master_res = mysqli_query($mysqli, $get_master_sql)
54:                        or die(mysqli_error($mysqli));
55:
56:      while ($name_info = mysqli_fetch_array($get_master_res)) {
57:          $display_name = stripslashes($name_info['display_name']);
58:      }
59:
60:      $display_block = "<h1>Showing Record for ".$display_name."</h1>";
61:
62:      //free result
63:      mysqli_free_result($get_master_res);
64:
65:      //get all addresses
66:      $get_addresses_sql = "SELECT address, city, state, zipcode, type
67:              FROM address WHERE master_id = '".$_POST["sel_id"]."'";
68:      $get_addresses_res = mysqli_query($mysqli, $get_addresses_sql)
69:                          or die(mysqli_error($mysqli));
70:
71:      if (mysqli_num_rows($get_addresses_res) > 0) {
72:          $display_block .= "<p><strong>Addresses:</strong><br/>
73:          <ul>";
74:
75:          while ($add_info = mysqli_fetch_array($get_addresses_res)) {
76:              address = stripslashes($add_info['address']);
77:              $city = stripslashes($add_info['city']);
78:              $state = stripslashes($add_info['state']);
79:              $zipcode = stripslashes($add_info['zipcode']);
80:              $address_type = $add_info['type'];
81:
82:              $display_block .= "<li>$address $city $state $zipcode
83:                              ($address_type)</li>";
84:          }
85:          $display_block .= "</ul>";
86:      }
87:      //free result
88:      mysqli_free_result($get_addresses_res);
```

Line 43 contains the else portion of the if...else statement and is invoked if the form wants to see a specific record. It first checks for a required field, in line 45; in this case, it is checking for the value of $_POST["sel_id"]. This value matches the ID from the master_name table to that of the selection made in the record selection form. If that value does not exist, the user is redirected back to the selection form—you can't very well gather information from a set of tables when the primary key isn't present!

Assuming that a value was present for $_POST["sel_id"], you issue a query in lines 51–54 that obtains the name of the user whose record you want to view. This information is placed in the now-familiar $display_block string, which will continue to be built as the script continues.

Lines 66–85 represent the query against the address table, and the resulting display that is built. If the selected individual has no records in the address table, nothing is added to the $display_block string. However, if there are one or more entries, the addresses for this person are added to the $display_block string as one or more unordered list elements, as shown in lines 73–85.

Lines 89–165 of Listing 20.4 perform the same type of looping and writing to the $display_block variable, but the tables are different. For instance, lines 90–105 look for information in the telephone table and create an appropriate string to be added to $display_block, if any information is present. The same structure is repeated in lines 111–126 for information from the fax table, lines 132–146 for information from the email table, and lines 152–162 for any content present in the personal_notes table.

LISTING 20.4   (continued)

```
89:      //get all tel
90:      $get_tel_sql = "SELECT tel_number, type FROM telephone WHERE
91:                      master_id = '".$_POST["sel_id"]."'";
92:      $get_tel_res = mysqli_query($mysqli, $get_tel_sql)
93:                      or die(mysqli_error($mysqli));
94:
95:      if (mysqli_num_rows($get_tel_res) > 0) {
96:          $display_block .= "<p><strong>Telephone:</strong><br/>
97:          <ul>";
98:
99:          while ($tel_info = mysqli_fetch_array($get_tel_res)) {
100:             $tel_number = stripslashes($tel_info['tel_number']);
101:             $tel_type = $tel_info['type'];
102:
103:             $display_block .= "<li>$tel_number ($tel_type)</li>";
104:          }
105:          $display_block .= "</ul>";
106:      }
107:      //free result
108:      mysqli_free_result($get_tel_res);
109:
110:      //get all fax
111:      $get_fax_sql = "SELECT fax_number, type FROM fax WHERE
112:                      master_id = '".$_POST["sel_id"]."'";
113:      $get_fax_res = mysqli_query($mysqli, $get_fax_sql)
114:                      or die(mysqli_error($mysqli));
115:
116:      if (mysqli_num_rows($get_fax_res) > 0) {
117:          $display_block .= "<p><strong>Fax:</strong><br/>
118:          <ul>";
119:
```

LISTING 20.4 Continued

```
120:          while ($fax_info = mysqli_fetch_array($get_fax_res)) {
121:              $fax_number =  stripslashes($fax_info['fax_number']);
122:              $fax_type = $fax_info['type'];
123:
124:              $display_block .= "<li>$fax_number ($fax_type)</li>";
125:          }
126:            $display_block .= "</ul>";
127:      }
128:      //free result
129:      mysqli_free_result($get_fax_res);
130:
131:      //get all email
132:      $get_email_sql = "SELECT email, type FROM email WHERE
133:                       master_id = '".$_POST["sel_id"]."'";
134:      $get_email_res = mysqli_query($mysqli, $get_email_sql)
135:                       or die(mysqli_error($mysqli));
136:      if (mysqli_num_rows($get_email_res) > 0) {
137:          $display_block .= "<p><strong>Email:</strong><br/>
138:          <ul>";
139:
140:          while ($email_info = mysqli_fetch_array($get_email_res)) {
141:              $email = stripslashes($email_info['email']);
142:              $email_type = $email_info['type'];
143:
144:              $display_block .= "<li>$email ($email_type)</li>";
145:          }
146:          $display_block .= "</ul>";
147:      }
148:      //free result
149:      mysqli_free_result($get_email_res);
150:
151:      //get personal note
152:      $get_notes_sql = "SELECT note FROM personal_notes WHERE
153:                       master_id = '".$_POST["sel_id"]."'";
154:      $get_notes_res = mysqli_query($mysqli, $get_notes_sql)
155:                       or die(mysqli_error($mysqli));
156:
157:      if (mysqli_num_rows($get_notes_res) == 1) {
158:          while ($note_info = mysqli_fetch_array($get_notes_res)) {
159:              $note = nl2br(stripslashes($note_info['note']));
160:          }
161:          $display_block .= "<p><strong>Personal Notes:</strong><br/>
162:          $note</p>";
163:      }
164:      //free result
165:      mysqli_free_result($get_notes_res);
```

You still have to do a little housekeeping and finish up the script, as shown in the last portion of Listing 20.4.

LISTING 20.4   (continued)

```
166:    $display_block .= "<br/>
167:    <p align=\"center\">
168:    <a href=\"".$_SERVER["PHP_SELF"]."\">select another</a></p>";
169: }
170: //close connection to MySQL
171: mysqli_close($mysqli);
172: ?>
173: <html>
174: <head>
175: <title>My Records</title>
176: </head>
177: <body>
178: <?php echo $display_block; ?>
179: </body>
180: </html>
```

Lines 166–168 simply print a link back to the selection form before closing up the
if...else statement in line 169 and the PHP block in the line following. Lines 172
through the end of the script are the generic HTML template that surround the contents of the $display_block string.

After selecting a record from the form shown in Figure 20.4, you will see a result like
that shown in Figure 20.5—your data will vary, of course.

FIGURE 20.5
An individual's
record.

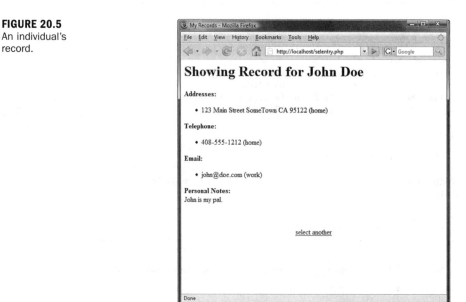

When you try this script for yourself, against your own records, you should see information only for those individuals who have additional data associated with them.

For example, if you have an entry for a friend, and all you have is an email address entered in the email table, you shouldn't see any text relating to address, telephone, fax, or personal notes—no associated records were entered in those tables.

Creating the Record Deletion Mechanism

The record deletion mechanism is virtually identical to the script used to view a record. In fact, you can just take the first 42 lines of Listing 20.4, paste them into a new file called `delentry.php`, and change "View" to "Delete" in lines 24 and 38. Starting with a new line 43, the remainder of the code for `delentry.php` is shown in Listing 20.5.

LISTING 20.5   Script Called `delentry.php` for Selecting and Deleting a Record

```
43: } else if ($_POST) {
44:     //check for required fields
45:     if ($_POST["sel_id"] == "")  {
46:         header("Location: delentry.php");
47:         exit;
48:     }
49:
50:     //issue queries
51:     $del_master_sql = "DELETE FROM master_name WHERE
52:                         id = '".$_POST["sel_id"]."'";
53:     $del_master_res = mysqli_query($mysqli, $del_master_sql)
54:                         or die(mysqli_error($mysqli));
55:
56:     $del_address_sql = "DELETE FROM address WHERE
57:                          id = '".$_POST["sel_id"]."'";
58:     $del_address_res = mysqli_query($mysqli, $del_address_sql)
59:                          or die(mysqli_error($mysqli));
60:
61:     $del_tel_sql = "DELETE FROM telephone WHERE id = '".$_POST["sel_id"]."'";
62:     $del_tel_res = mysqli_query($mysqli, $del_tel_sql)
63:                     or die(mysqli_error($mysqli));
64:
65:
66:     $del_fax_sql = "DELETE FROM fax WHERE id = '".$_POST["sel_id"]."'";
67:     $del_fax_res = mysqli_query($mysqli, $del_fax_sql)
68:                     or die(mysqli_error($mysqli));
69:
70:     $del_email_sql = "DELETE FROM email WHERE id = '".$_POST["sel_id"]."'";
71:     $del_email_res = mysqli_query($mysqli, $del_email_sql)
72:                       or die(mysqli_error($mysqli));
73:
74:     $del_note_sql = "DELETE FROM personal_notes WHERE
75:                       id = '".$_POST["sel_id"]."'";
76:     $del_note_res = mysqli_query($mysqli, $del_note_sql)
77:                      or die(mysqli_error($mysqli));
78:
```

LISTING 20.5   Continued

```
79:     $display_block = "<h1>Record(s) Deleted</h1>
80:     <p>Would you like to
81:     <a href=\"".$_SERVER["PHP_SELF"]."\">delete another</a>?</p>";
82: }
83: ?>
84: <html>
85: <head>
86: <title>My Records</title>
87: </head>
88: <body>
89: <?php echo $display_block; ?>
90: </body>
91: </html>
```

Picking up with line 45, the script looks for the required field, $_POST["sel_id"], just as it did in the selentry.php script. If that required value does not exist, the script redirects the user to the selection form. In lines 51–77, queries delete all information related to the selected individual from all tables. Lines 79–81 place a nice message in $display_block, and the script exits and prints the HTML to the screen. Figure 20.6 shows an output of the record deletion script.

FIGURE 20.6
Deleting a record.

When you go back to the record selection form after deleting a record, you'll note that the individual you deleted is no longer in the selection menu—as it should be!

Adding Subentries to a Record

At this point in the chapter, you've learned how to add, remove, and view records. What's missing is adding additional entries to the related tables after you've already entered a master record—entries for home versus work telephone number, for example. All you need to do is make a few changes to existing scripts.

In the `selentry.php` script in Listing 20.4, change lines 166–167 to read

```
$display_block .= "<p align=\"center\">
<a href=\"addentry.php?master_id=".$_POST["sel_id"]."\">add info</a> ...
<a href=\"".$_SERVER["PHP_SELF"]."\">select another</a></p>";
```

This change simply adds a link to the `addentry.php` script and also passes it a variable accessible via `$_GET["master_id"]`.

Now you need to modify the `addentry.php` script from Listing 20.3 to account for its dual purposes. Here is a summary of the changes to the original script.

Replace the first 10 lines of the original `addentry.php` script with the following snippet:

```php
<?php
include("ch20_include.php");
doDB();

if ((!$_POST) || ($_GET["master_id"] != "")) {
    //haven't seen the form, so show it
    $display_block = "
    <form method=\"post\" action=\"".$_SERVER["PHP_SELF"]."\">";

    if (isset($_GET["master_id"])) {
        //get first, last names for display/tests validity
        $get_names_sql = "SELECT concat_ws(' ', f_name, l_name) AS display_name
                        FROM master_name WHERE id = '".$_GET["master_id"]."'";
        $get_names_res = mysqli_query($mysqli, $get_names_sql)
                        or die(mysqli_error($mysqli));

        if (mysqli_num_rows($get_names_res) == 1) {
            while ($name_info = mysqli_fetch_array($get_names_res)) {
                $display_name = stripslashes($name_info['display_name']);
            }
        }
    }
}

if (isset($display_name)) {
    $display_block .= "<p>Adding information for
    <strong>$display_name</strong>:</p>";
} else {
    $display_block .= "
    <p><strong>First/Last Names:</strong><br/>
    <input type=\"text\" name=\"f_name\" size=\"30\" maxlength=\"75\">
    <input type=\"text\" name=\"l_name\" size=\"30\" maxlength=\"75\">";
}
$display_block .= "<p><strong>Address:</strong><br/>
```

This snippet simply moves around the form elements, printing the first and last name fields only if they contain a new record. If they contain an addition to a record, the individual's name is extracted from the database for aesthetic purposes as well as for a validity check of the ID.

Next, find this line in the original addentry.php script:

```
<p><input type=\"submit\" name=\"submit\" value=\"Add Entry\"></p>
```

Directly above it, add the following:

```
if ($_GET) {
    $display_block .= "<input type=\"hidden\" name=\"master_id\"
            value=\"".$_GET["master_id"]."\">";
}
```

This modification ensures that the known value of master_id is passed along to the next task, if it is present. Be sure to close the $display_block string in the line above this and restart the $display_block string in the line beneath this if statement.

Identify what were lines 49–75 of the original script, beginning with the comment time to add to tables and ending with obtaining the value of $master_id. Replace those lines with the following:

```
//time to add to tables, so check for required fields
if ((($_POST["f_name"] == "") || ($_POST["l_name"] == "")) &&
(!isset($_POST["master_id"]))) {
    header("Location: addentry.php");
    exit;
}

//connect to database
doDB();
if (!$_POST["master_id"]) {
    //add to master_name table
    $add_master_sql = "INSERT INTO master_name (date_added, date_modified,
                    f_name, l_name) VALUES (now(), now(),
                    '".$_POST["f_name"]."', '".$_POST["l_name"]."')";
    $add_master_res = mysqli_query($mysqli, $add_master_sql)
                    or die(mysqli_error($mysqli));

    //get master_id for use with other tables
    $master_id = mysqli_insert_id($mysqli);
} else {
    $master_id = $_POST["master_id"];
}
```

These lines modify the check for required fields, allowing the script to continue without values for first and last names, but only if it has a $_POST["master_id"] value. Then the script connects to the database to perform all the additions you want it to, but it skips the addition to the master_name table if a value for $_POST["master_id"] exists.

Finally, in the section of the script that handles the insertion into the personal_notes table, change INSERT into to UPDATE to handle an update of the notes field:

```
$add_notes_sql = "UPDATE personal_notes set note = '".$_POST["note"]."' WHERE
                  master_id = '".$master_id."'";
```

The new script should look like Listing 20.6.

LISTING 20.6   New addentry.php Script

```
1:   <?php
2:   include("ch20_include.php");
3:   doDB();
4:
5:   if ((!$_POST) || (isset($_GET["master_id"]))) {
6:       //haven't seen the form, so show it
7:       $display_block = "
8:       <form method=\"post\" action=\"".$_SERVER["PHP_SELF"]."\">";
9:
10:      if (isset($_GET["master_id"])) {
11:          //get first, last names for display/tests validity
12:          $get_names_sql = "SELECT concat_ws(' ', f_name, l_name) AS
13:                            display_name FROM master_name WHERE id =
14:                            '".$_GET["master_id"]."'";
15:          $get_names_res = mysqli_query($mysqli, $get_names_sql)
16:                           or die(mysqli_error($mysqli));
17:
18:          if (mysqli_num_rows($get_names_res) == 1) {
19:              while ($name_info = mysqli_fetch_array($get_names_res)) {
20:                  $display_name = stripslashes($name_info['display_name']);
21:              }
22:          }
23:      }
24:
25:      if (isset($display_name)) {
26:          $display_block .= "<p>Adding information for
27:          <strong>$display_name</strong>:</p>";
28:      } else {
29:        $display_block .= "
30:        <p><strong>First/Last Names:</strong><br/>
31:        <input type=\"text\" name=\"f_name\" size=\"30\" maxlength=\"75\">
32:        <input type=\"text\" name=\"l_name\" size=\"30\" maxlength=\"75\">";
33:      }
34:      $display_block .= "<p><strong>Address:</strong><br/>
35:      <input type=\"text\" name=\"address\" size=\"30\"></p>
36:
37:      <p><strong>City/State/Zip:</strong><br/>
38:      <input type=\"text\" name=\"city\" size=\"30\" maxlength=\"50\">
39:      <input type=\"text\" name=\"state\" size=\"5\" maxlength=\"2\">
40:      <input type=\"text\" name=\"zipcode\" size=\"10\" maxlength=\"10\"></p>
41:
42:      <p><strong>Address Type:</strong><br/>
43:      <input type=\"radio\" name=\"add_type\" value=\"home\" checked> home
44:      <input type=\"radio\" name=\"add_type\" value=\"work\"> work
45:      <input type=\"radio\" name=\"add_type\" value=\"other\"> other</p>
46:
```

LISTING 20.6 Continued

```
47:        <p><strong>Telephone Number:</strong><br/>
48:        <input type=\"text\" name=\"tel_number\" size=\"30\" maxlength=\"25\">
49:        <input type=\"radio\" name=\"tel_type\" value=\"home\" checked> home
50:        <input type=\"radio\" name=\"tel_type\" value=\"work\"> work
51:        <input type=\"radio\" name=\"tel_type\" value=\"other\"> other</p>
52:
53:        <p><strong>Fax Number:</strong><br/>
54:        <input type=\"text\" name=\"fax_number\" size=\"30\" maxlength=\"25\">
55:        <input type=\"radio\" name=\"fax_type\" value=\"home\" checked> home
56:        <input type=\"radio\" name=\"fax_type\" value=\"work\"> work
57:        <input type=\"radio\" name=\"fax_type\" value=\"other\"> other</p>
58:
59:        <p><strong>Email Address:</strong><br/>
60:        <input type=\"text\" name=\"email\" size=\"30\" maxlength=\"150\">
61:        <input type=\"radio\" name=\"email_type\" value=\"home\" checked> home
62:        <input type=\"radio\" name=\"email_type\" value=\"work\"> work
63:        <input type=\"radio\" name=\"email_type\" value=\"other\"> other</p>
64:
65:        <p><strong>Personal Note:</strong><br/>
66:        <textarea name=\"note\" cols=\"35\" rows=\"3\"
67:        wrap=\"virtual\"></textarea></p>
68:        <input type=\"hidden\" name=\"master_id\"
69:        value=\"".$_GET["master_id"]."\">
70:        <p><input type=\"submit\" name=\"submit\" value=\"Add Entry\"></p>
71:        </form>";
72:
73: } else if ($_POST) {
74:        //time to add to tables, so check for required fields
75:        if (((($_POST["f_name"] == "") || ($_POST["l_name"] == "")) &&
76:        (!isset($_POST["master_id"]))) {
77:              header("Location: addentry.php");
78:              exit;
79:        }
80:
81:        if (!$_POST["master_id"]) {
82:              //add to master_name table
83:              $add_master_sql = "INSERT INTO master_name (date_added,
84:                                  date_modified, f_name, l_name) VALUES
85:                                  (now(), now(), '".$_POST["f_name"]."',
86:                                  '".$_POST["l_name"]."')";
87:              $add_master_res = mysqli_query($mysqli, $add_master_sql)
88:                                  or die(mysqli_error($mysqli));
89:
90:              //get master_id for use with other tables
91:              $master_id = mysqli_insert_id($mysqli);
92:        } else {
93:              $master_id = $_POST["master_id"];
94: }
95:
96: if (($_POST["address"]) || ($_POST["city"]) || ($_POST["state"])
97: || ($_POST["zipcode"])) {
98:        //something relevant, so add to address table
99:        $add_address_sql = "INSERT INTO address (master_id, date_added,
```

LISTING 20.6   Continued

```
100:                          date_modified, address, city, state, zipcode,
101:                          type)  VALUES ('".$master_id."', now(), now(),
102:                          '".$_POST["address"]."', '".$_POST["city"]."',
103:                          '".$_POST["state"]."' , '".$_POST["zipcode"]."',
104:                          '".$_POST["add_type"]."')";
105:      $add_address_res = mysqli_query($mysqli, $add_address_sql)
106:                          or die(mysqli_error($mysqli));
107:   }
108:
109:   if ($_POST["tel_number"]) {
110:          //something relevant, so add to telephone table
111:          $add_tel_sql = "INSERT INTO telephone (master_id, date_added,
112:                          date_modified, tel_number, type) VALUES
113:                          ('".$master_id."', now(), now(),
114:                          '".$_POST["tel_number"]."',
115:                          '".$_POST["tel_type"]."')";
116:          $add_tel_res = mysqli_query($mysqli, $add_tel_sql)
117:                          or die(mysqli_error($mysqli));
118:   }
119:
120:   if ($_POST["fax_number"]) {
121:          //something relevant, so add to fax table
122:          $add_fax_sql = "INSERT INTO fax (master_id, date_added,
123:                          date_modified, fax_number, type)  VALUES
124:                          ('".$master_id."', now(), now(),
125:                          '".$_POST["fax_number"]."',
126:                          '".$_POST["fax_type"]."')";
127:          $add_fax_res = mysqli_query($mysqli, $add_fax_sql)
128:                          or die(mysqli_error($mysqli));
129:   }
130:
131:   if ($_POST["email"]) {
132:          //something relevant, so add to email table
133:          $add_email_sql = "INSERT INTO email (master_id, date_added,
134:                          date_modified, email, type)  VALUES
135:                          ('".$master_id."', now(), now(),
136:                          '".$_POST["email"]."',
137:                          '".$_POST["email_type"]."')";
138:          $add_email_res = mysqli_query($mysqli, $add_email_sql)
139:                          or die(mysqli_error($mysqli));
140:   }
141:
142:   if ($_POST["note"]) {
143:          //something relevant, so add to notes table
144:          $add_notes_sql = "UPDATE personal_notes set note =
145:                          '".$_POST["note"]."' WHERE
146:                          master_id = '".$master_id."'";
147:          $add_notes_res = mysqli_query($mysqli, $add_notes_sql)
148:                          or die(mysqli_error($mysqli));
149:   }
150:   mysqli_close($mysqli);
151:   $display_block = "<p>Your entry has been added.
152:   Would you like to <a href=\"addentry.php\">add another</a>?</p>";
153: }
154: ?>
155: <html>
```

LISTING 20.6   Continued

```
156: <head>
157: <title>Add an Entry</title>
158: </head>
159: <body>
160: <h1>Add an Entry</h1>
161: <?php echo $display_block; ?>
162: </body>
163: </html>
```

You can try out this revised script by selecting a record to view and then following the add info link. You should see a form like Figure 20.7.

FIGURE 20.7
Adding to a record.

After submitting this form, you can go back through the selection sequence and view the record to verify that your changes have been made.

Summary

In this hands-on chapter, you applied your basic PHP and MySQL knowledge to the creation of a personal address book. You learned how to create the database table and scripts for record addition, removal, and simple viewing. You also learned the process for adding multiple records attached to a single master entry.

Q&A

Q. *What do I do if I want to add additional sections to my address book, such as entries for a person's birthday or other information?*

A. Different tables are used for address, telephone, fax, email, and personal notes because it is possible for a person to have more than one record containing those types of information. In the case of a person's birthday, a person only has one of those so a relational database would be overkill since only one record would ever exist per user. So, to add a person's birthday you should add a field to the master_name table. In the case of adding tables for other information, ask yourself if a person will only ever have one instance of that information (such as birthday) or multiple instances (such as email addresses). If the latter, create a table much like the address, telephone, fax, email, or personal_notes tables, which use master_id as a foreign key.

Workshop

The workshop is designed to help you anticipate possible questions, review what you've learned, and begin putting your knowledge into practice.

Quiz

1. When passing a variable through the query string, which superglobal does it belong in?

2. How many records in the address, email, telephone, and fax tables can you have for each individual in your master_name table?

Answers

1. The $_GET superglobal.

2. As many as you want—it's relational!

Activities

1. Go through each of the administration scripts and modify the code so that a link to the menu prints at the bottom of each screen.

2. Use the second version of the addentry.php script to add secondary contact information to records in your database. Figure 20.8 shows how a record will look after the script adds secondary contact information to it.

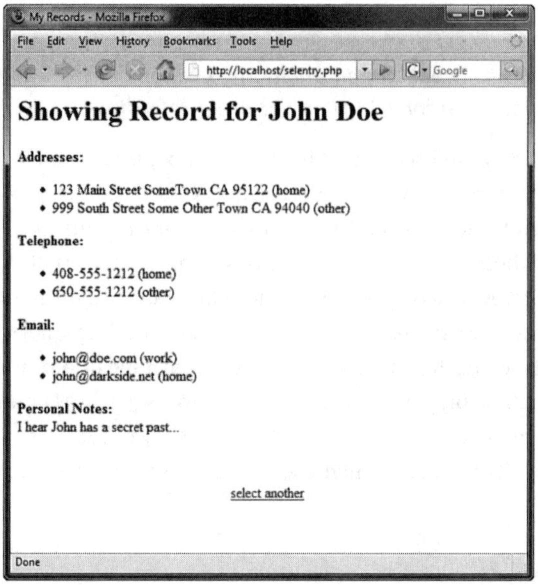

FIGURE 20.8
An individual's
record with mul-
tiple entries in
tables.

21

Creating a Simple Discussion Forum

In this chapter, you'll learn the design process behind a simple discussion forum. This includes developing the database tables and user input forms, and displaying the results. When broken into pieces like this, such a task seems simple—and it is! The ultimate goal is to understand the concepts and relationships that go into making something like a discussion forum, not to create the world's most full-functioned system—in fact, you'll see it's sparse, but it sure is relational.

In this chapter, you will learn

▶ How to create tables for a simple discussion forum

▶ How to create input forms for a simple discussion forum

▶ How to display a simple discussion forum

Designing the Database Tables

Think of the basic components of a forum: topics and posts. A forum—if properly used by its patrons—should have several topics, and each of those topics will have one or more posts submitted by users. Knowing that, you should realize that the posts are tied to the topics through a key field. This key forms the relationship between the two tables.

Think about the requirements for the topics themselves. You definitely need a field for the title, and subsequently you might want fields to hold the creation time and the identification of the user who created the topic. Similarly, think of the requirements for the posts: You'll want to store the text of the post, the time of its creation, and the identity of the person that created it. Most importantly, you need that key to tie the post to the topic.

The following two table creation statements create these tables, called `forum_topics` and `forum_posts`:

```
mysql> CREATE TABLE forum_topics (
    -> topic_id INT NOT NULL PRIMARY KEY AUTO_INCREMENT,
    -> topic_title VARCHAR (150),
    -> topic_create_time DATETIME,
    -> topic_owner VARCHAR (150)
    -> );
Query OK, 0 rows affected (0.03 sec)

mysql> CREATE TABLE forum_posts (
    -> post_id INT NOT NULL PRIMARY KEY AUTO_INCREMENT,
    -> topic_id INT NOT NULL,
    -> post_text TEXT,
    -> post_create_time DATETIME,
    -> post_owner VARCHAR (150)
    -> );
Query OK, 0 rows affected (0.00 sec)
```

By the Way

> This simple forum example will identify users by their email addresses and not require any sort of login sequence.

You should now have two empty tables, waiting for some input. In the next section, you'll create the input forms for adding a topic and a post.

Creating an Include File for Common Functions

Previous chapters used an included file of common functions to make your scripts more concise and to help manage information that might change over time, such as a database username and password. The same thing is true in this chapter. Listing 21.1 contains the code shared by the scripts in this chapter.

LISTING 21.1   Common Functions in an Included File

```
1:   <?php
2:
3:   function doDB() {
4:       global $mysqli;
5:
6:       //connect to server and select database; you may need it
7:       $mysqli = mysqli_connect("localhost", "joeuser",
8:           "somepass", "testDB");
9:
10:      //if connection fails, stop script execution
11:      if (mysqli_connect_errno()) {
12:          printf("Connect failed: %s\n", mysqli_connect_error());
```

LISTING 21.1   Continued

```
13:          exit();
14:      }
15:  }
16:  ?>
```

Lines 3–15 set up the database connection function, doDB. If the connection cannot be made, the script will exit when this function is called; otherwise, it will make the value of $mysqli available to other parts of your script.

Save this file as ch21_include.php and place it on your web server. The other code listings in this chapter will include this file within the first few lines of the script.

Creating the Input Forms and Scripts

Before you can add any posts, you must add a topic to the forum. It is common practice in forum creation to add the topic and the first post in that topic at the same time. From a user's point of view, it doesn't make much sense to add a topic and then go back, select the topic, and add a reply. You want the process to be as smooth as possible. Listing 21.2 shows the form for a new topic creation, which includes a space for the first post in the topic.

LISTING 21.2   Form for Adding a Topic

```
 1:  <html>
 2:  <head>
 3:  <title>Add a Topic</title>
 4:  </head>
 5:  <body>
 6:  <h1>Add a Topic</h1>
 7:  <form method="post" action="do_addtopic.php">
 8:  <p><strong>Your E-Mail Address:</strong><br/>
 9:  <input type="text" name="topic_owner" size="40" maxlength="150"/></p>
10:  <p><strong>Topic Title:</strong><br/>
11:  <input type="text" name="topic_title" size="40" maxlength="150"/></p>
12:  <p><strong>Post Text:</strong><br/>
13:  <textarea name="post_text" rows="8" cols="40" wrap="virtual"></textarea></p>
14:  <p><input type="submit" name="submit" value="Add Topic"/></p>
15:  </form>
16:  </body>
17:  </html>
```

Seems simple enough—the three fields shown in the form, which you can see in Figure 21.1, are all you need to complete both tables; your script and database can fill in the rest. Save Listing 21.2 as something like addtopic.html and put it in your web server document root so that you can follow along.

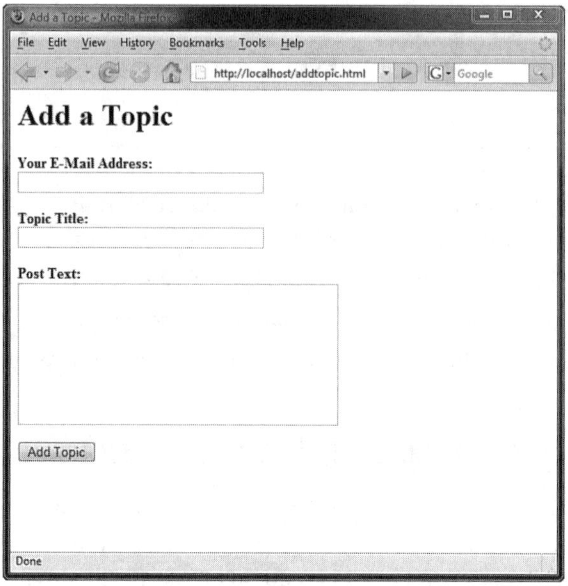

FIGURE 21.1
The topic
creation form.

To create the entry in the forum_topics table, you use the values from the $_POST["topic_title"] and $_POST["topic_owner"] variables from the input form. The topic_id and topic_create_time fields will be automatically incremented and added via the now() MySQL function, respectively.

Similarly, in the forum_posts table, you use the values of $_POST["post_text"] and $_POST["topic_owner"] from the input form, and the post_id, post_create_time, and the topic_id fields will be automatically incremented or otherwise supplied. Because you need a value for the topic_id field to be able to complete the entry in the forum_posts table, you know that query must happen after the query to insert the record in the forum_topics table. Listing 21.3 creates the script to add these records to the table.

LISTING 21.3   Script for Adding a Topic

```
1: <?php
2: include("ch21_include.php");
3: doDB();
4:
5: //check for required fields from the form
6: if ((!$_POST["topic_owner"]) || (!$_POST["topic_title"]) ||
7: (!$_POST["post_text"])) {
8:     header("Location: addtopic.html");
9:     exit;
10: }
11: //create and issue the first query
12: $add_topic = "INSERT INTO forum_topics (topic_title, topic_create_
13:              time, topic_owner) VALUES ('".$_POST["topic_title"]."',now(),
```

LISTING 21.3   Continued

```
14:                    '".$_POST["topic_owner"]."')";
15: $add_topic_res = mysqli_query($mysqli, $add_topic_sql)
16:                    or die(mysqli_error($mysqli));
17:
18: //get the id of the last query
19: $topic_id = mysqli_insert_id($mysqli);
20:
21: //create and issue the second query
22: $add_post_sql = "INSERT INTO forum_posts (topic_id,post_text,
23:                    post_create_time, post_owner) VALUES ('".$topic_id."',
24:                    '".$_POST["post_text"]."', now(),
25:                    '".$_POST["topic_owner"]."')";
26: $add_post_res = mysqli_query($mysqli, $add_post_sql)
27:                    or die(mysqli_error($mysqli));
28:
29:   //close connection to MySQL
30: mysqli_close($mysqli);
31:
32: //create nice message for user
33: $display_block = "<P>The <strong>".$_POST["topic_title"]."</strong>
34: topic has been created.</p>";
35: ?>
36: <html>
37: <head>
38: <title>New Topic Added</title>
39: </head>
40: <body>
41: <h1>New Topic Added</h1>
42: <?php echo $display_block; ?>
43: </body>
44: </html>
```

Lines 2–3 include the file of user-created functions and call the database connection function. Next, lines 6–10 check for the three required fields needed to complete both tables—the topic owner, a topic title, and some text for the post. If any one of these fields is not present, the user is redirected to the original form.

Lines 12–16 create and insert the first query, which adds the topic to the forum_top-ics table. Note that the first field is left blank, so the automatically incrementing value is added by the system per the original table definition. The MySQL now() function is used to timestamp the record with the current time, at insertion. The other fields in the record are completed using values from the form.

Line 19 shows the use of a handy function: mysqli_insert_id(). This function retrieves the primary key ID of the last record inserted into the database by this script. In this case, mysqli_insert_id() gets the id value from the forum_topics table, which will become the entry for the topic_id field in the forum_posts table.

Lines 22–27 create and insert the second query, again using a mixture of information known and supplied by the system. The second query adds the text of the user's post to the forum_posts table. Lines 33–34 simply create a display string for the user, and the rest of the script rounds out the display.

Save this listing as do_addtopic.php—the name of the action in the previous script—and place it in the document root of your web server. Complete the form and then submit it, and you should see the New Topic Added message. Figures 21.2 and 21.3 show the sequence of events.

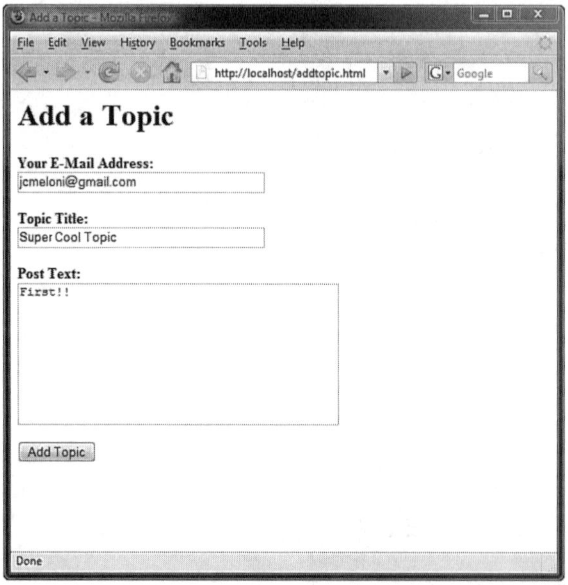

FIGURE 21.2
Adding a topic and first post.

FIGURE 21.3
Successful addition of a topic and first post.

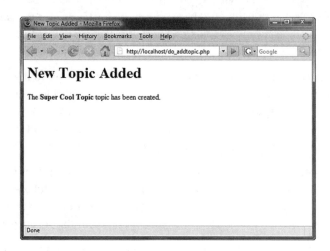

In the next section, you'll put together two more pieces of the puzzle: displaying the topics and posts, and replying to a topic.

Displaying the Topic List

Now that you have a topic and at least one post in your database, you can display this information and let people add new topics or reply to existing ones. In Listing 21.4, you take a step back and create a page that lists all the topics in the forum. This page shows the basic information of each topic and provides the user with a link to add a new topic; you have already created the form and script for that. The code in Listing 21.4 represents an entry page for your forum.

Although Listing 21.4 looks like a lot of code, it's actually many small, simple concepts you've already encountered, starting with the include() function and database connection function in lines 2–3.

LISTING 21.4 Topic Listing Script

```
1:  <?php
2:  include("ch21_include.php");
3:  doDB();
4:
5:  //gather the topics
6:  $get_topics_sql = "SELECT topic_id, topic_title,
7:                     DATE_FORMAT(topic_create_time,  '%b %e %Y at %r') AS
8:                     fmt_topic_create_time, topic_owner FROM forum_topics
9:                     ORDER BY topic_create_time DESC";
10: $get_topics_res = mysqli_query($mysqli, $get_topics_sql)
11:                   or die(mysqli_error($mysqli));
12:
13: if (mysqli_num_rows($get_topics_res) < 1) {
14:     //there are no topics, so say so
15:     $display_block = "<p><em>No topics exist.</em></p>";
16: } else {
17:     //create the display string
18:     $display_block = "
19:     <table cellpadding=\"3\" cellspacing=\"1\" border=\"1\">
20:     <tr>
21:     <th>TOPIC TITLE</th>
22:     <th># of POSTS</th>
23:     </tr>";
24:
25:     while ($topic_info = mysqli_fetch_array($get_topics_res)) {
26:         $topic_id = $topic_info['topic_id'];
27:         $topic_title = stripslashes($topic_info['topic_title']);
28:         $topic_create_time = $topic_info['fmt_topic_create_time'];
29:         $topic_owner = stripslashes($topic_info['topic_owner']);
30:
```

LISTING 21.4   Continued

```
31:        //get number of posts
32:        $get_num_posts_sql = "SELECT COUNT(post_id) AS post_count FROM
33:                             forum_posts WHERE topic_id = '".$topic_id."'";
34:        $get_num_posts_res = mysqli_query($mysqli, $get_num_posts_sql)
35:                             or die(mysqli_error($mysqli));
36:
37:        while ($posts_info = mysqli_fetch_array($get_num_posts_res)) {
38:            $num_posts = $posts_info['post_count'];
39:        }
40:
41:        //add to display
42:        $display_block .= "
43:        <tr>
44:        <td><a href=\"showtopic.php?topic_id=".$topic_id."\"><strong>".
45:        $topic_title."</strong></a><br/>
46:        Created on ".$topic_create_time." by ".$topic_owner."</td>
47:        <td align=center>".$num_posts."</td>
48:        </tr>";
49:    }
50:    //free results
51:    mysqli_free_result($get_topics_res);
52:    mysqli_free_result($get_num_posts_res);
53:
54:    //close connection to MySQL
55:    mysqli_close($mysqli);
56:
57:    //close up the table
58:    $display_block .= "</table>";
59: }
60: ?>
61: <html>
62: <head>
63: <title>Topics in My Forum</title>
64: </head>
65: <body>
66: <h1>Topics in My Forum</h1>
67: <?php echo $display_block; ?>
68: <p>Would you like to <a href="addtopic.html">add a topic</a>?</p>
69: </body>
70: </html>
```

Lines 6–11 show the first of the database queries, and this particular one selects all the topic information in order by descending date. In other words, these lines gather the data in such a way that the topic that was created most recently will appear at the top of the list. In the query, notice the use of the date_format() function to create a much nicer date display than the raw value stored in the database.

Line 13 checks for the presence of any records returned by the query. If no records are returned, and therefore no topics are in the table, you'll want to tell the user. Line 15 creates this message. At this point, if no topics existed, the script would break out of the if...else construct and be over with; the next action would occur at line 61, which is the start of the static HTML. If the script ended here, the message created in line 15 would be printed in line 67.

If, however, you have topics in your forum_topics table, the script continues at line 16. At line 18, a block of text is assigned to the $display_block variable, containing the beginnings of an HTML table. Lines 19–23 set up a table with two columns: one for the title and one for the number of posts. At line 25, you begin to loop through the results of the original query.

The while loop in line 25 says that while there are elements to be extracted from the resultset, extract each row as an array called $topic_info, and use the field names as the array element to assign the value to a new variable. So, the first element the script tries to extract is the topic_id field, on line 26. It assigns the value of $topic_info['topic_id'] to the $topic_id variable, meaning that it gets a local value for $topic_id from an array called $topic_info, containing a field called topic_id. Continue doing this for the $topic_title, $topic_create_time, and $topic_owner variables in lines 27–29. The stripslashes() function removes any escape characters that were input into the table at the time of record insertion.

Lines 32–35 issue another query, in the context of the while loop, to get the number of posts for that particular topic. In line 42, the script continues the creation of the $display_block string, using the concatenation operator (.=) to make sure that this string is tacked on to the end of the display string we have built so far. In line 44, you create the HTML table column to display the link to the file that will show the topic (showtopic.php) and print the topic owner and creation time.

The second HTML table column, on line 47, shows the number of posts. The script breaks out of the while loop on line 49, and in line 58 adds the last bit to the $display_block string to close the table. The remaining lines print the HTML for the page, including the value of the $display_block string.

If you save this file as topiclist.php and place it in your web server document root, and if you have topics in your database tables, you might see something like Figure 21.4.

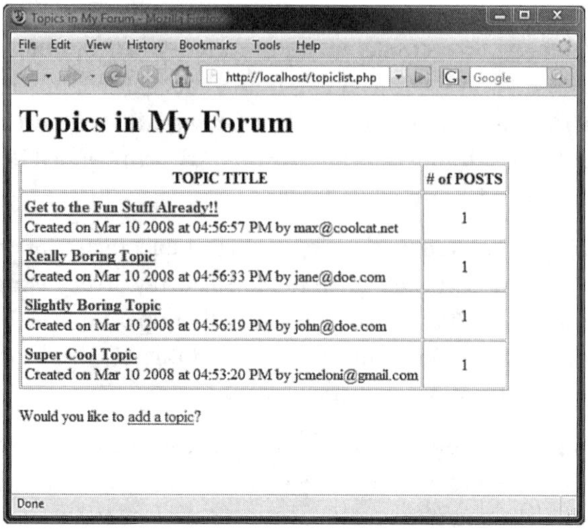

FIGURE 21.4
Topics are
available.

Displaying the Posts in a Topic

As you might have guessed, the next item on the task list is to build that show-topic.php file to show the topic's postings. Listing 21.5 does just that. In this listing, lines 3–6 check for the existence of a value for topic_id in the GET query string. Because you intend to show all the posts within a selected topic, you need to know which topic to use in your query, and this is the manner in which the information is given to you. If a value in $_GET["topic_id"] does not exist, the user is redirected back to the topic listing page, presumably to try again.

LISTING 21.5   Script to Show Topic Posts

```
1:  <?php
2:  include("ch21_include.php");
3:  doDB();
4:
5:  //check for required info from the query string
6:  if (!isset($_GET["topic_id"])) {
7:      header("Location: topiclist.php");
8:      exit;
9:  }
10:
11: //verify the topic exists
12: $verify_topic_sql = "SELECT topic_title FROM forum_topics
13:                     WHERE topic_id = '".$_GET["topic_id"]."'";
14: $verify_topic_res =  mysqli_query($mysqli, $verify_topic_sql)
15:                     or die(mysqli_error($mysqli));
16:
17: if (mysqli_num_rows($verify_topic_res) < 1) {
18:     //this topic does not exist
19:     $display_block = "<p><em>You have selected an invalid topic.<br/>
```

LISTING 21.5 Continued

```
20:     Please <a href=\"topiclist.php\">try again</a>.</em></p>";
21: } else {
22:     //get the topic title
23:     while ($topic_info = mysqli_fetch_array($verify_topic_res)) {
24:         $topic_title = stripslashes($topic_info['topic_title']);
25:     }
26:
27:     //gather the posts
28:     $get_posts_sql = "SELECT post_id,post_text, DATE_FORMAT(post_create_time,
29:                         '%b %e %Y at %r') AS fmt_post_create_time, post_owner
30:                         FROM forum_posts
31:                         WHERE topic_id = '".$_GET["topic_id"]."'
32:                         ORDER BY post_create_time ASC";
33:     $get_posts_res = mysqli_query($mysqli, $get_posts_sql)
34:                         or die(mysqli_error($mysqli));
35:
36:     //create the display string
37:     $display_block = "
38:     <p>Showing posts for the <strong>".$topic_title."</strong> topic:</p>
39:     <table width=\"100%\" cellpadding=\"3\" cellspacing=\"1\" border=\"1\">
40:     <tr>
41:     <th>AUTHOR</th>
42:     <th>POST</th>
43:     </tr>";
44:
45:     while ($posts_info = mysqli_fetch_array($get_posts_res)) {
46:         $post_id = $posts_info['post_id'];
47:         $post_text = nl2br(stripslashes($posts_info['post_text']));
48:         $post_create_time = $posts_info['fmt_post_create_time'];
49:         $post_owner = stripslashes($posts_info['post_owner']);
50:
51:         //add to display
52:         $display_block .= "
53:         <tr>
54:         <td width=\"35%\" valign=\"top\">".$post_owner."<br/>
55:         [".$post_create_time."]</td>
56:         <td width=\"65%\" valign=\"top\">".$post_text."<br/><br/>
57:         <a href=\"replytopost.php?post_id=".$post_id."\">
58:         <strong>REPLY TO POST</strong></a></td>
59:         </tr>";
60:     }
61:
62:     //free results
63:     mysqli_free_result($get_posts_res);
64:     mysqli_free_result($verify_topic_res);
65:
66:     //close connection to MySQL
67:     mysqli_close($mysqli);
68:
69:     //close up the table
70:     $display_block .= "</table>";
71: }
72: ?>
73: <html>
74: <head>
75: <title>Posts in Topic</title>
```

LISTING 21.5 Continued

```
76: </head>
77: <body>
78: <h1>Posts in Topic</h1>
79: <?php echo $display_block; ?>
80: </body>
81: </html>
```

Lines 12–15 show the first of these queries, and this one is used to validate that the `topic_id` sent in the query string is actually a valid entry by selecting the associated `topic_title` for the topic in question. If the validation fails the test in line 17, a message is created in lines 19–20, and the script breaks out of the `if...else` statement and finishes up by printing HTML. This output looks like Figure 21.5.

FIGURE 21.5
Invalid topic
selected.

If, however, the topic is valid, extract the value of `topic_title` in line 24, again using `stripslashes()` to remove any escape characters. Next, the script issues a query in lines 28–34 to gather all the posts associated with that topic in ascending order by time. In this case, newest posts are at the bottom of the list. Line 37 starts a block of text, containing the beginnings of an HTML table. Lines 38–43 set up a table with two columns: one for the author of the post and one for the post text itself. The script stops writing the text block momentarily, and at line 45 begins to loop through the results of the original query.

The `while` loop in line 45 says that although there are elements to be extracted from the resultset, extract each row as an array called `$posts_info`, and use the field names as the array element to assign the value to a new variable. So, the first element the script tries to extract is the post_id field on line 46. It assigns the value of $posts_info['post_id'] to the variable $post_id, meaning that it gets a local value for $post_id from an array called $posts_info, containing a field called post_id. Continue doing this for the $post_text, $post_create_time, and $post_owner variables in lines 47–49. The stripslashes() function is again used to remove any escape characters, and the nl2br() function is used on the value of $posts_info['post_text'] to replace all newline characters with XHTML-compliant line break characters.

In line 52, the script continues to write to the $display_block string, using the concatenation operator (.=) to make sure that this string is tacked on to the end of the string we have created so far. Line 54 creates the HTML table column to display the author and creation time of the post. The second HTML table row, on line 56, shows the text of the post as well as a link to reply to the post. The script breaks out of the while loop on line 60, and on line 70 adds the last bit to the $display_block string to close the table. The remaining lines print the HTML for the page, including the value of the $display_block string.

If you save this file as showtopic.php and place it in your web server document root, and if you have posts in your database tables, you might see something like Figure 21.6.

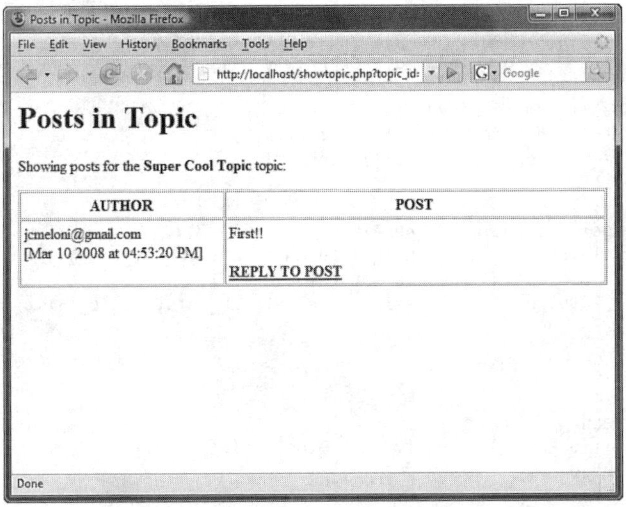

FIGURE 21.6
Posts in a topic.

A one-post topic is boring, so let's finish up this chapter by creating the script to add a post to a topic.

Adding Posts to a Topic

In this final step, you will create the `replytopost.php` script, which contains code that looks similar to the script used to add a new topic. Listing 21.6 shows the code for this all-in-one form and script, which begins with the inclusion of the functions file and the initiation of the database connection on lines 2–3. Although the script performs different tasks depending on the status of the form (whether it's being shown or submitted), both conditions require database interaction at some point.

LISTING 21.6   Script to Add Replies to a Topic

```
1:   <?php
2:   include("ch21_include.php");
3:   doDB();
4:
5:   //check to see if we're showing the form or adding the post
6:   if (!$_POST) {
7:       // showing the form; check for required item in query string
8:       if (!isset($_GET["post_id"])) {
9:           header("Location: topiclist.php");
10:          exit;
11: }
12:
13:      //still have to verify topic and post
14:      $verify_sql = "SELECT ft.topic_id, ft.topic_title FROM forum_posts
15:                     AS fp LEFT JOIN forum_topics AS ft ON fp.topic_id =
16:                     ft.topic_id WHERE fp.post_id = '".$_GET["post_id"]."'";
17:
18:      $verify_res = mysqli_query($mysqli, $verify_sql)
19:                    or die(mysqli_error($mysqli));
20:
21:      if (mysqli_num_rows($verify_res) < 1) {
22:          //this post or topic does not exist
23:          header("Location: topiclist.php");
24:          exit;
25:      } else {
26:          //get the topic id and title
27:          while($topic_info = mysqli_fetch_array($verify_res)) {
28:              $topic_id = $topic_info['topic_id'];
29:              $topic_title = stripslashes($topic_info['topic_title']);
30:          }
31:
32:          echo "
33:          <html>
34:          <head>
35:          <title>Post Your Reply in ".$topic_title."</title>
36:          </head>
37:          <body>
38:          <h1>Post Your Reply in $topic_title</h1>
39:          <form method=\"post\" action=\"".$_SERVER["PHP_SELF"]."\">
40:          <p><strong>Your E-Mail Address:</strong><br/>
41:          <input type=\"text\" name=\"post_owner\" size=\"40\"
42:          maxlength=\"150\"></p>
43:          <p><strong>Post Text:</strong><br/>
44:          <textarea name=\"post_text\" rows=\"8\" cols=\"40\"
```

LISTING 21.6   Continued

```
45;          wrap=\"virtual\"></textarea>
46:          <input type=\"hidden\" name=\"topic_id\" value=\"$topic_id\">
47:          <p><input type=\"submit\" name=\"submit\" value=\"Add Post\"></p>
48:          </form>
49:          </body>
50:          </html>";
51: }
52:
53: //free result
54: mysqli_free_result($verify_res);
55:
56: //close connection to MySQL
57: mysqli_close($mysqli);
58:
59: } else if ($_POST) {
60:      //check for required items from form
61:      if ((!$_POST["topic_id"]) || (!$_POST["post_text"]) ||
62:      (!$_POST["post_owner"])) {
63:           header("Location: topiclist.php");
64:           exit;
65:      }
66:
67:      //add the post
68:      $add_post_sql = "INSERT INTO forum_posts (topic_id,post_text,
69:                       post_create_time,post_owner) VALUES
70:                       ('".$_POST["topic_id"]."', '".$_POST["post_text"]."',
71:                       now(),'".$_POST["post_owner"]."')";
72:      $add_post_res = mysqli_query($mysqli, $add_post_sql)
73:                       or die(mysqli_error($mysqli));
74:
75:      //close connection to MySQL
76:      mysqli_close($mysqli);
77:
78:      //redirect user to topic
79:      header("Location: showtopic.php?topic_id=".$_POST["topic_id"]);
80:      exit;
81: }
82: ?>
```

Line 6 checks to see whether the form is being submitted. If $_POST does not have a value, the form has not yet been submitted, and it must be shown. Before showing the form, however, you must check for that one required item; lines 8–11 check for the existence of a value for post_id in the GET query string. If a value in $_GET["post_id"] does not exist, the user is redirected back to the topic listing page.

If you made it past the check for a value in $_GET["post_id"], lines 14–19 issue a complicated-looking query that gets the values of the topic_id and topic_title fields from the forum_topics table, based on the only value that you know: the value of $_GET["post_id"]. This query both validates the existence of the post and gets information you will need later in the script. Lines 21–24 act on the results of this validity test, again redirecting the user back to the topiclist.php page if the test fails.

If the value of $_GET["post_id"] represents a valid post, you extract the value of topic_id and topic_title in lines 27–30, again using stripslashes() to remove any escape characters. Next, the script prints to the screen the entirety of the form for adding a post, and that's it for this script until the user clicks the form submission button. In the form, you see that the action is $_SERVER["PHP_SELF"] on line 39, indicating that this script will be recalled into action. A hidden field in line 46 holds the information that needs to be passed along to the next iteration of the script.

Moving on to line 53, this block of code is executed when the script is reloaded and $_POST contains a value. This block checks for the presence of all required fields from the form (lines 61–65) and then, if they are all present, issues the query to add the post to the database (lines 68–73). After the post is added to the database, the user is redirected to the showtopic.php page (lines 79–80), using the appropriate query string to display the active topic.

If you save this file as replytopost.php and place it in your web server document root, try it out and you may see something like Figures 21.7 and 21.8.

FIGURE 21.7
Preparing to add a post.

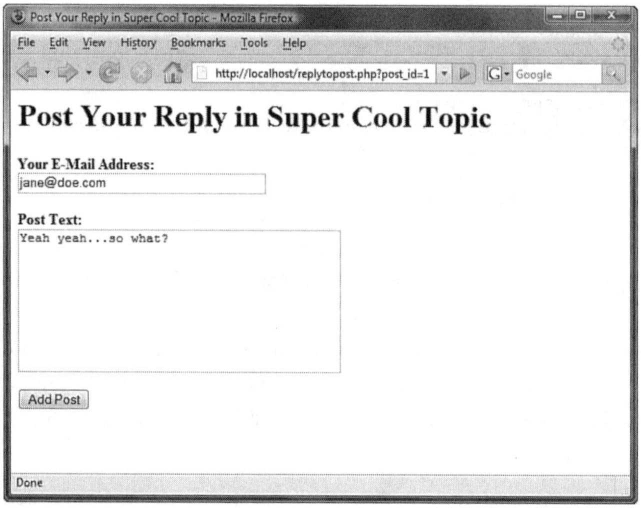

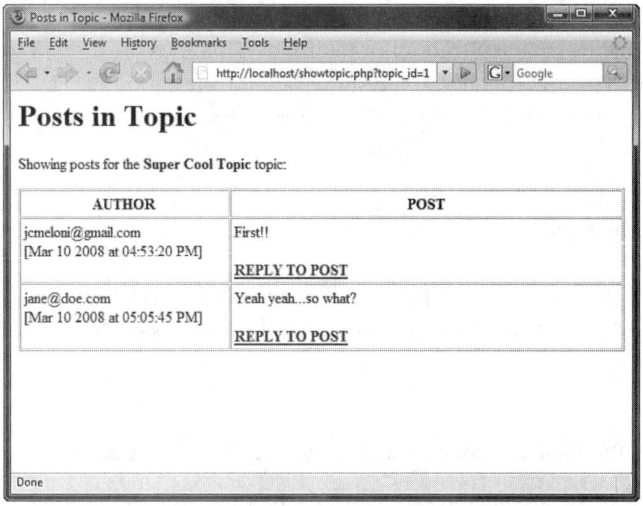

FIGURE 21.8
A post was
added to the
list.

Summary

To take an idea from inception through to fruition, you should follow a design process. This process essentially says, "Think before you act." Discuss rules, requirements, and objectives; then create the final version of your normalized tables.

In this chapter, you saw how forums are hierarchical in nature—forums contain topics; topics contain posts. You can't have a topic without a post, and posts don't exist in forums without belonging to a topic. You applied this knowledge to the creation of tables to hold forum topics and posts, and used PHP scripts to create the input and display pages for these items.

Q&A

Q. *What if I want multiple forums? This sequence assumes that only one forum is available.*

A. If you want to have multiple forums in your discussion board, create a table called forums (or something to that effect) containing fields for an ID, name, and perhaps a forum description. Then, in the forum_topics and forum_posts tables, add a field called forum_id so that these elements lower in the hierarchy are tied to the master forum. Be sure to amend the SQL queries for record insertion to account for the value of the forum_id.

Next, instead of starting your display at the topic level, begin it at the forum level. Just as you created a script to display topics, create a script to show the forums. The link to the forum display would contain the forum_id, and the page itself would show all the topics within that forum.

Workshop

The workshop is designed to help you anticipate possible questions, review what you've learned, and begin putting your knowledge into practice.

Quiz

1. How is the topic ID value passed to the showtopic.php script?

2. What else, besides telling the user that the topic was successfully added, could we do at the end of the do_addtopic.php script?

Answers

1. Through the $_GET superglobal, named as the the value of $_GET["topic_id"].

2. Just as with the replytopost.php script, we could eliminate the message display and simply redirect the user to the topic she just created, showing the new topic and post in all its glory.

Activity

You'll notice that none of these pages are really tied together with any sort of navigation. Take these basic framework scripts and apply some navigational flow to them. Make sure that users can always add a topic or return to the topic list from any given page, for example.

If you're feeling really ambitious, use the information provided in the Q&A section to integrate and display multiple forums into your tidy little discussion board.

22

Creating an Online Storefront

In this short, hands-on chapter, you will create a generic online storefront. You will learn the methods for creating the relevant database tables as well as the scripts for displaying the information to the user. The examples used in this chapter represent one of an infinite number of possibilities to complete these tasks and are meant to provide a foundation of knowledge rather than a definitive method for completing this task.

In this chapter, you will learn how to

▶ Create relational tables for an online store

▶ Create scripts to display store categories

▶ Create scripts to display individual items

Planning and Creating the Database Tables

Before you tackle the process of creating database tables for an online store, think about the real-life shopping process. When you walk into a store, items are ordered in some fashion: The hardware and the baby clothes aren't mixed together, the electronics and the laundry detergent aren't side by side, and so on. Applying that knowledge to database normalization, already you can see that you will need a table to hold categories and a table to hold items. In this simple store, each item will belong to one category.

Next, think about the items themselves. Depending on the type of store you have, your items might or might not have colors, and might or might not have sizes. But all your items will have a name, a description, and a price. Again, thinking in terms of normalization, you can imagine that you might have one general items table and two additional tables that relate to the general items table.

Table 22.1 shows sample table and field names to use for your online storefront. In a minute, you'll create the actual SQL statements, but first you should look at this information and try to see the relationships. Ask yourself which of the fields should be primary or unique keys.

TABLE 22.1   Storefront Table and Field Names

Table Name	Field Names
store_categories	id, cat_title, cat_desc
store_items	id, cat_id, item_title, item_price, item_desc, item_image
store_item_size	item_id, item_size
store_item_color	item_id, item_color

As you can see in the following SQL statements, the store_categories table has two fields besides the id field: cat_title and cat_desc, for title and description, respectively. The id field is the primary key, and cat_title is a unique field because there's no reason you would have two identical categories.

```
mysql> CREATE TABLE store_categories (
    -> id INT NOT NULL PRIMARY KEY AUTO_INCREMENT,
    -> cat_title VARCHAR (50) UNIQUE,
    -> cat_desc TEXT
    -> );
Query OK, 0 rows affected (0.03 sec)
```

Next we tackle the store_items table, which has five fields besides the id field—none of which are unique keys. The lengths specified in the field definitions are arbitrary; you should use whatever best fits your store.

The cat_id field relates the item to a particular category in the store_categories table. This field is not unique because you will want more than one item in each category. The item_title, item_price, and item_desc (for description) fields are self-explanatory. The item_image field will hold a filename (in this case, the file is assumed to be local to your server) that you will use to build an HTML <img> tag when it's time to display your item information.

```
mysql> CREATE TABLE store_items (
    -> id INT NOT NULL PRIMARY KEY AUTO_INCREMENT,
    -> cat_id INT NOT NULL,
    -> item_title VARCHAR (75),
    -> item_price FLOAT (8,2),
    -> item_desc TEXT,
    -> item_image VARCHAR (50)
    -> );
Query OK, 0 rows affected (0.00 sec)
```

Both the store_item_size and store_item_color tables contain optional information: If you sell books, they won't have sizes or colors, but if you sell shirts, they will. For each of these tables, the item_id and item_size fields are not unique keys because you can associate as many colors and sizes with a particular item as you want.

```
mysql> CREATE TABLE store_item_size (
    -> id INT NOT NULL PRIMARY KEY AUTO_INCREMENT,
    -> item_id INT NOT NULL,
    -> item_size VARCHAR (25)
    -> );
Query OK, 0 rows affected (0.00 sec)

mysql> CREATE TABLE store_item_color (
    -> id INT NOT NULL PRIMARY KEY AUTO_INCREMENT,
    -> item_id INT NOT NULL,
    -> item_color VARCHAR (25)
    -> );
Query OK, 0 rows affected (0.00 sec)
```

These are all the tables necessary for a basic storefront—that is, for displaying the items you have for sale. Chapter 23, "Creating a Shopping Cart Mechanism," integrates the user experience into the mix. For now, just concentrate on your inventory.

In Chapter 20, "Creating an Online Address Book," you learned how to use PHP forms and scripts to add or delete records in your tables. If you apply the same principles to this set of tables, you can easily create an administrative front end to your storefront. We won't go through that process in this book, but feel free to do it on your own. At this point, you know enough about PHP and MySQL to complete the tasks.

For now, you can simply issue MySQL queries, via the MySQL monitor or other interface, to add information to your tables. Following are some examples, if you want to follow along with sample data.

Inserting Records into the store_categories Table

The following queries create three categories in your store_categories table: hats, shirts, and books.

```
mysql> INSERT INTO store_categories VALUES
    -> ('1', 'Hats', 'Funky hats in all shapes and sizes!');
Query OK, 1 row affected (0.01 sec)

mysql> INSERT INTO store_categories VALUES ('2', 'Shirts', 'From t-shirts to
    -> sweatshirts to polo shirts and beyond.');
Query OK, 1 row affected (0.00 sec)

mysql> INSERT INTO store_categories VALUES ('3', 'Books', 'Paperback, hardback,
    -> books for school or play.');
Query OK, 1 row affected (0.00 sec)
```

In the next section, we'll add some items to the categories.

Inserting Records into the `store_items` Table

The following queries add three item records to each category. Feel free to add many more.

```
mysql> INSERT INTO store_items VALUES ('1', '1', 'Baseball Hat', '12.00',
    -> 'Fancy, low-profile baseball hat.', 'baseballhat.gif');
Query OK, 1 row affected (0.00 sec)

mysql> INSERT INTO store_items VALUES ('2', '1', 'Cowboy Hat', '52.00',
    -> '10 gallon variety', 'cowboyhat.gif');
Query OK, 1 row affected (0.01 sec)

mysql> INSERT INTO store_items VALUES ('3', '1', 'Top Hat', '102.00',
    -> 'Good for costumes.', 'tophat.gif');
Query OK, 1 row affected (0.00 sec)

mysql> INSERT INTO store_items VALUES ('4', '2', 'Short-Sleeved T-Shirt',
    -> '12.00', '100% cotton, pre-shrunk.', 'sstshirt.gif');
Query OK, 1 row affected (0.00 sec)

mysql> INSERT INTO store_items VALUES ('5', '2', 'Long-Sleeved T-Shirt',
    -> '15.00', 'Just like the short-sleeved shirt, with longer sleeves.',
    -> 'lstshirt.gif');
Query OK, 1 row affected (0.00 sec)

mysql> INSERT INTO store_items VALUES ('6', '2', 'Sweatshirt', '22.00',
    -> 'Heavy and warm.', 'sweatshirt.gif');
Query OK, 1 row affected (0.00 sec)

mysql> INSERT INTO store_items VALUES ('7', '3', 'Jane\'s Self-Help Book',
    -> '12.00', 'Jane gives advice.', 'selfhelpbook.gif');
Query OK, 1 row affected (0.00 sec)

mysql> INSERT INTO store_items VALUES ('8', '3', 'Generic Academic Book',
    -> '35.00', 'Some required reading for school, will put you to sleep.',
    -> 'boringbook.gif');
Query OK, 1 row affected (0.00 sec)

mysql> INSERT INTO store_items VALUES ('9', '3', 'Chicago Manual of Style',
    -> '9.99', 'Good for copywriters.', 'chicagostyle.gif');
Query OK, 1 row affected (0.00 sec)
```

By the Way

> The queries above refer to various graphics such as "baseballhat.gif", which are not included in the code. You can find sample images or make some placeholder graphics of your own.

Inserting Records into the `store_item_size` Table

The following queries associate sizes with one of the three items in the `shirts` category and a generic "one size fits all" size to each of the hats (assume that they're strange hats). On your own, insert the same set of size associations for the remaining items in the `shirts` category.

```
mysql> INSERT INTO store_item_size VALUES ('',1,'One Size Fits All');
Query OK, 1 row affected (0.00 sec)

mysql> INSERT INTO store_item_size VALUES ('',2,'One Size Fits All');
Query OK, 1 row affected (0.00 sec)

mysql> INSERT INTO store_item_size VALUES ('',3,'One Size Fits All');
Query OK, 1 row affected (0.00 sec)

mysql> INSERT INTO store_item_size VALUES ('',4,'S');
Query OK, 1 row affected (0.00 sec)

mysql> INSERT INTO store_item_size VALUES ('',4,'M');
Query OK, 1 row affected (0.00 sec)

mysql> INSERT INTO store_item_size VALUES ('',4,'L');
Query OK, 1 row affected (0.00 sec)

mysql> INSERT INTO store_item_size VALUES ('',4,'XL');
Query OK, 1 row affected (0.00 sec)
```

Inserting Records into the `store_item_color` Table

The following queries associate colors with one of the three items in the `shirts` category. On your own, insert color records for the remaining shirts and hats.

```
mysql> INSERT INTO store_item_color VALUES ('',1,'red');
Query OK, 1 row affected (0.00 sec)

mysql> INSERT INTO store_item_color VALUES ('',1,'black');
Query OK, 1 row affected (0.00 sec)

mysql> INSERT INTO store_item_color VALUES ('',1,'blue');
Query OK, 1 row affected (0.00 sec)
```

Displaying Categories of Items

Believe it or not, the most difficult task in this project is now complete. Compared to thinking up categories and items, creating the scripts used to display the information is easy!

The first script you will make is one that lists categories and items. Obviously, you wouldn't want to list all categories and all items all at once as soon as the user walks in the door, but you do want to give the user the option of immediately picking a category, seeing its items, and then picking another category. In other words, this script serves two purposes: It shows the categories and then shows the items in that category. Listing 22.1 shows the code for `seestore.php`.

LISTING 22.1 Script to View Categories

```
1:  <?php
2:  //connect to database
3:  $mysqli = mysqli_connect("localhost", "joeuser", "somepass", "testDB");
4:
5:  $display_block = "<h1>My Categories</h1>
6:  <p>Select a category to see its items.</p>";
7:
8:  //show categories first
9:  $get_cats_sql = "SELECT id, cat_title, cat_desc FROM
10:                  store_categories ORDER BY cat_title";
11: $get_cats_res = mysqli_query($mysqli, $get_cats_sql)
12:                 or die(mysqli_error($mysqli));
13:
14: if (mysqli_num_rows($get_cats_res) < 1) {
15:     $display_block = "<p><em>Sorry, no categories to browse.</em></p>";
16: } else {
17:     while ($cats = mysqli_fetch_array($get_cats_res)) {
18:         $cat_id    = $cats['id'];
19:         $cat_title = strtoupper(stripslashes($cats['cat_title']));
20:         $cat_desc  = stripslashes($cats['cat_desc']);
21:
22:         $display_block .= "<p><strong><a href=\"".$_SERVER["PHP_SELF"].
23:         "?cat_id=".$cat_id."\">".$cat_title."</a></strong><br/>"
24:         .$cat_desc."</p>";
25:
26:         if (isset($_GET["cat_id"])) {
27:             if ($_GET["cat_id"] == $cat_id) {
28:             //get items
29:             $get_items_sql = "SELECT id, item_title, item_price FROM
30:                              store_items WHERE cat_id = '".$cat_id."'
31:                              ORDER BY item_title";
32:             $get_items_res = mysqli_query($mysqli, $get_items_sql)
33:                              or die(mysqli_error($mysqli));
34:
35:             if (mysqli_num_rows($get_items_res) < 1) {
36:                 $display_block = "<p><em>Sorry, no items in this
37:                 category.</em></p>";
38:             } else {
39:                 $display_block .= "<ul>";
40:                 while ($items = mysqli_fetch_array($get_items_res)) {
41:                     $item_id    = $items['id'];
42:                     $item_title = stripslashes($items['item_title']);
43:                     $item_price = $items['item_price'];
44:
45:                     $display_block .= "<li><a href=\"showitem.php?
46:                     item_id=".$item_id."\">".$item_title."</a>
47:                     </strong> (\$".$item_price.")</li>";
48:                 }
49:                 $display_block .= "</ul>";
50:             }
51:             //free results
52:             mysqli_free_result($get_items_res);
53:         }
54:     }
55:  }
56: }
```

LISTING 22.1   Continued

```
57: //free results
58: mysqli_free_result($get_cats_res);
59: //close connection to MySQL
60: mysqli_close($mysqli);
61: ?>
62: <html>
63: <head>
64: <title>My Categories</title>
65: </head>
66: <body>
67: <?php echo $display_block; ?>
68: </body>
69: </html>
```

Given the length of scripts you saw in Chapter 20, these 69 fully functional lines should be a welcome change. Line 3 opens the database connection because regardless of which action the script is taking—showing categories or showing items in categories—the database is necessary.

Line 5 starts the $display_block string, with some basic page title information added to it. Lines 9–12 create and issue the query to retrieve the category information. Line 14 checks for categories; if none are in the table, a message is printed to the user, and that's all this script does. However, if categories are found, the script moves on to line 17, which begins a while loop to extract the information.

In the while loop, lines 18–20 retrieve the ID, title, and description of the category. String operations are performed to ensure that no slashes are in the text and that the category title is in uppercase for display purposes. Lines 22–24 place the category information, including a self-referential page link, in the $display_block string. If a user clicks the link, she will return to this same script, except with a category ID passed in the query string. The script checks for this value in line 26.

If a $_GET["cat_id"] value has been passed to the script because the user clicked on a category link in hopes of seeing listed items, the script builds and issues another query (lines 29–33) to retrieve the items in the category. Lines 35–47 check for items and then build an item string as part of $display_block. Part of the information in the string is a link to a script called showitem.php, which you'll create in the next section.

After reaching that point, the script has nothing left to do, so it prints the HTML and value of $display_block. Figure 22.1 shows the outcome of the script when accessed directly; only the category information shows.

FIGURE 22.1
Categories in the store.

In Figure 22.2, you see what happens when the user clicks on the HATS link: The script gathers all the items associated with the category and prints them on the screen. The user can still jump to another category on this same page, and the script will gather the items for that category.

FIGURE 22.2
Items within a category in the store.

The last piece of the puzzle for this chapter is the creation of the item display page.

Displaying Items

The item display page in this chapter simply shows all the item information. In Chapter 23, you'll add a few lines to it to make it function with an Add to Cart button. Listing 22.2 shows the code for showitem.php.

LISTING 22.2   Script to View Item Information

```
1:  <?php
2:  //connect to database
3:  $mysqli = mysqli_connect("localhost", "joeuser", "somepass", "testDB");
4:
5:  $display_block = "<h1>My Store - Item Detail</h1>";
6:
7:  //validate item
8:  $get_item_sql = "SELECT c.id as cat_id, c.cat_title, si.item_title,
9:                   si.item_price, si.item_desc, si.item_image FROM store_items
10:                  AS si LEFT JOIN store_categories AS c on c.id = si.cat_id
11:                  WHERE si.id = '".$_GET["item_id"]."'";
12: $get_item_res = mysqli_query($mysqli, $get_item_sql)
13:                 or die(mysqli_error($mysqli));
14:
15: if (mysqli_num_rows($get_item_res) < 1) {
16:     //invalid item
17:     $display_block .= "<p><em>Invalid item selection.</em></p>";
18: } else {
19:     //valid item, get info
20:     while ($item_info = mysqli_fetch_array($get_item_res)) {
21:         $cat_id = $item_info['cat_id'];
22:         $cat_title = strtoupper(stripslashes($item_info['cat_title']));
23:         $item_title = stripslashes($item_info['item_title']);
24:         $item_price = $item_info['item_price'];
25:         $item_desc = stripslashes($item_info['item_desc']);
26:         $item_image = $item_info['item_image'];
27:     }
28:
29:     //make breadcrumb trail
30:     $display_block .= "<p><strong><em>You are viewing:</em></strong><br/>
31:     <a href=\"seestore.php?cat_id=".$cat_id."\">".$cat_title."</a>
32     &gt; ".$item_title."</strong></p>
33:     <table cellpadding=\"3\" cellspacing=\"3\">
34:     <tr>
35:     <td valign=\"middle\" align=\"center\">
36:     <img src=\"".$item_image."\"/></td>
37:     <td valign=\"middle\"><p><strong>Description:</strong><br/>".
38:     $item_desc."</p>
39:     <p><strong>Price:</strong> \$".$item_price."</p>";
40:
41:     //free result
42:     mysqli_free_result($get_item_res);
43:
44:     //get colors
45:     $get_colors_sql = "SELECT item_color FROM store_item_color WHERE
46:                        item_id = '".$_GET["item_id"]."' ORDER BY item_color";
```

LISTING 22.2   Continued

```
47:     $get_colors_res = mysqli_query($mysqli, $get_colors_sql)
48:                           or die(mysqli_error($mysqli));
49:
50:     if (mysqli_num_rows($get_colors_res) > 0) {
51:         $display_block .= "<p><strong>Available Colors:</strong><br/>";
52:         while ($colors = mysqli_fetch_array($get_colors_res)) {
53:             item_color = $colors['item_color'];
54:             $display_block .= $item_color."<br/>";
55:         }
56:     }
57:     //free result
58:     mysqli_free_result($get_colors_res);
59:
60:     //get sizes
61:     $get_sizes_sql = "SELECT item_size FROM store_item_size WHERE
62:                         item_id = ".$_GET["item_id"]." ORDER BY item_size";
63:     $get_sizes_res = mysqli_query($mysqli, $get_sizes_sql)
64:                           or die(mysqli_error($mysqli));
65:
66:     if (mysqli_num_rows($get_sizes_res) > 0) {
67:         $display_block .= "<p><strong>Available Sizes:</strong><br/>";
68:         while ($sizes = mysqli_fetch_array($get_sizes_res)) {
69:             $item_size = $sizes['item_size'];
70:             $display_block .= $item_size."<br/>";
71:         }
72:     }
73:     //free result
74:     mysqli_free_result($get_sizes_res);
75:
76:     $display_block .= "
77:     </td>
78:     </tr>
79:     </table>";
80: }
81: ?>
82: <html>
83: <head>
84: <title>My Store</title>
85: </head>
86: <body>
87: <?php echo $display_block; ?>
88: </body>
89: </html>
```

Line 3 makes the database connection because information in the database forms
all the content of this page. Line 5 starts the $display_block string with some basic
page title information.

Lines 8–13 create and issue the query to retrieve the category and item information.
This particular query is a table join. Instead of selecting the item information from
one table and then issuing a second query to find the name of the category, this
query simply joins the table on the category ID to find the category name.

Line 15 checks for a result; if there is no matching item in the table, a message is printed to the user and that's all this script does. However, if item information is found, the script moves on and gathers the information in lines 20–27.

In lines 30–32, you create what's known as a *breadcrumb trail*. This is simply a navigational device used to get back to the top-level item in the architecture. Those are fancy words that mean "print a link so that you can get back to the category." The category ID, retrieved from the master query in this script, is appended to the link in the breadcrumb trail.

In lines 33–39, you continue to add to the $display_block, setting up a table for information about the item. You use the values gathered in lines 21–26 to create an image link, print the description, and print the price. What's missing are the colors and sizes, so lines 44–56 select and print any colors associated with this item, and lines 61–72 gather the sizes associated with the item.

Lines 76–80 wrap up the $display_block string and the master if...else statement. Because the script has nothing left to do, it prints the HTML (lines 82–89) including the value of $display_block. Figure 22.3 shows the outcome of the script when selecting the baseball hat from the hats category. Of course, your display will differ from mine because you won't have the same images I used, but you get the idea.

FIGURE 22.3
The baseball hat item page.

That's all there is to creating a simple item display. In Chapter 23, you'll modify this script so that it can add the item to a shopping cart.

Summary

In this chapter, you applied your basic PHP and MySQL knowledge to the creation of a storefront display. You learned how to create the database table and scripts for viewing categories, item lists, and single items.

Workshop

The workshop is designed to help you anticipate possible questions, review what you've learned, and begin putting your knowledge into practice.

Q&A

Q. *In the item detail record, you use single filenames in the `item_image` field. What if I want to link to items on a different server?*

A. You can enter a URL in the `item_image` field as long as you define the field to hold a long string such as a URL.

Quiz

1. Which PHP function was used to uppercase the category title strings?

2. Why don't the `store_item_size` and `store_item_color` tables contain any unique keys?

Answers

1. `strtoupper()`

2. Presumably, you will have items with more than one color and more than one size. Therefore, `item_id` is not a unique key. Also, items may have the same colors or sizes, so the `item_color` and `item_size` fields must not be primary or unique either.

23

Creating a Shopping Cart Mechanism

In this chapter, you will integrate a shopping cart mechanism and checkout procedure into the basic storefront display that you created in Chapter 22, "Creating an Online Storefront." You will see the methods for creating the relevant database tables as well as the scripts for adding and deleting cart items. The examples used in this chapter again represent only a few of an infinite number of possibilities to complete these tasks and are meant as working examples rather than the definitive guide for building an online store.

In this chapter, you will learn

- ▶ How to create relational tables for the shopping cart and checkout portion of an online store
- ▶ How to create the scripts to add and remove cart items
- ▶ Some methods for processing transactions, and how to create your checkout sequence

Planning and Creating the Database Tables

Because the goal of this chapter is to provide the user with a way to select and order items, you can imagine what the tables will be—first and foremost, you need a table to hold the shopping cart information. In addition to the cart table, you'll need a table to store orders, along with one to store the items purchased as part of each order.

The following SQL statements were used to create the three new tables, starting with the store_shoppertrack table. This is the table used to hold items as users add them to their shopping cart.

> The field lengths used to define these tables were chosen arbitrarily to accommodate several possible inputs. Feel free to modify the lengths to meet your specific needs.

```
mysql> CREATE TABLE store_shoppertrack (
    -> id INT NOT NULL PRIMARY KEY AUTO_INCREMENT,
    -> session_id VARCHAR (32),
    -> sel_item_id INT,
    -> sel_item_qty SMALLINT,
    -> sel_item_size VARCHAR(25),
    -> sel_item_color VARCHAR(25),
    -> date_added DATETIME
    -> );
Query OK, 0 rows affected (0.01 sec)
```

In this table, the only key is the id field for the record. The session_id cannot be unique; otherwise, users could order only one item from your store, which is not a good business practice.

The value stored in the session_id field identifies the user; it matches the value of the PHP session ID assigned to that particular user. The sel_* fields hold the selections by the user: the selected item, the selected quantity of the item, and the selected color and size of the item. Finally, there's a date_added field. Many times, users place items in their cart and never go through the checkout process. This practice leaves straggling items in your tracking table, which you might want to clear out periodically. For example, you might want to delete all cart items more than a week old—this is where the date_added field is helpful.

The next table holds the order information:

```
mysql> CREATE TABLE store_orders (
    -> id INT NOT NULL PRIMARY KEY AUTO_INCREMENT,
    -> order_date DATETIME,
    -> order_name VARCHAR (100),
    -> order_address VARCHAR (255),
    -> order_city VARCHAR (50),
    -> order_state CHAR(2),
    -> order_zip VARCHAR(10),
    -> order_tel VARCHAR(25),
    -> order_email VARCHAR(100),
    -> item_total FLOAT(6,2),
    -> shipping_total FLOAT(6,2),
    -> authorization VARCHAR (50),
    -> status ENUM('processed', 'pending')
    -> );
Query OK, 0 rows affected (0.00 sec)
```

The only key field in the store_orders table is the id. For the sake of brevity in this chapter, we make assumptions that the billing and shipping addresses of the user are the same and that this store sells only to United States addresses. It's simple enough for you to add another block of fields for shipping address information, if you want to do so.

Also, this table assumes that you are not storing credit card information, which you shouldn't do unless you have superencrypted the information and are sure that your firewalled server is secure. Instead, this table is based on the idea of real-time, credit card processing. You'll learn a few transaction options at the end of this lesson.

The final table holds the line items in each order, store_orders_items:

```
mysql> CREATE TABLE store_orders_items (
    -> id INT NOT NULL PRIMARY KEY AUTO_INCREMENT,
    -> order_id INT,
    -> sel_item_id INT,
    -> sel_item_qty SMALLINT,
    -> sel_item_size VARCHAR(25),
    -> sel_item_color VARCHAR(25),
    -> sel_item_price FLOAT(6,2)
    -> );
Query OK, 0 rows affected (0.00 sec)
```

The sel_* fields should look familiar—with the exception of sel_item_price, they are the same fields that appear in the store_shoppertrack table! The primary key is the id field, and the order_id field ties each line item to the appropriate record in store_orders.

The sel_item_price field is included here, as opposed to simply relating to the item record, because you might have occasion to change the pricing in your item record. If you change the price in the item record, and you relate the sold line items to the current catalog price, your line item prices won't reflect what the user actually paid.

With your tables all squared away, we can move on to adding an item to the user's shopping cart.

Integrating the Cart with Your Storefront

In this section, you'll make modifications to the showitem.php script from Chapter 22. The goal is to transform the item information page into an item information page with a form for selecting colors, sizes, and quantities.

In the original script, insert the following before line 2:

```
session_start();
```

Because the shopping cart elements are attached to the user through a session ID, the session must be started. The next changes don't occur until what was line 39 of the showitem.php script from Chapter 22, so that's where we start in Listing 23.1.

LISTING 23.1   New Lines in showitem.php

```
39:    <p><strong>Price:</strong> \$".$item_price."</p>
40:    <form method=\"post\" action=\"addtocart.php\">";
41:
42:    //free result
43:    mysqli_free_result($get_item_res);
44:
45:    //get colors
46:    $get_colors_sql = "SELECT item_color FROM store_item_color WHERE
47:                        item_id = '".$_GET["item_id"]."' ORDER BY item_color";
48:    $get_colors_res = mysqli_query($mysqli, $get_colors_sql)
49:                        or die(mysqli_error($mysqli));
50:
51:    if (mysqli_num_rows($get_colors_res) > 0) {
52:        $display_block .= "<p><strong>Available Colors:</strong><br/>
53:        <select name=\"sel_item_color\">";
54:
55:        while ($colors = mysqli_fetch_array($get_colors_res)) {
56:            $item_color = $colors['item_color'];
57:            $display_block .= "<option value=\"".$item_color."\">".
58:            $item_color."</option>";
59:        }
60:        $display_block .= "</select>";
61:    }
62:
63:    //free result
64:    mysqli_free_result($get_colors_res);
65:
66:    //get sizes
67:    $get_sizes_sql = "SELECT item_size FROM store_item_size WHERE
68:                        item_id = ".$_GET["item_id"]." ORDER BY item_size";
69:    $get_sizes_res = mysqli_query($mysqli, $get_sizes_sql)
70:                        or die(mysqli_error($mysqli));
71:
72:    if (mysqli_num_rows($get_sizes_res) > 0) {
73:        $display_block .= "<p><strong>Available Sizes:</strong><br/>
74:        <select name=\"sel_item_size\">";
75:
76:        while ($sizes = mysqli_fetch_array($get_sizes_res)) {
77:            $item_size = $sizes['item_size'];
78:            $display_block .= "<option value=\"".$item_size."\">".
79:            $item_size."</option>";
80:        }
81:    }
82:
83:    $display_block .= "</select>";
84:
85:    //free result
86:    mysqli_free_result($get_sizes_res);
87:
88:    $display_block .= "
89:    <p><strong>Select Quantity:</strong>
```

LISTING 23.1 Continued

```
90:      <select name=\"sel_item_qty\">";
91:
92:      for($i=1; $i<11; $i++) {
93:          $display_block .= "<option value=\"".$i."\">".$i."</option>";
94:      }
95:
96:      $display_block .= "
97:      </select>
98:      <input type=\"hidden\" name=\"sel_item_id\"
99:      value=\"".$_GET["item_id"]."\"/>
100:     <p><input type=\"submit\" name=\"submit\" value=\"Add to Cart\"/></p>
101:     </form>
102:     </td>
103:     </tr>
104:     </table>";
105: }
106: //close connection to MySQL
107: mysqli_close($mysqli);
108: ?>
109: <html>
110: <head>
111: <title>My Store</title>
112: </head>
113: <body>
114: <?php echo $display_block; ?>
115: </body>
116: </html>
```

The first change is at the new line 40, where the $display_block string is continued to include the beginning <form> element. The action of the form is a script called addtocart.php, which you will create in the next section.

The next change occurs at line 53, where the $display_block string is continued to include the opening tag of a <select> element named sel_item_color. In lines 57–58, the colors are put into <option> elements for the user to choose from instead of simply printing on the screen. Line 60 closes the <select> element.

The same types of changes are made for item sizes. Lines 73–74 reflect the continuation of the $display_block string to include the <select> element, named sel_item_size. Lines 78–79 write the colors in <option> elements, and line 83 closes the <select> element.

Lines 88–94 are additions to the script. These lines create a <select> element, called sel_item_qty, for the user to pick how many items to purchase. Line 97 closes this <select> element, and line 98 adds a hidden field for the item_id. Line 100 adds the submit button, and line 101 closes the form. We close the connection to MySQL in line 107, and the remaining lines are unchanged from the original script.

When viewing the baseball hat item using the new version of showitem.php, you would see Figure 23.1, reflecting the addition of the form elements.

FIGURE 23.1
The new base-
ball hat item
page.

The next step is to create the addtocart.php script.

Adding Items to Your Cart

The addtocart.php script simply writes information to the store_shoppertrack table and redirects the user to the view of the shopping cart. We'll create the addto-cart.php script first in Listing 23.2 and then tackle the showcart.php script next.

LISTING 23.2   The addtocart.php **Script**

```
1:  <?php
2:  session_start();
3:
4:  //connect to database
5:  $mysqli = mysqli_connect("localhost", "joeuser", "somepass", "testDB");
6:
7:  if (isset($_POST["sel_item_id"])) {
8:      //validate item and get title and price
9:      $get_iteminfo_sql = "SELECT item_title FROM store_items WHERE
10:                       id = '".$_POST["sel_item_id"]."'";
11:     $get_iteminfo_res = mysqli_query($mysqli, $get_iteminfo_sql)
12:                       or die(mysqli_error($mysqli));
13:
14:     if (mysqli_num_rows($get_iteminfo_res) < 1) {
15:         //invalid id, send away
16:         header("Location: seestore.php");
17:         exit;
```

LISTING 23.2   Continued

```
18:      } else {
19:          //get info
20:          while ($item_info = mysqli_fetch_array($get_iteminfo_res)) {
21:              $item_title = stripslashes($item_info['item_title']);
22:          }
23:
24:          //add info to cart table
25:          $addtocart_sql = "INSERT INTO store_shoppertrack
26:                            (session_id, sel_item_id, sel_item_qty,
27:                            sel_item_size, sel_item_color, date_added)
28:                            VALUES ('".$_COOKIE["PHPSESSID"]."',
29:                            '".$_POST["sel_item_id"]."',
30:                            '".$_POST["sel_item_qty"]."',
31:                            '".$_POST["sel_item_size"]."',
32:                            '".$_POST["sel_item_color"]."', now())";
33:          $addtocart_res = mysqli_query($mysqli, $addtocart_sql)
34:                            or die(mysqli_error($mysqli));
35:
36:          //redirect to showcart page
37:          header("Location: showcart.php");
38:          exit;
39:      }
40:
41: } else {
42:      //send them somewhere else
43:      header("Location: seestore.php");
44:      exit;
45: }
46: ?>
```

Line 2 continues the user session, which is important because you need to capture the user's session ID to write to the `store_shoppertrack` table. Line 5 makes the database connection, and line 7 begins the validation of the actions.

In line 7, the script verifies that a value is present in `$_POST["sel_item_id"]`, meaning that the user came to this script after submitting the proper form. If there is no value, the script jumps down to line 41 and sends the user away in line 43, and that's it for the script.

However, if there is a value in `$_POST["sel_item_id"]`, the next action is to verify that it is a valid value. Lines 9–12 create and issue a SQL query to gather the title of the selected item. Line 14 checks for a result; if there is no result, the user is again redirected away in line 16 because the item selection was not valid.

If the item selection is valid, the script continues to line 20 and extracts this value from the resultset. The script now has enough information to add the item selection to the `store_shoppertrack` table, which it does in lines 25–34.

After the query has been issued, the user is redirected to `showcart.php`, which contains all cart items. You'll create this script in the next section.

Viewing the Cart

Now that you can add items to a cart, you'll want to see them! Listing 23.3 shows
the code for showcart.php.

LISTING 23.3 The showcart.php Script

```
1:    <?php
2:    session_start();
3:
4:    //connect to database
5:    $mysqli = mysqli_connect("localhost", "joeuser", "somepass", "testDB");
6:
7:    $display_block = "<h1>Your Shopping Cart</h1>";
8:
9:    //check for cart items based on user session id
10:   $get_cart_sql = "SELECT st.id, si.item_title, si.item_price,
11:                   st.sel_item_qty, st.sel_item_size, st.sel_item_color FROM
12:                   store_shoppertrack AS st LEFT JOIN store_items AS si ON
13:                   si.id = st.sel_item_id WHERE session_id =
14:                   '".$_COOKIE["PHPSESSID"]."'";
15:   $get_cart_res = mysqli_query($mysqli, $get_cart_sql)
16:                   or die(mysqli_error($mysqli));
17:
18:   if (mysqli_num_rows($get_cart_res) < 1) {
19:       //print message
20:       $display_block .= "<p>You have no items in your cart.
21:       Please <a href=\"seestore.php\">continue to shop</a>!</p>";
22:   } else {
23:       //get info and build cart display
24:       $display_block .= "
25:       <table celpadding=\"3\" cellspacing=\"2\" border=\"1\" width=\"98%\">
26:       <tr>
27:       <th>Title</th>
28:       <th>Size</th>
29:       <th>Color</th>
30:       <th>Price</th>
31:       <th>Qty</th>
32:       <th>Total Price</th>
33:       <th>Action</th>
34:       </tr>";
35:
36:       while ($cart_info = mysqli_fetch_array($get_cart_res)) {
37:           $id = $cart_info['id'];
38:           $item_title = stripslashes($cart_info['item_title']);
39:           $item_price = $cart_info['item_price'];
40:           $item_qty = $cart_info['sel_item_qty'];
41:           $item_color = $cart_info['sel_item_color'];
42:           $item_size = $cart_info['sel_item_size'];
43:           $total_price = sprintf("%.02f", $item_price * $item_qty);
44:
45:           $display_block .= "
46:           <tr>
47:           <td align=\"center\">$item_title <br></td>
48:           <td align=\"center\">$item_size <br></td>
49:           <td align=\"center\">$item_color <br></td>
50:           <td align=\"center\">\$ $item_price <br></td>
```

LISTING 23.3 Continued

```
51:              <td align=\"center\">$item_qty <br></td>
52:              <td align=\"center\">\$ $total_price</td>
53:              <td align=\"center\"><a href=\"removefromcart.php?id=".
54:              $id."\">remove</a></td>
55:              </tr>";
56:      }
57:
58:      $display_block .= "</table>";
59: }
60: ?>
61: <html>
62: <head>
63: <title>My Store</title>
64: </head>
65: <body>
66: <?php echo $display_block; ?>
67: </body>
68: </html>
```

Line 2 continues the user session, which is important because you need to match the user's session ID with the records in the store_shoppertrack table. Line 5 makes the database connection, and line 7 begins the $display_block string, with a heading for the page.

Lines 10–14 represent a joined query, in which the user's saved items are retrieved. The id, sel_item_qty, sel_item_size, and sel_item_color fields are extracted from store_shoppertrack, and the item_title and item_price fields are retrieved from the store_items table based on the matching information from store_shoppertrack. In other words, instead of printing 2 for the selected item, Baseball Hat is shown as the title. Lines 15–16 issue the query, and line 18 checks for results.

If there are no results, the user has no items in the store_shoppertrack table. A message is written to the $display_block string, and the script exits and shows the message.

If there are indeed results, the beginning of an HTML table is created in lines 24–34, with columns defined for all the information in the cart (and then some). Line 36 begins the while loop to extract each item from the store_shoppertrack, and this loop continues until line 56, printing the information in the proper table cell.

In lines 53–54, you see a link created for an item removal script, which you will create in the next section. Line 58 closes the table, and the script finishes and prints HTML to the screen in lines 61–68.

Now, go back to an item page and add the item to your cart. After the items are written to the store_shoppertrack table, you should be redirected to the showcart.php page, and your newly selected items should be displayed. Figure 23.2 shows my cart after adding some items.

FIGURE 23.2
Items added to
cart.

The next step is to create the removefromcart.php script.

Removing Items from Your Cart

The removefromcart.php script is short because all it does is issue a query and redirect the user to another script. Inevitably, a user will want to weed items out of his cart, and this script enables him to do just that. Listing 23.4 shows the complete script.

LISTING 23.4 The removefromcart.php **Script**

```
1:  <?php
2:  session_start();
3:
4:  //connect to database
5:  $mysqli = mysqli_connect("localhost", "joeuser", "somepass", "testDB");
6:
7:  if (isset($_GET["id"])) {
8:      $delete_item_sql = "DELETE FROM store_shoppertrack WHERE
9:                          id = '".$_GET["id"]."' and session_id =
10:                         '".$_COOKIE["PHPSESSID"]."'";
11:     $delete_item_res = mysqli_query($mysqli, $delete_item_sql)
12:                         or die(mysqli_error($mysqli));
13:
```

LISTING 23.4   Continued

```
14:       //redirect to showcart page
15:       header("Location: showcart.php");
16:       exit;
17:   } else {
18:       //send them somewhere else
19:       header("Location: seestore.php");
20:       exit;
21:   }
22:   ?>
```

Line 2 continues the user session because you need to match the user's session ID
with the records in the store_shoppertrack table. Line 5 makes the database connection, and line 7 checks for a value in $_GET["id"]. If a value does not exist in
$_GET["id"], the user is not clicking the link from her cart and, thus, is sent away
in line 19.

If a value exists in $_GET["id"], a SQL query (lines 8–10) is issued (lines 11–12),
and the user is redirected to the showcart.php script (line 15), where the item
should no longer show up. Try it and see!

Payment Methods and the Checkout Sequence

Several commerce methods exist when it comes time to pay for the purchases in the
shopping cart. The "right" method for you depends on your business—merchant
accounts through banking institutions often require you to have a business license,
a reseller's permit, and other pieces of paper proving that you're a legitimate business. If you're simply a person who has a few items to sell, you might not want to
go through all that paperwork. However, you still have options!

Regardless of the payment method you choose, one thing is certain: If you are passing credit card information over the Web, you must do so over an SSL (Secure
Sockets Layer) connection. Obtaining an SSL certificate and installing it on your system is covered in Chapter 30, "Setting Up a Secure Web Server." You do not have to
use this secure connection during the user's entire shopping experience, just from
the point at which sensitive information will be captured, such as when you send
the user to the checkout form.

Creating the Checkout Form

At this point in the book, you should be well versed in creating a simple form. At the beginning of this chapter, you created the `store_orders` table with fields to use as a guideline for your form:

- ▶ `order_name`

- ▶ `order_address`

- ▶ `order_city`

- ▶ `order_state`

- ▶ `order_zip`

- ▶ `order_tel`

- ▶ `order_email`

Additionally, your form will need fields for the credit card number, expiration date, and the name on the credit card. Another nice feature is to repeat the user's shopping cart contents with an item subtotal so that the customer remembers what he's paying for and approximately how much the order will cost. Also at this point of the checkout sequence, you offer any shipping options you might have. Shipping and sales tax would be calculated in the next step of the process.

From the point of clicking the submit button on the form, the checkout sequence depends on the payment method you are using. The next section goes through the basic steps and offers suggestions on various methods of payment processing.

Performing the Checkout Actions

If you have obtained a merchant account through your bank, you can utilize real-time payment services such as PayPal's PayFlo or Authorize.Net's payment gateway services. PHP does not contain built-in functions that enable direct access to the these payment gateways, but when you have an account with merchant services of these types you will be able to download scripts that you can use in your own applications, or you will be given information on an API for application developers.

PayPal and Authorize.Net are two of several transaction-processing gateways that exist for use by merchants—I include them here because I have personally (and successfully) used both gateway services since they have existed. Your bank will usually provide a list of merchants it prefers you to use. If you stray from your bank's list of preferred vendors, be sure to research your selected vendor thoroughly to avoid any delays with deposits and to ensure that you're getting the best deal.

After you have selected a transaction processor, your checkout script should follow a path such as the following:

1. Total the items, add tax, and add shipping. This gives you the total amount to authorize from the credit card.

2. Perform credit card authorization for the total amount.

3. You will receive either a success or failure response from your card-processing routine. If the response is a failure, print a message to the user and the transaction is over. If the response is a success, continue to step 4.

4. Write the basic order information to a table such as `store_orders`, including the authorization code you will receive on successful authorization. Get the `id` value of this record using `mysql_insert_id()`.

5. For each item in the shopping cart tied to this user, insert a record into `store_orders_itemmap`. Each record will reference the `id` (as `order_id`) gathered in the previous step.

6. Delete the shopping cart items for this user.

7. Display the order with the authorization code in place of the credit card information on the screen so that the user can print it and hold it as a receipt. You can also send this information via email to the user.

The steps listed previously—with the exception of the actual payment authorization code—are the same simple steps you have been using throughout this book, and there's no reason to make them more difficult than they need to be!

Summary

In this chapter, you applied your basic PHP and MySQL knowledge to the integration of a shopping cart into the storefront from Chapter 22. Included were the database table creation, modifications to the item detail page, and new scripts for adding and removing cart items.

Workshop

The workshop is designed to help you anticipate possible questions, review what you've learned, and begin putting your knowledge into practice.

Quiz

1. When removing an item from the cart, why do you suppose that the query validates the session ID of the user against the record?

2. What would be a reason not to store the price in a hidden field when adding to the cart?

Answers

1. Users should be able to remove only their own items.

2. If you stored the price in a hidden field, a rogue user could change that value before posting the form, therefore writing whatever price he wanted into the store_shoppertrack table, as opposed to the actual price.

24

Creating a Simple Calendar

This chapter will pull together the skills you've learned so far regarding the PHP language and building small applications. In this chapter, you'll continue your learning in the context of creating a small calendar.

In this chapter, you will learn

- ▶ How to build a simple calendar script
- ▶ How to view and add events in your calendar
- ▶ How to build a class library to generate date pull-downs in HTML forms

Building a Simple Display Calendar

You'll use the date and time functions you learned in Chapter 10, "Working with Strings, Dates, and Time," to build a calendar that displays the dates for any month between 1980 and 2010. Those are randomly selected years and have no significance—you can make your calendar go from 1990 to 2005 if you want, or any other range of dates that make sense to you. The user will be able to select both month and year with pull-down menus, and the dates for the selected month will be organized according to the days of the week.

In this script, we will be working with two variables—one for month and one for year—which will be supplied by user input. These pieces of information will be used to build a time stamp based on the first day of the selected month. If user input is invalid or absent, the default value will be the first day of the current month.

Checking User Input

When the user accesses the calendar application for the first time, no information will have been submitted. Therefore, we must ensure that the script can handle the fact that the variables for month and year might not be defined. We could use the isset() function for this because it returns false if the variable passed to it has not been defined. However, let's use the checkdate() function instead, which not only will see whether the variable exists but will also do something meaningful with it, namely, validate that it is a date. Listing 24.1 shows the fragment of code that checks for month and year variables coming from a form, and builds a time stamp based on them.

LISTING 24.1   Checking User Input for the Calendar Script

```
 1: <?php
 2: if ((!isset($_POST["month"])) || (!isset($_POST["year"]))) {
 3:     $nowArray = getdate();
 4:     $month = $nowArray["mon"];
 5:     $year = $nowArray["year"];
 6: } else {
 7:     $month = $_POST["month"];
 8:     $year = $_POST["year"];
 9: }
10: $start = mktime (12, 0, 0, $month, 1, $year);
11: $firstDayArray = getdate($start);
12: ?>
```

Listing 24.1 is a fragment of a larger script, so it does not produce any output itself. But it's an important fragment to understand, which is why it sits all alone here, ready for an explanation.

In the if statement on line 2, we test whether the month and year have been provided by a form. If the month and year have not been defined, the mktime() function used later in the fragment will not be able to make a valid date from undefined month and year arguments.

If the values are present, we use getdate() on line 3 to create an associative array based on the current time. We then set values for $month and $year ourselves, using the array's mon and year elements (lines 4 and 5). If the variables have been set from the form, we put the data into $month and $year variables so as not to touch the values in the original $_POST superglobal.

Now that we are sure that we have valid data in $month and $year, we can use mktime() to create a time stamp for the first day of the month (line 10). We will need information about this time stamp later on, so on line 11, we create a variable called $firstDayArray that will store an associative array returned by getdate() and based on this time stamp.

Building the HTML Form

We now need to create an interface by which users can ask to see data for a month and year. For this, we will use SELECT elements. Although we could hard-code these in HTML, we must also ensure that the pull-downs default to the currently chosen month, so we will dynamically create these pull-downs, adding a SELECT attribute to the OPTION element where appropriate. The form is generated in Listing 24.2.

LISTING 24.2   Building the HTML Form for the Calendar Script

```
1:  <?php
2:  if ((!isset($_POST["month"])) || (!isset($_POST["year"]))) {
3:      $nowArray = getdate();
4:      $month = $nowArray["mon"];
5:      $year = $nowArray["year"];
6:  } else {
7:      $month = $_POST["month"];
8:      $year = $_POST["year"];
9:  }
10: $start = mktime (12, 0, 0, $month, 1, $year);
11: $firstDayArray = getdate($start);
12: ?>
13: <html>
14: <head>
15: <title><?php echo "Calendar:".$firstDayArray["month"]."
16:    ".$firstDayArray["year"]; ?></title>
17: <head>
18: <body>
19: <h1>Select a Month/Year Combination</h1>
20: <form method="post" action="<?php echo $_SERVER["PHP_SELF"]; ?>">
21: <select name="month">
22: <?php
23: $months = Array("January", "February", "March", "April", "May",
24: "June", "July", "August", "September", "October", "November", "December");
25: for ($x=1; $x <= count($months); $x++) {
26:     echo"<option value=\"$x\"";
27:     if ($x == $month) {
28:         echo " selected";
29:     }
30:     echo ">".$months[$x-1]."</option>";
31: }
32: ?>
33: </select>
34: <select name="year">
35: <?php
36: for ($x=1980; $x<=2010; $x++) {
37:     echo "<option";
38:     if ($x == $year) {
39:         echo " selected";
40:     }
41:     echo ">$x</option>";
42: }
43: ?>
44: </select>
45: <input type="submit" name="submit" value="Go!">
46: </form>
47: </body>
48: </html>
```

Having created the $start time stamp and the $firstDayArray date array in lines
2–11, let's begin to write the HTML for the page. Notice that we use $firstDayArray
to add the month and year to the TITLE element on lines 15 and 16.

Line 20 is the beginning of our form. To create the SELECT element for the month pull-down, we drop back into PHP mode on line 22 to write the individual OPTION tags. First, for display purposes, we create in lines 23 and 24 an array called $months that contains the names of the 12 months. We then loop through this array, creating an OPTION tag for each name (lines 25–31).

This would be an overcomplicated way of writing a simple SELECT element were it not for the fact that we are testing $x (the counter variable in the for statement) against the $month variable on line 27. If $x and $month are equivalent, we add the string SELECTED to the OPTION tag, ensuring that the correct month will be selected automatically when the page loads. We use a similar technique to write the year pull-down on lines 36–42. Finally, back in HTML mode, we create a submit button on line 45.

We now have a form that can send the month and year parameters to itself and will default either to the current month and year or the month and year previously chosen. If you save this listing as dateselector.php, place it in your web server document root, and access it with your web browser, you should see something like Figure 24.1 (your month and year might differ).

FIGURE 24.1
The calendar
form.

Creating the Calendar Table

We now need to create a table and populate it with dates for the chosen month. We do this in Listing 24.3, which represents the complete calendar display script.

Although line 2 is new, lines 3–47 come right from Listing 24.2. Line 2 simply defines a constant variable, in this case ADAY (for example, "a day") with a value of 86400. This value represents the number of seconds in a day, which the script uses later.

LISTING 24.3   The Complete Calendar Display Script

```
1: <?php
2: define("ADAY", (60*60*24));
3: if ((!isset($_POST["month"])) || (!isset($_POST["year"]))) {
4:      $nowArray = getdate();
5:      $month = $nowArray["mon"];
6:      $year = $nowArray["year"];
7: } else {
8:      $month = $_POST["month"];
9:      $year = $_POST["year"];
10: }
11: $start = mktime (12, 0, 0, $month, 1, $year);
12: $firstDayArray = getdate($start);
13: ?>
14: <html>
15: <head>
16: <title><?php echo "Calendar: ".$firstDayArray["month"]."
17:    ".$firstDayArray["year"]; ?></title>
18: <head>
19: <body>
20: <h1>Select a Month/Year Combination</h1>
21: <form method="post" action="<?php echo $_SERVER["PHP_SELF"]; ?>">
22: <select name="month">
23: <?php
24: $months = Array("January", "February", "March", "April", "May",
25: "June", "July", "August", "September", "October", "November", "December");
26: for ($x=1; $x <= count($months); $x++) {
27:      echo"<option value=\"$x\"";
28:      if ($x == $month) {
29:          echo " selected";
30:      }
31:      echo ">".$months[$x-1]."</option>";
32: }
33: ?>
34: </select>
35: <select name="year">
36: <?php
37: for ($x=1980; $x<=2010; $x++) {
38:      echo "<option";
39:      if ($x == $year) {
40:          echo " selected";
41:      }
42:      echo ">$x</option>";
43: }
44: ?>
45: </select>
46: <input type="submit" value="Go!">
47: </form>
48: <br/>
49: <?php
50: $days = Array("Sun", "Mon", "Tue", "Wed", "Thu", "Fri", "Sat");
51: echo "<table border=\"1\" cellpadding=\"5\"><tr>\n";
52: foreach ($days as $day) {
53:      echo "<td style=\"background-color: #CCCCCC;
54:      text-align: center;width: 14%\"><strong>$day</strong></td>\n";
55: }
```

LISTING 24.3   Continued

```
56: for ($count=0; $count < (6*7); $count++) {
57:     $dayArray = getdate($start);
58:     if (($count % 7) == 0) {
59:         if ($dayArray["mon"] != $month) {
60:             break;
61:         } else {
62:             echo "</tr><tr>\n";
63:         }
64:     }
65:     if ($count < $firstDayArray["wday"] || $dayArray["mon"] != $month) {
66:         echo "<td> </td>\n";
67:     } else {
68:         echo "<td>".$dayArray["mday"]."    </td>\n";
69:         $start += ADAY;
70:     }
71: }
72: echo "</tr></table>";
73: ?>
74: </body>
75: </html>
```

We pick up the new code at line 48. Because the table will be indexed by days of the week, we loop through an array of day names in lines 52–55, printing each in its own table cell, on lines 53–54. All the real magic of the script happens in the final for statement beginning on line 56.

In line 56, we initialize a variable called $count and ensure that the loop will end after 42 iterations. This is to make sure that we will have enough cells to populate with date information, taking into consideration that a four-week month might actually have partial weeks at the beginning and the end, thus the need for six seven-day weeks (rows).

Within this for loop, we transform the $start variable into a date array with get-date(), assigning the result to $dayArray (line 57). Although $start is the first day of the month during the loop's initial execution, we will increment this time stamp by the value of ADAY (24 hours) for every iteration (see line 69).

On line 58, we test the $count variable against the number 7, using the modulus operator. The block of code belonging to this if statement will therefore be run only when $count is either zero or a multiple of 7. This is our way of knowing whether we should end the loop altogether or start a new row, where rows represent weeks.

After we have established that we are in the first iteration or at the end of a row, we can go on to perform another test on line 59. If the mon (month number) element of the $dayArray is no longer equivalent to the $month variable, we are finished. Remember that $dayArray contains information about the $start time stamp, which is the current place in the month that we are displaying. When $start goes beyond the current month, $dayArray["mon"] will hold a different figure than the $month number provided by user input. Our modulus test demonstrated that we are at the end of a row, and the fact that we are in a new month means that we can leave the loop altogether. Assuming, however, that we are still in the month that we are displaying, we end the row and start a new one on line 62.

In the next if statement, on line 65, we determine whether to write date information to a cell. Not every month begins on a Sunday, so it's likely that our rows will contain an empty cell or two. Similarly, few months will finish at the end of one of our rows, so it's also likely that we will have a few empty cells before we close the table.

We have stored information about the first day of the month in $firstDayArray; in particular, we can access the number of the day of the week in $firstDayArray["wday"]. If the value of $count is smaller than this number, we know that we haven't yet reached the correct cell for writing. By the same token, if the value of the $month variable is no longer equal to $dayArray["mon"], we know that we have reached the end of the month (but not the end of the row, as we determined in our earlier modulus test). In either case, we write an empty cell to the browser on line 66.

In the final else clause on line 67, we can do the fun stuff. We have already determined that we are within the month that we want to list, and that the current day column matches the day number stored in $firstDayArray["wday"]. Now we must use the $dayArray associative array that we established early in the loop to write the day of the month and some blank space into a cell.

Finally, on line 69, we need to increment the $start variable, which contains our date stamp. We simply add the number of seconds in a day to it (we defined this value in line 2), and we're ready to begin the loop again with a new value in $start to be tested. If you save this listing as showcalendar.php, place it in your web server document root, and access it with your web browser, you should see something like Figure 24.2 (your month and year might differ).

Adding Events to the Calendar

Displaying the calendar is great, but with just a few extra lines of code, you can make it interactive—that is, you can add and view events on a given day. To begin, let's create a simple database table that holds event information. For purposes of simplicity, these events will occur on only a single day and only their start date and time will be shown. Although you can make the event entries as complex as you want, this example is here just to show the basic process involved.

FIGURE 24.2
The calendar
form and script.

The `calendar_events` table will include fields for the start date and time, the event title, and an event short description:

```
mysql>  CREATE TABLE calendar_events (
    -> id INT NOT NULL PRIMARY KEY AUTO_INCREMENT,
    -> event_title VARCHAR (25),
    -> event_shortdesc VARCHAR (255),
    -> event_start DATETIME
    -> );
Query OK, 0 rows affected (0.01 sec)
```

We can use the code in Listing 24.3 as our base (the script called `showcalendar.php`). In this new script, we'll add a link to a pop-up window as part of the calendar display. Each date will be a link; the pop-up window will call another script that will display the full text of an event as well as provide the capability to add an event. To begin, add the following JavaScript code after the opening <head> tag—after line 18 of the original script:

```
<script type="text/javascript">
function eventWindow(url) {
    event_popupWin = window.open(url, 'event', 'resizable=yes, scrollbars=yes,
            toolbar=no,width=400,height=400');
    event_popupWin.opener = self;
}
</script>
```

This JavaScript function defines a 400×400 window that will call a URL we provide. We use this JavaScript function at what was line 68 of the original script; we now wrap the date display in this link to the JavaScript-based pop-up window, which calls a script named event.php. The new code is as follows:

```
echo "<td valign=\"top\">
<a href=\"javascript:eventWindow('event.php?m=".$month."
&d=".$dayArray["mday"]."&y=$year');\">".$dayArray["mday"]."</a>
<br/><br/>".$event_title."</td>\n";
```

Not only do we call the event.php file, but we also have to send along with it the date information for the particular link that is clicked. This is done via the query string, and you can see we're sending along three variables—what will become $_GET["m"] for the month, $_GET["d"] for the day, and $_GET["y"] for the year.

Only one change remains for this particular script before we tackle the event.php script—adding an indicator to this particular view, if events do indeed exist. To do this, we have to connect to the database, so after the opening PHP tag at the original line 1, add the database connection code:

```
$mysqli = mysqli_connect("localhost", "joeuser", "somepass", "testDB");
```

The query that checks for existing events on a given day appears at the onset of the else statement that was originally found at line 7. An entirely new else statement is shown; you can see that the query is issued, and, if results are found, text is printed within the table cell for that day:

```
} else {
    $chkEvent_sql = "SELECT event_title FROM calendar_events WHERE
                     month(event_start) = '".$month."' AND
                     dayofmonth(event_start) = '".$dayArray["mday"]."'
                     AND year(event_start) = '".$year."' ORDER BY event_start";
    $chkEvent_res = mysqli_query($mysqli, $chkEvent_sql)
                    or die(mysqli_error($mysqli));

    if (mysqli_num_rows($chkEvent_res) > 0) {
        while ($ev = mysqli_fetch_array($chkEvent_res)) {
            $event_title = stripslashes($ev["event_title"]);
        }
    } else {
        $event_title = "";
    }

    echo "<td valign=\"top\"><a href=\"javascript:eventWindow('event.php?m=".
    $month."&d=".$dayArray["mday"]."&y=$year');\">".$dayArray["mday"]."</a>
    <br/><br/>".
    $event_title."</td>\n";

    unset($event_title);

    $start += ADAY;
}
```

In Listing 24.4, you can see the entirely new script, which we'll call showcalendar_
withevent.php.

LISTING 24.4   Calendar Display Script with Entry-Related Modifications

```
 1:  <?php
 2:  $mysqli = mysqli_connect("localhost", "joeuser", "somepass", "testDB");
 3:
 4:  define("ADAY", (60*60*24));
 5:  if ((!isset($_POST["month"])) || (!isset($_POST["year"]))) {
 6:      $nowArray = getdate();
 7:      $month = $nowArray["mon"];
 8:      $year = $nowArray["year"];
 9:  } else {
10:      $month = $_POST["month"];
11:      $year = $_POST["year"];
12:  }
13:  $start = mktime (12, 0, 0, $month, 1, $year);
14:  $firstDayArray = getdate($start);
15:  ?>
16:  <html>
17:  <head>
18:  <title><?php echo "Calendar: ".$firstDayArray["month"]." ".
19:  $firstDayArray["year"] ?></title>
20:  <head>
21:  <script type="text/javascript">
22:  function eventWindow(url) {
23:      event_popupWin = window.open(url, 'event',
24:        'resizable=yes,scrollbars=yes,toolbar=no,width=400,height=400');
25:          event_popupWin.opener = self;
26:  }
27:  </script>
28:  <body>
29:  <h1>Select a Month/Year Combination</h1>
30:  <form method="post" action="<?php echo $_SERVER["PHP_SELF"]; ?>">
31:  <select name="month">
32:  <?php
33:  $months = Array("January", "February", "March", "April", "May", "June",
34:  "July", "August", "September", "October", "November", "December");
35:  for ($x=1; $x <= count($months); $x++) {
36:      echo"<option value=\"$x\"";
37:      if ($x == $month) {
38:          echo " selected";
39:      }
40:      echo ">".$months[$x-1]."</option>";
41:  }
42:  ?>
43:  </select>
44:  <select name="year">
45:  <?php
46:  for ($x=1980; $x<=2010; $x++) {
47:      echo "<option";
48:      if ($x == $year) {
49:          echo " selected";
50:      }
51:      echo ">$x</option>";
52:  }
53:  ?>
```

LISTING 24.4   Continued

```
54:  </select>
55:  <input type="submit" name="Submit" value="Go!">
56:  </form>
57:  <br/>
58:  <?php
59:  $days = Array("Sun", "Mon", "Tue", "Wed", "Thu", "Fri", "Sat");
60:  echo "<table border=\"1\" cellpadding=\"5\"><tr>\n";
61:  foreach ($days as $day) {
62:      echo "<td style=\"background-color: #CCCCCC;
63:      text-align: center; width: 14%\"><strong>$day</strong></td>\n";
64:  }
65:
66:  for ($count=0; $count < (6*7); $count++) {
67:      $dayArray = getdate($start);
68:      if (($count % 7) == 0) {
69:          if ($dayArray["mon"] != $month) {
70:              break;
71:          } else {
72:              echo "</tr><tr>\n";
73:          }
74:      }
75:      if ($count < $firstDayArray["wday"] || $dayArray["mon"] != $month) {
76:          echo "<td> </td>\n";
77:      } else {
78:          $chkEvent_sql = "SELECT event_title FROM calendar_events WHERE
79:                          month(event_start) = '".$month."' AND
80:                          dayofmonth(event_start) = '".$dayArray["mday"]."'
81:                          AND year(event_start) = '".$year."'
82:                          ORDER BY event_start";
83:          $chkEvent_res = mysqli_query($mysqli, $chkEvent_sql)
84:                          or die(mysqli_error($mysqli));
85:
86:          if (mysqli_num_rows($chkEvent_res) > 0) {
87:              $event_title = "<br/>";
88:              while ($ev = mysqli_fetch_array($chkEvent_res)) {
89:                  $event_title = stripslashes($ev["event_title"])."<br/>";
90:              }
91:              mysqli_free_result($chkEvent_res);
92:          } else {
93:              $event_title = "";
94:          }
95:          echo "<td valign=\"top\"><a href=\"javascript:eventWindow
96:          ('event.php?m=".$month."&d=".$dayArray["mday"]."&y=$year');\">".
97:          $dayArray["mday"]."</a><br/>".$event_title."</td>\n";
98:
99:          unset($event_title);
100:         $start += ADAY;
101:     }
102: }
103: echo "</tr></table>";
104: mysqli_close($mysqli);
105: ?>
106: </body>
107: </html>
```

In Figure 24.3, you can see the new calendar, including the representation of the event title on a date that is prepopulated with an event.

FIGURE 24.3
Showing the cal-
endar with an
event.

All that remains is adding the all-in-one event.php script used in the pop-up window to display and also add an event to the calendar (on a particular day). Listing 24.5 contains all the necessary code; the fun part starts at lines 8–9, which connect to the MySQL database. Lines 12–19 look to see whether the event entry form has been submitted; if it has, an INSERT statement is used to add the event to the calendar_events table before continuing.

LISTING 24.5   Showing Events/Adding Events Via Pop-Up

```
1:  <html>
2:  <head>
3:  <title>Show/Add Events</title>
4:  <head>
5:  <body>
6:  <h1>Show/Add Events</h1>
7:  <?php
8:  $mysqli = mysqli_connect("localhost", "joeuser", "somepass", "testDB");
9:
10: //add any new event
11: if ($_POST) {
12:     $m = $_POST["m"];
13:     $d = $_POST["d"];
14:     $y = $_POST["y"];
15:
16:     $event_date = $y."-".$m."-".$d." ".$_POST["event_time_hh"].":
17:     ".$_POST["event_time_mm"].":00";
18:     $insEvent_sql = "INSERT INTO calendar_events (event_title,
```

LISTING 24.5   Continued

```
19:      event_shortdesc, event_start) VALUES('".$_POST["event_title"]."',
20:      '".$_POST["event_shortdesc"]."', '$event_date')";
21:      $insEvent_res = mysqli_query($mysqli, $insEvent_sql)
22:                     or die(mysqli_error($mysqli));
23: } else {
24:      $m = $_GET["m"];
25:      $d = $_GET["d"];
26:      $y = $_GET["y"];
27: }
28: //show events for this day
29: $getEvent_sql = "SELECT event_title, event_shortdesc,
30:                  date_format(event_start, '%l:%i %p') as fmt_date FROM
31:                  calendar_events WHERE month(event_start) = '".$m."'
32:                  AND dayofmonth(event_start) = '".$d."' AND
33:                  year(event_start)= '".$y."' ORDER BY event_start";
34: $getEvent_res = mysqli_query($mysqli, $getEvent_sql)
35:                 or die(mysqli_error($mysqli));
36:
37: if (mysqli_num_rows($getEvent_res) > 0) {
38:      $event_txt = "<ul>";
39:      while ($ev = @mysqli_fetch_array($getEvent_res)) {
40:          $event_title = stripslashes($ev["event_title"]);
41:          $event_shortdesc = stripslashes($ev["event_shortdesc"]);
42:          $fmt_date = $ev["fmt_date"];
43:          $event_txt .= "<li><strong>".$fmt_date."</strong>:
44:          ".$event_title."<br/>".$event_shortdesc."</li>";
45:      }
46:      $event_txt .= "</ul>";
47:      mysqli_free_result($getEvent_res);
48: } else {
49:      $event_txt = "";
50: }
51:
52: mysqli_close($mysqli);
53:
54: if ($event_txt != "") {
55:      echo "<p><strong>Today's Events:</strong></p>
56:      $event_txt
57:      <hr/>";
58: }
59:
60: // show form for adding an event
61: echo "
62: <form method=\"post\" action=\"".$_SERVER["PHP_SELF"]."\">
63: <p><strong>Would you like to add an event?</strong><br/>
64: Complete the form below and press the submit button to add
65: the event and refresh this window.</p>
66: <p><strong>Event Title:</strong><br/>
67: <input type=\"text\" name=\"event_title\" size=\"25\"
68:      maxlength=\"25\"/>
69: <p><strong>Event Description:</strong><br/>
70: <input type=\"text\" name=\"event_shortdesc\" size=\"25\"
71:      maxlength=\"255\"/>
72: <p><strong>Event Time (hh:mm):</strong><br/>
73: <select name=\"event_time_hh\">";
74: for ($x=1; $x <= 24; $x++) {
75:      echo "<option value=\"$x\">$x</option>";
76: }
```

LISTING 24.5   Continued

```
77: echo "</select> :
78: <select name=\"event_time_mm\">
79: <option value=\"00\">00</option>
80: <option value=\"15\">15</option>
81: <option value=\"30\">30</option>
82: <option value=\"45\">45</option>
83: </select>
84: <input type=\"hidden\" name=\"m\" value=\"".$m."\">
85: <input type=\"hidden\" name=\"d\" value=\"".$d."\">
86: <input type=\"hidden\" name=\"y\" value=\"".$y."\">
87: <br/><br/>
88: <input type=\"submit\" name=\"submit\" value=\"Add Event\">
89: </form>";
90: ?>
91: </body>
92: </html>
```

Lines 29–35 issue the query and retrieve all records that correspond to events on this given day. The text block used to display entries is created in lines 37–51. However, users also need to see the form for adding an event, and this is built in lines 61–89, effectively the end of the script.

Figure 24.4 shows how a pop-up looks when a link is followed from the calendar and an entry is already present. In this example, we wanted to add another event on this day, so the form has been completed in preparation for adding the additional event.

FIGURE 24.4
Showing the day detail, ready to add another event.

In Figure 24.5, a second event has been added to this particular day.

FIGURE 24.5
A second event
has been
added.

Obviously, this is a simple example, but it shows that it is indeed easy to build a calendar type of system in just a few short scripts.

Creating a Calendar Library

Because dates are ubiquitous in web-based application interfaces, and because working with dates can be complicated, let's look at creating a class library to automate some of the work you might do with dates. Along the way, we will revisit some of the techniques we have already covered in this book.

The simple date_pulldown library created in this instance will consist of three separate select elements: one for day of the month, one for month, and one for year. When a user submits a page, the script will verify the form input. If there is a problem with the input, we will refresh the page with the user's input still in place. This is easy to accomplish with text boxes but is more of a chore with pull-down menus.

Pages that display information pulled from a database present a similar problem. Data can be entered straight into the value attributes of text-type input elements. Dates will need to be split into month, day, and year values, and then the correct option elements selected.

The date_pulldown class aims to make date pull-downs sticky (so that they will remember settings from page to page) and easy to set. To create our class, we first need to declare it and create a constructor.

By the
~~Way~~

> A *constructor* is a function that exists within a class and is automatically called when a new instance of the class is created.

We can also declare some class properties. We will step through Listing 24.6; this first snippet shows the beginning of the class.

LISTING 24.6   Creating a Calendar Library

```
 1: class date_pulldown {
 2:      var $name;
 3:      var $timestamp = -1;
 4:      var $months = array("Jan", "Feb", "Mar", "Apr", "May", "Jun",
 5:           "Jul", "Aug", "Sep", "Oct", "Nov", "Dec");
 6:      var $yearstart = -1;
 7:      var $yearend = -1;
 8:
 9:      function date_pulldown($name) {
10:          $this->name = $name;
11:      }
```

We first declare the $name property on line 2. We'll use it to name the HTML select elements. The $timestamp property, defined on line 3, will hold a UNIX time stamp. The $months array property, defined on lines 4–5, contains the strings we will display in our month pull-down. The $yearstart and $yearend properties (lines 6 and 7) are both set to –1, pending initialization. They will eventually hold the first and last years of the range that will be presented in the year pull-down.

The constructor is simple. It accepts a string, which we assign to the $name property. Now that we have the basis of our class, we need a set of methods by which the client code can set the date. Listing 24.6 continues as follows.

LISTING 24.6 (continued)

```
12:     function setDate_global( ) {
13:         if (!$this->setDate_array($GLOBALS[$this->name])) {
14:             return $this->setDate_timestamp(time());
15:         }
16:         return true;
17:     }
18:
19:     function setDate_timestamp($time) {
20:         $this->timestamp = $time;
21:         return true;
22:     }
23:
24:     function setDate_array($inputdate) {
25:         if (is_array($inputdate) &&
26:             isset($inputdate['''"mon"]) &&
```

LISTING 24.6 Continued

```
27:              isset($inputdate['''"mday"]) &&
28:              isset($inputdate['''"year"])) {
29:
30:              $this->timestamp = mktime(11, 59, 59,
31:                  $inputdate["mon"], $inputdate["mday"], $inputdate["year"]);
32:              return true;
33:          }
34:          return false;
35:      }
```

Of the methods shown here, setDate_timestamp() is the simplest (lines 19–22). It requires a UNIX time stamp, which it assigns to the $timestamp property. But let's not forget the others.

The setDate_array() method (lines 24–35) expects an associative array with at least three keys: mon, mday, and year. These keys will have data values in the same format as in the array returned by getdate(). This means that setDate_array() will accept a hand-built array such as

```
array("mday"=> 12, "mon"=>4, "year"=> 2008);
```

or the result of a call to getdate():

```
getdate(1208052013);
```

It is no accident that the pull-downs we will build later will be constructed to produce an array containing mon, mday, and year keys. The method uses the mktime() function to construct a time stamp, which is then assigned to the $timestamp variable.

The setDate_global() method (lines 12–17) is called by default. It attempts to find a global variable with the same name as the object's $name property. This is passed to setDate_array(). If this method discovers a global variable of the right structure, it uses that variable to create the $timestamp variable. Otherwise, the current date is used.

The ranges for days and months are fixed, but years are a different matter. As Listing 24.6 continues, we create a few methods to allow the client code to set a range of years, although we also provide default behavior.

LISTING 24.6 (continued)

```
36:    function setYearStart($year) {
37:        $this->yearstart = $year;
38:    }
39:
40:    function setYearEnd($year) {
41:        $this->yearend = $year;
42:    }
43:
44:    function getYearStart() {
45:        if ($this->yearstart < 0) {
46:            $nowarray = getdate(time());
47:            $this->yearstart = $nowarray["year"]-5;
48:        }
49:
50:        return $this->yearstart;
51:    }
52:
53:    function getYearEnd() {
54:        if ($this->yearend < 0) {
55:            $nowarray = getdate(time());
56:            $this->yearend = $nowarray["year"]+5;
57:        }
58:        return $this->yearend;
59:    }
```

The setYearStart() and setYearEnd() methods (lines 36–43) are straightforward in that a year is directly assigned to the appropriate property. The getYearStart() method tests whether the $yearstart property has been set, and if it has not, the method assigns a $yearstart value five years before the current year. The getYearEnd() method performs a similar operation.

We're now ready to create the business end of the class as Listing 24.6 continues.

LISTING 24.6 (continued)

```
60:    function output() {
61:        if ($this->timestamp < 0) {
62:            $this->setDate_global();
63:        }
64:        $datearray = getdate($this->timestamp);
65:        $out  = $this->day_select($this->name, $datearray);
66:        $out .= $this->month_select($this->name, $datearray);
67:        $out .= $this->year_select($this->name, $datearray);
68:        return $out;
69:    }
70:
71:    function day_select($fieldname, $datearray)  {
72:        $out = "<select name=\"$fieldname"."[\"mday\"]\">\n";
73:        for ($x=1; $x<=31; $x++) {
74:            $out .= "<option value=\"$x\"".($datearray["mday"]==($x)
75:                ?" selected":"").">".sprintf("%02d", $x) ."</option>\n";
76:        }
77:        $out .= "</select>\n";
78:        return $out;
```

LISTING 24.6   Continued

```
79:     }
80:
81:     function month_select($fieldname, $datearray) {
82:         $out = "<select name=\"$fieldname"."[\"mon\"]\">\n";
83:         for ($x = 1; $x <= 12; $x++) {
84:             $out .= "<option value=\"".($x)."\"".($datearray["mon"]==($x)
85:             ?" SELECTED":"")."> ".$this->months[$x-1]."</option>\n";
86:         }
87:         $out .= "</select>\n";
88:         return $out;
89:     }
90:
91:     function year_select($fieldname, $datearray) {
92:         $out = "<select name=\"$fieldname"."[\"year\"]\">";
93:         $start = $this->getYearStart();
94:         $end = $this->getYearEnd();
95:         for ($x= $start; $x < $end; $x++) {
96:             $out .= "<option value=\"$x\"".($datearray['''"year"]==($x)
97:             ?" SELECTED":"").">".$x."</option>\n";
98:         }
99:         $out .= "</select>\n";
100:        return $out;
101:    }
102: }
```

The output() method orchestrates most of this code (lines 60–69). It first checks the $timestamp property, and, unless one of the setDate methods has been called, the value of $timestamp will be set to –1 and setDate_global() will be called by default. The time stamp is passed to the getdate() function to construct a date array, and a method is called to produce each pull-down.

The day_select() method (lines 71–79) simply constructs an HTML select element with an option element for each of the 31 possible days in a month. The object's current date is stored in the $datearray argument variable, which is used during the construction of the element to set the selected attribute of the relevant option element. The sprintf() function formats the day number, adding a leading zero to days 1–9. The month_select() and year_select() methods (lines 81–101) use similar logic to construct the month and year pull-downs.

Why did we break down the output code into four methods, rather than simply creating one block of code? When we build a class, we have two kinds of programmer in mind: one who will want to instantiate a date_pulldown object, and one who will want to subclass the date_pulldown class to refine its functionality.

For the former, we want to provide a simple and clear interface to the class's functionality. The programmer can then instantiate an object, set its date, and call the output() method. For the latter, we want to make it easy to change discrete elements of the class's functionality. By putting all the output code into one method, we would force a child class that needed to tweak output to reproduce a lot of code that is perfectly usable. By breaking this code into discrete methods, we allow for subclasses that can change limited aspects of functionality without disturbing the whole. If a child class needs to represent the year pull-down as two radio buttons, for example, you can simply override the year_select() method.

Listing 24.7 contains some code that calls the library class. Before you try to execute this code, take the code from Listing 24.6, surround it with PHP opening and closing tags, and save it into a file called date_pulldown.class.php. Place this file in the document root of your web server because Listing 24.7 uses it and it had better be there!

LISTING 24.7   Using the date_pulldown **Class**

```
 1:  <html>
 2:  <head>
 3:  <title>Using the date_pulldown Class</title>
 4:  </head>
 5:  <?php
 6:  include("date_pulldown.class.php");
 7:  $date1 = new date_pulldown("fromdate");
 8:  $date2 = new date_pulldown("todate");
 9:  $date3 = new date_pulldown("foundingdate");
10: $date3->setYearStart("1972");
11: if (empty($foundingdate)) {
12:     $date3->setDate_array(array('mday'=>26, 'mon'=>4, 'year'=>1984));
13: }
14: ?>
15: <body>
16: <form>
17: <p><strong>From:</strong><br/>
18: <?php echo $date1->output(); ?>
19: <p><strong>To:</strong><br/>
20: <?php echo $date2->output(); ?>
21: <p><strong>Company Founded:</strong><br/>
22: <?php echo $date3->output(); ?>
23: <p><input type="submit" name="submit" value="submit"/></p>
24: </form>
25: </body>
26: </html>
```

On line 6, we include the date_pulldown.class.php; after we have included the class file, we can use all of its methods. We use the class's default behavior for all the pull-downs, apart from "foundingdate". For this particular object, we override the default year start, setting it to 1972 on line 10. On line 12, we assign this pull-down an arbitrary date that will be displayed until the form is submitted (see Figure 24.6).

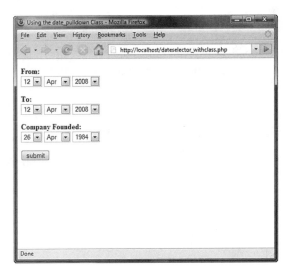

FIGURE 24.6
The pull-downs
generated by
the date_
pulldown class.

This is only the front end of a form, with no action or method; you need to supply your own action or method for this to actually do something!

By the Way

Summary

In this chapter, you pulled together the PHP date-related functions you learned about earlier in the book to work within a basic calendar application display. You learned how to test the validity of an input date using checkdate(), and you worked through a sample script that applied some of the tools you have learned. You also saw one method for adding and viewing events within your calendar application. You also learned how to build a date-related class library that can be used to automate some of the more tedious aspects of working with dates within HTML forms.

Q&A

Q. *Are there any functions for converting between different calendars?*

A. Yes. PHP provides an entire suite of functions that cover alternative calendars. You can read about these in the official PHP manual at http://www.php.net/manual/en/ref.calendar.php.

Workshop

The workshop is designed to help you anticipate possible questions, review what you've learned, and begin putting your knowledge into practice.

Quiz

1. What PHP function did we use to create a time stamp?

2. What PHP function did we use to create an associative array of date-related information?

Answers

1. `mktime()`

2. `getdate()`

Activity

Use your fancy new date pull-down class in the context of your own form. Create a back-end script that takes the selected dates and displays their input.

25

Restricting Access to Your Applications

This chapter explains how to use Apache to restrict access to parts of a website based on the identity of the user or on information about the request. On the application side of things, you can create your own mechanism for user validation and check the validity of your users through cookies.

In this chapter, you will learn

- ▶ How to restrict access based on the user, client IP address, domain name, and browser version
- ▶ How to use the user management tools provided with Apache
- ▶ How to store and retrieve cookie information
- ▶ How to use cookies for authentication

Authentication Overview

Authorization and authentication are common requirements for many websites. Before continuing, a few definitions are in order.

Authentication establishes the identity of parties in a communication. You can authenticate yourself through something you know such as a password or a cookie, through something tangible such as an ID card or a key, through something intrinsically part of you such as your fingerprint or your retina, or through any combination of these elements. In the context of a website, authentication is usually restricted to the use of passwords and certificates.

Authorization deals with protecting access to resources. You can authorize access based on several factors, such as the IP address the user is coming from, the user's browser type, the content the user is trying to access, or who the user is (previously determined via authentication).

Apache includes several modules that provide authentication and access control and that you can use to protect both dynamic and static content. You can either use one of these modules or implement your own access control at the application level and provide customized login screens, single sign-on, and other advanced functionality.

Client Authentication

Users are authenticated for tracking or authorization purposes. The HTTP specification provides two authentication mechanisms: basic and digest. In both cases, the process is the following:

1. A client tries to access restricted content in the web server.

2. Apache checks whether the client is providing a username and password. If not, Apache returns an HTTP 401 status code, indicating that user authentication is required.

3. The client reads the response and prompts the user for the required username and password (usually with a pop-up dialog box).

4. The client retries accessing the web page, this time transmitting the username and password as part of the HTTP request. The client remembers the username and password and transmits them in later requests to the same site, so the user does not need to retype them for every request.

5. Apache checks the validity of the credentials and grants or denies access based on the user identity and other access rules.

In the basic authentication scheme, the username and password are transmitted in clear text, as part of the HTTP request headers. This poses a security risk because an attacker could easily peek at the conversation between server and browser, learn the username and password, and reuse them freely afterward.

The digest authentication provides increased security because it transmits a digest instead of the clear text password. The digest is based on a combination of several parameters, including the username, password, and request method. The server can calculate the digest on its own and check that the client knows the password, even when the password itself is not transmitted over the network.

By the Way

A *digest algorithm* is a mathematical operation that takes a text and returns another text, a digest, which uniquely identifies the original one. A good digest algorithm should make sure that, at least for practical purposes, different input texts produce different digests and that the original input text cannot be derived from the digest. MD5 is the name of a commonly used digest algorithm.

Unfortunately, although the specification has been available for some time, only very recent browsers support digest authentication. This means that for practical purposes, digest authentication is restricted to scenarios in which you have control over the browser software of your clients, such as in a company intranet.

In any case, for both digest and basic authentication, the requested information itself is transmitted unprotected over the network. A better choice to secure access to your website involves using the HTTP over SSL protocol, as described in Chapter 30, "Setting Up a Secure Web Server."

User Management Methods

When the authentication module receives the username and password from the client, it needs to verify that they are valid against an existing repository of users. The usernames and passwords can be stored in a variety of ways, including the file- and database-based mechanisms provided for by Apache. Third-party modules provide support for additional mechanisms such as Lightweight Directory Access Protocol (LDAP) and Network Information Services (NIS).

Apache Authentication Module Functionality

Apache provides the basic framework and directives to perform authentication and access control. The authentication modules provide support for validating passwords against a specific back-end method (file, database, and so on). Users can optionally be organized in groups, easing management of access control rules.

Apache provides three built-in directives related to authentication that can be used with any of the authentication modules: AuthName, AuthType, and Require.

AuthName accepts a string argument, the name for the authentication realm. A *realm* is a logical area of the web server that you are asking the password for. It will be displayed in the browser pop-up window.

AuthType specifies the type of browser authentication: basic or digest.

Require enables you to specify a list of users or groups that will be allowed access. The syntax is Require user followed by one or more usernames, or Require group followed by one or more group names. For example

```
Require user joe bob
```

or

```
Require group employee contractor
```

If you want to grant access to anyone who provides a valid username and password, you can do so with

```
Require valid-user
```

With the preceding directives, you can control who has access to specific virtual hosts, directories, files, and so on. Although authentication and authorization are separate concepts, in practice they intertwine in Apache. Access is granted based on specific user identity or group membership. Some third-party modules, such as certain LDAP-based modules, allow for clearer separation between authentication and authorization.

The authentication modules included with Apache provide

▶ **Back-end storage**—Provides text or database files containing the username and group information

▶ **User management**—Supplies tools for creating and managing users and groups in the back-end storage

▶ **Authoritative information**—Specifies whether the results of the module are authoritative

By the
Way

Sometimes users will not be allowed access to a particular realm because their information is not found in the user database provided by the module, or because no authentication rules matched their information. In that case, one of two situations will occur:

▶ If the module specifies its results as authoritative, a user will be denied access and Apache will return an error.

▶ If the module specifies its results as not authoritative, other modules can have a chance of authenticating the user.

This enables you to have a main authorization module that knows about most users, and to be able to have additional modules that can authenticate the rest of the users.

File-Based Authentication

The mod_auth Apache module provides basic authentication via text files containing usernames and passwords, similar to how traditional UNIX authentication works with the /etc/passwd and /etc/groups files.

Back-End Storage

When using back-end storage methods, you need to specify the file containing the list of usernames and passwords and, optionally, the file containing the list of groups.

The users file is a UNIX-style password file, containing names of users and encrypted passwords. The entries look like the following, on UNIX, using the crypt algorithm:

```
admin:iFrlxqg0Q6RQ6
```

and on Windows, using the MD5 algorithm:

```
admin:$apr1$Ug3.....$jVTedbQWBKTfXsn5jK6UX/
```

The groups file contains a list of groups and the users who belong to each one of them, separated by spaces, such as in the following entry:

```
web: admin joe Daniel
```

The AuthUserFile and the AuthGroupFile directives take a path argument, pointing to the users file and the groups file. The groups file is optional.

User Management

The Apache distribution includes the htpasswd utility on UNIX and htpasswd.exe on Windows; they are designed to help you manage user password files. Both versions are functionally identical, but the Windows version uses a different method to encrypt the password. The encryption is transparent to the user and administrator. On Linux/UNIX, the first time you add a user, you need to type

```
/usr/local/apache2/bin/htpasswd -c file userid
```

where *file* is the password file that will contain the list of usernames and passwords, and *userid* is the username you want to add. You will be prompted for a password, and the file will be created. For example, on Linux/UNIX, the command

```
/usr/local/apache2/bin/htpasswd -c /usr/local/apache2/conf/htusers admin
```

creates the password file /usr/local/apache2/conf/htusers and adds the admin user.

Similar functionality exists on Windows, where the command-line operation might look something like the following:

```
htpasswd -c "C:\Program Files\Apache Software Foundation\Apache2.2\conf\htusers"
admin
```

The -c command-line option tells the htpasswd executable that it should create the file. When you want to add users to an existing password file, do not use the -c option; if you do so, the file will be overwritten.

It is important that you store the password file outside the document root and thus make it inaccessible via a web browser. Otherwise, an attacker could download the file and get a list of your usernames and passwords. Although the passwords are encrypted, when you have the file, it is possible to perform a brute-force attack to try to guess them.

Authoritative

The Authoritative directive takes a value of on or off. By default, it is on, meaning that the module authentication results are authoritative. That is, if the user is not found or does not match any rules, access will be denied.

Using mod_auth

Listing 25.1 shows a sample configuration, restricting access to the private directory in the document root to authenticated users present in the htusers password file. Note that the optional AuthGroupFile directive is not present.

LISTING 25.1   File-Based Authentication Example

```
1: <Directory /usr/local/apache2/htdocs/private>
2: AuthType Basic
3: AuthName "Private Area"
4: AuthUserFile /usr/local/apache2/conf/htusers
5: AuthAuthoritative on
6: Require valid-user
7: </Directory>
```

Database File-Based Access Control

Storing usernames and passwords in plain text files is convenient, but this method does not scale well. Apache would need to open and read the files sequentially to look for a particular user. When the number of users grows, this operation becomes very time-consuming. The mod_auth_dbm module enables you to replace the text-based files with indexed database files, which can handle a much greater number of users without performance degradation. The mod_auth_dbm module is included with Apache but is not enabled by default. Enabling this module occurs when configuring Apache to be built using the --enable-module=dbm option.

Back-End Storage

The mod_auth_dbm module provides two directives, AuthDBMUserFile and AuthDBMGroupFile, that point to the database files containing the usernames and groups. Unlike plain text files, both directives can point to the same file, which combines both users and groups.

User Management

Apache provides a Perl script (dbmmanage on UNIX and dbmmanage.pl on Windows) that allows you to create and manage users and groups stored in a database file. Under UNIX, you might need to edit the first line of the script to point to the location of the Perl interpreter in your system. On Windows, you need to install the additional MD5 password package. If you are using ActiveState Perl, start the Perl package manager and type

```
install Crypt-PasswdMD5
```

To add a user to a database on Linux/UNIX, type

```
dbmmanage dbfile adduser userid
```

On Windows, type

```
perl dbmmanage.pl dbfile adduser userid
```

You will be prompted for the password, and the user will be added to the existing database file or a new file will be created if one does not exist.

When adding a user, you can optionally specify the groups the user belongs to as comma-separated arguments. The following command adds the user daniel to the database file /usr/local/apache2/conf/dbmusers and makes it a member of the groups employee and engineering:

```
dbmmanage /usr/local/apache2/conf/dbmusers adduser daniel employee,engineering
```

If you ever need to delete the user daniel, you can issue the following command:

```
dbmmanage dbfile delete daniel
```

The dbmmanage program supports additional options. You can find complete syntax information in the dbmmanage manual page or by invoking dbmmanage without any arguments.

Apache 2 provides an additional utility, htdbm, that does not depend on Perl and provides all the functionality that dbmmanage does.

Did you Know?

Using Apache for Access Control

The mod_access module, enabled by default, allows you to restrict access to resources based on parameters of the client request, such as the presence of a specific header or the IP address or hostname of the client.

Implementing Access Rules

You can specify access rules using the Allow and Deny directives. Each of these directives takes a list of arguments such as IP addresses, environment variables, and domain names.

Allow/Deny Access by IP Addresses

You can deny or grant access to a client based on its IP address:

```
Allow from 10.0.0.1 10.0.0.2 10.0.0.3
```

You can also specify IP address ranges with a partial IP address or a network/mask pair. Additionally, you can specify the first one, two, or three bytes of an IP address. Any IP address containing those will match this rule. For example, the rule

```
Deny from 10.0
```

matches any address starting with 10.0, such as 10.0.1.0 and 10.0.0.1.

You can also utilize the IP address and the netmask; the IP address specifies the network, and the mask specifies which bits belong to the network prefix and which ones belong to the nodes. The rule

```
Allow from 10.0.0.0/255.255.255.0
```

matches IP addresses 10.0.0.1, 10.0.0.2, and so on, to 10.0.0.254.

You can also specify the network mask via high-order bits. For example, you could write the previous rule as

```
Allow from 10.0.0.0/24
```

Allow/Deny Access by Domain Name

You can control access based on specific hostnames or partial domain names. For example, Allow from example.com will match www.example.com, foo.example.com, and so on.

> Enabling access rules based on domain names forces Apache to do a reverse
> DNS lookup on the client address, bypassing the settings of the
> HostNameLookups directive. This has performance implications.

Allow/Deny Access Based on Environment Variables

You can specify access rules based on the presence of a certain environment variable
by prefixing the name of the variable with the string env=. You can use this feature
to grant or deny access to certain browsers or browser versions, to prevent specific
sites from linking to your resources, and so on. For this example to work as intended, the client needs to transmit the User-Agent header.

For example:

```
BrowserMatch MSIE iexplorer
Deny from env=iexplorer
```

Because the client sends the User-Agent header, it could possibly be omitted or
manipulated, but most users will not do so, and this technique will work in most
cases.

Allow/Deny Access to All Clients

The keyword all matches all clients. You can specify Allow from all or Deny
from all to grant or deny access to all clients.

Evaluating Access Rules

You can have several Allow and Deny access rules. You can choose the order in
which the rules are evaluated by using the Order directive. Rules evaluated later
have higher precedence. Order accepts one argument, which can be Deny,Allow,
Allow,Deny, or Mutual-Failure. Deny,Allow is the default value for the Order
directive. Note that there is no space in the value.

Deny,Allow

Deny,Allow specifies that Deny directives are evaluated before Allow directives. With
Deny,Allow, the client is granted access by default if there are no Allow or Deny
directives or the client does not match any of the rules. If the client matches a Deny
rule, it will be denied access unless it also matches an Allow rule, which will take
precedence because Allow directives are evaluated last and have greater priority.

Listing 25.2 shows how to configure Apache to allow access to the /private location to clients coming from the internal network or the domain example.com and
deny access to everyone else.

LISTING 25.2   Sample Deny,Allow Access Control Configuration

```
1: <Location /private>
2:   Order Deny,Allow
3:   Deny from all
4:   Allow from 10.0.0.0/255.255.255.0  example.com
5: </Location>
```

Allow,Deny

Allow,Deny specifies that Allow directives are evaluated before Deny directives. With Allow,Deny, the client is denied access by default if there are no Allow or Deny directives or if the client does not match any of the rules. If the client matches an Allow rule, it will be granted access unless it also matches a Deny rule, which will take precedence.

Note that the presence of Order Allow,Deny without any Allow or Deny rules causes all requests to the specified resource to be denied because the default behavior is to deny access.

Listing 25.3 allows access to everyone except a specific host.

LISTING 25.3   Sample Allow,Deny Access Control Configuration

```
1: <Location /some/location/>
2:   Order Allow,Deny
3:   Allow from all
4:   Deny from host.example.com
5: </Location>
```

Mutual-Failure

In the case of Mutual-Failure, the host will be granted access only if it matches an Allow directive *and* does not match any Deny directive.

Combining Apache Access Methods

In previous sections, you learned how to restrict access based on user identity or request information. The Satisfy directive enables you to determine whether both types of access restrictions must be satisfied to grant access. Satisfy accepts one parameter, which can be either all or any.

Satisfy all means that the client will be granted access if it provides a valid username and password *and* passes the access restrictions. Satisfy any means the client will be granted access if it provides a valid username and password *or* passes the access restrictions.

Why is this directive useful? For example, you might want to provide free access to your website to users coming from an internal, trusted address, but require users coming from the Internet to provide a valid username and password. Listing 25.4 demonstrates just that.

LISTING 25.4   Mixing Authentication and Access Control Rules

```
1: <Location /restricted>
2: Allow from 10.0.0.0/255.255.255.0
3: AuthType Basic
4: AuthName "Intranet"
5: AuthUserFile /usr/local/apache2/conf/htusers
6: AuthAuthoritative on
7: Require valid-user
8: Satisfy any
9: </Location>
```

> **By the Way**
>
> Access control based on connection or request information is not completely secure. Although it provides an appropriate level of protection for most cases, the rules rely on the integrity of your DNS servers and your network infrastructure. If an attacker gains control of your DNS servers, or your routers or firewalls are incorrectly configured, he can easily change authorized domain name records to point to his machine or pretend he is coming from an authorized IP address.

Limiting Access Based on HTTP Methods

In general, you want your access control directives to apply to all types of client requests, and this is the default behavior. In some cases, however, you want to apply authentication and access rules to only certain HTTP methods such as GET and HEAD.

The <Limit> container takes a list of methods and contains the directives that apply to requests containing those methods. The complete list of methods that you can use is GET, POST, PUT, DELETE, CONNECT, OPTIONS, TRACE, PATCH, PROPFIND, PROPPATCH, MKCOL, COPY, MOVE, LOCK, and UNLOCK.

The <LimitExcept> section provides complementary functionality, containing directives that will apply to requests not containing the listed methods.

Listing 25.5 shows an example from the default Apache configuration file. The <Limit> and <LimitExcept> sections allow read-only methods but deny requests to any other methods that can modify the content of the file system, such as PUT. For more information on the myriad options available here, see the Apache documentation at http://httpd.apache.org/docs-2.2/mod/core.html.

LISTING 25.5   Restricting Access Based on Rule

```
 1: <Directory /home/*/public_html>
 2:   AllowOverride FileInfo AuthConfig Limit
 3:   Options MultiViews Indexes SymLinksIfOwnerMatch IncludesNoExec
 4:   <Limit GET POST OPTIONS PROPFIND>
 5:     Order Allow,Deny
 6:     Allow from all
 7:   </Limit>
 8:   <LimitExcept GET POST OPTIONS PROPFIND>
 9:     Order Deny,Allow
10:     Deny from all
11:   </LimitExcept>
12: </Directory>
```

In the next section, you'll learn about restricting access on the application side based on information found in cookies.

Restricting Access Based on Cookie Values

In Chapter 12, "Working with Cookies and User Sessions," you learned all about the structure of a cookie and how to set and access cookie variables in PHP. The next few sections show some practical uses of cookies for authentication purposes.

Suppose that you created a login form that checked for values against a database. If the user is authorized, you send a cookie that says as much. Then, for all pages you want to restrict only to authorized users, you check for the specific cookie. If the cookie is present, the user can see the page. If the cookie is not present, the user is either sent back to the login form, or a message regarding access restrictions can be printed to the screen. The next few sections go through each of these steps.

Creating the Authorized Users Table

When you're integrating user accounts into a web-based application, it is common to store the user-specific information in a database table. The information in this table can then be used to authorize the user and grant access to areas of the site specifically for these "special" users.

The following table creation command will create a table called auth_users in your MySQL database, with fields for the ID, first name, last name, email address, username, and password:

```
mysql> CREATE TABLE auth_users (
    -> id int NOT NULL PRIMARY KEY AUTO_INCREMENT,
    -> f_name VARCHAR(50),
    -> l_name VARCHAR(50),
    -> email VARCHAR(150),
    -> username VARCHAR(25),
    -> password VARCHAR (75)
    -> );
Query OK, 0 rows affected (0.03 sec)
```

The following INSERT command puts a record in the auth_users table for a user named John Doe, with an email address of john@doe.com, a username of jdoe, and a password of doepass:

```
mysql> INSERT INTO auth_users VALUES ('1', 'John', 'Doe', 'john@doe.com',
    -> 'jdoe', PASSWORD('doepass'));
Query OK, 1 row affected (0.00 sec)
```

This INSERT command should be self-explanatory, with the exception of the use of the PASSWORD() function. When this function is used in the INSERT command, what is stored in the table is in fact not the actual password, but a hash of the password.

When you view the contents of the auth_users table, you will see the hash in the password field, as follows:

```
mysql> select username, password from auth_users;
+----------+-------------------------------------------+
| username | password                                  |
+----------+-------------------------------------------+
| jdoe     | *0AAD744979343D58A7F17A50E514E6AD6533D04B |
+----------+-------------------------------------------+
1 row in set (0.03 sec)
```

Although it may look like it is encrypted, a *hash* is in fact not an encrypted bit of information. Instead, it is a "fingerprint" of the original information. Hashes are generally used, like fingerprints, to perform matches. In this case, when you check your user's password, you check that the hash of the input matches the stored hash. Using hashes alleviates the need—and security risk—of storing actual passwords.

Creating the Login Form and Script

After you authorize users in your table, you need to give them a mechanism for proving their authenticity. In this case, a simple two-field form will do, as shown in Listing 25.6.

LISTING 25.6   User Login Form

```
 1: <html>
 2: <head>
 3: <title>Login Form</title>
 4: </head>
 5: <body>
 6: <h1>Login Form</h1>
 7: <form method="post" action="userlogin.php">
 8: <p><strong>username:</strong><br/>
 9: <input type="text" name="username"/></p>
10: <p><strong>password:</strong><br/>
11: <input type="password" name="password"/></p>
12: <p><input type="submit" name="submit" value="login"/></p>
13: </form>
14: </body>
15: </html>
```

Put these lines into a text file called `loginform.html`, and place it in your web server document root. Next, you'll create the script itself, which the form expects to be called `userlogin.php` (see Listing 25.7).

LISTING 25.7   User Login Script

```
 1: <?php
 2: //check for required fields from the form
 3: if ((!isset($_POST["username"])) || (!isset($_POST["password"]))) {
 4:      header("Location: userlogin.html");
 5:      exit;
 6: }
 7:
 8: //connect to server and select database
 9: $mysqli = mysqli_connect("localhost", "joeuser", "somepass", "testDB");
10:
11: //create and issue the query
12: $sql = "SELECT f_name, l_name FROM auth_users WHERE
13:         username = '".$_POST["username"]."' AND
14:         password = PASSWORD('".$_POST["password"]."')";
15: $result = mysqli_query($mysqli, $sql) or die(mysqli_error($mysqli));
16:
17: //get the number of rows in the result set; should be 1 if a match
18: if (mysqli_num_rows($result) == 1) {
19:
20:     //if authorized, get the values of f_name l_name
21:     while ($info = mysqli_fetch_array($result)) {
22:         $f_name = stripslashes($info['f_name']);
23:         $l_name = stripslashes($info['l_name']);
24:     }
25:
```

LISTING 25.7   Continued

```
26:        //set authorization cookie
27:        setcookie("auth", "1", 0, "/", "yourdomain.com", 0);
28:
29:        //create display string
30:        $display_block = "
31:        <p>".$f_name." ".$l_name." is authorized!</p>
32:        <p>Authorized Users' Menu:</p>
33:        <ul>
34:        <li><a href=\"secretpage.php\">secret page</a></li>
35:        </ul>";
36: } else {
37:        //redirect back to login form if not authorized
38:        header("Location: userlogin.html");
39:        exit;
40: }
41: ?>
42: <html>
43: <head>
44: <title>User Login</title>
45: </head>
46: <body>
47: <?php echo "$display_block"; ?>
48: </body>
49: </html>
```

Put these lines into a text file called userlogin.php, modify line 27 so that "yourdomain.com" is your actual domain name, and place this file in your web server document root. In a moment, you'll try it out, but first let's examine what the script is doing.

Line 3 checks for the two required fields—the only two fields in the form: $_POST["username"] and $_POST["password"]. If either of these fields is not present, the script redirects the user back to the original login form. If the two fields *are* present, the script moves along to line 9, which connects to the database server in preparation for issuing the SQL query to check the authenticity of the user. This query, and its execution, is found in lines 12–15. Note that the query checks the hash of the password input from the form against the password stored in the table. These two elements must match each other, and belong to the username in question, to authorize the user.

Line 18 tests the result of the query by counting the number of rows in the resultset. The row count should be exactly 1 if the username and password pair represents a valid login. If this is the case, the mysqli_fetch_array() function is used in lines 22–23 to extract the first and last names of the user. These names are used for aesthetic purposes only.

Line 27 sets the authorization cookie. The name of the cookie is auth, and the value is 1. If a 0 is put in the time slot, the cookie will last as long as this user's web browser session is open. When the user closes the browser, the cookie expires. Lines 30–35 create a message for display, including a link to a file you will create in a moment.

Finally, lines 36–40 handle a failed login attempt. In this case, the user is simply redirected back to the original login form.

Go ahead and access the login form, and input the valid values for the John Doe user. When you submit the form, the result should look like Figure 25.1.

FIGURE 25.1
Successful login result.

Try to log in with an invalid username and password pair, and you should be redirected to the login form. In the next (and final) section, you will create the secret-page.php script, which will read the authentication cookie you have just set and act accordingly.

Testing for the auth Cookie

The last piece of this puzzle is to use the value of the auth cookie to allow a user to access a private file. In this case, Listing 25.8 shows the file in question.

LISTING 25.8　Checking for auth Cookie

```
1: <?php
2: if ($_COOKIE["auth"] == "1") {
3:     $display_block = "<p>You are an authorized user.</p>";
4: } else {
5:     //redirect back to login form if not authorized
6:     header("Location: userlogin.html");
7:     exit;
8: }
```

LISTING 25.8   Continued

```
 9: ?>
10: <html>
11: <head>
12: <title>Secret Page</title>
13: </head>
14: <body>
15: <?php echo "$display_block"; ?>
16: </body>
17: </html>
```

From the menu shown in Figure 25.1, click the Secret Page link. Because you are an authorized user, you should see a result like Figure 25.2.

FIGURE 25.2
Accessing the secret page as an authorized user.

Close your browser and attempt to access `secretpage.php` directly. You will find that you cannot, and you will be redirected to the original login form because the authentication cookie has not been set after a successful login.

Summary

This chapter explained how to use Apache features to restrict access to your website based on the identity of the remote user and information from the HTTP request or network connection. It also covered some authentication modules included with Apache and additional tools that you can use to create and manage your user and group databases.

Additionally, you learned one method for using cookie values to allow access to specific parts of your PHP application.

Q&A

Q. *I have a UNIX system. Can I use /etc/passwd as my user database?*

A. Although using /etc/passwd might seem convenient, it is advisable that you do not use the existing /etc/passwd file for authenticating users of your website. Otherwise, an attacker who gains access to a user of your website will also gain access to the system. Keep separate databases and encourage users to choose different passwords for their system accounts and web access. Periodically run password checkers that scan for weak passwords and accounts in which the username is also the password.

Q. *Why am I asked for my password twice in some websites?*

A. Your browser keeps track of your password so that you do not have to type it for every request. The stored password is based on the realm (AuthName directive) and the hostname of the website. Sometimes you can access a website via different names, such as yourdomain.com and www.yourdomain.com. If you are authorized to access a certain restricted area of yourdomain.com but are redirected or follow a link to www.yourdomain.com, you will be asked again to provide the username and password because your browser thinks it is a completely different website.

Q. *Are there any serious security or privacy issues raised by cookies?*

A. A server can access a cookie set only from its own domain. Although a cookie can be stored on the user's hard drive, there is no other access to the user's file system. It is possible, however, to set a cookie in response to a request for an image. So, if many sites include images served from a third-party ad server or counter script, the third party may be able to track a user across multiple domains.

Workshop

The workshop is designed to help you anticipate possible questions, review what you've learned, and begin putting your knowledge into practice.

Quiz

1. What are the advantages of database files over plain text files for storing user authentication information?

2. Can you name some disadvantages of HTTP basic authentication?

3. What function is designed to allow you to set a cookie on a visitor's browser?

Answers

1. Database files are much more scalable because they can be indexed. This means that Apache does not need to read the file sequentially until a match is found for a particular user but rather can jump to the exact location.

2. One disadvantage is that the information is transmitted in clear text over the network. This means that unless you are using SSL, it is possible for an attacker to read the packets your browser sends to the server and steal your password. Another disadvantage is that HTTP authentication does not provide a means for customizing the login (except the realm name). It is common for websites to implement custom login mechanisms using HTML forms and cookies.

3. The setcookie() function allows you to set a cookie (although you could also output a Set-Cookie header using the header() function).

Activity

Practice using the various types of authentication—both server-based and with PHP—on your development server. Get a feel for the differences between basic HTTP authentication and something you devise on your own.

26

Logging and Monitoring Web Server Activity

This chapter describes how the logging system in Apache works and how you can customize it—which information to store and where to do it. Additionally, you will learn a quick way to use PHP and MySQL to log specific items of interest to you outside the realm of the Apache log files.

In this chapter, you will learn

- ▶ How to understand Apache log formats and logging levels

- ▶ How to rotate and analyze Apache logs

- ▶ How to interpret common errors that might appear in your logs

- ▶ How to create scripts that log specific items to database tables

- ▶ How to create custom reports based on these logging tables

Standard Apache Access Logging

Using Apache's basic logging features, you can keep track of who visits your websites by logging accesses to the servers hosting them. You can log every aspect of the browser requests and server responses, including the IP address of the client, user, and resource accessed. You need to take three steps to create a request log:

1. Define *what* you want to log—your log format.

2. Define *where* you want to log it—your log files, a database, an external program.

3. Define *whether* to log—conditional logging rules.

The next few sections take a closer look at these steps.

Defining What to Log

As well as logging nearly every aspect associated with the request, you can define how your log entries appear by creating a log format. A *log format* is a string that contains text mixed with log-formatting directives. Log-formatting directives start with a % followed by a directive name or identifier, usually a letter indicating the piece of information to be logged.

When Apache logs a request, it scans the string and substitutes the value for each directive. For example, if the log format is This is the client address %a, the log entry is something like This is the client address 10.0.0.2. That is, the logging directive %a replaces the IP address of the client making the request. Table 26.1 provides a comprehensive list of all formatting directives.

TABLE 26.1   Log Formatting Directives

Formatting Options	Explanation
Data from the Client	
%a	Remote IP address, from the client.
%h	Hostname or IP address of the client making the request. Whether or not the hostname is logged depends on two factors: The IP address of the client must resolve to a hostname via a reverse DNS lookup, and Apache must be configured to do that lookup using the HostNameLookups directive, explained later in this chapter. If these conditions are not met, the IP address of the client will be logged instead of the hostname.
%l	Remote user, obtained via the identd protocol. This option is not very useful because the majority of the client machines do not support this protocol.
%u	Remote user, from the HTTP basic authentication protocol.
Data from the Server	
%A	Local IP address, from the server.
%D	Time it took to serve the request, in microseconds.
%{env_variable}e	Value for an environment variable named *env_variable* (there are many).
%{time_format}t	Current time. If {time_format} is present, it will be interpreted as an argument to the UNIX strftime function. See the logresolve Apache manual page for details.
%T	Time it took to serve the request, in seconds.
%v	Canonical name of the server that answered the request.

TABLE 26.1 Continued

Formatting Options	Explanation
Data from the Server	
%V	Server name according to the UseCanonicalName directive.
%X	Status of the connection to the server. A value of x means the connection was aborted before the server could send the data. A + means the connection will be kept alive for further requests from the same client. A - means the connection will be closed.
Data from the Request	
%{cookie_name}C	Value for a cookie named cookie_name.
%H	Request protocol, such as HTTP or HTTPS.
%m	Request method such as GET, POST, PUT, and so on.
%{header_name}i	Value for a header named header_name in the request from the client. This information can be useful, for example, to log the names and versions of your visitors' browsers.
%r	Text of the original HTTP request.
%q	Query parameters, if any, prefixed by a ?.
%U	Requested URL, without query parameters.
%y	Username for the HTTP authentication (basic or digest).
Data from the Response	
%b, %B	Size, in bytes, of the body of the response sent back to the client (excluding headers). The only difference between the options is that if no data was sent, %b will log a - and %B will log 0.
%f	Path of the file served, if any.
%t	Time when the request was served.
%{header_name}o	Value for a header named header_name in the response to the client.
%>s	Final status code. Apache can process several times the same request (internal redirects). This is the status code of the final response.

The Common Log Format (CLF) is a standard log format. Most websites can log requests using this format, and many log processing and reporting tools understand the format. Its format is the following:

```
"%h %l %u %t \"%r\" %>s %b"
```

That is, it includes the hostname or IP address of the client, remote user via identd, remote user via HTTP authentication, time when the request was served, text of the request, status code, and size in bytes of the content served.

By the Way

> You can read the Common Log Format documentation of the original W3C server at http://www.w3.org/Daemon/User/Config/Logging.html.

The following is a sample CLF entry:

```
10.0.0.1 - - [23/Jan/2008:11:27:56 -0800] "GET / HTTP/1.1" 200 1456
```

You are now ready to learn how to define log formats using the LogFormat directive. This directive takes two arguments: The first argument is a logging string, and the second is a nickname that will be associated with that logging string.

For example, the following directive from the default Apache configuration file defines the CLF and assigns it the nickname common:

```
LogFormat "%h %l %u %t \"%r\" %>s %b" common
```

You can also use the LogFormat directive with only one argument, either a log format string or a nickname. This will have the effect of setting the default value for the logging format used by the TransferLog directive, explained in "Logging Accesses to Files" later in this chapter.

The HostNameLookups **Directive**

When a client makes a request, Apache knows only the IP address of the client. Apache must perform what is called a *reverse DNS lookup* to find out the hostname associated with the IP address. This operation can be time-consuming and can introduce a noticeable lag in the request processing. The HostNameLookups directive allows you to control whether to perform the reverse DNS lookup.

The HostNameLookups directive can take one of the following arguments: on, off, or double. The default is off. The double lookup argument means that Apache will find out the hostname from the IP and then will try to find the IP from the hostname. This process is necessary if you are really concerned with security, as described in http://httpd.apache.org/docs-2.0/dns-caveats.html. If you are using hostnames as part of your Allow and Deny rules, a double DNS lookup is performed regardless of the HostNameLookups settings.

If HostNameLookups is enabled (on or double), Apache will log the hostname. This causes extra load on your server, which you should be aware of when making the decision to turn HostNameLookups on or off. If you choose to keep HostNameLookups off, which is recommended for medium-to-high traffic sites, Apache logs only the associated IP address. There are plenty of tools to resolve the IP addresses in the logs later. See the "Managing Apache Logs" section later in this chapter. Additionally, the result will be passed to CGI scripts via the environment variable REMOTE_HOST.

The IdentityCheck Directive

At the beginning of the chapter, you learned how to log the remote username via the identd protocol using the %l log formatting directive. The IdentityCheck directive takes a value of on or off to enable or disable checking for that value and making it available for inclusion in the logs. Because the information is not reliable and takes a long time to check, it is switched off by default and should probably never be enabled. %l was mentioned only because it is part of the CLF. For more information on the identd protocol, see RFC 1413 at http://www.rfc-editor.org/rfc/rfc1413.txt.

Status Code

You can specify whether to log specific elements in a log entry. At the beginning of the chapter, you learned that log directives start with a %, followed by a directive identifier. In between, you can insert a list of status codes, separated by commas. If the request status is one of the listed codes, the parameter will be logged; otherwise, a - will be logged.

For example, the following directive identifier logs the browser name and version for malformed requests (status code 400) and requests with methods not implemented (status code 501). This information can be useful for tracking which clients are causing problems.

```
%400,501{User-agent}i
```

You can precede the method list with an ! to log the parameter if the methods are implemented:

```
%!400,501{User-agent}i
```

Logging Accesses to Files

Logging to files is the default way of logging requests in Apache. You can define the name of the file using the TransferLog and CustomLog directives.

The TransferLog directive takes a file argument and uses the latest log format defined by a LogFormat directive with a single argument (the nickname or the format string). If no log format is present, it defaults to the CLF.

The following example shows how to use the `LogFormat` and `TransferLog` directives to define a log format that is based on the CLF but that also includes the browser name:

```
LogFormat "%h %l %u %t \"%r\" %>s %b \"%{User-agent}i\""
TransferLog logs/access_log
```

The `CustomLog` directive enables you to specify the logging format explicitly. It takes at least two arguments: a logging format and a destination file. The logging format can be specified as a nickname or as a logging string directly.

For example, the directives

```
LogFormat "%h %l %u %t \"%r\" %>s %b \"%{User-agent}i\"" myformat
CustomLog logs/access_log myformat
```

and

```
CustomLog logs/access_log "%h %l %u %t \"%r\" %>s %b \"%{User-agent}i\""
```

are equivalent.

The `CustomLog` directive accepts an environment variable as a third argument. If the environment variable is present, the entry will be logged; otherwise, it will not. If the environment variable is negated by prefixing an ! to it, the entry will be logged if the variable is *not* present.

The following example shows how to avoid logging images in GIF and JPEG format in your logs:

```
SetEnvIf Request_URI "(\.gif|\.jpg)$" image
CustomLog logs/access_log common env=!image
```

> The regular expression used for pattern matching in this and other areas of the `httpd.conf` file follow the same format for regular expressions in PHP and other programming languages.

Logging Accesses to a Program

Both `TransferLog` and `CustomLog` directives can accept an executable program, prefixed by a pipe sign, |, as an argument. Apache will write the log entries to the standard input of this program. The program will, in turn, process the input by logging the entries to a database, transmitting them to another system, and so on.

If the program dies for some reason, the server makes sure that it restarts. If the server stops, the program stops as well. The `rotatelogs` utility, bundled with Apache and explained later in this chapter, is an example of a logging program.

As a general rule, unless you have a specific requirement for using a particular program, it is easier and more reliable to log to a file on disk and do the processing, merging, analysis of logs, and so on, at a later time, possibly on a different machine.

> **By the Way**
>
> Make sure that the program you use for logging requests is secure because it runs as the user Apache was started with. On UNIX, this usually means root because the external program will be started before the server changes its user ID to the value of the User directive, typically nobody or www.

Standard Apache Error Logging

Apache can be configured to log error messages and debugging information, in addition to client requests. In addition to errors generated by Apache itself, CGI errors can be logged.

Each error log entry is prefixed by the time the error occurred and the client IP address or hostname, if available. As with HTTP request logging, you can log error information to a file or program. On UNIX systems, you can also log to the syslog daemon. On Windows, errors can be logged in the Windows event log and would then be viewable via the Windows Event Viewer. Use the ErrorLog directive to define where you want your logs to go.

Logging Errors to a File

A file argument indicates the path to the error log file. If the path is relative, it is assumed to be relative to the server root. By default, the error log file will be located in the logs directory and will be named error_log on UNIX and error.log on Windows. The following is an example:

```
ErrorLog logs/my_error_log
```

Logging Errors to a Program

You can specify the path to a program, prefixed by a pipe ¦. Apache will log errors to the standard input of the program, and the program will further process them. The following is an example:

```
ErrorLog "¦/usr/local/bin/someprogram"
```

The syslog **Daemon Argument**

On a UNIX system, if you specify syslog as an argument, you can log error messages to the UNIX system log daemon syslogd. By default, log errors are logged to the syslog facility local7. The facility is the part of the system generating the error. You can specify a facility by providing syslog:*facility* as an argument. Examples of syslog facilities are mail, uucp, local0, local1, and so on. For a complete list, look at the documentation for syslog included with your system (try man syslogd or man syslogd.conf at the command line). The following is an example of logging to syslog:

```
ErrorLog syslog:local6
```

The LogLevel **Directive**

The error information provided by Apache has several degrees of importance. You can choose to log only important messages and disregard informational or trivial warning messages. The LogLevel directive takes an error-level argument. Only errors of that level of importance or higher will be logged.

Table 26.2 specifies the valid values for the LogLevel directive, as specified by the Apache documentation. By default, the LogLevel value is warn. That should be enough for most Apache installations. If you are trying to troubleshoot a specific configuration, you can alter the level to debug.

TABLE 26.2   LogLevel **Options as Described in the Apache Documentation**

Setting	Description	Example
emerg	Emergencies—system is unusable	Child cannot open lock file. Exiting.
alert	Action must be taken immediately	getpwuid: couldn't determine user name from uid.
crit	Critical conditions	socket: Failed to get a socket, exiting child.
error	Error conditions	Premature end of script headers.
warn	Warning conditions	Child process 1234 did not exit, sending another SIGHUP.

TABLE 26.2 Continued

Setting	Description	Example
notice	Normal but significant conditions	httpd: caught SIGBUS, attempting to dump core in...
info	Informational	Server seems busy, (You may need to increase StartServers, or Min/MaxSpareServers)...
debug	Debug-level messages	Opening config file...

Managing Apache Logs

Apache provides several tools for managing your logs. Other Apache-specific third-party tools are available and mentioned here. Because Apache can log requests in the CLF, you can use most generic log-processing tools with Apache as well.

Resolving Hostnames

Earlier in the chapter, you learned how to use the HostNameLookups directive to enable or disable hostname resolution at the time the request is made. If HostNameLookups is set to off (the default), the log file will contain only IP addresses. Later, you can use the command-line logresolve utility on UNIX or logresolve.exe on Windows to process the log file and convert the IP addresses to hostnames.

The logresolve utility reads log entries from standard input and outputs the result to its standard output. To read to and from a file, you can use redirection on both UNIX and Windows:

```
logresolve < access.log > resolved.log
```

Log-resolving tools are efficient because they can cache results and do not cause any delay when serving requests to clients.

Log Rotation

In websites with high traffic, access log files can quickly grow in size. You should have a mechanism to rotate logs periodically, archiving and compressing older logs at defined intervals.

Log files should not be removed while Apache is running because the server is writing directly to them. A solution would be to use an intermediate program to log the requests. The program will, in turn, take care of rotating the logs.

Apache provides the `rotatelogs` program on UNIX and `rotatelogs.exe` on Windows for this purpose. It accepts three arguments: a filename, a rotate interval in seconds, and an optional offset in minutes against UTC (Coordinated Universal Time).

For example,

```
TransferLog "¦bin/rotatelogs /var/logs/apachelog 86400"
```

creates a new log file and moves the current log to the /var/logs directory daily. (At the end of the command, 86400 is the number of seconds in one day.)

> If the path to the program includes spaces, you might need to escape them by prefixing them with a \ (backslash)—for example, My\ Documents. This is especially common in the Windows platform.

If the name of the file includes % prefixed options, the name will be treated as input to the `strftime` function that converts the % options to time values. The manual page for the `rotatelogs` utility contains a complete listing of options, but here's an example:

```
TransferLog "¦bin/rotatelogs /var/logs/apachelog%m_%d_%y 86400"
```

This command adds the current month, day, and year to the log filename.

If the name does not include any %-formatted options, the current time in seconds is added to the name of the archived file.

Merging and Splitting Logs

When you have a cluster of web servers serving similar content, perhaps behind a load balancer, you often need to merge the logs from all the servers in a unique log stream before passing the log to analysis tools.

Similarly, if a single Apache server instance handles several virtual hosts, sometimes it is useful to split a single log file into different files, one per each virtual host.

Logtools is a collection of log-manipulation tools at http://www.coker.com.au/logtools/. Additionally, Apache includes the `split-file` Perl script for splitting logs. You can find it in the `support` subdirectory of the Apache distribution.

Log Analysis

After you collect the logs, you can analyze them and gain information about traffic and visitor behavior.

Many commercial, shareware, and freeware applications are available for log analysis and reporting. Two popular open source applications are Webalizer (http://www.mrunix.net/webalizer/) and awstats (http://awstats.sourceforge.net/).

Wusage is a nice, inexpensive commercial alternative at http://www.boutell.com/wusage/.

Monitoring Error Logs

If you run Apache on a UNIX system, you can use the `tail` command-line utility to monitor in real-time log entries to both your access and error logs. The syntax is

```
tail -f logname
```

where `logname` is the path to the Apache log file. It will print onscreen the last few lines of the log file and will continue to print entries as they are added to the file.

You can find additional programs that enable you to identify problems quickly by scanning your error log files for specific errors, malformed requests, and so on, and reporting on them. Here are links to a few:

▶ Logscan can be found at http://www.garandnet.net/security.php.

▶ ScanErrLog can be found at http://www.librelogiciel.com/software/.

Logging Custom Information to a Database

Creating your own logging tables in MySQL, matched up with snippets of PHP code, can help you to capture access-related information for specific pages of your site. Using this information, you can create customized reports. This method can be much less cumbersome than wading through Apache log files, especially when you are just searching for a subset of access information. The following sections outline a simple version of this process.

Creating the Database Table

The first step in your custom logging method is to create the database table. The following table creation command creates a table called `access_tracker` in your MySQL database, with fields for an ID, page title, user agent, and date of access:

```
mysql> CREATE TABLE access_tracker (
    ->  id INT NOT NULL PRIMARY KEY AUTO_INCREMENT,
    ->  page_title VARCHAR(50),
    ->  user_agent TEXT,
    ->  date_accessed DATE
    ->  );
```

Next, you'll create the code snippet that will write to this table.

Creating the PHP Code Snippet

As you may have gathered already, *code snippet* essentially means *a little bit of code*. In other words, something that doesn't qualify as a long script but just serves a simple purpose. In this case, the code snippet in Listing 26.1 writes some basic information to the access_tracker table.

LISTING 26.1   Code Snippet for Access Tracking

```
 1:  <?php
 2:  //set up static variables
 3:  $page_title = "sample page A";
 4:  $user_agent = getenv("HTTP_USER_AGENT");
 5:
 6:  //connect to server and select database
 7:  $mysqli = mysqli_connect("localhost", "joeuser", "somepass", "testDB");
 8:
 9:  //create and issue query
10: $sql = "INSERT INTO access_tracker (page_title,user_agent,date_accessed)
11:          VALUES ('$page_title', '$user_agent', now())";
12: $result = mysqli_query($mysqli, $sql) or die(mysqli_error($mysqli));
13:
14: //close connection to MySQL
15: mysqli_close($mysqli);
16: ?>
```

What you do with this snippet is simple: Place it at the beginning of every page you want to track. For each page, change the value of $page_title in the snippet to represent the actual title of the page.

Now create a sample script called sample1.php, containing the contents of Listing 26.1 and then the content in Listing 26.2.

LISTING 26.2   Sample HTML Page

```
1: <html>
2: <head>
3: <title>Sample Page A</title>
4: </head>
5: <body>
6: <h1>Sample Page A</h1>
7: <p>blah blah blah.</p>
8: </body>
9: </html>
```

Create a few copies of this file with different filenames and values for $page_title. Then access these different pages with your web browser to fill up your logging table.

Creating Sample Reports

When you have the data in your access_tracker table, you can create a simple report screen to disseminate this information. The code in Listing 26.3 creates a report that issues queries to count total results as well as the breakdown of browsers in use. Each of these blocks will be explained after the code listing.

LISTING 26.3   Creating an Access Report

```
1:   <?php
2:   //connect to server and select database
3:   $mysqli = mysqli_connect("localhost", "joeuser", "somepass", "testDB");
4:
5:   //issue query and select results for counts
6:   $count_sql = "SELECT count(page_title) AS p_count FROM access_tracker";
7:   $count_res = mysqli_query($mysqli, $count_sql)
8:               or die(mysqli_error($mysqli));
9:   while ($count_info = mysqli_fetch_array($count_res)) {
10:      $all_count = $count_info['p_count'];
11:  }
12:
13:  //issue query and select results for user agents
14:  $user_agent_sql = "SELECT DISTINCT user_agent, count(user_agent) AS
15:                     ua_count FROM access_tracker GROUP BY user_agent
16:                     ORDER BY ua_count desc";
17:  $user_agent_res = mysqli_query($mysqli, $user_agent_sql)
18:               or die(mysqli_error($mysqli));
19:
20:  //start user agent display block
21:  $user_agent_block = "<ul>";
22:
23:  //loop through user agent results
24:  while ($row_ua = mysqli_fetch_array($user_agent_res)) {
25:      $user_agent = $row_ua['user_agent'];
26:      $user_agent_count = $row_ua['ua_count'];
27:      $user_agent_block .= "
28:      <li>".$user_agent."
29:         <ul>
30:         <li><em>accesses per browser: ".$user_agent_count."</em>
31:         </ul>
32:      </li>";
33:  }
34:
35:  //finish up the user agent block
36:  $user_agent_block .= "</ul>";
37:
38:  //issue query and select results for pages
39:  $page_title_sql = "SELECT DISTINCT page_title, count(page_title) AS
40:                     pt_count FROM access_tracker GROUP BY page_title
```

LISTING 26.3   Continued

```
41:                     ORDER BY pt_count desc";
42:  $page_title_res = mysqli_query($mysqli, $page_title_sql)
43:                     or die(mysqli_error($mysqli));
44:
45:  //start page title display block
46:  $page_title_block = "<ul>";
47:
48:  //loop through results
49:  while ($row_pt = mysqli_fetch_array($page_title_res)) {
50:     $page_title = $row_pt['page_title'];
51:     $page_count = $row_pt['pt_count'];
52:     $page_title_block .= "
53:     <li>".$page_title."
54:        <ul>
55:        <li><em>accesses per page: ".$page_count."</em>
56:        </ul>
57:     </li>";
58:  }
59:
60:  //finish up the page title block
61:  $page_title_block .= "</ul>";
62:  ?>
63:  <html>
64:  <head>
65:  <title>Access Report</title>
66:  </head>
67:  <body>
68:  <h1>Access Report</h1>
69:  <p><strong>Total Accesses Tracked:</strong> <?php echo "$all_count"; ?></p>
70:  <p><strong>Web Browsers Used:</strong>
71:  <?php echo "$user_agent_block"; ?></p>
72:  <p><strong>Individual Pages:</strong>
73:  <?php echo "$page_title_block"; ?></p>
74:  </body>
75:  </html>
```

Line 3 connects to the database so that you can issue the queries against the access_tracker table. Lines 6–8 issue the query to select the count of all pages, and lines 14–18 count the user agent accesses. Line 21 starts an unordered list block for the results of the user agent query, while lines 24–33 loop through the results and create the list, which is closed in line 36.

Lines 39–43 create and issue the query to count the individual pages. Line 46 starts an unordered list block for the results of this query, and lines 49–58 loop through the results and create the list of accessed pages, which is closed in line 61.

Put these lines into a text file called accessreport.php, and place this file in your web server document root. When you access this report, you will see something like Figure 26.1—your page names, counts, and browsers will be different, but you get the idea.

FIGURE 26.1
Custom access report for tracked pages.

This sort of tracking is a lot easier than wading through Apache access logs, but I wouldn't recommend completely replacing your access logs with a database-driven system. That's a bit too much database-connection overhead, even if MySQL is particularly nice on your system. Instead, target your page tracking to something particularly important.

Summary

This chapter explained how to log specific information about the requests and errors generated by Apache. You can store the logs in files or databases, or pass them to external programs. You learned about the different utilities available for managing, processing, and analyzing logs, both the ones included with Apache and those available from third parties.

Finally, you saw a simple method for using PHP code snippets and a MySQL database to perform simple access tracking of specific pages. This information was displayed in a simple access report, built with PHP.

Q&A

Q. *Why wouldn't I want to log images?*

A. In heavily loaded servers, logging can become a bottleneck. If the purpose of logging is to count the number of visitors and analyze their usage of the website, you can achieve this result by logging only the HTML pages, not the images contained in them. This reduces the number of hits stored in the logs and the time spent writing them.

Workshop

The workshop is designed to help you anticipate possible questions, review what you've learned, and begin putting your knowledge into practice.

Quiz

1. How would you avoid logging hits from a client accessing your website from a particular network?

2. How can you log images to a different file?

Answers

1. In some situations, you may want to ignore requests coming from a particular network, such as your own, so that they do not skew the results. You can do this either by post-processing the logs and removing them or by using the SetEnvIf directive:

```
SetEnvIf Remote_Addr 10\.0\.0\. intranet
CustomLog logs/access_log "%h %l %u %t \"%r\" %>s %b" !intranet
```

2. Earlier in the chapter, you learned how to avoid logging images. Instead of ignoring images altogether, you can easily log them to a separate file, using the same environment variable mechanism:

```
SetEnvIf Request_URI "(\.gif|\.jpeg)$" image
CustomLog logs/access_log common env=!image
CustomLog logs/images_log common env=image
```

27

Application Localization

The key phrase in *World Wide Web* is *World Wide*. Creating a website useful to speakers of different languages is a breeze using PHP and MySQL. The process of preparing your applications for use in multiple locales is called *internationalization*; customizing your code for each locale is called *localization*. In this chapter, you will learn some basic tips for performing localization tasks, including

- ▶ How to recognize and prepare for character set differences
- ▶ How to prepare the structure of your application and produce localized sites

About Internationalization and Localization

First and foremost, neither internationalization nor localization is the same thing as translation. In fact, you can have a fully translated website—all in German, all in Japanese, or all in whatever language you want—and it will not be considered an internationalized or localized website. It will just be a translated one. The key aspects to internationalization are as follows:

- ▶ Externalizing all strings, icons, and graphics
- ▶ Modifying the display of formatting functions (dates, currency, numbers, and so on)

After you have constructed your application so that your strings are externalized and your formatting functions can change per locale, you can begin the process of localization. Translation happens to be a part of that.

A *locale* is essentially a grouping—in this case, a grouping of the translated strings, graphics, text, and formatting conventions that will be used in the application or website to be localized. These groupings are usually referred to by the name of the pervasive language of the application, such as the German locale. Although it might be obvious that the German locale includes text translated into German, it does not mean that the website is applicable only to people in Germany—Austrians who speak German would probably utilize a localized German website, but it would not be referred to as the Austrian locale.

In the next few sections, you learn about working with different character sets and how to modify your environment to successfully prepare your applications for localization.

About Character Sets

Character sets are usually referred to as *single-byte* or *multibyte*, referring to the number of bytes needed to define a relationship with a character used in a language. English, German, and French (among many others) are single-byte languages; only one byte is necessary to represent a character such as the letter *a* or the number *9*. Single-byte code sets have, at most, 256 characters, including the entire set of ASCII characters, accented characters, and other characters necessary for formatting.

Multibyte code sets have more than 256 characters, including all single-byte characters as a subset. Multibyte languages include traditional and simplified Chinese, Japanese, Korean, Thai, Arabic, Hebrew, and so forth. These languages require more than 1 byte to represent a character. A good example is the word *Tokyo*, the capital of Japan. In English, it is spelled with four different characters, using a total of 5 bytes. However, in Japanese, the word is represented by two syllables, *tou* and *kyou*, each of which uses 2 bytes, for a total of 4 bytes used.

This is a complete simplification of character sets and the technology behind them, but the relevance is this: To properly interpret and display the text of web pages in their intended language, it is up to you to tell the web browser which character set to use. This is achieved by sending the appropriate headers before all content.

If you have a set of pages that include Japanese text and you do not send the correct headers regarding language and character set, those pages will render incorrectly in web browsers whose primary language is not Japanese. In other words, because no character set information is included, the browser assumes that it is to render the text using its own default character set. For example, if your Japanese pages use the Shift_JIS or UTF-8 character set and your browser is set for ISO-8859-1, your browser will try to render the Japanese text using the single-byte ISO-8859-1 character set. It will fail miserably in this unless the headers alert it to use Shift_JIS or UTF-8 and you have the appropriate libraries and language packs installed on your operating system.

The headers in question are the Content-type and Content-language headers, and these can also be set as META tags. Because you have all the tools for a dynamic environment, it's best to both send the appropriate headers before your text and print the correct META tags in your document. The following is an example of the header() function outputting the proper character information for an English site:

```
header("Content-Type: text/html;charset=ISO-8859-1");
header("Content-Language: en");
```

The accompanying META tags would be these:

```
<META HTTP-EQUIV="Content-Type" content="text/html; charset=ISO-8859-1">
<META HTTP-EQUIV="Content-Language" content="en">
```

A German site would use the same character set but a different language code:

```
header("Content-Type: text/html;charset=ISO-8859-1");
header("Content-Language: de");
```

The accompanying META tags would be these:

```
<META HTTP-EQUIV="Content-Type" content="text/html; charset=ISO-8859-1">
<META HTTP-EQUIV="Content-Language" content="de">
```

A Japanese site uses both a different character set and different language code:

```
header("Content-Type: text/html;charset=Shift_JIS");
header("Content-Language: ja");
```

The accompanying META tags would be these:

```
<META HTTP-EQUIV="Content-Type" content="text/html; charset=Shift_JIS">
<META HTTP-EQUIV="Content-Language" content="ja">
```

Environment Modifications

Your environment, as defined in the installation chapters of this book, need not change to handle localized websites. Although you can use several language-related settings in Apache, PHP, and MySQL to accommodate localized websites, you can also perform all the tasks in this chapter without making any language-related changes to your configuration. Just for your own information, the next few sections point you to the appropriate documentation for internationalization using Apache, PHP, and MySQL.

Configuration Changes to Apache

In Chapter 29, "Apache Performance Tuning and Virtual Hosting," you will learn about the concept of content negotiation using the mod_mime or mod_negotiation modules and the AddLanguage and AddCharset directives (among others). You use these directives when you manually change the extension of your file and want Apache to interpret the character set to be used, based on that extension. However, that is not what this chapter discusses. You want all your localized websites to have the same file-naming conventions (such as index.html and company_info.html) and not have to manually create multiple pages with different language-based extensions to accommodate translated files. Your goal regarding website localization is to have a single set of pages filled with the appropriately translated text running from one web server.

By the Way

There's nothing wrong with Apache-based content negotiation using multiple files with language-based naming conventions. It's just not the focus of this chapter. You can read more about Apache-based content negotiation at http://httpd.apache.org/docs-2.2/content-negotiation.html.

Configuration Changes to PHP

As with Apache, no configuration changes in PHP are required for any tasks in this chapter. However, you can use a host of functions related to the handling of multibyte characters, if you want. These functions are in the PHP manual at http://www.php.net/mbstring and must be enabled during the configuration process using this code:

```
--enable-mbstring=LANG
```

Here, LANG is a language code, such as ja for Japanese, cn for Simplified Chinese, and so forth. Or, you can use this line to enable all available languages:

```
--enable-mbstring=all
```

When you enable mbstring functions in PHP, you can set several options in the php.ini configuration file to use these functions properly. After this is configured, you can use any of the more than 40 mbstring-related functions for handling multibtye input in PHP.

The manual entries for these functions are comprehensive and recommended reading for advanced work with multibyte character sets and dynamic content. You will get by just fine in this chapter without them, although it is recommended that at some point you peruse the PHP manual for your own edification.

Configuration Changes to MySQL

No explicit changes are needed in MySQL for the localization examples used in this chapter because the examples are not database-driven. The default character set used in MySQL is ISO-8859-1, but that does not mean that you are limited only to storing single-byte characters in your database tables. For more information on the current language-related elements of MySQL, read the MySQL manual entry at http://www.mysql.com/doc/en/Localisation.html.

Creating a Localized Page Structure

In this section, you look at a functioning example of a localized welcome page that uses PHP to enable a user to select a target language and then receive the appropriate text. The goal of this section is to show an example of externalizing the strings used in this script, which is one of the characteristics of internationalization.

In this script, the user happens upon your English-based website but is also presented with an option to browse within the locale of his choice—English, German, or Japanese. Three elements are involved in this process:

▶ Creating and using a master file for sending locale-specific header information

▶ Creating and using a master file for displaying the information based on the selected locale

▶ Using the script itself

Listing 27.1 shows the contents of the master file used for sending locale-specific header information.

LISTING 27.1   Language Definition File

```
1:    <?php
2:    if ((!isset($_SESSION["lang"])) || (!isset($_GET["lang"]))) {
3:        $_SESSION["lang"] = "en";
4:        $currLang = "en";
5:    } else {
6:        $currLang = $_GET["lang"];
7:        $_SESSION["lang"] = $currLang;
8:    }
9:
10:   switch($currLang) {
11:       case "en":
12:             define("CHARSET","ISO-8859-1");
13:             define("LANGCODE", "en");
14:       break;
15:
16:       case "de":
17:             define("CHARSET","ISO-8859-1");
18:             define("LANGCODE", "de");
19:       break;
20:
```

LISTING 27.1   Continued

```
21:        case "ja":
22:            define("CHARSET","UTF-8");
23:            define("LANGCODE", "ja");
24:        break;
25:
26:        default:
27:            define("CHARSET","ISO-8859-1");
28:            define("LANGCODE", "en");
29:        break;
30:    }
31:
32:    header("Content-Type: text/html;charset=".CHARSET);
33:    header("Content-Language: ".LANGCODE);
34:    ?>
```

Lines 2–8 of Listing 27.1 set up the session value needed to store the user's selected language choice.

The session_start() function is not used in the define_lang.php or the lang_strings.php file listed in the following paragraphs because these files are included via the include() function from within the master file. The master file, which you will create shortly, calls the session_start() function, which will be valid for these included files as well.

If no session value exists, the English locale settings will be used. If your site were a German site by default, you would change this file to use the German locale by default. This script prepares for the next script, which contains an input-selection mechanism, by setting the value of $currLang to the result of this input in line 6.

The switch statement beginning on line 10 contains several case statements designed to assign the appropriate values to the constant variables CHARSET and LANGCODE. Lines 32–33 actually utilize these variables for the first time when dynamically creating and sending the headers for Content-type and Content-language.

Save this file as define_lang.php and place it in the document root of your web browser. This file defines two constants used in the next script, which is the actual display script. The constants are CHARSET and LANGCODE, corresponding to the character set and language code for each locale. The display script uses these constants to create the proper META tags regarding character set and language code. Although this script sends the headers, it's a good idea to ensure that they are part of the page itself to aid in any necessary input from forms.

Listing 27.2 creates a function that simply stores the externalized strings used in the display script. This example uses two: one to welcome the user to the page (WELCOME_TXT) and one to introduce the language selection process (CHOOSE_TXT) .

LISTING 27.2   String Definition File

```
1:  <?php
2:  function defineStrings() {
3:    switch($_SESSION["lang"]) {
4:        case "en":
5:            define("WELCOME_TXT","Welcome!");
6:            define("CHOOSE_TXT","Choose Language");
7:        break;
8:
9:        case "de":
10:            define("WELCOME_TXT","Willkommen!");
11:            define("CHOOSE_TXT","Sprache auswählen");
12:        break;
13:
14:        case "ja":
15:            define("WELCOME_TXT","[unprintable characters]");
16:            define("CHOOSE_TXT","[unprintable characters]");
17:        break;
18:
19:        default:
20:            define("WELCOME_TXT","Welcome!");
21:            define("CHOOSE_TXT","Choose Language");
22:        break;
23:    }
24: }
25: ?>
```

Use the file lang_strings.php from the CD included with this book to use the actual Japanese characters that cannot be displayed here. Place this file in the document root of your web browser. This file defines two constants, WELCOME_TXT and CHOOSE_TXT, which are used in the display script. These constants are defined within the context of the function called defineStrings(), although you could just as easily make this file a long switch statement outside the context of the function structure. I've simply put it in a function for the sake of organization and for ease of explanation when it comes time to use the display script.

Finally, it's time to create the display script. Remember, one key element of internationalization is to externalize all strings so that only one master file needs to be used. Listing 27.3 is such an example.

LISTING 27.3   Localized Welcome Script

```
1:  <?php
2:  session_start();
3:  include("define_lang.php");
4:  include("lang_strings.php");
5:  defineStrings();
6:  ?>
7:  <html>
8:  <head>
9:  <title><?php echo WELCOME_TXT; ?></title>
10: <META HTTP-EQUIV="Content-Type" content="text/html;
11:     charset=<?php echo CHARSET; ?>"/>
12: <META HTTP-EQUIV="Content-Language" content="<?php echo LANGCODE; ?>"/>
13: <body>
14: <h1 align="center"><?php echo WELCOME_TXT; ?></h1>
15: <p align="center"><strong><?php echo CHOOSE_TXT; ?></strong><br/><br/>
16: <a href="<?php echo $_SERVER["PHP_SELF"]."?lang=en"; ?>">
17:    <img src="en_flag.gif" border="0"/></a>
18: <a href="<?php echo $_SERVER["PHP_SELF"]."?lang=de"; ?>">
19:    <img src="de_flag.gif" border="0"/></a>
20: <a href="<?php echo $_SERVER["PHP_SELF"]."?lang=ja"; ?>">
21:    <img src="ja_flag.gif" border="0"/></a>
22: </p>
23: </body>
24: </html>
```

You'll notice that Listing 27.3 is a basic template because all the language-related elements are externalized in the define_lang.php or lang_strings.php files. All this third file does is display the appropriate results, depending on the selected (or default) locale.

Line 5 calls the defineStrings() function, which then makes available the appropriate values for the two constant variables. Lines 15–18 display the flags representing the English, German, and Japanese locales, which are clickable. When the user clicks one of the flags, the locale changes to the new, selected locale, and the strings used are those appropriate to the new locale. These links contain the lang variable, which is passed to the script as $_GET["lang"]. If you look at line 6 of Listing 27.1, you will see how the code uses this to change the setting regarding the user's preferred locale.

Save this file as lang_selector.php and place it in the document root of your web browser. When visited for the first time, it should look something like Figure 27.1.

Until another language is selected, the default is English; accordingly, the Welcome and Choose Language text appears in English. When the user clicks the German flag, he sees Figure 27.2; when the user clicks the Japanese flag, he sees Figure 27.3.

The use of the flag of Great Britain might seem unusual for a book written by an American and with primary distribution in the United States. However, when using flags (instead of names of countries) as locale selectors, it is more common for the English locale to be represented by the flag of Great Britain rather than the United

States of America. As you can imagine, the use of flags for locale selection can get very political.

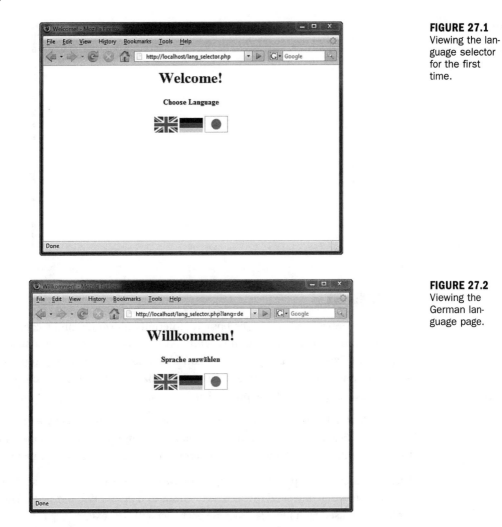

FIGURE 27.1
Viewing the language selector for the first time.

FIGURE 27.2
Viewing the German language page.

Companies that offer localized versions of their websites often have long discussions about how to represent the locale selections—flags, names of countries, names of languages, and so forth. There is no clear-cut answer; the websites for Sun Microsystems, Cisco Systems, and IBM use country names, whereas other large corporations use language names, but even Google uses flags. How to display the language selection can definitely be a business decision, but if you have gone through the process of externalizing strings, text, and images and created an internationalized website template that is ready to be localized, the format of your locale selection is the least of your concerns.

FIGURE 27.3
Viewing the Japanese language page.

FIGURE 27.3
Viewing the Japanese language page.

Summary

This chapter introduced you to the basics of internationalization and localization. You learned the two keys to creating an internationalized site: All strings, text, and graphics are externalized, as is number, currency, and date formatting. You also learned that neither internationalization nor localization is equivalent to translating text; translation is just one part of localization.

You also learned a little bit about character sets: They can be single-byte or multibyte. You also learned the importance of sending the appropriate language-related headers so that your web browser can interpret and display your text properly.

Finally, you created a practical example of how to store a locale-related session variable, to determine and send the localized strings to a preexisting template. This template can be used by all locales because each element was externalized.

Q&A

Q. *How do I go about localizing numbers, dates, and currency using PHP?*

A. Two functions will prove very useful to you in this regard: number_format() and date(). You have already learned about the date() function. To use it in a localized environment, you simply rearrange the month, day, and year elements as appropriate to the locale (MM-DD-YYYY, DD-MM-YYYY, and so forth). The number_format() function is used for numbers and currency; it groups the thousandths with a comma, period, or space, as appropriate to the locale. Read the PHP manual entry at http://www.php.net/number_format for possible uses.

Workshop

The workshop is designed to help you anticipate possible questions, review what you've learned, and begin putting your knowledge into practice.

Quiz

1. Is English a single-byte or multibyte language? What about Japanese?

2. What two headers related to character encoding are crucial in a localized site?

Answers

1. English is single-byte; Japanese is double-byte.

2. Content-Type with the charset indicator, Content-Language.

28

Working with XML

This chapter introduces you to working with XML documents via PHP, but in no way is it comprehensive—entire books have been written on this topic alone because there are several methods for accessing XML data using PHP functions. However, for people new to XML, or new to XML manipulation via PHP, some sets of functions are more manageable than others—this chapter introduces you to two of them.

In this chapter you will learn

- ▶ How to create a basic XML document structure
- ▶ How to access XML in PHP using DOM functions
- ▶ How to access XML in PHP using SimpleXML functions

What Is XML?

The name *XML* comes from the full name of the language, *Extensible Markup Language*. Although *markup* is in the name of the language, do not think of XML as you do HTML because, aside from the fact that both languages are based on tag pairs, there are no similarities. XML is used for the storage and exchange of data within its tag pairs, whereas HTML couldn't care less what is contained in the content or how it is structured—its only purpose is to display the content to the browser. In other words, XML defines and carries the content, whereas HTML makes it visually appealing to the reader.

Basic XML Document Structure

XML documents contain two major elements, the prolog and the body. The *prolog* contains the XML declaration statement, and any processing instructions and comments you want to add.

By the
Way

For a complete definition of XML documents, read the XML specification at
http://www.w3.org/TR/REC-xml.

The following snippet is a valid prolog:

```
<?xml version="1.0" ?>
<!-- Sample XML document -->
```

After the prolog comes the content structure. XML is hierarchical, like a book—books
have titles and chapters, each of which contain paragraphs, and so forth. There is
only one root element in an XML document. Continuing the book example, the element might be called Books, and the tags <Books></Books> surround all other
information.

```
<Books>
```

Next, add any subsequent elements—called *children*—to your document. Continuing
the book example, you will need a master book element and then within it elements
for title, author, and publishing information. Call these child elements Title,
Author, and PublishingInfo. But the publishing information will likely contain
more than one bit of information—you'll need a publisher's name, location, and
year of publication. Not a problem—just create another set of child elements within
your parent element (which also happens to be a child elements of the root element). For example, just the <PublishingInfo> element could look like this:

```
<PublishingInfo>
    <PublisherName>Sams Publishing</PublisherName>
    <PublisherCity>Indianapolis</PublisherCity>
    <PublishedYear>2008</PublishedYear>
</PublishingInfo>
```

All together, a sample books.xml document with one entry could look something
like this:

```
<?xml version="1.0" ?>
<!--Sample XML document -->
<Books>
    <Book>
        <Title>A Very Good Book</Title>
        <Author>Jane Doe</Author>
        <PublishingInfo>
            <PublisherName>Sams Publishing</PublisherName>
            <PublisherCity>Indianapolis</PublisherCity>
            <PublishedYear>2008</PublishedYear>
        </PublishingInfo>
    </Book>
</Books>
```

Keep in mind two important rules for creating valid XML documents:

- ▶ XML is case sensitive, so <Book> and <book> are considered different elements.

- ▶ All XML tags must be properly closed, XML tags must be properly nested, and no overlapping tags are allowed.

Add some dummy entries to the books.xml file and place it in the document root of your web server for use in later examples. You will use the same XML file throughout the different interface examples shown in the rest of this chapter.

When Might You Use XML and PHP?

The short (and snarky) answer to this question is "anytime you want," but the serious answer is, as you can imagine, a little more complex than that. Earlier in this section, I noted that XML defines and carries content. This is still true. But what does that look like in "real life"?

The examples in this chapter use XML to store a small catalog of books. Imagine a large catalog of books stored in a proprietary database format, but one which has the capability to output data in XML format. If you need to get your hands on that catalog of books, but have no intention of purchasing or using the proprietary software in which it lives, XML would be the answer. The owner of that data would export the catalog into XML format, which you could then parse and display however you wanted, using one of the formats described in this chapter.

Another use of XML has seen a recent growth in popularity—for use in data exchange when creating "add-on" applications to popular social networking sites such as Facebook. The following XML snippet is an example of how error messages are communicated to external scripts using the Facebook API.

```xml
<?xml version="1.0" encoding="UTF-8"?>
<error_response xmlns="http://api.facebook.com/1.0/"
xmlns:xsi=http://www.w3.org/2001/XMLSchema-instance
xsi:schemaLocation="http://api.facebook.com/1.0/
http://api.facebook.com/1.0/facebook.xsd">
  <error_code>5</error_code>
  <error_msg>Unauthorized source IP address (ip was: 10.1.2.3)</error_msg>
  <request_args list="true">
    <arg>
      <key>method</key>
      <value>facebook.friends.get</value>
    </arg>
  </request_args>
</error_response>
```

For information on becoming a Facebook developer or working with the Facebook developer platform, please visit http://developers.facebook.com/.

The use of XML to relay this type of information eliminates the need for developers to be part of internal systems, while still providing crucial information necessary for rich application development.

Accessing XML in PHP Using DOM Functions

The DOM XML extension has been part of PHP since version 4 but was completely overhauled in PHP 5. The primary change was to include the DOM functionality within a default installation of PHP, which is to say that no additional libraries or extensions need to be installed or configured to use these functions.

DOM stands for *Document Object Model*. For more information on DOM, visit http://www.w3.org/TR/DOM-Level-2-Core/core.html.

The purpose of DOM functions is to allow you to work with data stored in an XML document using the DOM API. The most basic DOM function is DOMDocument->load(), which creates a new DOM tree from the contents of a file. After you create the DOM tree, you can use other DOM functions to manipulate the data. In Listing 28.1, DOM functions are used to loop through a DOM tree and retrieve stored values for later display.

LISTING 28.1   Loop Through an XML Document Using DOM Functions

```
1:   <?php
2:   $dom = new DomDocument;
3:   $dom->load("books.xml");
4:
5:   foreach ($dom->documentElement->childNodes as $books) {
6:       if (($books->nodeType == 1) && ($books->nodeName == "Book")) {
7:
8:           foreach ($books->childNodes  as $theBook) {
9:               if (($theBook->nodeType == 1) &&
10:               ($theBook->nodeName == "Title")) {
11:                   $theBookTitle = $theBook->textContent;
12:               }
13:
14:               if (($theBook->nodeType == 1) &&
15:               ($theBook->nodeName == "Author")) {
16:                   $theBookAuthor = $theBook->textContent;
17:               }
18:
```

LISTING 28.1   Continued

```
19:            if (($theBook->nodeType == 1) &&
20:            ($theBook->nodeName == "PublishingInfo")) {
21:
22:                foreach ($theBook->childNodes as $thePublishingInfo) {
23:                    if (($thePublishingInfo->nodeType == 1) &&
24:                    ($thePublishingInfo->nodeName == "PublisherName")) {
25:                        $theBookPublisher = $thePublishingInfo->textContent;
26:                    }
27:
28:                    if (($thePublishingInfo->nodeType == 1) &&
29:                    ($thePublishingInfo->nodeName == "PublishedYear")) {
30:                        $theBookPublishedYear =
31:                            $thePublishingInfo->textContent;
32:                    }
33:                }
34:            }
35:        }
36:
37:        echo "
38:        <p><span style=\"text-decoration:underline\">".$theBookTitle."</span>
39:        by ".$theBookAuthor."<br/>
40:        published by ".$theBookPublisher." in ".$theBookPublishedYear."</p>";
41:
42:        unset($theBookTitle);
43:        unset($theBookAuthor);
44:        unset($theBookPublisher);
45:        unset($theBookPublishedYear);
46:    }
47: }
48: ?>
```

Line 2 creates a new DOM document, and line 3 loads the contents of books.xml into this document. The document tree is now accessible through $dom, as you can see in later lines. Line 5 begins the master loop through the document tree, as it places each node of the document into an array called $books.

Line 6 looks for an element called "Book", and processing continues if it finds one. Remember, the <Book></Book> tag pair surrounds each entry for a book in the books.xml file. If processing continues, line 8 gathers all the child nodes into an array called $theBook, and the if statements in lines 9–12 and 14–17 look for specific nodes called "Title" and "Author", respectively, and place the values into the variables $theBookTitle and $theBookAuthor for later use.

Line 19 begins a similar if statement, but because this line looks for a node called "Publishing Info" and you know that the <PublishingInfo></PublishingInfo> tag pair contains its own set of child nodes, another looping construct is needed to obtain the information in the next level of data. On line 22, child nodes are found and placed in the array called $thePublishingInfo, and then if statements in lines 23–26 and lines 28–32 look for specific nodes called "PublisherName" and "PublishedYear", respectively, and place the values into the variables $theBookPublisher and $theBookPublishedYear for later use.

After the loop created in line 8 is closed in line 35, lines 37–40 echo a marked-up string to the browser, using values stored in $theBookTitle, $theBookAuthor, $theBookPublisher, and $theBookPublishedYear variables. After these values are used, they are unset in lines 42–45, and the loop continues for the next "Book" entry in the document tree.

Save this listing as domexample.php and place it in the document root of your web server. When viewed through your web browser you should see something like Figure 28.1.

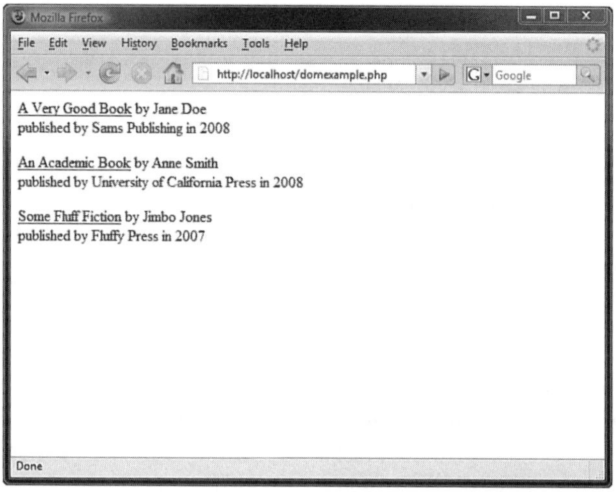

FIGURE 28.1
Text extracted and displayed using DOM functions.

For a complete listing of the more than 80 DOM-related functions in PHP, including functions to add to your XML document and save the new version, visit the PHP Manual at http://www.php.net/dom.

In the next section, you'll use the same books.xml file but will retrieve and display its values using the SimpleXML family of functions.

Accessing XML in PHP Using SimpleXML Functions

SimpleXML is a new addition to PHP 5; it is enabled by default and requires no additional installation or configuration steps. It lives up to its description in the PHP Manual of being "a very simple and easily usable toolset to convert XML" while still being powerful.

Unlike the DOM family of functions, there are only a few SimpleXML functions and methods—seven, at current count. The most basic SimpleXML function parses the XML data into an object that you can directly access and manipulate without special functions to do so. The first function you need to know about is simplexml_load_file(), which loads a file and creates an object out of the data:

```
$object_with_data = simplexml_load_file("somefile.xml");
```

Listing 28.2 uses a short bit of code to create a SimpleXML object and then displays the hierarchy of the data stored in the object.

LISTING 28.2   Load and Display Data Using SimpleXML

```
1: <?php
2: $theData = simplexml_load_file("books.xml");
3: echo "<pre>";
4: print_r($theData);
5: echo "</pre>";
6: ?>
```

Line 2 uses simple_load_file() to load the contents of books.xml into an object called $theData. In line 4, the print_r() function outputs a human-readable version of the data stored in the object, surrounded by the <pre></pre> tag pair.

Save this listing as simplexml_dump.php and place it in the document root of your web server. When viewed through your web browser, you should see something like Figure 28.2.

Dumping out data isn't all that spectacular, but it does show you the structure of the object, which in turn lets you know how to access the data in a hierarchical fashion. For instance, the output of simplexml_dump.php shows the entry for a book:

```
[0] => SimpleXMLElement Object
(
    [Title] => A Very Good Book
    [Author] => Jane Doe
    [PublishingInfo] => SimpleXMLElement Object
    (
        [PublisherName] => Sams Publishing
        [PublisherCity] => Indianapolis
```

```
            [PublishedYear] => 2008
        )
)
```

To reference this record directly, you would use

`$theData->Book`

FIGURE 28.2
Data dumped
from a
SimpleXML
object.

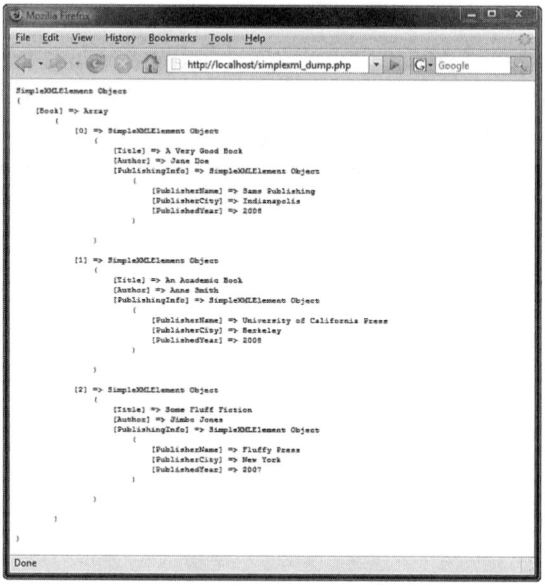

You would access the elements in the record like this:

▶ `$theData->Book->Title` for the Title

▶ `$theData->Book->Author` for the Author

▶ `$theData->Book->PublishingInfo->PublisherName` for the Publisher Name

▶ `$theData->Book->PublishingInfo->PublisherCity` for the Publisher City

▶ `$theData->Book->PublishingInfo->PublishedYear` for the Published year

But because you likely would want to loop through all the records and not just the
first one, the references to the data are a little different, as you can see in Listing 28.3.

LISTING 28.3   Through an XML Document Using SimpleXML

```
1:   <?php
2:   $theData = simplexml_load_file("books.xml");
3:
4:   foreach($theData->Book as $theBook) {
5:         $theBookTitle = $theBook->Title;
6:         $theBookAuthor = $theBook->Author;
7:         $theBookPublisher = $theBook->PublishingInfo->PublisherName;
8:         $theBookPublisherCity = $theBook->PublishingInfo->PublisherCity;
9:         $theBookPublishedYear = $theBook->PublishingInfo->PublishedYear;
10:
11:        echo "
12:        <p><span style=\"text-decoration:underline\">".$theBookTitle."</span>
13:        by ".$theBookAuthor."<br/>
14:        published by ".$theBookPublisher." (".$theBookPublisherCity.")
15:        in ".$theBookPublishedYear."</p>";
16:
17:        unset($theBookTitle);
18:        unset($theBookAuthor);
19:        unset($theBookPublisher);
20:        unset($theBookPublishedYear);
21: }
22: ?>
```

In line 2, the contents of books.xml are loaded using simple_load_file() into an
object called $theData. In line 4, the contents of $theData->Book, which is to say
all the individual records, are put into an array called $theBook. Lines 5–9 gather
the value of specific elements, beginning at the level of $theBook, and these values
are output in lines 11–15. Lines 17–20 unset the value of the variables for the next
pass through the loop.

Save this listing as simplexmlexample.php and place it in the document root of
your web server. When viewed through your web browser, you should see something
like Figure 28.3.

For more information on the SimpleXML functions in PHP, visit the PHP Manual at
http://www.php.net/simplexml.

FIGURE 28.3
Text extracted
and displayed
using
SimpleXML
functions.

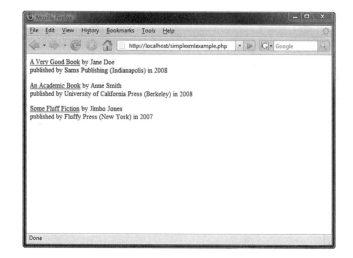

Summary

This brief chapter introduced you to two sets of PHP functions used to manipulate XML: the DOM functions and the SimpleXML functions. In addition to a brief overview of both topics, you saw examples of displaying information stored in XML files using each set of these functions. The overall purpose of this chapter was to introduce you to the concept of working with XML using PHP. If you are interested in using XML and PHP together, you might also want to look into AJAX (Asynchronous JavaScript and XML), which often uses PHP to produce or modify XML data before it is displayed to the client. For more information, I recommend the *Ajax Starter Kit*.

Q&A

Q. *Why would I use XML to store data when MySQL is a great (and free) database?*

A. XML can be used not only as a storage method, but also as an intermediary for data transfer. For instance, you might use XML in conjunction with a database, by extracting data and sending it to a third-party function that only interprets XML data. Additionally, while it is true that MySQL is great (and free), some users might not have access to MySQL or any other database, in which case XML files can play the role of a database system.

Workshop

The workshop is designed to help you anticipate possible questions, review what you've learned, and begin putting your knowledge into practice.

Quiz

1. What should be the opening line of a valid XML document?

2. Does the following code put your XML content into a new DOM document?

   ```
   $dom = new DomDocument;
   ```

3. What code would be used to load the contents of a file called my.xml into a SimpleXML object called $myData?

Answers

1. `<?xml version="1.0">`

2. No, it just creates a DOM document referenced as $dom. To load the content you must also use something like this:

   ```
   $dom->load("books.xml");
   ```

3. `$myData = simplexml_load_File("my.xml");`

PART VI

Administration and Fine-Tuning

29

Apache Performance Tuning and Virtual Hosting

In this administration-related chapter, the focus will be on increasing the performance and scalability of your Apache server. Additionally, you will learn about name-based and IP-based virtual hosting, as well as DNS-related issues and issues related to the web browser itself. This chapter also explains different mechanisms that can be used to isolate clients from each other and the associated security trade-offs.

In this chapter, you will learn

- ▶ Which operating system and Apache-related settings can limit the server's scalability or degrade performance

- ▶ About several tools for load testing Apache

- ▶ How to fine-tune Apache for optimum performance

- ▶ How to configure Apache to detect and prevent abusive behavior from clients

- ▶ How to configure name-based virtual hosts, IP-based virtual hosts, and the difference between the two

- ▶ About the dependencies virtual hosting has on DNS

- ▶ How to set up scaled-up cookie-cutter virtual hosts

Scalability Issues

This section covers scalability problems and how to prevent them. This section is more of a "don't do this" list, explaining limiting factors that can degrade performance or prevent the server from scaling. You also learn about the proactive tuning of Apache for optimal performance.

Operating System Limits

Several operating system factors can prevent Apache from scaling. These factors relate to process creation, memory limits, and maximum simultaneous number of open files or connections.

By the
Way

> The UNIX `ulimit` command enables you to set several of the limits covered in this section on a per-process basis. Refer to your operating system documentation for details on `ulimit`'s syntax.

Processes

Apache provides settings for preventing the number of server processes and threads from exceeding certain limits. These settings affect scalability because they limit the number of simultaneous connections to the web server, which in turn affects the number of visitors you can service simultaneously.

The Apache Multi-Processing Module (MPM) settings are in turn constrained by OS settings limiting the number of processes and threads. How to change those limits varies from operating system to operating system. In Linux 2.0.x and 2.2.x kernels, it requires changing the `NR_TASKS` defined in `/usr/src/linux/include/linux/tasks.h` and recompiling the kernel. In the 2.4.x series, the limit can be accessed at runtime from the `/proc/sys/kernel/threads-max` file. You can read the contents of the file with this command:

```
# cat /proc/sys/kernel/threads-max
```

You can write to the file using this command:

```
# echo value > /proc/sys/kernel/threads-max
```

In Linux (unlike most other UNIX versions), there is a mapping between threads and processes, and they are similar from the point of view of the OS.

In Solaris, those parameters can be changed in the `/etc/system` file. Those changes don't require rebuilding the kernel but might require a reboot to take effect. You can change the total number of processes by changing the `max_nprocs` entry and the number of processes allowed for a given user with `maxuproc`.

File Descriptors

Whenever a process opens a file (or a socket), a structure called a *file descriptor* is assigned until the file is closed. The OS limits the number of file descriptors that a given process can open, thus limiting the number of simultaneous connections the web server can have. How those settings are changed depends on the operating system. On Linux systems, you can read or modify /proc/sys/fs/file-max. On Solaris systems, you must edit the value for rlim_fd_max in the /etc/system file. This change requires a reboot to take effect.

You can find additional information at http://httpd.apache.org/docs/2.2/vhosts/fd-limits.html.

Controlling External Processes

Apache provides several directives to control the amount of resources external processes use. Such processes include CGI scripts spawned from the server and programs executed via server-side includes, but do not include PHP scripts that are invoked using the module version because the module is part of the server process.

> Following the installation instructions in the initial chapters of this book will result in PHP being installed as a module. Thus, these directives will not apply in your situation, unless you modified the installation type on your own.

By the Way

Support for the following Apache directives (used in httpd.conf) is available only on UNIX and varies from system to system:

- ▶ **RLimitCPU**—Accepts two parameters: the soft limit and the hard limit for the amount of CPU time in seconds that a process is allowed. If the max keyword is used, it indicates the maximum setting allowed by the operating system. The hard limit is optional. The soft limit can be changed between restarts, and the hard limit specifies the maximum allowed value for that setting.

- ▶ **RLimitMem**—The syntax is identical to RLimitCPU, but this directive specifies the amount (in bytes) of memory used per process.

- ▶ **RLimitNProc**—The syntax is identical to RLimitCPU, but this directive specifies the number of processes.

These three directives are useful to prevent malicious or poorly written programs from running out of control.

Performance-Related Apache Settings

This section presents different Apache settings that affect performance.

File System Access

From a resource standpoint, accessing files on disk is an expensive process, so you should try to minimize the number of disk accesses required for serving a request.

Symbolic links, per-directory configuration files, and content negotiation are some of the factors that affect the number of disk accesses:

▶ **Symbolic links**—In UNIX, a *symbolic link* (or *symlink*) is a special kind of file that points to another file. It is created with the UNIX `ln` command and is useful for making a certain file appear in different places.

Two of the parameters that the `Options` directive allows are `FollowSymLinks` and `SymLinksIfOwnerMatch`. By default, Apache won't follow symbolic links because they can be used to bypass security settings. For example, you can create a symbolic link from a public part of the website to a restricted file or directory not otherwise accessible via the Web. So, also by default, Apache needs to perform a check to verify that the file isn't a symbolic link. If `SymLinksIfOwnerMatch` is present, it will follow a symbolic link if the same user who created the symbolic link owns the target file.

Because those tests must be performed for every path element and for every path that refers to a filesystem object, they can be taxing on your system. If you control the content creation, you should add an `Options` `+FollowSymLinks` directive to your configuration and avoid the `SymLinksIfOwnerMatch` argument. In this way, the tests won't take place, and performance isn't affected.

▶ **Per-directory configuration files**—As explained in Chapter 3, "Installing and Configuring Apache," it is possible to have per-directory configuration files. These files, usually named `.htaccess`, provide a convenient way of configuring the server and allow for some degree of delegated administration. However, if this feature is enabled, Apache has to look for these files in each directory in the path leading to the file being requested, resulting in taxing filesystem accesses. If you don't have a need for per-directory configuration files, you can disable this feature by adding `AllowOverride none` to your configuration. Doing so will avoid the performance penalty associated with accessing the filesystem looking for `.htaccess` files.

▶ **Content negotiation**—Apache can serve different versions of a file depending on client language or preferences. This can be accomplished using specific language-related file extensions, but in that case, Apache must access the filesystem for every request, looking for files such as extensions. If you need to use content negotiation, make sure that you at least use a type-map file, minimizing accesses to disk. Alternatives to Apache-based content negotiation for internationalization purposes can be found in Chapter 27, "Application Localization."

▶ **Scoreboard file**—This is a special file that the main Apache process uses to communicate with its child processes on older operating systems. You can specify its location using the ScoreBoardFile directive, but most modern platforms do not require the use of this file. If this file is required, you might find improved performance if you place it on a RAM disk. A *RAM disk* is a mechanism that allows a portion of the system memory to be accessed as a filesystem. The details on creating a RAM disk vary from system to system.

Network and Status Settings

A number of network-related Apache options can degrade performance:

▶ `HostnameLookups`—When HostnameLookups is set to on or double, Apache will perform a DNS lookup to capture the hostname of the client each time the client makes a request. This constant lookup will introduce a delay into the response process. The default setting for this directive is off. If you want to capture the hostname of the requestor, you can always process the request logs with a log resolver later, offline, and not in real-time.

▶ **Accept mechanism**—Apache can use different mechanisms to control how Apache children arbitrate requests. The optimal mechanism depends on the specific platform and number of processors. You can find additional information at http://httpd.apache.org/docs-2.2/misc/perf-tuning.html.

▶ `mod_status`—This module collects statistics about the server, connections, and requests, which slow down Apache. For optimal performance, disable this module, or at least make sure that ExtendedStatus is set to off, which is the default.

Load Testing with ApacheBench

You can test the scalability and performance of your site with benchmarking and traffic generation tools. Many commercial and open-source tools are available, each with varying degrees of sophistication. In general, it is difficult to accurately simulate real-world request traffic because visitors have different navigation patterns, access the Internet using connections with different speeds, stop a download if it is taking too long, press the reload button repeatedly if they get impatient, and so on. As such, some tools record actual network traffic for later replay.

However, for a quick—but accurate—glimpse at basic information regarding your server's capability to handle heavy traffic, the Apache server comes with a simple,

but useful, load-testing tool called ApacheBench, or ab. You can find it in the bin
directory of the Apache distribution.

This tool enables you to request a certain URL a number of times and display a
summary of the result. The following command requests the main page of the
www.example.com server 1,000 times, with 10 simultaneous clients at any given
time:

```
# /usr/local/apache2/bin/ab -n 1000 -c 10 http://www.example.com/
```

By the
~~Way~~

| If you invoke ab without any arguments, you will get a complete listing of com-
| mand-line options and syntax. Additionally, the trailing slash on the target URL is
| required, unless a specific page is named.

The result will look similar to the following:

```
This is ApacheBench, Version 2.0.40-dev <$Revision: 1.121.2.8 $> apache-2.0
Copyright (c) 1996 Adam Twiss, Zeus Technology Ltd, http://www.zeustech.net/
Copyright (c) 1998-2002 The Apache Software Foundation, http://www.apache.org/

Benchmarking www.example.com (be patient)
Completed 100 requests
Completed 200 requests
Completed 300 requests
Completed 400 requests
Completed 500 requests
Completed 600 requests
Completed 700 requests
Completed 800 requests
Completed 900 requests
Finished 1000 requests


Server Software:        Apache/2.2.8
Server Hostname:        www.example.com
Server Port:            80

Document Path:          /
Document Length:        16 bytes

Concurrency Level:      10
Time taken for tests:   2.269667 seconds
Complete requests:      1000
Failed requests:        0
Write errors:           0
Total transferred:      252255 bytes
HTML transferred:       16080 bytes
Requests per second:    440.59 [#/sec] (mean)
Time per request:       22.697 - (mean)
Time per request:       2.270 - (mean, across all concurrent requests)
Transfer rate:          108.39 [Kbytes/sec] received
```

```
Connection Times (ms)
              min   mean[+/-sd] median    max
Connect:        0     0    1.9      0      15
Processing:     1    20   61.9     15     689
Waiting:        0    19   60.6     14     687
Total:          1    21   61.9     15     689

Percentage of the requests served within a certain time (ms)
    50%      15
    66%      16
    75%      17
    80%      18
    90%      19
    95%      22
    98%     224
    99%     422
   100%     689 (longest request)
```

These requests were made over the Internet to a sample server. You should get many more requests per second if you conduct the test against a server in the same machine or over a local network. The output of the tool is self-explanatory. Some of the relevant results are the number of requests per second and the average time it takes to service a request. You can also see how more than 95% of the requests were served in less than one second.

You can play with different settings for the number of requests and with the number of simultaneous clients to find the point at which your server slows down significantly.

Proactive Performance Tuning

Although previous sections explained which settings might prevent Apache from scaling, the following are some techniques for proactively increasing the performance of your server.

Mapping Files to Memory

As explained previously, accesses to disk affect performance significantly. Although most modern operating systems keep a cache of the most frequently accessed files, Apache also enables you to explicitly map a file into memory so that access to disk isn't necessary. The module that performs this mapping is mod_file_cache. You can specify a list of files to memory map by using the MMapFile directive, which applies to the server as a whole. An additional directive in Apache 2.x, CacheFile, takes a list of files, caches the file descriptors at startup, and keeps them around between requests, saving time and resources for frequently requested files.

Distributing the Load

Another way to increase performance is to distribute the load among several servers. This can be done in a variety of ways:

▶ Utilize a hardware load balancer to direct network and HTTP traffic across several servers, making it look like a single server from the outside.

▶ Utilize a software load balancer solution using a reverse proxy with `mod_rewrite`.

▶ Utilize separate servers to provide images, large download files, and other static material. For example, you can place your images in a server called `images.example.com` and link to them from your main server.

Caching

The fastest way to serve content is not to serve it at all! This can be achieved by using appropriate HTTP headers that instruct clients and proxies of the validity in time of the requested resources. In this way, some resources that appear in multiple pages but don't change frequently, such as logos or navigation buttons, are transmitted only once for a certain period of time.

Additionally, you can use `mod_cache` in Apache 2.x to cache dynamic content so that it doesn't have to be created for every request. This is potentially a big performance boost because dynamic content usually requires accessing databases, processing templates, and so on, which can take significant resources.

By the Way

> Apache 2.2 has many caching features that were considered experimental in previous versions of Apache. Please see the Apache Caching Guide for more information on this topic: http://httpd.apache.org/docs/2.2/caching.html.

Reducing Transmitted Data

Another method for reducing server load is to reduce the amount of data being transferred to the client. This in turn makes your clients' websites operate faster, especially for those over slow links. You can do a number of things to achieve this:

▶ Reduce the number of images.

▶ Reduce the size of your images.

▶ Compress large, downloadable files.

▶ Precompress static HTML and use content negotiation.

▶ Use mod_deflate to compress HTML content. This can be useful if CPU power is available and clients are connecting over slow links. The content will be delivered quicker, and the process will be free sooner to answer additional requests.

Network Settings

HTTP 1.1 allows multiple requests to be served over a single connection. HTTP 1.0 enables the same thing with keep-alive extensions. The KeepAliveTimeout directive enables you to specify the maximum time in seconds that the server will wait before closing an inactive connection. Increasing the timeout means that you increase the chance of the connection being reused. On the other hand, it also ties up the connection and Apache process during the waiting time, which can prevent scalability, as discussed earlier in the chapter.

Preventing Abuse

Denial of service (DoS) attacks work by swamping your web server with a great number of simultaneous requests, slowing down the server or preventing access altogether. DoS attacks are difficult to prevent in general, and usually the most effective way to address them is at the network or operating system level. One example would be to block specific addresses from making requests to the server; although you can block addresses at the web server level, it is more efficient to block them at the network firewall/router or with the operating system network filters.

Other kinds of abuse include posting extremely big requests or opening many simultaneous connections. You can limit the size of requests and timeouts to minimize the effect of attacks. The default request timeout is 300 seconds, but you can change it with the TimeOut directive. A number of directives enable you to control the size of the request body and headers: LimitRequestBody, LimitRequestFields, LimitRequestFieldSize, LimitRequestLine, and LimitXMLRequestBody.

Robots

Robots, *web spiders*, and *web crawlers* are names that describe a category of programs that access pages in your website, recursively following your site's links. Web search engines use these programs to scan the Internet for web servers, download their content, and index it. Real-life users use these types of programs to download an entire website or portion of a website for later offline browsing. Normally, these programs are well behaved, but sometimes they can be aggressive and swamp your website with too many simultaneous connections or become caught in cyclic loops.

Well-behaved spiders will request a special file, called `robots.txt`, that contains instructions about how to access your website and which parts of the website won't be available to them. The syntax for the file can be found at http://www.robotstxt.org/. By placing a properly formatted `robots.txt` file in your web server document root, you can control spider activity. Additionally, you can stop the requests at the router or operating system level.

Implementing Virtual Hosting

The first generation of web servers was designed to handle the contents of a single site. The standard way of hosting several websites in the same machine was to install and configure separate web server instances for each site. As the Internet grew, so did the need for hosting multiple websites, and a more efficient solution was developed: virtual hosting. Virtual hosting allows a single instance of Apache to serve different websites, identified by their domain names or IP addresses. *IP-based* virtual hosting means that each domain is assigned a different IP address; *name-based* virtual hosting means that several domains share a single IP address.

Web clients use the domain name server system (DNS) to translate hostnames into IP addresses and vice versa. Several mappings are possible:

▶ **One to one**—Each hostname is assigned a single, unique IP address. This is the foundation for IP-based virtual hosting.

▶ **One to many**—A single hostname is assigned to several IP addresses. This is useful for having several Apache instances serving the same website. If each of the servers is installed in a different machine, it is possible to balance the web traffic among them, improving scalability.

▶ **Many to one**—You can assign the same IP address to several hostnames. The client will specify the website it is accessing by using the `Host:` header in the request. This is the foundation for name-based virtual hosting.

By the Way

When a many-to-one mapping is in place, a DNS server usually can be configured to respond with a different IP address for each DNS query, which helps to distribute the load. This is known as *round robin DNS*. However, if you have the opportunity to utilize a load-balancing device instead of relying on a DNS server, doing so will alleviate any problems that may arise when tying your web server to your DNS server. Utilizing a load balancer eliminates the possibility that high traffic to your web server will bring down your DNS server as well.

IP-Based Virtual Hosting

The simplest virtual host configuration is when each host is assigned a unique IP address. Each IP address maps the HTTP requests that Apache handles to separate content trees in their own VirtualHost containers, as shown in the following snippet:

```
Listen 192.168.128.10:80
Listen 192.168.129.10:80

<VirtualHost 192.168.128.10:80>
    DocumentRoot /usr/local/apache2/htdocs/host1
</VirtualHost>

<VirtualHost 192.168.129.10:80>
    DocumentRoot /usr/local/apache2/htdocs/host2
</VirtualHost>
```

If a DocumentRoot is not specified for a given virtual host, the global setting, specified outside any <VirtualHost> section, will be used. In the previous example, each virtual host has its own DocumentRoot. When a request arrives, Apache uses the destination IP address to direct the request to the appropriate host. For example, if a request comes for IP 192.168.128.10, Apache returns the documents from /usr/local/apache2/htdocs/host1.

If the host operating system cannot resolve an IP address used as the VirtualHost container's name and there's no ServerName directive, Apache will complain at server startup time that it can't map the IP addresses to hostnames. This complaint is not a fatal error. Apache will still run, but the error indicates that there might be some work to be done with the DNS configuration so that web browsers can find your server. A fully qualified domain name (FQDN) can be used instead of an IP address as the VirtualHost container name and the Listen directive binding (if the domain name resolves in DNS to an IP address configured on the machine and Apache can bind to it).

Name-Based Virtual Hosts

As a way to mitigate the consumption of IP addresses for virtual hosts, the HTTP/1.1 protocol version introduced the Host: header, which enables a browser to specify the exact host for which the request is intended. This allows several hostnames to share a single IP address. Most browsers nowadays provide HTTP/1.1 support.

Although Host: usage was standardized in the HTTP/1.1 specification, some older HTTP/1.0 browsers also provided support for this header.

By the Way

Listing 29.1 shows a typical set of request headers from the Mozilla Firefox browser. If the URL were entered with a port number, it would be part of the Host header contents as well.

LISTING 29.1   Request Headers

```
GET / HTTP/1.1
Accept: image/gif, image/x-xbitmap, image/jpeg, image/pjpeg, */*
Accept-Language: en-us
Accept-Encoding: gzip, deflate
Mozilla/5.0 (Windows; U; Windows NT 6.0; en-US; rv:1.8.1.11) Gecko/20071127
Firefox/2.0.0.11
Host: host1.example.com
Connection: Keep-Alive
```

Apache uses the Host: header for configurations in which multiple hostnames can be shared by a single IP address—the many-to-one scenario outlined earlier this chapter—thus, the description *name-based virtual hosts*.

The NameVirtualHost directive enables you to specify IP address and port combinations on which the server will receive requests for name-based virtual hosts. This is a required directive for name-based virtual hosts. Listing 29.2 has Apache dispatch all connections to 192.168.128.10 based on the Host header contents.

LISTING 29.2   Name-Based Virtual Hosts

```
NameVirtualHost 192.168.128.10
Listen 192.168.128.10:80

<VirtualHost 192.168.128.10>
    ServerName host1.example.com
    DocumentRoot /usr/local/apache2/htdocs/host1
</VirtualHost>

<VirtualHost 192.168.128.10>
    ServerName host2.example.com
    DocumentRoot /usr/local/apache2/htdocs/host2
</VirtualHost>
```

For every hostname that resolves to 192.168.128.10, Apache can support another name-based virtual host. If a request comes for that IP address for a hostname that is not included in the configuration file, say host3.example.com, Apache simply associates the request to the first container in the configuration file; in this case, host1.example.com. The same behavior is applied to requests that are not accompanied by a Host header; whichever container is first in the configuration file is the one that gets the request.

An end user from the example.com domain might have his machine set up with example.com as his default domain. In that case, he might direct his browser to http://host1/ instead of the fully qualified http://host1.example.com/. The Host header would simply have host1 in it instead of host1.example.com. To make sure that the correct virtual host container gets the request, you can use the ServerAlias directive as shown in Listing 29.3.

LISTING 29.3   The ServerAlias **Directive**

```
NameVirtualHost 192.168.128.10
Listen 192.168.128.10:80

<VirtualHost 192.168.128.10>
    ServerName host1.example.com
    ServerAlias host1
    DocumentRoot /usr/local/apache2/htdocs/host1
</VirtualHost>

<VirtualHost 192.168.128.10>
    ServerName host2.example.com
    ServerAlias host2
    DocumentRoot /usr/local/apache2/htdocs/host2
</VirtualHost>
```

In fact, you can give ServerAlias a space-separated list of other names that might show up in the Host header so that you don't need a separate VirtualHost container with a bunch of common directives just to handle all the name variants.

HTTP 1.1 forces the use of the Host header. If the protocol version is identified as 1.1 in the HTTP request line, the request *must* be accompanied by a Host header. In the early days of name-based virtual hosts, Host headers were considered a trade-off: Fewer IP resources were required, but legacy browsers that did not send Host headers were still in use and, therefore, could not access all the server's virtual hosts. Today, that is not a consideration; there is no statistically significant number of such legacy browsers in use.

Mass Virtual Hosting

In the previous listings, the DocumentRoot directives follow a simple pattern:

```
DocumentRoot /usr/local/apache2/htdocs/hostname
```

where *hostname* is the hostname portion of the fully qualified domain name used in the virtual host's ServerName. For just a few virtual hosts, this configuration is fine. But what if there are dozens, hundreds, or even thousands of these virtual hosts? The configuration file can become difficult to maintain. Apache provides a good solution for cookie-cutter virtual hosts with mod_vhost_alias. You can configure Apache to map the virtual host requests to separate content trees with pattern-matching rules in the VirtualDocumentRoot directive. This functionality is especially useful for ISPs that want to provide a virtual host for each one of their users. The following example provides a simple mass virtual host configuration:

```
NameVirtualHost 192.168.128.10
Listen 192.168.128.10:80

VirtualDocumentRoot /usr/local/apache2/htdocs/%1
```

The %1 token used in this example's VirtualDocumentRoot directive will be substituted for the first portion of the fully qualified domain name. The mod_vhost_alias directives have a language for mapping FQDN components to filesystem locations, including characters within the FQDN.

If all the VirtualHost containers are eliminated and our configuration is simplified to the one shown here, the server would serve requests for any subdirectories created in the /usr/local/apache2/htdocs directory. If the hostname portion of the FQDN is matched as a subdirectory, Apache will look there for content when it translates the request to a filesystem location.

Although virtual hosts normally inherit directives from the main server context, some of them, such as Alias directives, do not get propagated. For instance, the virtual hosts will not inherit this filesystem mapping:

```
Alias /icons /usr/local/apache2/icons
```

The FollowSymLinks flag for the Options directive is also disabled in this context. However, a variant of the ScriptAlias directive is supported.

The VirtualScriptAlias directive shown in the following snippet treats requests for any resources under /cgi-bin as containing CGI scripts:

```
NameVirtualHost 192.168.128.10
Listen 192.168.128.10:80
VirtualDocumentRoot /usr/local/apache2/htdocs/%1/docs
VirtualScriptAlias /usr/local/apache2/htdocs/%1/cgi-bin
```

Note that cgi-bin is a special token for that directive; calling the directory just cgi won't work; it must be cgi-bin.

For IP-based virtual hosting needs, there are variants of these directives: VirtualDocumentRootIP and VirtualScriptAliasIP.

Summary

This chapter provided information on Apache and operating system settings that can affect scalability and performance. In most cases, the problems in website scalability relate to dynamic content generation and database access. Writing efficient scripts will alleviate issues in those categories. Hardware-related improvements, such as high-quality network cards and drivers, increased memory, and disk arrays can also provide enhanced performance.

With regard to virtual hosting, Apache can be configured to handle virtual hosts in a variety of ways. Whether you need a large number of cookie-cutter virtual hosts, a varied set of different virtual host configurations, or the number of IP addresses you can use is limited, there's a way to configure Apache for your application. Name-based virtual hosting is a common technique for deploying virtual hosts without using up IP addresses. IP-based virtual hosting is another method when you have plenty of IPs available and you want to keep your configuration tidy, with a one-to-one balance of IPs to virtual hosts. In addition, if you cannot change your DNS configuration, you have the recourse of using separate port numbers for your virtual hosts.

Q&A

Q. *How can I measure whether my site is fast enough?*

A. Many developers test their sites locally or over an internal network, but if you run a public website, chances are good that many of your users will access it over slow links. Try navigating your website from a dialup account and make sure that your pages load fast enough, with the rule of thumb being that pages should load in less than three seconds.

Q. *How can I migrate an existing name-based virtual host to its own machine while maintaining continuous service?*

A. If a virtual host is destined to move to a neighboring machine, which by definition cannot have the same IP address, there are some extra measures to take. A common practice is to do something like the following, although many variations on these steps are possible:

1. Set the time-to-live (TTL) of the DNS mapping to a very low number. This increases the frequency of client lookups of the hostname.

2. Configure an IP alias on the old host with the new IP address.

3. Configure the virtual host's content to be served by both name- and IP-address–based virtual hosts.

4. After all the requests for the virtual host at the old IP address diminish (due to DNS caches expiring their old lookups), the server can be migrated.

Q. *Can I mix IP- and name-based virtual hosting?*

A. Yes. If multiple IP addresses are bound, you can allocate their usage a number of different ways. A family of name-based virtual hosts might be associated with each; just use a separate `NameVirtualHost` directive for each IP. One IP might be dedicated as an IP-based virtual host for SSL, for instance, whereas another might be dedicated to a family of name-based virtual hosts.

Workshop

The workshop is designed to help you anticipate possible questions, review what you've learned, and begin putting your knowledge into practice.

Quiz

1. Name some Apache settings that might limit scalability or affect Apache performance.

2. Name some operating system settings that might limit scalability.

3. Name some approaches to improve performance.

4. Which `VirtualHost` container gets a request if the connection uses `NameVirtualHost`, but no `Host` header is sent?

5. Is the `ServerName` directive necessary in a `VirtualHost` container?

Answers

1. Some of the Apache settings that might affect scalability include `FollowSymLinks`, `SymLinksIfOwnerMatch` arguments to the `Options` directive, enabling per-directory configuration files, hostname lookups, having a scoreboard file, and statistics collection with `mod_status`.

2. Some operating system settings that might affect scalability include limits for number of processes, open file descriptors, and memory allowed per process.

3. The following are some suggestions for improving performance: load distribution via a hardware load balancer or reverse proxy, data compression, caching, mapping files to memory, and compiling modules statically.

4. Reading the configuration top-to-bottom, the first `VirtualHost` container is favored. The same behavior occurs if there is a `Host` header, but no `VirtualHost` container that matches it.

5. The `ServerName` directive is necessary in a `VirtualHost` container only when name-based virtual hosts are used. The `Host` header contents are compared to the contents of the `ServerName` directive. If a match isn't satisfied, the `VirtualHost` containers' `ServerAlias` directive value(s) are checked for matches.

30

Setting Up a Secure Web Server

This chapter explains how to set up an Apache server capable of secure transactions. If you are using shared server space with a hosting provider, you will not have access to these configuration options—the process of setting up a secure web server will be specific to the provider and usually is not something you can do yourself. However, if you have root access to your server, use this chapter to learn

▶ The SSL/TLS family of protocols and the underlying cryptography concepts

▶ What secure certificates are and how to create and manage them

▶ How to activate the mod_ssl Apache module in Apache 2.2

The Need for Security

Several types of Internet-related transactions require a high level of security. These include financial transactions, such as banking operations and electronic commerce, but also any exchange of sensitive information, such as medical records and corporate documents. Secure transactions over the Internet require three main elements:

▶ **Confidentiality**—If you are transmitting or accessing sensitive information such as your credit card number or your personal medical history, you certainly don't want a stranger to get hold of it.

▶ **Integrity**—Transmitted information must be protected from external manipulation—if you place an order online to buy 100 shares of stock, you don't want anyone to intercept the message and change it to an order to buy 1,000 shares.

▶ **Authentication**—You need to trust that the organization or individual you are communicating with is who they say they are.

The SSL Protocol

SSL stands for *Secure Sockets Layer*, and TLS stands for *Transport Layer Security*. These two families of protocols were originally designed to provide security for HTTP trans-actions, but they also can be used for a variety of other Internet protocols such as IMAP (Internet Message Access Protocol) and NNTP (Network News Transfer Protocol). HTTP running over SSL is referred to as *secure HTTP*.

Netscape released SSL version 2 in 1994 and SSL version 3 in 1995. TLS is an IETF (Internet Engineering Task Force) standard designed to standardize SSL as an Internet protocol, but it is just a modification of SSL version 3 with a small number of added features and minor cleanups. The TLS acronym is the result of arguments between Microsoft and Netscape over the naming of the protocol because each com-pany proposed its own name. However, the name has not stuck, and most people refer to these protocols simply as SSL. Unless otherwise specified, the rest of this chapter refers to SSL/TLS as *SSL*.

You specify that you want to connect to a server using SSL by replacing http with https in the protocol component of a URI (uniform resource identifier). The default port for HTTP over SSL is 443.

The following sections explain how SSL addresses the confidentiality, integrity, and authentication requirements outlined previously. You also learn a bit about the underlying mathematical and cryptographic principles at the core of SSL.

Addressing the Need for Confidentiality

The SSL protocol protects data by encrypting it. *Encryption* is the process of convert-ing a message, the *plaintext*, into a new encrypted message, the *ciphertext*. Although the plaintext is readable by everyone, the ciphertext is completely unintelligible to anyone who might intercept it. Decryption is the reverse process, which transforms the ciphertext back into the original plaintext.

Usually, the encryption and decryption process involves an additional piece of infor-mation: a *key*. If both sender and receiver share the same key, the process is referred to as *symmetric* cryptography. If sender and receiver have different, complementary keys, the process is called *asymmetric* or *public key* cryptography.

Symmetric Cryptography

If the key used to both encrypt and decrypt the message is the same, the process is known as *symmetric cryptography*. DES, Triple-Des, RC4, and RC2 are algorithms used for symmetric key cryptography. Many of these algorithms can have different key sizes, measured in bits. In general, given an algorithm, the greater the number of bits in the key, the more secure the algorithm is and the slower it will run because of the increased computational needs of performing the algorithm.

Symmetric cryptography is relatively fast compared to public key cryptography, which is explained in the next section. Symmetric cryptography has two main drawbacks, however. One is that keys must be changed periodically to avoid providing an eavesdropper with access to large amounts of material encrypted with the same key. The other issue is the key distribution problem: How do you get the keys to each one of the parties, and do so in a safe manner? This was one of the original limiting factors of symmetric cryptography; the problem was solved by periodically having people traveling around with suitcases full of keys. Then along came public key cryptography.

Public Key Cryptography

Public key cryptography takes a different approach than its symmetric predecessor. Instead of both parties sharing the same key, a pair of keys exists: one public and the other private. The public key can be widely distributed, whereas the owner keeps the private key secret. These two keys are complementary—a message encrypted with one of the keys can be decrypted only by the other key.

Using this method, anyone wanting to transmit a secure message to you can encrypt the message using your public key, assured that only the owner of the private key—you—can decrypt it. Even if an eavesdropper has access to the public key, he cannot decrypt the communication meant for you. In fact, you want the public key to be as widely available as possible so that more people can send encrypted messages to you. Public key cryptography can also be used to provide message integrity and authentication. People with public keys will place these keys on public key servers or simply send the keys to others with whom they want to have secure email exchanges. Using the appropriate software tools, such as PGP or GnuPG, the sender will encrypt the outgoing message based on the recipient's public key.

The assertion that only the owner of the private key can decrypt a message meant for her means that with the current knowledge of cryptography and availability of computing power, brute force alone will not break the encryption in a reasonable time frame; however, if the underlying algorithm or its implementation is flawed, such attacks are possible.

Public key cryptography is similar to giving away many identical padlocks and retaining the master key. Anybody who wants to send you a message privately can do so by putting it in a safe and locking it with one of those padlocks (public keys) before sending it to you. Only you have the appropriate key (private key) to open that padlock (decrypt the message).

By the Way

The SSL protocol uses public key cryptography in the initial handshake phase to securely exchange symmetric keys that can then be used to encrypt the communication.

Addressing the Need for Integrity

Data integrity is preserved by performing a special calculation on the contents of the message and storing the result with the message itself. When the message arrives at its destination, the recipient then performs the same calculation and compares the results. If the contents of the message changed, the results of the calculation will be different—and you'll know someone else has tampered with it.

Digest algorithms perform just that process: creating message digests. A *message digest* is a method of creating a fixed-length representation of an arbitrary message that uniquely identifies it—like a fingerprint. A good message digest algorithm should be irreversible and collision resistant, at least for practical purposes. *Irreversible* means that the original message cannot be obtained from the digest, and *collision resistant* means that no two different messages should have the same digest. Examples of digest algorithms are MD5 and SHA.

Message digests alone, however, do not guarantee the integrity of the message—an attacker could change the text *and* the message digest. Message authentication codes, or MACs, are similar to message digests, but incorporate a shared secret key in the process. The result of the algorithm depends both on the message and the key used. Because the attacker has no access to the key, he cannot modify both the message and the digest. HMAC (Hash Message Authentication Code) is an example of a message authentication code algorithm.

The SSL protocol uses MAC codes to avoid replay attacks and to ensure integrity of the transmitted information.

Addressing the Need for Authentication

SSL uses certificates to authenticate the parties in a communication. Public key cryptography can be used to digitally sign messages. In fact, just the act of your encrypting a message with your secret key guarantees the receiver that the message came from you. Other digital signature algorithms involve first calculating a digest of the message and then signing the digest.

You can tell that the person who created that public and private key pair is the one sending the message, but how do you tie that key to a person or organization that you can trust in the real world? It's plausible that an attacker could impersonate a sender's identity and distribute a different public key, claiming it is the legitimate one.

Trust can be achieved by using digital certificates. *Digital certificates* are electronic documents that contain a public key and information about its owner (name, address, and so on). To be useful, the certificate must be signed by a trusted third party (certification authority, or CA) who certifies that the information is correct. There are many different kinds of CAs, as described later in the chapter. Some of them are commercial entities, providing certification services to companies conducting business over the Internet. Companies providing internal certification services create other CAs.

The CA guarantees that the information in the certificate is correct, and that the key belongs to that individual or organization. Certificates have a period of validity and can expire or be revoked. Certificates can be chained so that the certification process can be delegated. For example, a trusted entity can certify companies, which in turn can take care of certifying their own employees.

If this whole process is to be effective and trusted, the certificate authority must require appropriate proof of identity from individuals and organizations before it issues a certificate.

By default, browsers include a collection of root certificates for trusted certificate authorities.

SSL and Certificates

The main standard defining certificates is X.509, adapted for Internet usage. An X.509 certificate contains the following information:

- ▶ **Issuer**—The name of the signer of the certificate
- ▶ **Subject**—The person holding the key being certified
- ▶ **Subject public key**—The public key of the subject
- ▶ **Control information**—Data such as the dates for which the certificate is valid
- ▶ **Signature**—The signature that covers the previous data

You can check a real-life certificate by connecting to a secure server with your browser. If the connection has been successful, a little padlock icon or another visual clue will be added to the status bar of your browser. Depending on your browser, you should be able to click the representative icon to view information on the SSL connection and the remote server certificate. In the following example, the SSL certificate is examined for https://www.amazon.com/. You can see that the issuer of the certificate is VeriSign (see Figure 30.1). The page downloaded seamlessly because VeriSign is a trusted certification authority.

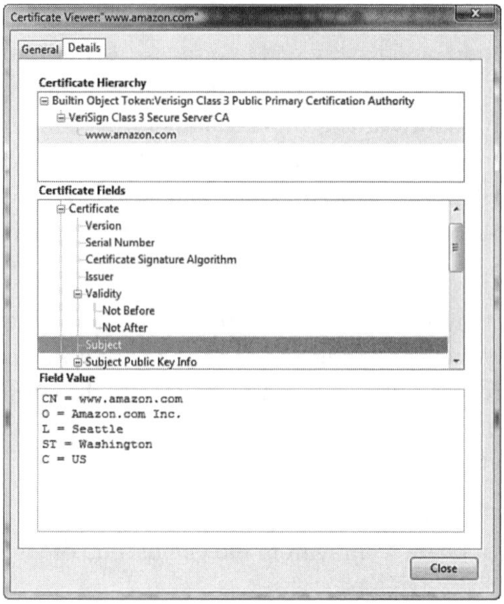

FIGURE 30.1
SSL certificate
in use at www.
amazon.com.

You can see that both issuer and subject are provided as distinguished names (DN), a structured way of providing a unique identifier for every element on the network. In the case of the certificate in Figure 30.1, the DN is C=US, ST=Washington, L=Seattle, O=Amazon.com, Inc., and CN=www.amazon.com.

C stands for *country*, ST for *state*, L for *locality*, O for *organization*, and CN for *common name*. In a website certificate, the common name identifies the fully qualified domain name of the website. This is the server name part of the URL; in this case, the www.amazon.com domain and the hostname "www". If this address does not match what you typed in the location bar, the browser will issue an error.

By the Way

If the CN were *.amazon.com, the SSL certificate would be valid for any host on the amazon.com domain.

SSL Protocol Summary

You have seen how SSL achieves confidentiality via encryption, integrity via message authentication codes, and authentication via certificates and digital signatures.

The process to establish an SSL connection is the following:

1. The user uses his browser to connect to the remote web server.

2. The handshake phase begins—the browser and server exchange keys and certificate information.

3. The browser checks the validity of the server certificate, including that it has not expired, that it has been issued by a trusted CA, and so on.

4. Optionally, the server can require the client to present a valid certificate as well.

5. Server and client use each other's public key to securely agree on a symmetric key.

6. The handshake phase concludes and transmission continues using symmetric cryptography.

Obtaining and Installing SSL Tools

SSL support is provided by mod_ssl, an Apache module. This module requires the OpenSSL library—an open-source implementation of the SSL/TLS protocols and a variety of other cryptographic algorithms. OpenSSL is based on the SSLeay library developed by Eric A. Young and Tim J. Hudson.

Because of the restrictions on the distribution of string cryptography and patented intellectual property worldwide, the installation of SSL-related tools varies in its ease from platform to platform. The following sections provide an overview for obtaining and installing SSL-related tools.

OpenSSL

All files and instructions necessary for installing OpenSSL can be found at http://www.openssl.org/. Users of UNIX/Linux (and their variants) will find the installation of the OpenSSL software to be similar to installing other system tools. However, the casual Windows user will discover that there are currently no freely distributed precompiled binaries. As such, Windows users must compile the OpenSSL tools on their own. After you have installed the OpenSSL toolkit, you will have all the necessary elements for creating and manipulating certificates and keys, as well as interfacing with the mod_ssl Apache module.

Installation for Windows Users

Windows users familiar with the process of building their own binaries may do so with the OpenSSL source code provided at the OpenSSL website. The instructions for compiling OpenSSL on Windows are in the INSTALL.W32 file found in the source distribution. Restating these instructions is beyond the scope of this book; however, you will find they are comprehensive and well written. The required tools are ActiveState Perl for Windows and one of the following C compilers:

- ▶ Visual C++

- ▶ Borland C

- ▶ GNU C (Cygwin or MinGW)

Be sure to follow the instructions appropriate to your compiler of choice because they are different for each. You can also find tips from Apache for compiling OpenSSL as part of the Apache compilation instructions at http://httpd.apache.org/docs/2.2/platform/win_compiling.html.

Installation for UNIX/Linux Users

If you are running a recent Linux or FreeBSD distribution, OpenSSL might already be installed in your system. Should you need to install OpenSSL, you can download the source from the OpenSSL website. After you have downloaded the file, uncompress it and cd into the created directory (replace -*version* in the following commands with your particular, current version of OpenSSL):

```
# gunzip < openssl-version.tar.gz ¦ tar xvf -
# cd openssl-version
```

Complete installation instructions are found in the INSTALL file, but in short, the config script will help you build the software, which is followed by the make and make install processes.

The mod_ssl Apache Module

In the past, SSL extensions for Apache had to be distributed separately because of export restrictions. Currently, mod_ssl is bundled with Apache 2.2, but only as part of the source distributions. Although this is not an issue for UNIX/Linux users, Windows users will find they must build Apache from source to build the mod_ssl module; mod_ssl is not distributed in the precompiled and distributed binaries. The mod_ssl module depends on the OpenSSL library, so a valid OpenSSL installation is required.

For Windows Users

When downloading the precompiled installation binaries, be sure to select the version with "openssl" in the filename. For instance, apache_2.2.8-win32-x86-openssl-0.9.8e.msi is the name of the Windows installer for Apache 2.2.8.

If you would like to build OpenSSL and Apache with mod_ssl from source, follow the Apache documentation found at http://httpd.apache.org/docs/2.2/platform/win_compiling.html. Again, restating these instructions is beyond the scope of this book, but they will provide you with all the information you need if you choose to go that route. The core requirements for building from source are as follows:

▶ Installed OpenSSL toolkit

▶ Microsoft Visual C++ 5.0 or higher

▶ The Windows Platform SDK

▶ The awk utility (awk, gawk, or similar)

For UNIX/Linux Users

The source distribution used in Chapter 3, "Installing and Configuring Apache," should already include the files necessary to use mod_ssl. As such, for UNIX/Linux users to use mod_ssl, you only need to follow the configure and make/make install process again, with the following addition as part of the configure command:

```
--enable-ssl --with-ssl=/usr/local/ssl/
```

This assumes that you installed OpenSSL in the listed location; if it resides in another directory on your server, simply substitute the location in the preceding command.

If you compiled mod_ssl statically into Apache, you can check whether it is present by issuing the following command, which provides a list of compiled-in modules:

```
# /usr/local/apache2/bin/httpd -l
```

> The preceding command assumes that you installed Apache in the /usr/local/ apache2 directory.

By the Way

If mod_ssl was compiled as a dynamic loadable module, the following line must be added to or uncommented in the Apache configuration file (httpd.conf):

```
LoadModule ssl_module modules/libmodssl.so
```

When you have finished making changes to the httpd.conf file, restart Apache so that your changes take effect. If you look in your error_log after restarting, mod_ssl will be part of your server signature, such as

```
Apache/2.2.8 (Unix) mod_ssl/2.2.8 OpenSSL/0.9.8g PHP/5.2.5
```

Managing Certificates

After installing and configuring OpenSSL and mod_ssl, the next step for a working SSL server implementation is to create a server certificate. This section explains in detail how to create and manage certificates and keys by using the openssl command-line tool. If you are using SSL for an e-commerce site, encryption protects customer data from eavesdroppers, and the certificate enables customers to verify that you are who you claim to be.

By the Way

> The examples refer to the UNIX version of the command-line program openssl. If you are running under Windows, you need to use openssl.exe instead and change the paths of the examples to use back slashes instead of forward slashes. In addition, if you installed OpenSSL in a directory unlike the one listed here, simply substitute that directory in the examples.

Creating a Key Pair

You must have a public/private key pair before you can create a certificate request. Assume that the fully qualified domain name (FQDN) for the certificate you want to create is www.example.com. You can create the keys by issuing the following command:

```
# openssl genrsa -des3 -out www.example.com.key 1024
```

▶ The genrsa switch indicates to OpenSSL that you want to generate a key pair.

▶ The -des3 switch indicates that the private key should be encrypted and protected by a pass phrase.

▶ The -out switch indicates where to store the results.

▶ 1024 indicates the number of bits of the generated key.

The result of invoking this command looks like this:

```
Generating RSA private key, 1024 bit long modulus
...............++++++
.....................++++++
e is 65537 (0x10001)
Enter pass phrase for www.example.com.key:
```

As you can see, you will be asked to provide a pass phrase; choose a secure one. The pass phrase is necessary to protect the private key, and you will be asked for it whenever you want to start the server.

> You can choose not to password-protect the key. This is convenient because you will not need to enter the pass phrase during reboots, but it is highly insecure, and a compromise of the server means a compromise of the key as well. In any case, you can choose to unprotect the key either by leaving out the -des3 switch in the generation phase or by issuing the following command:
>
> ```
> # openssl rsa -in www.example.com.key -out www.example.com.key.unsecure
> ```

Did you Know?

It is a good idea to back up the www.example.com.key file. You can learn about the contents of the key file by issuing the following command:

```
# openssl rsa -noout -text -in www.example.com.key
```

Elements of the key will then be displayed to you.

Creating a Certificate Signing Request

To get a certificate issued by a CA, you must submit a *certificate signing request*. To create a request, issue the following command:

```
#  req -new -key www.example.com.key -out www.example.com.csr
```

You will be prompted for the certificate information, something like the following:

```
Using configuration from /usr/local/ssl/install/openssl/openssl.cnf
Enter PEM pass phrase:
You are about to be asked to enter information that will be incorporated
into your certificate request.
What you are about to enter is what is called a Distinguished Name or a DN.
There are quite a few fields but you can leave some blank
For some fields there will be a default value,
If you enter '.', the field will be left blank.
-----
Country Name (2 letter code) [AU]:US
State or Province Name (full name) [Some-State]:CA
Locality Name (eg, city) []: San Francisco
Organization Name (eg, company) [Internet Widgits Pty Ltd]:.
Organizational Unit Name (eg, section) []:.
Common Name (eg, YOUR name) []:www.example.com
Email Address []:administrator@example.com
Please enter the following 'extra' attributes
to be sent with your certificate request
A challenge password []:
An optional company name []:
```

It is important that the Common Name field entry matches the address that visitors to your website will type in their browsers. This is one of the checks that the browser will perform for the remote server certificate. If the names differ, a warning indicating the mismatch will be issued to the user.

The certificate is now stored in www.example.com.csr. You can learn about the contents of the certificate using the following command:

```
# openssl req -noout -text -in www.example.com.csr
```

You can submit the certificate signing request file to a CA for processing. VeriSign and Thawte are two of those CAs, but many CAs are available. You can learn more about the VeriSign and Thawte submission procedures at their websites for their products:

▶ **VeriSign**—http://www.verisign.com/products-services/security-services/ssl/

▶ **Thawte**—http://www.thawte.com/ssl-digital-certificates/ssl/

Creating a Self-Signed Certificate

You can also create a self-signed certificate. That is, you can be both the issuer and the subject of the certificate. Although this is not useful for a commercial website, it will enable you to test your installation of mod_ssl and to have a secure web server while you wait for the official certificate from the CA.

```
# openssl x509 -req -days 30 -in www.example.com.csr -signkey
www.example.com.key -out www.example.com.cert
```

You need to copy your certificate www.example.com.cert (either the one returned by the CA or your self-signed one) to /usr/local/ssl/openssl/certs/ and your key to /usr/local/ssl/openssl/private/.

Protect your key file by issuing the following command:

```
# chmod 400 www.example.com.key
```

This command makes the key readable only by the root user.

SSL Configuration

The previous sections introduced the (not-so-basic) concepts behind SSL, and you have learned how to generate keys and certificates. Now you can configure Apache to support SSL. As you learned earlier in the chapter, the mod_ssl module must either be compiled statically, or, if you have compiled as a loadable module, the appropriate LoadModule directive must be present in the httpd.conf file.

Apache 2.2.x ships with an "extra" configuration file specifically for running an SSL-aware server. To use this extra file, simply uncomment this line in httpd.conf:

```
Include conf/extra/httpd-ssl.conf
```

Next, modify the standard configuration snippet in `httpd-ssl.conf`, replacing the information with your own, of course:

```
UseCanonicalName On
<VirtualHost www.examle.com:443>
ServerName www.example.com
SSLEngine on
SSLCertificateFile  /usr/local/ssl/openssl/certs/www.example.com.cert
SSLCertificateKeyFile /usr/loca/ssl/openssl/certs/www.example.com.key
</VirtualHost>
```

This snippet configures a new virtual host that will listen to port 443 (the default port for HTTPS); you enable SSL on that virtual host with the `SSLEngine` directive. The `SSLCertificateFile` and `SSLCertificateKeyfile` directives indicate where to find the server's certificate and the file containing the associated key.

Starting the Server

Previous versions of Apache required you to issue the `apachectl startssl` command when you wanted to start Apache in secure mode. However, given the configuration methods defined in the previous section, starting Apache in secure mode is no different from starting Apache without SSL: issue the `apachectl start` command. As long as the `httpd-ssl.conf` file is included in `httpd.conf` via directive, per the earlier instructions, Apache will start the SSL-enabled server. If your server is already running and you restart it, you will be prompted for your pass phrase if your key is protected by one. After entering the correct pass phrase, Apache will start, and you should be able to connect securely to it using the https://www.example.com/ URL. Substitute your own domain name, of course. If you are unable to successfully start your server, check the Apache error log for clues about what might have gone wrong. For example, if you cannot bind to the port, make sure that another Apache instance is not running already. You must have administrator privileges to bind to port 443.

Summary

This chapter explained the fundamentals of the SSL protocol and `mod_ssl`, the Apache module that implements support for SSL. You were given an introduction to installing and configuring OpenSSL and `mod_ssl`, and how to use the `openssl` command-line tool for certificate and key generation and management. You can access the `mod_ssl` reference documentation at http://httpd.apache.org/docs/2.2/mod/mod_ssl.html for in-depth syntax explanation and additional configuration information. Bear in mind also that SSL is just part of maintaining a secure server, which includes applying security patches, OS configuration, access control, physical security, and so on.

Q&A

Q. *Can I have SSL with name-based virtual hosting?*

A. A question that comes up frequently is how to make name-based virtual hosts work with SSL. The answer is that you currently cannot. Name-based virtual hosts depend on the Host header of the HTTP request, but the certificate verification happens when the SSL connection is being established and no HTTP request can be sent. There is a protocol for upgrading an existing HTTP connection to TLS, but it is mostly unsupported by current browsers (see RFC 2817, at http://www.rfc-editor.org/rfc/rfc2817.txt).

Q. *Can I use SSL with other protocols?*

A. The mod_ssl module implements the SSL protocol as a filter. Other protocols using the same Apache server can easily take advantage of the SSL.

Workshop

The workshop is designed to help you anticipate possible questions, review what you've learned, and begin putting your knowledge into practice.

Quiz

1. Name three requirements to carry on secure communications on the Internet.

2. How do you start an SSL-enabled instance of Apache?

Answers

1. Confidentiality, integrity, and authentication.

2. Ensure that the httpd-ssl.conf file is included via directive in the httpd.conf file, and issue the command apachectl.

31

Optimizing and Tuning MySQL

Proper care and feeding of your MySQL server will keep it running happily and without incident. The optimization of your system consists of proper hardware maintenance and software tuning. In this chapter, you will learn the basics of optimizing and tuning your server, including

- ► Basic hardware and software optimization tips for your MySQL server

- ► Key startup parameters for your MySQL server

- ► How to use the OPTIMIZE TABLE command

- ► How to use the EXPLAIN command

- ► How to use the FLUSH command to clean up tables, caches, and log files

- ► How to use SHOW commands to retrieve information about databases, tables, and indexes

- ► How to use SHOW commands to find system status information

For additional methods of maintaining and administering your MySQL server, review the MySQL Administrator Console product from MySQL AB. You can find information and screenshots of this full-featured graphical interface at http://www.mysql.com/products/tools/administrator/.

By the Way

Building an Optimized Platform

Designing a well-structured, normalized database schema is just half of the optimization puzzle (albeit an important half). The other half is building and fine-tuning the server that will house your database. Think about the four main components of a server: CPU, memory, hard drive, and operating system. Each of these components must be up to speed or no amount of design or programming will make your database faster!

▶ **CPU**—The faster the CPU, the faster MySQL will be able to process your data. There's no real secret to this, but a 3.0GHz processor is significantly faster than a 1.0GHz processor. With processor speeds consistently increasing, and with reasonable prices all around, it's not difficult to get a good bang for your buck.

▶ **Memory**—Put as much RAM in your machine as you can. You can never have enough, and RAM is cheap these days. Having available RAM can help balance out sluggish CPUs.

▶ **Hard drive**—The proper hard drive will be both large enough and fast enough to accommodate your database server and its traffic. An important measurement of hard-drive speed is its *seek time*, or the amount of time it takes for the drive to spin around and find a specific piece of information. Seek time is measured in milliseconds, and an average disk-seek time is around 8 or 9 milliseconds. When buying a hard drive, make sure that it's big enough to accommodate all the data you'll eventually store in your database and fast enough to find it quickly.

▶ **Operating system**—If you use an operating system that's a resource hog (for example, Windows), you have two choices: buy enough resources so that it doesn't matter, or use an operating system that doesn't suck away all your resources.

If you put the proper pieces together at the system level, you'll have taken several steps toward overall server optimization.

Using the benchmark() **Function**

You can perform a quick test of your server speed using the benchmark() MySQL function to see how long it takes to process a given expression. You can make the expression something simple, such as 10+10, or something more extravagant, such as extracting pieces of dates.

No matter the result of the expression, the result of benchmark() will always be 0. The purpose of benchmark() is not to retrieve the result of an expression, but to see how long it takes to repeat the expression for a specific number of times. For example, the following command executes the expression 10+10 one million times:

```
mysql> select benchmark(1000000,10+10);
+-------------------------+
| benchmark(1000000,10+10) |
+-------------------------+
|                       0 |
+-------------------------+
1 row in set (0.0326sec)
```

This command executes the date extraction expression also one million times:

```
mysql> select benchmark(1000000, extract(year from now()));
+----------------------------------------------+
| benchmark(1000000, extract(year from now())) |
+----------------------------------------------+
|                                            0 |
+----------------------------------------------+
1 row in set (0.0242sec)
```

The important number is the time in seconds, which is the elapsed time for the execution of the function; the first test took 0.0326 seconds, and the second took 0.0242 seconds. You might want to run the same uses of benchmark() multiple times during different parts of the day (when your server is under different loads) to get a better idea of how your server is performing.

> **By the Way**
> A few time-tested benchmarking suites are the Open Source Database Benchmark (http://osdb.sourceforge.net/) and MySQL Super Smack (http://vegan.net/tony/supersmack/).

MySQL Startup Options

MySQL AB provides a wealth of information regarding the tuning of server parameters, much of which the average user will never need to use. And frankly, if you are using MySQL in a virtual hosting environment, you won't be able to use the information except to ask for changes in your server setup. So as not to completely overwhelm you with information, this section contains only a few of the common startup options for a finely tuned MySQL server.

> **By the Way**
> You can read more in the MySQL Manual, at http://dev.mysql.com/doc/refman/5.0/en/system.html.

When you start MySQL, a configuration file called my.cnf is loaded. This file contains information ranging from port number to buffer sizes but can be overruled by command-line startup options.

In the support-files subdirectory of your MySQL installation directory (or in the installation directory itself on Windows), you'll find sample configuration files, each tuned for a specific range of installed memory:

- **my-small.cnf**—For systems with less than 64MB of RAM, where MySQL is used occasionally.

- **my-medium.cnf**—For systems with less than 64MB of RAM, where MySQL is the primary activity on the system, or for systems with up to 128MB of RAM, where MySQL shares the box with other processes. This is the most common configuration, where MySQL is installed on the same box as a web server and receives a moderate amount of traffic.

- **my-large.cnf**—For a system with 128MB to 512MB of RAM, where MySQL is the primary activity.

- **my-huge.cnf**—For a system with 1GB to 2GB of RAM, where MySQL is the primary activity.

To use any of these as the base configuration file, simply copy the file of your choice to /etc/my.cnf (or wherever my.cnf is on your system) and change any system-specific information, such as port or file locations.

Key Startup Parameters

Two primary startup parameters will affect your system the most: key_buffer_size and table_cache. If you get only two server parameters correctly tuned, make sure they're these two!

The value of key_buffer_size is the size of the buffer used with indexes. The larger the buffer, the faster the SQL command will finish and a result will be returned. Try to find the fine line between finely tuned and over-optimized; you might have a key_buffer_size of 256MB on a system with 512MB of RAM, but any more than 256MB could cause degraded server performance.

A simple way to check the actual performance of the buffer is to examine four additional variables: key_read_requests, key_reads, key_write_requests, and key_writes. You can find the values of these variables by issuing the SHOW STATUS command:

```
mysql> SHOW STATUS;
```

A long list of variables and values will be returned, listed in alphabetical order. Find the rows that look something like this (your values will differ):

```
¦ Key_read_requests      ¦ 10182771  ¦
¦ Key_reads              ¦ 9326      ¦
¦ Key_write_requests     ¦ 48487     ¦
¦ Key_writes             ¦ 2287      ¦
```

If you divide the value of key_reads by the value of key_read_requests, the result should be less than 0.01. Also, if you divide the value of key_writes by the value of key_write_requests, the result should be less than 1. Using the previous values yields results of 0.000915861721998 and 0.047167281951863, respectively, well within the acceptable parameters. You could try to get these numbers even smaller by increasing the value of key_buffer_size, but these numbers are fine as they are.

The other important server parameter is table_cache, which is the number of open tables for all threads. The default is 64, but you might need to adjust this number. Using the SHOW STATUS command, look for a variable called open_tables in the output. If this number is large, the value of table_cache should be increased.

The sample configuration files included with your MySQL installation use various combinations of key_buffer_size and table_cache. You can use these combinations as a baseline for any modifications you need to make. Whenever you modify your configuration, you have to restart your server for changes to take effect—sometimes with no knowledge of the consequences of your changes. In this case, be sure to try your modifications in a development environment before rolling the changes into production.

Optimizing Your Table Structure

An optimized table structure is different from a well-designed table. Table structure optimization has to do with reclaiming unused space after deletions and basically cleaning up the table after structural modifications have been made. The OPTIMIZE TABLE SQL command takes care of this, using the following syntax:

```
OPTIMIZE TABLE table_name[,table_name]
```

For example, if you want to optimize the grocery_inventory table in the testDB database, use

```
mysql> OPTIMIZE TABLE grocery_inventory;
+----------------------------+----------+----------+----------+
¦ Table                      ¦ Op       ¦ Msg_type ¦ Msg_text ¦
+----------------------------+----------+----------+----------+
¦ testDB.grocery_inventory   ¦ optimize ¦ status   ¦ OK       ¦
+----------------------------+----------+----------+----------+
1 row in set (0.08 sec)
```

The output doesn't explicitly state what was fixed, but the text in the Msg_text column shows that the grocery_inventory table was indeed optimized. If you run the command again, you might see a message such as this one:

```
mysql> OPTIMIZE TABLE grocery_inventory;
+----------------------------+----------+----------+----------------------------+
| Table                      | Op       | Msg_type | Msg_text                   |
+----------------------------+----------+----------+----------------------------+
| testDB.grocery_inventory   | optimize | status   | Table is already up to date |
+----------------------------+----------+----------+----------------------------+
1 row in set (0.03 sec)
```

Be aware that tables are locked while undergoing optimization, so if your table is large, perform the optimization during scheduled downtime or when little traffic is flowing to your system.

Optimizing Your Queries

Query optimization has a lot to do with the proper use of indexes. The EXPLAIN command examines a given SELECT statement to see whether it's optimized the best that it can be, using indexes wherever possible. This is especially useful when looking at complex queries involving JOINs. The syntax for EXPLAIN is

EXPLAIN SELECT *statement*

The output of the EXPLAIN command is a table of information containing the following columns:

- ▶ **id**—The select identifier ID.
- ▶ **select_type**—The type of SELECT statement, of which there are several.
- ▶ **table**—The name of the table.
- ▶ **type**—The join type, of which there are several.
- ▶ **possible_keys**—This column indicates which indexes MySQL could use to find the rows in this table. If the result is NULL, no indexes would help with this query. You should then take a look at your table structure and see whether there are any indexes you could create that would increase the performance of this query.
- ▶ **key**—The key actually used in this query, or NULL if no index was used.
- ▶ **key_len**—The length of the key used, if any.
- ▶ **ref**—Any columns used with the key to retrieve a result.
- ▶ **rows**—The number of rows MySQL must examine to execute the query.

▶ **extra**—Additional information regarding how MySQL will execute the query. There are several options, such as `Using index` (an index was used) and `Where` (a WHERE clause was used).

There's not much optimizing you can do with a "select all" query except add a WHERE clause with the primary key. The `possible_keys` column would then show PRIMARY, and the Extra column would show `Where used`.

When using EXPLAIN on statements involving JOIN, a quick way to gauge the optimization of the query is to look at the values in the rows column. Suppose that you have 2 and 1 as results; multiply these numbers together and you have 2 as your answer. This is the number of rows that MySQL must look at to produce the results of the query. You want to get this number as low as possible, and 2 is as low as it can go!

For a great deal more information on the EXPLAIN command, visit the MySQL Manual at http://dev.mysql.com/doc/refman/5.0/en/explain.html.

Using the FLUSH **Command**

Users with reload privileges for a specific database can use the FLUSH command to clean up the internal caches used by MySQL. Often, only the root-level user has the appropriate permissions to issue administrative commands such as FLUSH.

The FLUSH syntax is

```
FLUSH flush_option
```

There are nine different options for the FLUSH command; the most common are

▶ PRIVILEGES

▶ TABLES

▶ HOSTS

▶ LOGS

You've used the FLUSH PRIVILEGES command before, after adding new users. This command simply reloads the grant tables in your MySQL database, enabling the changes to take effect without stopping and restarting MySQL. When you issue a FLUSH PRIVILEGES command, the `Query OK` response assures you that the cleaning process occurred without a hitch.

```
mysql> FLUSH PRIVILEGES;
Query OK, 0 rows affected (0.10 sec)
```

The FLUSH TABLES command closes all tables currently open or in use and essentially gives your MySQL server a millisecond of breathing room before starting back to work. When your caches are empty, MySQL can better utilize available memory. Again, you're looking for the Query OK response:

```
mysql> FLUSH TABLES;
Query OK, 0 rows affected (0.21 sec)
```

The FLUSH HOSTS command works specifically with the host cache tables. If you are unable to connect to your MySQL server, a common reason is that the maximum number of connections has been reached for a particular host, and it's throwing errors. When MySQL sees numerous errors on connection, it assumes that something is amiss and simply blocks any additional connection attempts to that host. The FLUSH HOSTS command resets this process and again allows connections to be made:

```
mysql> FLUSH HOSTS;
Query OK, 0 rows affected (0.00 sec)
```

The FLUSH LOGS command closes and reopens all log files. If your log file is getting to be a burden, and you want to start a new one, this command creates a new, empty log file. Weeding through a year's worth of log entries in one file looking for errors can be a chore, so try to flush your logs at least monthly.

```
mysql> FLUSH LOGS;
Query OK, 0 rows affected (0.04 sec)
```

For more information on FLUSH, visit the MySQL Manual page at http://dev.mysql.com/doc/refman/5.0/en/flush.html.

Using the SHOW Command

There are several different uses of the SHOW command, which produces output displaying a great deal of useful information about your MySQL database, users, and tables. Depending on your access level, some of the SHOW commands will not be available to you or will provide only minimal information. The root-level user has the ability to use all the SHOW commands, with the most comprehensive results. The common uses of SHOW include the following, which you'll soon learn about in more detail:

```
SHOW GRANTS FOR user
SHOW DATABASES [LIKE something]
SHOW [OPEN] TABLES [FROM database_name] [LIKE something]
SHOW CREATE TABLE table_name
SHOW [FULL] COLUMNS FROM table_name [FROM database_name] [LIKE something]
SHOW INDEX FROM table_name [FROM database_name]
SHOW TABLE STATUS [FROM db_name] [LIKE something]
SHOW STATUS [LIKE something]
SHOW VARIABLES [LIKE something]
```

The SHOW GRANTS command displays the privileges for a given user at a given host. This is an easy way to check on the current status of a user, especially if you have a request to modify a user's privileges. With SHOW GRANTS, you can check first to see that the user doesn't already have the requested privileges. For example, examine the privileges available to the joeuser user:

```
mysql> SHOW GRANTS FOR joeuser@localhost;
+----------------------------------------------------------------------+
| Grants for joeuser@localhost                                         |
+----------------------------------------------------------------------+
| GRANT ALL PRIVILEGES ON *.* TO 'joeuser'@'localhost' IDENTIFIED|
| BY  PASSWORD ' *13883BDDBE566ECEFF0501CDE9B293303116521A'            |
+----------------------------------------------------------------------+
1 rows in set (0.00 sec)
```

If you're not the root-level user or the joeuser user, you'll get an error; unless you're the root-level user, you can see only the information relevant to yourself. For example, the joeuser user isn't allowed to view information about the root-level user:

```
mysql> SHOW GRANTS FOR root@localhost;
ERROR 1044: Access denied for user:'joeuser@localhost' to database 'mysql'
```

Be aware of your privilege level throughout the remainder of this chapter. If you are not the root-level user, some of these commands will not be available to you or will display only limited information.

Some popular SHOW commands follow; for more information, see the MySQL Manual at http://dev.mysql.com/doc/refman/5.0/en/show.html.

Retrieving Information About Databases and Tables

You've used a few of the basic SHOW commands earlier in this book to view the list of databases and tables on your MySQL server. As a refresher, the SHOW DATABASES command does just that—it lists all the databases on your MySQL server:

```
mysql> SHOW DATABASES;
+--------------------+
| Database           |
+--------------------+
| testDB             |
| mysql              |
+--------------------+
2 rows in set (0.00 sec)
```

After you've selected a database to work with, you can also use SHOW to list the tables in the database. This example uses testDB (your table listing may vary):

```
mysql> SHOW TABLES;
+---------------------+
| Tables_in_testDB    |
+---------------------+
| grocery_inventory   |
| email               |
| master_name         |
| myTest              |
| testTable           |
+---------------------+
5 rows in set (0.01 sec)
```

If you add OPEN to your SHOW TABLES command, you get a list of all the tables in the table cache, showing how many times they're cached and in use:

```
mysql> SHOW OPEN TABLES;
+----------+-------------------+--------+-------------+
| Database | Table             | In_use | Name_locked |
+----------+-------------------+--------+-------------+
| mysql    | procs_priv        | 0      | 0           |
| mysql    | db                | 0      | 0           |
| mysql    | host              | 0      | 0           |
| testdb   | grocery_inventory | 0      | 0           |
| mysql    | user              | 0      | 0           |
| mysql    | tables_priv       | 0      | 0           |
| mysql    | columns_priv      | 0      | 0           |
+----------+-------------------+--------+-------------+
7 rows in set (0.00 sec)
```

Using this information in conjunction with the FLUSH TABLES command you learned earlier in this chapter helps keep your database running smoothly. If SHOW OPEN TABLES shows that tables are cached numerous times but aren't currently in use, go ahead and use FLUSH TABLES to free up that memory.

Retrieving Table Structure Information

A helpful command is SHOW CREATE TABLE, which does what it sounds like—it shows you the SQL statement used to create a specified table:

```
mysql> SHOW CREATE TABLE grocery_inventory;
+-------------------+------------------------------------------------------+
| Table             | Create Table                                         |
+-------------------+------------------------------------------------------+
| grocery_inventory | CREATE TABLE 'grocery_inventory' (                   |
|                   |   'id' int(11) NOT NULL auto_increment,              |
|                   |   'item_name' varchar(50) NOT NULL default ",        |
|                   |   'item_desc' text,                                  |
|                   |   'item_price' float NOT NULL default '0',           |
|                   |   'curr_qty' int(11) NOT NULL default '0',           |
|                   |   PRIMARY KEY  ('id')                                |
|                   | ) ENGINE=InnoDB DEFAULT CHARSET=latin1               |
+-------------------+------------------------------------------------------+
1 row in set (0.00 sec)
```

This is essentially the same information you'd get if you dumped the table schema, but the SHOW CREATE TABLE command can be used quickly if you're just looking for a reminder or a simple reference to a particular table-creation statement.

If you need to know the structure of the table but don't necessarily need the SQL command to create it, you can use the SHOW COLUMNS command:

```
mysql> SHOW COLUMNS FROM grocery_inventory;
+------------+-------------+------+-----+---------+----------------+
| Field      | Type        | Null | Key | Default | Extra          |
+------------+-------------+------+-----+---------+----------------+
| id         | int(11)     | NO   | PRI |         | auto_increment |
| item_name  | varchar(50) | NO   |     |         |                |
| item_desc  | text        | YES  |     |         |                |
| item_price | float       | NO   |     |         |                |
| curr_qty   | int(11)     | NO   |     |         |                |
+------------+-------------+------+-----+---------+----------------+
5 rows in set (0.01 sec)
```

> The SHOW COLUMNS and DESCRIBE commands are aliases for one another and, therefore, do the same thing.

By the Way

The SHOW INDEX command displays information about all the indexes present in a particular table. The syntax is

```
SHOW INDEX FROM table_name [FROM database_name]
```

This command produces a table full of information, ranging from the column name to the cardinality of the index. Table 31.1 describes the columns returned from this command.

TABLE 31.1 Columns in the SHOW INDEX Result

Column Name	Description
Table	The name of the table.
Non_unique	1 or 0.
	1 = Index can contain duplicates.
	0 = Index can't contain duplicates.
Key_name	The name of the index.
Seq_in_index	The column sequence number for the Index; starts at 1.
Column_name	The name of the column.
Collation	The sort order of the column, either A (ascending) or NULL (not sorted).
Cardinality	Number of unique values in the index.

TABLE 31.1   Continued

Column Name	Description
Sub_part	On a partially indexed column, this shows the number of indexed characters, or NULL if the entire key is indexed.
Packed	The size of numeric columns.
Null	Displays whether the column can contain NULL values.
Index_type	The index method used.
Comment	Any additional comments.

Another command that produces a wide table full of results is the SHOW TABLE STATUS command. The syntax of this command is

```
SHOW TABLE STATUS [FROM database_name] LIKE 'something'
```

This command produces a table full of information, ranging from the size and number of rows to the next value to use in an auto_increment field. Table 31.2 describes the columns returned from this command.

TABLE 31.2   Columns in the SHOW TABLE STATUS Result

Column Name	Description
Name	The name of the table.
Engine	The storage engine used for this table.
Version	The version of the table's *.frm file.
Row_format	The row storage format: fixed, dynamic, or compressed.
Rows	The number of rows.
Avg_row_length	The average row length.
Data_length	The length of the data file.
Max_data_length	The maximum length of the data file.
Index_length	The length of the index file.
Data_free	The number of bytes allocated but not used.
Auto_increment	The next value to use in an auto_increment field.
Create_time	The date and time when the table was created (in datetime format).
Update_time	The date and time when the data file was last updated (in datetime format).
Check_time	The date and time when the table was last checked (in datetime format).

TABLE 31.2   Continued

Column Name	Description
Collation	The character set and collation type for the table.
Checksum	The checksum value of the table, if applicable.
Create_options	Any extra options used in the CREATE TABLE statement.
Comment	Any comments added when the table was created. Additionally, InnoDB tables use this column to report the free space in the tablespace.

Retrieving System Status

The SHOW STATUS and SHOW VARIABLES commands quickly provide important infor-mation about your database server. The syntax for these commands is simply SHOW STATUS or SHOW VARIABLES—nothing fancy.

There are more than 200 status variables that will appear as the output of SHOW STATUS, but the most useful are these:

▶ **Aborted_connects**—The number of failed attempts to connect to the MySQL server. Anytime you see an aborted connection, you should investigate the problem. It could be related to a bad username and password in a script, or the number of allowable simultaneous connections could be set too low for the flood of traffic to your site.

▶ **Connections**—The aggregate number of connection attempts to the MySQL server during the current period of uptime.

▶ **Max_used_connections**—The maximum number of connections that have been in use simultaneously during the current period of uptime.

▶ **Slow_queries**—The number of queries that have taken more than long_query_time, which defaults to 10 seconds. If you have more than one slow query, it's time to investigate your SQL syntax!

▶ **Uptime**—Total number of seconds the server has been up during the current period of uptime.

You can find a comprehensive list of SHOW STATUS variables and an explanation of their values in the MySQL Manual, located at http://dev.mysql.com/doc/ref-man/5.0/en/show-status.html.

The SHOW VARIABLES command produces 212 results that control the general operation of MySQL and include the following useful tidbits:

- ▶ **connect_timeout**—Shows the number of seconds the MySQL server will wait during a connection attempt before it gives up

- ▶ **max_connections**—The allowable number of simultaneous connections to MySQL before a connection is refused

- ▶ **port**—The port on which MySQL is running

- ▶ **table_type**—The table type for MySQL

- ▶ **version**—The MySQL version number

You can find a comprehensive list of the variables returned by the SHOW VARIABLES results and an explanation of their values in the MySQL Manual at http://dev.mysql.com/doc/refman/5.0/en/show-variables.html. After you know the values you have, you can change them in your MySQL configuration file or startup command.

Summary

Running an optimized MySQL server starts with the hardware and operating system in use. Your system's CPU should be sufficiently fast, and you should have enough RAM in use to pick up the slack when your CPU struggles. This is especially true if MySQL shares resources with other processes, such as a web server.

Additionally, the hard drive in use is important because a small hard drive limits the amount of information you can store in your database. The seek time of your hard drive is important—a slow seek time causes the overall performance of the server to be slower. Your operating system should not overwhelm your machine and should share resources with MySQL rather than using all the resources itself.

Some key startup parameters for MySQL are the values of key_buffer_size and table_cache, among others. You can find baseline values in sample MySQL configuration files, or you can modify the values of these variables and watch the server performance to see whether you hit on the right result for your environment.

Beyond hardware and software optimization is the optimization of tables, as well as SELECT queries. Table optimization, using the OPTIMIZE command, enables you to reclaim unused space. You can see how well (or not) optimized your queries are by using the EXPLAIN command. The resulting output will show if and when indexes are used, and whether you can use any indexes to speed up the given query.

Paying attention to your MySQL server ensures that it continues to run smoothly. Basic administration commands, such as FLUSH and SHOW, help you to recognize and quickly fix potential problems. All these commands are designed to give MySQL a millisecond of rest time and breathing room if it's under a heavy load. Numerous SHOW commands display structural information about databases, tables, and indexes, as well as how the system is performing.

Q&A

Q. Can MySQL take advantage of multiple CPUs in a single server?

A. Absolutely. If your operating system supports multiple CPUs, MySQL will take advantage of them. However, the performance and tuning of MySQL using multiple processors varies, depending on the operating system. For more information, see the MySQL Manual section for your specific operating system: http://dev.mysql.com/doc/refman/5.0/en/operating-system-specific-notes.html.

Q. What permission level must I have to use the OPTIMIZE command?

A. Any user with INSERT privileges for a table can perform OPTIMIZE commands. If a user has only SELECT permissions, the OPTIMIZE command will not execute.

Workshop

The workshop is designed to help you anticipate possible questions, review what you've learned, and begin learning how to put your knowledge into practice.

Quiz

1. Which MySQL function enables you to run an expression many times over to find the speed of the iterations?

2. Which SQL command cleans up the structure of your tables?

3. Which FLUSH command resets the MySQL log files?

4. To quickly determine whether MySQL has support for InnoDB tables, would you use SHOW STATUS or SHOW VARIABLES?

5. Write a SQL statement that enables you to see the SQL statement used to create a table called myTable.

Answers

1. The benchmark() function

2. OPTIMIZE

3. FLUSH LOGS

4. SHOW VARIABLES

5. SHOW CREATE TABLE myTable

Activities

1. If you have root-level access to your server, change the values of key_buffer_size and table_cache, and run benchmark() functions after each change to see how the execution times differ.

2. Use OPTIMIZE on all the tables you have created in your database to clean up any structural issues.

3. Use the SHOW STATUS command to retrieve information about your MySQL server and then issue FLUSH commands to clean up the server. After each command, use SHOW STATUS again to see which commands affect which results in the SHOW STATUS results display.

32

Software Upgrades

Throughout this book, you've been reminded to seek out information regarding new versions of PHP, Apache, and MySQL, and to be mindful of updates. Also, you've been shown how to add functionality to PHP at build time but only in the context of installing the software. In this short chapter, you'll learn how to update your already-installed software over the normal course of time, without wreaking havoc on your system, including

▶ How to keep up-to-date with new software releases

▶ How to upgrade between minor versions of MySQL

▶ How to upgrade between minor versions of Apache

▶ How to upgrade between minor versions of PHP

Staying in the Loop

You should already have bookmarked the websites for Apache, PHP, and MySQL. It doesn't matter whether you've been using these technologies for six days or six years—there will always be a need to refer back to the sites (I do, all the time!). If the primary reason for visiting the websites is to obtain information regarding updates, you could always subscribe to an announcements-only mailing list:

▶ For MySQL announcements, go to http://lists.mysql.com/ and subscribe to the MySQL Announcements list.

▶ For Apache announcements, go to http://www.apache.org/foundation/mailinglists.html and subscribe to the Apache News and Announcements list.

▶ For PHP announcements, go to http://www.php.net/mailing-lists.php and subscribe to the Announcements list.

When to Upgrade

As indicated in the installation chapters, minor version changes occur whenever the developers find it necessary to do so—not on any particular schedule. But just because a minor version change has occurred, that doesn't necessarily mean you should run right out and upgrade your software. Sometimes, however, you should upgrade.

The primary instance in which you should immediately upgrade your software is when a security fix is announced. Usually, security issues are not discovered until they are exploited—sometimes in a testing environment but sometimes by a rogue user who just wants to cause trouble for the world. After verification of a security issue, you can bet that it becomes the top priority for developers to fix, and quickly you will see an announcement of an upgrade. When that occurs, you should upgrade immediately—even if you don't use the particular element that is the cause of the security issue. A hole is a hole—why leave it uncovered?

Here is an example of the Apache changelog, documenting a change that occurred between version 2.0.61 and 2.0.63 (version 2.0.62 was not released to the public) that would be an indicator of a need to upgrade:

```
SECURITY: CVE-2007-6388 (cve.mitre.org)
mod_status: Ensure refresh parameter is numeric to prevent a possible XSS
attack caused by redirecting to other URLs.
```

A good rule of thumb is that if the word *security* appears anywhere in the changelog, you should upgrade.

However, if the release is simply a maintenance release, meaning that it contains bugfixes and general enhancements that occur through normal development, you probably don't need to drop everything and upgrade your software. Here are some examples of maintenance items from the Apache and PHP changelogs:

```
mpm_winnt: Eliminate wait_for_many_objects.  Allows the clean shutdown of the
server
when the MaxClients is higher then 257,  in a more responsive manner.
Fixed bug #43137 (rmdir() and rename() do not clear statcache). (from PHP
changelog)
```

If nothing in the list of changes is relevant to you, your work, or your environment, you could probably put off the upgrade until scheduled downtime or a rainy day. For example, if all the bugs fixed in a maintenance release of PHP have to do with the Windows platform and you run PHP on Linux, you can put the task aside, worry-free.

Even if you don't immediately upgrade your software, it's a good idea to stay at least within one or two minor versions of the current production version of the software. Anything past that and it becomes more likely that new features would be added or bugs fixed that are indeed relevant to your work or your environment.

Upgrading MySQL

Whether you use UNIX/Linux or Windows, upgrading minor versions of MySQL is simple—install the new version as if the other version does not exist.

> Before upgrading to a new minor version of MySQL, back up your existing databases.

MySQL AB has made it easy to upgrade within the same base version; 5.0 is a base version, 5.1 is a base version, and so on. This means that upgrading any minor version in the 5.0.x family is as simple as installing the new software on top of the old software. With the Windows Installer, this is all invisible to you but is exactly what occurs. UNIX/Linux users who install from the binary distribution will simply be relinking the mysql symbolic directory to the new, unpacked distribution, as part of the installation process.

If you run into problems during the upgrade process, refer to the troubleshooting tips at http://dev.mysql.com/doc/refman/5.0/en/upgrade.html. However, upgrading minor versions of MySQL has always been a painless experience for me, on multiple platforms.

> If you change character sets when upgrading, you will have to run the following command to adjust the collation of your existing data:
>
> ```
> myisamchk -r -q --set-collation=new_collation_name
> ```

By the Way

Upgrading Apache

Like MySQL, upgrading or rebuilding Apache follows the same process as installing the software in the first place. Windows users have the benefit of an Installer application that automatically detects the previous version, removes core components, and installs new ones. The Windows Installer will, however, retain existing configuration files. You are responsible for upgrading any other version-specific modules, such as mod_ssl, which are tied to specific versions of Apache.

For UNIX/Linux users, the process also follows the same path as the original installation. When you unpack your new distribution, it creates a directory named with the new version number. For example, if your previous version was 2.2.6 and you are upgrading to 2.2.8, your directories will be named `httpd-2.2.6` and `httpd-2.2.8`, respectively.

The actual installation directory for Apache is determined by you, when you run the `configure` script, as in this example:

```
# ./configure --prefix=/usr/local/apache2
```

After running the `configure` script to build the new version of Apache, just go through the `make` and `make install` process as you did when installing Apache in the first place.

Now, should you want to install your new version of Apache directly over your old version, you can—even with the old `httpd` binary still running. Just be sure to back up your configuration files in case something goes awry. However, if you are more comfortable installing your new version in a different directory, that's fine, too—you'll just have to move all your web-related files (that is, everything in the document root) to the new directory and make all appropriate edits to your fresh, new `httpd.conf` file. Whichever method you choose is up to you; one method just requires more file movement and reconfiguration than the other.

After upgrading Apache on UNIX/Linux, you should also rebuild your PHP module. Windows users do not have a module to rebuild but should ensure that the appropriate PHP-related changes are still present in the `httpd.conf` file related to loading the module residing in the PHP directory tree.

Modifying Apache Without Upgrading

Suppose that you need to add or remove functionality from Apache but are not upgrading to a new minor version. An example would be to add a new module or to upgrade the version of OpenSSL used on your system.

In this case, UNIX/Linux users should go to the existing source directory (such as `httpd-2.2.8`) and type **make clean** at the prompt. This will, essentially, reset the makefiles so that you can rebuild Apache without relying on previous, cached values. After the `make clean` command, run the `configure` script with your new parameters, and go through the `make` and `make install` process again. You do not need to rebuild the PHP module in this situation.

Windows users would activate the prebuilt modules by uncommenting the appropriate lines in `httpd.conf` or by adding the lines if they do not already exist.

Upgrading PHP

Given that UNIX/Linux users can add so much functionality to PHP through various build options, it is likely that you will upgrade or modify PHP more often than Apache or MySQL. Regardless of whether you are upgrading to a new minor version or simply adding new functionality (or removing some you no longer need), the process for modifying an existing version is exactly the same as installing it in the first place: `configure`, `make`, `make install`. The `make install` step places the PHP module in the appropriate place in the Apache directory tree. When your new module is in place, restart Apache—the new version of PHP should be in use.

If you are upgrading to a new minor version of PHP, when you extract the distribution archive you will have a completely distinct directory tree, based on the version number. Perform the `configure`, `make`, `make install` steps within this new directory structure, and a new PHP module will be built, independent of the other.

Windows users have a different set of tasks to perform: Adding new functionality to an existing module requires only that you activate the module by uncommenting its entry in `php.ini` and then restart Apache. Upgrading to a new minor version requires you to download a new distribution file. The contents of this file extract into a directory named for the version it represents. You must then follow the steps required for installation, regarding the configuration of `php.ini`, because each version produces a different file. Finally, change any PHP-related pathnames in the Apache `httpd.conf` file and restart the server—the new version of PHP should be in use.

Using PECL and PEAR to Extend PHP

A wealth of user-created extensions and applications can be obtained from PECL (the PHP Extension Community Library, at http://pecl.php.net/), and PEAR (the PHP Extension and Application Repository, at http://pear.php.net/). These sites are governed by rules and style guides, so anything you download from these sites will be of high quality.

If you are looking for additional extensions for your PHP installation, look to PECL. If you are looking for a library of open source code to integrate in your application, look to PEAR.

Summary

This short chapter provided some guidelines for keeping your installations of MySQL, Apache, and PHP current. You learned where to look for updates and how to weigh the importance of upgrading to a new version. Additionally, you learned the step-by-step processes for upgrading or modifying MySQL, Apache, and PHP.

Workshop

The workshop is designed to help you anticipate possible questions, review what you've learned, and begin putting your knowledge into practice.

Quiz

1. What is considered the primary reason for upgrading to a new minor version of any software?

2. What command will clean up previous `makefiles` and cached settings?

Answers

1. Security issues that have been found and fixed by the developers

2. The `make clean` command

Index

SYMBOLS

&& (and) operators, 103

* (asterisks)

    multiplication operators, 98

    table creation, 313

    wildcards, 38

\ (backslashes)

    converting time stamps to dates, 195

    directives, 51

\n (newline) character, 124, 214, 250

$ COOKIE superglobal, 90, 225

$ FILES superglobal, 90, 217

$ GET superglobal, 89

$ POST superglobal, 89

$ POST value, 379

$ REQUEST superglobal, 90

$ SERVER superglobal, 90

$ SESSION superglobal, 90

$cat id value, 439

$check result value, 381

$check result values, 380

$count variable, 464

$dayArray variable, 464

$display block strings

    online address books, 399, 402

    topic posts (discussion forums), 427

$display block value, 442-443

$display value, 439

$ENV superglobal, 90

$file array variable, 220

$file dir variable, 219

$file name variable, 220

$firstDayArray variable, 465

$name variable, 474

$newnum variable, 133

$SESSION superglobal, 229-232, 235

$start variable, 464

$txt variable, 135

= (equal sign)

    assignment operators, 89, 97

    concatenation operators, 214

== (equivalence) operators, 102, 316, 322

=== (identical) operators, 102

! (not operators), 103

!= (nonequivalence) operators, 102, 316

> (greater than) operators, 102, 316

NUMBERS

J - K

L

mysql insert id() function, 397

MySQL Installation wizard, 26

mysql result() function, 495

MySQL Setup Wizard, 26

mysqladmin status command, MySQL installation, 8

mysqli * functions, 361

mysqli close() function, 363

mysqli connect error() function, 362

mysqli error() function, 364-365

mysqli fetch array() function, 370

mysqli get host info() function, 362

mysqli num rows() function, 369

mysqli query() function, 363-366

mysql_insert_id() function, 419

N

name-based virtual hosting, 552-555

NameVirtualHost directive, 554

naming

constants, 105-106

domains, access control rules, 488

error log files, 507

functions, 134-135

logging files, 505

uploaded files, 220

variables, 88

navigating files via fseek() function, 252-253

negative terms, 73

nesting loops, 124-125

network settings

Apache performance, 551

scalability, 547

network/mask pairs, control access rules, 488

Networking Options screen (MySQL Configuration Wizard), 30

newline character (\n), 124, 214, 250

newlines, removing from strings, 185

NIS (Network Information Services), client authentication, 483

nl2br() function, 189

nonequivalence operators (!=), 102, 316

normal forms, 298

first normal form rules, 299

second normal form rules, 300

third normal form rules, 301

normalization, 293

defining, 298

flat tables, 298-299

normal forms, 298-301

redundancy, 299

not operators (!), 103

NOW() function, 346, 419

NULL data types, 91

numberedHeading() function, 141-142

numeric data types, 306-307

O

objects

constructors, 164

creating, 159

instances of, 160-161

methods, 163-164

data types, 91

declaring, 160

inheritance, 164-165

methods, 162-163

properties

changing, 162

viewing, 161

ON clause, 320

one to many mappings, DNS virtual hosting, 552

one to one mappings, DNS virtual hosting, 552

one to many table relationships, 296

one to one table relationships, 295

online address books

database tables, planning/creating, 389

email tables, 391

fax tables, 391

field names, 390

master name tables, 390

personal notes tables, 392

telephone tables, 391

include files, creating, 392

menus, creating, 393

records

adding subentries to, 407-412

record addition mechanism, 394-397

record deletion mechanism, 405-406

viewing, 398-405

online storefront database table example

cat id field, 434

category of items, displaying, 437-440

planning process, 433-434

store categories field, 434-435

store item color field, 434-437

store item size table, 436

store items field, 434-436

opendir() function, 257-258

openssl command-line tool (certificates), 570

OpenSSL libraries, 567-569

operands, 97